THE WORLD ENCYCLOPEDIA OF SERIAL KILLERS

VOLUME TWO:
E - L

WRITTEN AND COMPILED BY

SUSAN HALL

WILDBLUE PRESS

WildBluePress.com

THE WORLD ENCYCLOPEDIA OF SERIAL KILLERS:
Volume Two: E-L published by:
WILDBLUE PRESS
P.O. Box 102440
Denver, Colorado 80250

WILDBLUE PRESS is registered at the U.S. Patent and Trademark Offices.

ISBN 978-1-952225-21-5 Trade Paperback
ISBN 978-1-952225-20-8 eBook

Interior Formatting/Book Cover Design by Elijah Toten
www.totencreative.com

Solved
Serial Killer
Cases

Book 2
E - L

7th Earl of Pembroke/4th Earl of Montgomery aka **Herbert, Philip** (1652/3 – August 29, 1683) was an English nobleman and a serial killer. In spite of the fact that he held titles and estates of two earldoms, he committed at least three murders.

In 1677, he murdered a man in a brawl in a tavern, was tried and found guilty of manslaughter. "Privilege of peerage" was granted and he was released upon payment of all fees. The Duke of Ormond, the Lord High Steward of Ormonde, warned the earl that, "the Earl of Pembroke should take notice that no man could have the benefit of 'privilege of peerage' but once."

On October 17, 1678, the man who had prosecuted Herbert for murder was found dead in a ditch on Primrose Hill. He had been impaled with his own sword. It was concluded that he had been murdered by the Earl of Pembroke, but the earl was never taken to court.

On August 18, 1680, the earl killed William Smeeth following a drunken evening. Smeeth was an officer of the watch. On June 21, 1681, the grand jury of Middlesex indicted the Earl for murder. He could not claim "privilege of peerage" this time, but upon petition to the king, signed by 24 of his fellow peers, the Earl of Pembroke was granted a pardon.

Philip Herbert, 7th Earl of Pembroke, died on August 29, 1683. He is buried in Salisbury Cathedral in Salisbury, England.

East Harlem Rapist aka **Kee, Arohn** (b. September 18, 1973) was a serial killer/rapist who murdered at least three of his rape victims between 1991 and 1998 in New York.

Authorities believe that one of his victims was burned alive on a rooftop, one was strangled to death, and the third girl, only 13, was strangled and stabbed three times. DNA found on six victims matched Kee's DNA. Arohn Kee was arrested at the Sun Hotel in Miami, Florida, and extradited back to New York. He testified in his own defense against his lawyer's advice, saying that the police "planted his DNA on the victims."

On December 20, 2000, Arohn Kee was convicted of three murders and four rapes. He was sentenced to three terms of life imprisonment without the possibility of parole. He is incarcerated at Attica Correctional Facility in Attica, New York.

Eberling, Richard George (December 8, 1929 – July 25, 1998) was the son of Louise Lenardic, an unmarried woman, who was placed in foster care after his mother realized she could no longer care for him. As a ward of the State of Ohio, he was passed from family to family due to his behavior—tantrums, compulsive masturbation, and his inability to learn language. Louise refused to give up her rights to him, giving him no chance for adoption. He was placed with the Eberlings, George and Christine, who used foster children as cheap labor for their farm near Bay Village, Ohio. He was Mrs. Eberling's favorite child and preferred to stay inside with her to clean, rearrange the rooms, and wear Mrs. Eberling's clothing. He refused to play outside with the other boys and showed homosexual tendencies at an early age. Mr. Eberling died of a stroke in 1946.

After Richard graduated from high school, he began a house-cleaning and redecorating company. His clients included the home of Dr. Sam Sheppard, whose wife was found bludgeoned to death in her bed the morning of July 4, 1954. He became successful and eventually purchased the Eberling farm and legally changed his name to Richard George Eberling. His house cleaning service made it easy to steal from his clients.

Sometime after starting his house-cleaning business, Eberling met Obie Henderson who became his ever-present companion.

One of his clients was the wife of Cleveland Mayor Ralph Perk, with whom he developed a friendship and acted as an aide to the mayor. Eberling's companion, Henderson, became Perk's executive secretary. In 1973, Eberling was named the head of the committee for remodeling City Hall in Cleveland, even though he lacked the credentials.

Due to his association with Mayor Perk and his wife, Lucille, Eberling was always in attendance at Republican fund-raising parties. It was at one of these parties that he met Patricia Bogar, who claimed that she dated Henderson, but when Henderson showed up for their date, Eberling was always with him. He also met Ethel May Durkin, a wealthy childless widow, who hired him to do some decorating for her, and a friendship developed. Durkin's sisters, Myrtle Fray and Sarah Belle Farrow, took a dislike to Eberling.

On May 20, 1962, Myrtle was savagely beaten about her head and strangled to death at her apartment. In March 1970, Sarah, Ethel's older sister, died supposedly by falling down the basement steps at Ethel's home where she was living. The fall broke both of her legs and both arms.

Eberling, with help from Patricia Bogar, forged documents giving Eberling complete control of Ethel Durkin's finances. He promised Patricia 10% of the estimated $500,000. Eberling used the documents to make financial and medical decisions for Ethel. To ensure that she get her promised 10% Eberling had promised her, Patricia wrote a letter, with all the details of the forgery, had her signature notarized, and mailed it to her attorney with instructions to place the unopened letter in a secure place until she asked that it be given back to her.

Ethel's health declined and she began to have a series of accidents, including falling down the stairs as her sister Sarah had done. Eberling hired Kathy Wagner, a health aide. She claimed that Eberling had told her he had murdered Marilyn Sheppard and assaulted Dr. Sam Sheppard. He said to her, "You didn't hear that."

On November 15, 1983, the emergency squad was called to find Ethel face down on the floor. Eberling told the paramedics that Ethel had risen from her chair and fallen. Eberling told them he thought she had suffered a heart attack, but paramedics checking her vital signs and noting the wounds on her face were led to believe she had been attacked. An X-ray showed that one of her neck bones was broken in the same exact spot as that of Marilyn Sheppard's. Eberling did have one of Marilyn's rings, but he claimed that he had helped himself to it while cleaning the home.

Ethel May Durkin died from her injuries on January 3, 1984. Her death and the deaths of her two sisters caused authorities to become suspicious of Eberling. Ethel had requested that she be buried with her jewelry and wearing her favorite mink coat. Her estate was reviewed by the Cuyahoga County Probate Court who found irregularities in the estate accounting signatures and this information was turned over to the authorities for investigation.

Patricia Bogar began turning on Eberling and Henderson, after they seemingly deserted her. Eberling and Henderson and two others were indicted in July 1988 for forgery, perjury, aggravated grand theft, and tampering with evidence and records. Patricia was not charged.

When Durkin's body was exhumed, detectives saw that she was not wearing her mink coat and there was no jewelry buried with her. The autopsy revealed that she had been hit in the neck very hard from behind. Eberling and Henderson were charged with murder. Both were convicted.

Eberling was given a life term on one count of murder in Ohio. While in prison, he was linked to the suspicious deaths of George Eberling, who died in 1946, and Barbara Kinzel, supposedly a girlfriend and nurse at Bay View Hospital, where Dr. Sam Sheppard practiced, who died as the result of an automobile accident when Eberling was driving her Ford convertible and slammed it into the back of a parked truck. Eberling told investigators that Barbara had hit the windshield, but there was no blood anywhere on her, there was no internal bleeding, and there was no blood on the windshield. Her autopsy showed that she died of a broken neck at the second vertebra, the same as Ethel May Durkin and Marilyn Sheppard.

Eberling also wrote to Sam Reese Sheppard, son of Dr. Sam Sheppard, referencing the murder of Marilyn Sheppard and promising to reveal all of the details at a later date. He was also interviewed by reporters and authors. It should be noted that Eberling suffered from male pattern baldness and in his younger days, he wore what could easily be called a bushy hairpiece, as Dr. Sheppard had described the killer of his wife.

Eberling was never charged with any of the other murders. He died in prison on July 25, 1998.

Eckert, Volker (July 1, 1959 – July 2, 2007) was a lorry (truck) driver and a serial killer in the European countries of France, Germany, Italy, and Spain, and possibly the Czech Republic.

Eckert murdered for the first time when he was only 15. As a younger boy, he sometimes played with his sister's doll. He especially liked running his fingers through its hair, and eventually he had orgasms while stroking the doll's hair. By his early teens, he had grown tired of doll's hair and fantasized running his fingers through the hair of his 14-year-old classmate, Silvia Unterdorfel, who lived in the same building. On May 7, 1974, Eckert went to the Unterdorfels' flat and Silvia answered the door. Realizing she was alone in the home, he put his hands around her neck and squeezed until she lost consciousness. He then buried his hands in her hair. Eckert soon realized that Silvia could get him in bad trouble for his actions. He found some clothesline and pulling it tight around her neck, he killed her.

In April 1987, Heike Wunderlich was on her way to college after work when she was strangled to death and left naked in the woods outside Plauen. Eckert was arrested after attacking two young Plauen women who were able to identify him. He was sentenced to 12 years for attempted murder, but his sentence was overturned on appeal and he received only a few hours of therapy and served six years in jail.

Nothing more is known about Eckert until 1999, when he qualified to be a long-distance lorry driver. He later admitted that he chose this profession for the opportunity it provided him to carry out his fantasy. By this time, he was not only addicted to running his fingers through women's hair, but also to the act of strangulation.

On June 21, 2001, he stopped in Bordeaux in southwestern France and picked up Sandra Osifo, a Nigerian prostitute. He picked her because of her long hair, which he later discovered was a wig. She was dead within an hour. Her body was found on June 25 in a ditch along a road about 90 km (about 56 miles) north of where Eckert had picked her up.

In August, Eckert picked up Isabel Beatriz Diaz in Lloret de Mar, along the coast of Spain. He later told police that as he started to strangle her in the cab of his truck, she fought back with great strength and he had sex with her as he killed her. Her body was found near the junction at Macanet de la Selva about two months later.

The following year in August, Benedicta Edwards, from Sierra Leone, was working as a prostitute in Troyes, France. Her naked body was found near a local footpath.

In June 2003, police in the Czech Republic found the naked body of a woman, still unidentified, by the motorway near Pilsen.

In September 2004, Ahhiobe Gali, from Ghana, was murdered in northeast Italy; in February 2005, Mariy Veselova, from Russia, was found murdered in Figueras near Gerona; in October 2006, Agneska Bos, a Polish woman was found murdered in northeastern France; and in November 2006, the body of Miglena Petrova Rahim, from Bulgaria, was found at Sant Julia de Ramis, near Gerona.

It was found later that Eckert took photos of the bodies, cut off the hair, and took "trophies" such as clothing, handbags, or makeup.

When Eckert was caught on November 17, 2006, it was a fluke. He parked his lorry outside a football stadium in a small town in northeastern Spain and was waiting for dark to get rid of his latest victim's body. By sheer chance, a technician was installing a CCTV camera on the wall of a neighboring factory and while adjusting the camera, he panned across the stadium parking lot and picked out the lone lorry with the owner's logo splashed across its side. The following day, the Spanish police found the body of the murdered woman, checked the local CCTV cameras, and found the footage of the lorry parked in the stadium lot. They traced the lorry to Germany and asked the German police to pick up the driver who was possibly a witness, or the murderer.

Volker Eckert was convicted of this murder. On July 2, 2007, he was found hanging in his cell in Germany; his death was ruled a suicide. The police have found evidence that he murdered nine women across Germany, France, Spain, and Italy. They also strongly suspect that he committed four other murders, one of which was in the Czech Republic.

Edwards, Edward (June 14, 1933 – April 7, 2011) was a serial killer in Wisconsin and Ohio. He was raised in an orphanage where he claimed he was beaten by the nuns. He told the nuns he wanted to be a crook when he grew up and he would be a good one. He supposedly escaped jail in Akron, Ohio, in 1955 by pushing past a guard, and fled across the country holding up gas stations for money.

He never covered his face during the robberies because he wanted to be famous.

Edwards admitted to killing Bill Lavaco, age 21, and Judith Straub, age 18, in 1977 by shooting them in the neck at close range. He also admitted to killing Tim Hack and Kelly Drew, both 19, in 2007 after DNA found on Kelly's pants matched Edward Edwards. They disappeared from a wedding reception in Jefferson County, Wisconsin. Their bodies were found several weeks later.

Edwards also admitted to murdering his foster son, age 25, in 1996 for his life insurance of $250,000.

Edward Edwards died on April 7, 2011 at the Corrections Medical Center in Columbus, Ohio, of natural causes.

Edwards, Mack Ray (October 17, 1918 – October 30, 1971) was a serial killer of children during the years of 1953 – 1970 in Los Angeles County, California. He was born and raised in Arkansas and moved to California in 1941, where he worked as a heavy equipment operator on the freeway system.

On June 20, 1953, Stella Darlene Nolan, age 8, disappeared from Compton.

On August 6, 1956, Don Baker, age 13, and Brenda Howell, age 11, both of Azusa, disappeared.

On November 26, 1968, Gary Rochet, age 16, of Granada Hills, was shot to death. His body was found shortly afterward.

On December 16, 1968, Roger Madison, age 16, of Sylmar, disappeared.

On May 16, 1969, Donald Allen Todd, age 13, of Pomona, disappeared.

The body of one of Edwards' victims was found under the Santa Ana Freeway. He claimed that another of his victims was buried under the Ventura Freeway.

In 1970, Edwards and a teenage male accomplice kidnapped three girls from their home in Sylmar, but the girls managed to escape. Edwards and his accomplice were arrested. Edwards confessed to the murders of Stella Darlene Nolan, Gary Rochet, and Donald Allen Todd. He was convicted of these murders and sentenced to death. He also confessed to the murders of Don Baker, Brenda Howell, and Roger Madison, but he was never officially charged with these murders.

On October 30, 1971, Edwards committed suicide at San Quentin Prison by hanging himself with the cord from his television.

Edwards is suspected by police in the disappearances of Tommy Bowman, age 8, in Pasadena on March 23, 1957; Bruce Kremen, age 6, from a YMCA camp in the Angeles National Forest on July 12, 1960; Karen Lynn Tompkins, age 11, on August 18, 1961; and Dorothy Gale Brown, age 11, of Torrance who disappeared on July 3, 1962. Dorothy had been molested and drowned. Her body was found in the ocean near Corona del Mar.

Edwards had, at one time, claimed to have murdered 18 children. From his last known murders in 1956 to his next known murder in 1968 is a span of 12 years. Serial killers do not normally take a respite from their murders. They usually increase in numbers and frequency, over time.

Egypt Bluebeard is the name given to the person arrested in April 1920 for the murders of numerous women in Tanta, Egypt. When police raided his residence on April 28, they found at least 20 severed heads on display in his home. It is thought that he lured women to his home to rob them of their cash and jewelry and then murder them. The bodies were not found, and authorities believed he disposed of them by burning. Nothing more found on this killer.

El Coqueta aka **Legorreta, Cesar Armando Librado** (b. February 5, 1980) was born in Tenango del Valle, Mexico. He, his wife, and two children lived in Tultitlan where he worked as a driver of a minibus on the public transport between Metro Chapultepec and Tlalnepantla de Baz during the late-night hours.

Beginning on July 14, 2011, he claimed to his passengers that his vehicle had broken down and he could not finish delivering them to their destinations. He would get everyone off the bus except for one girl. He would offer to take this girl to her destination if she would help him fix the problem. Before arriving at her destination, he would change the route, then rape and murder the girl and drop her into the Tlalnepantla channel. Sometimes, the victim would be the last passenger on the bus. Over the next 17 months, he murdered seven more girls.

Legorreta was finally arrested on February 26, 2012, and transferred to the Deputy Attorney General's Office in Barrientos de la Vega, where he escaped under the watch of three guards. Knowing that they would be blamed for his escape, they also fled. The guards were discharged with negligence and attempting to flee. Legorreta was recaptured on March 3 by agents of the Attorney General's Office of the State of Mexico in Magdalena Contreras.

On December 12, 2012, Cesar Armando Librado Legorreta was convicted and sentenced to 240 years in prison for the rape and murder of six girls/women.

El Gato Imperial aka **Marroquin, Raul Osiel** (b. September 1, 1980) and **Manuel, Juan Enrique Madrid** (c. 1980) were serial killers of gay men in Mexico City.

Claiming that homosexuality harmed society, they lured the men from bars and took them to Marroquin's apartment. They asked the victims' families for ransom and then they either hanged or strangled the victims. They claimed they had released two men after they had received the ransom payment.

The two were arrested. On September 4, 2008, Raul Osiel Marroquin and Juan Enrique Madrid Manuel were sentenced to nearly 300 years in prison. They will probably be paroled after 50 years, if they are still alive, in accordance with current Mexican laws.

El Loco/La Bestia (The Crazy One/The Beast) aka **Garavito, Luis Alfredo** (b. January 25, 1957) is a rapist and serial killer in Colombia, South America. He was the oldest of seven brothers and is said to have suffered physical, sexual, and emotional abuse during his childhood.

All of his victims were poor, peasant or street children ranging in age from 5 to 16. Garavito enticed them to accompany him with offers of candy, small gifts, or money. He would take them for a walk to some secluded place where he raped them, slashed their throats, and dismembered most of the bodies, which often showed signs of torture.

The possibility of a serial killer operating in Colombia was first brought to the attention of the police with the discovery of 36 bodies in the western city of Pereira. More bodies were found in at least 10 more counties.

Garavito was captured on April 22, 1999. A total of 114 skeletons had been discovered by the time of his capture. He confessed to murdering 140 children. He was investigated for the murder of 172 children in more than 59 counties in Colombia and is being investigated to see if there is any connection to disappearances of children in Ecuador.

He was found guilty of 138 murders. Other cases are still ongoing. His sentences added up to 1,853 years, but because of Colombian law, he can serve no more than 30 years. Because he assisted officials in locating the bodies, his sentence was reduced to 22 years.

A review of the cases against Garavito by the Courts in different jurisdictions found that his sentence could be extended legally, so he will serve many more years in prison.

Ellebracht Sr., Walter Wesley (August 22, 1931 – February 21, 2003), his son **Ellebracht Jr., Walter Wesley** (b. 1953), and ranch foreman **Caldwell, Robert Carlton** (b. 1965) were suspected of the kidnapping, torture, and murder of several male drifters in the 1980s in Kerr County, Texas, on what became known as the Texas Slave Ranch. Each was convicted on one count of murder in 1986. William Jr. was given a sentence of 15 years, Caldwell was given a sentence of 14 years, and William Sr. was given seven years' probation.

Ellwood, Russell (c. 1950) grew up in Massillon, Ohio, and moved to New Orleans about 1990. He first worked as a freelance photographer, then as a taxi driver. He was also a serial killer whom investigators in Jefferson Parish believe may be responsible for as many as 15 murders across southern Louisiana between 1991 and 1996.

Ellwood was a loner, had few friends, and was constantly coming up with get-rich-quick schemes that never worked. He slept in his cab when he could not afford a room at a boarding house. When Ellwood's mother passed away, he inherited $15,000 which he quickly lost investing in penny stocks.

There were 26 murders in the 1990s, but authorities believe more than one person is responsible for these murders. Most of the victims were women with histories of drug abuse and prostitution. Some were transsexuals, some were strangled, and others apparently died of drug overdoses. Police believe Ellwood is responsible for several of these murders.

On March 2, 1998, Russell Ellwood was arrested and charged with the murders of Cheryl Lewis and Delores Mack, who were found on February 21-22, 1993. Cheryl drowned in the canal while under the influence of cocaine and amphetamines. Delores had been strangled and suffocated and cocaine was found in her blood. Although prosecutors admitted they had no physical evidence to tie Ellwood to these murders, they did have the testimony of his former girlfriend who said that Ellwood took her to the swamp and showed her both bodies. They also had the testimony of several jailhouse snitches.

Ellwood was a meticulous record keeper and authorities tracked his activities for years through the receipts he kept, but the year 1993 has no records for the two-week period when Delores Mack was murdered. Ellwood claims he was in Ohio with relatives during this time. Jefferson Parish Sheriff Harry Lee acknowledged that their investigation proved that Ellwood was in Ohio when Delores Mack was murdered.

Russell Ellwood was tried and convicted of Cheryl Lewis' murder. On August 17, 1999, he was sentenced to life in prison.

Emory, Joseph (b. 1920) was an osteopath in Los Angeles who performed a large number of illegal abortions in the 1950s. In 1960, he was convicted of second-degree murder, after one of his patients died during an illegal abortion. He was paroled in 1964.

In 1967, Emory was arrested on new abortion charges and jailed from 1967 to 1969. His medical license was revoked. In May 1974, his medical license was reinstated, and he opened a clinic called Highland Medical Center. He catered mainly to pregnant illegal immigrants and charged about half of what a hospital would charge for deliveries. He delivered more than 700 babies between 1974 and June 8, 1976. The clinic recorded 25 infant deaths during that time. Another died in the hospital just hours after being removed from the clinic for emergency treatment.

On June 8, 1976, Emory and his wife, Harriett, were arrested and booked on 10 counts of murder. Their son, Alan, was arrested and booked on five counts of murder.

No further information was found.

Engleman, Glennon Edward aka *Killing Dentist* (February 6, 1927 – March 3, 1999) was born into a US Air Corps family, the youngest of four children. He was raised in a nice home in middle class neighborhoods. He was an above average student, but did not excel in any one subject. After graduating from high school, he served in the US Army Air Corps and attended the Washington University in St. Louis under the GI Bill. He graduated with a degree in dentistry in 1954. Engelman practiced dentistry in the city of St. Louis, Missouri.

Engleman had a side-line—he moonlighted as a hitman. He carried out at least seven murders for monetary gain over the course of 30 years. He was a sociopath; he had the talent to kill without remorse and enjoyed the planning of the kill, the kill itself, and the disposing of the remains. His exact number of victims is unknown, but his methods included shooting, bludgeoning with a sledgehammer, and explosives.

His known victims include:

James Stanley Bullock, age 27, a clerk for Union Electric Company of Missouri, whose wife was actually Engleman's ex-wife. He was murdered in 1958. She collected $64,000 from his life insurance.

Eric Frey, a business partner of Engleman's at Pacific Drag Strip, was murdered in 1963. Engleman struck him with a rock, pushed him down a well, and used dynamite to blow up the well with Frey in it. Engleman divided the insurance proceeds with Frey's widow.

Peter J. Halm was shot to death in Pacific, Missouri, in 1976. Carmen Miranda Halm, his wife, was a former dental assistant trainee who worked for Engleman and had known him since childhood. She ordered the hit and collected $60,000 from his life insurance policy.

Arthur Gusewelle was shot and his wife, Vernita, bashed to death at their farmhouse near Edwardsville, Illinois, in

1977. Their son, Ronald Gusewelle, was murdered in East St. Louis, Illinois, about 17 months later. He was the sole heir to his parents' oil business. Ronald's wife, Barbara, collected roughly $340,000 following her husband's murder. She was convicted of her husband's murder and sentenced to 50 years in prison. She was tried for the murders of Arthur and Vernita Gusewelle, but was acquitted. She was released from prison on October 10, 2009.

Sophie Marie Barrera, owner of a south St. Louis dental laboratory, was killed in a car bomb explosion. Engleman owed her over $14,000.

Glennon Edward Engleman died on March 3, 1999, at the Jefferson City Correctional Center in Jefferson City, Missouri where he was serving two life sentences for the murder of a man and his wealthy parents.

Erskine, Scott (b. December 22, 1962) murdered two boys in California. On March 27, 1993, the bodies of Charlie Keever, age 13, and Jonathan Sellers, age 9, were found. Sellers' body was hanging from a tree. The boys had been molested, tortured, and strangled. Erskine was not caught for 11 years. At that time, he was in prison serving 70 years for rape. It was found that he had quite a long record of sexual assaults. After he was arrested, he confessed to murdering a woman in 1989 in Florida. Scott Erskine was sentenced to death and is currently on death row at San Quentin prison in California.

Note: On March 13, 2019, Governor Gavin Newsom ordered a moratorium on executions in California.

Escalero, Francisco Garcia (b. May 24, 1954) was a serial killer in the country of Spain. Born in Madrid, Escalero was a sickly boy who received very little education. Often beaten by his father, he was a strange youngster who enjoyed walking through cemeteries. When he was 16 years old, he was confined to a psychiatric hospital. He was sent to a reformatory for stealing a motorbike in 1973. He raped a girl in 1975 and was sentenced to 12 years in prison. Upon his release, he became a beggar and used alcohol spiked with some kind of pills which caused hallucinations accompanied by violent and aggressive behavior. In August 1987, Escalero decapitated and burned the body of Paula Martinez. In March 1988, he stabbed and used a large rock to crush the head of Juan, another beggar. Another beggar was found burned to death a few months later. Escalero also began practicing necrophilia and cannibalism. In March 1989, Angel, another beggar, was found decapitated and his fingerprints removed. In May 1989, a beggar named Julio was found stabbed, his penis cut off and burned.

In 1994, two patients escaped from a psychiatric hospital. They were Victor Luis Criado and Francisco Garcia Escalero. Criado was found two days later with his head crushed and his body burned. Escalero was arrested in April. At his trial in February 1995, Escalero was judged to be insane with severe mental disorders and sent to a psychiatric hospital. He is considered a dangerous person and is not likely to ever be released from the psychiatric hospital.

Etheridge, Ellen (b. 1866) murdered four of her stepchildren with poison in Meridian, Texas, (and attempted to murder another) because she was jealous of the attention they received from her husband, J. D. Etheridge. They had been married less than a year. On December 23, 1913, Etheridge was given four life sentences plus five years at the Goree State Farm for Women. She was reportedly a model prisoner until she died there when she was in her 60s.

Evans, Donald Leroy (July 5, 1957 – January 5, 1999) made claims of murdering over 70 people in parks and rest areas in 20 states.

Discharged from the Marine Corps in 1980, Evans began drifting across the US and killing those whom he could kidnap or lure away from a busy area to a more secluded area to do his evil business. He was arrested in 1991 for the kidnapping, rape, strangulation, and murder of Beatrice Routh, age 10, in Gulfport, Mississippi. He led authorities to her body. He was convicted and sentenced to death.

In 1995, he was convicted of the rape and murder of Ira Jean Smith in Florida and sentenced to life imprisonment.

On January 5, 1999, while on death row at the Mississippi State Penitentiary, Donald Leroy Evans was stabbed to death in the shower by fellow death row inmate, Jimmy Mack. At the time of his death, Evans was considered by police to be the prime suspect in at least 12 unsolved murders.

Evans, Gary Charles (October 7, 1954 – August 14, 1998) was a thief of antiques, coins, and jewelry. He was also a confessed serial killer.

Gary Evans was born in Troy, New York, to Roy Evans, a father who punished his son with beatings and who allegedly raped him when he was eight years old, and Flora May Evans, a mentally ill woman who also beat her son. They divorced in 1968. Evans went to live with his older sister and her husband, where he continued to be physically abused. Evans moved back with his mother because of the abuse. Flora married and divorced four more times before "coming out" as a lesbian in 1971.

Evans studied antiques and jewelry, and would talk to antique dealers posing as an antiques dealer. He was really casing the place to find ways of breaking into the establishment. Evans was convicted of at least 15 antique robberies. His roommates, **Michael Falco** (c. 1955), who practiced zoo sadism and bestiality, and **Timothy**

Rysedorph (c. 1958) were his "sometime" accomplices. Falco disappeared in February 1985, the first known associate of Gary Evans to "disappear." Thirteen years later, Evans told authorities that he had shot Falco to death, put his body in a sleeping bag, and disposed of it in a swamp near his sister's home in Lake Worth, Florida. Evans said he believed that Falco had stolen merchandise from him, and that Falco would report him to the authorities.

Another of Evans' accomplices was **Damien Cuomo** (b. September 10, 1961) with whom he teamed up after being paroled from Sing Sing on March 1, 1988. He and Cuomo robbed a coin and jewelry store in September in Watertown, New York, and shot the owner to death. On December 27, 1989, Cuomo was seen leaving his apartment with Evans and was never seen again. Evans confessed to Cuomo's murder in 1998. Evans said that he shot Cuomo to death shortly after they left Cuomo's apartment and buried the body nearby.

Evans spent the better part of the first two weeks in October 1991 on the roof of a building, casing a coin and jewelry shop in Herkimer County. On October 17, 1991, he walked into the shop, asked for a price on a piece of jewelry, and then shot the owner to death. In 1993, he stole more than 800 antiques from a shop in Quechee, Vermont. He was arrested after his "fence" became nervous and turned him in to police. In 1994, Evans agreed to assist police in catching the killer in the high-profile murder of Karolyn Lonczak. He was to obtain information on Jeffrey Williams, who was a suspect in the murder. He was also to "stay clean" at least until he testified against Williams. But he did not. On March 20, 1994, Evans stole John James Audubon's *Birds of America* out of a library in Woodstock, Vermont. He was arrested when he tried to sell the book through a fellow inmate. The inmate turned him in, and he was sent to federal prison. He was released on June 6, 1996, a shortened sentence because he had returned the book.

Upon his release he again teamed up with Rysedorph. They stole approximately $80,000 worth of merchandise from a shop in Great Barrington, Massachusetts, in January 1997. In July, Evans stole some antique jewelry from a shop in Albany. Police later linked that burglary to the one in Great Barrington. On October 4, 1997, Rysedorph telephoned his wife. He was never seen or heard from again. Evans had shot Rysedorph to death when he had his back turned and then dismembered him with a chain saw. Evans left the area and went to Texas where he worked in building and construction. He then disappeared again. On May 27, 1998, Evans was arrested near St. Johnsbury, Vermont, where he was living in a tent. Police had little evidence and little hope that they could bring murder charges against Evans, so they were surprised when he confessed to the murders of Falco, Cuomo, and Rysedorph. He aided the police in recovering the bodies. Evans also confessed to the murders of Douglas J. Berry, the owner of the coin and jewelry store in Watertown, New York, and Gregory Jouben at the coin and jewelry shop in Herkimer County.

Gary Evans was indicted in Rensselaer County, New York, on August 12, 1998, for the deaths of Falco, Cuomo, and Rysedorph. On August 13, he was indicted for Jouben's murder. The next day, August 14, as he was being transported back to Rensselaer County Jail, Evans managed to free his hands with a key he had hidden in his sinus cavity. As they reached the Troy-Menands Bridge, Evans kicked out the side window of the vehicle, jumped out, and ran. When he was cornered by the police, he jumped off the bridge and plunged to his death in the Hudson River, a fall of more than 60 feet. When his body was recovered, authorities found the key in his nose and a razor blade taped to his ankle.

Evonitz, Richard Marc (July 29, 1963 – June 27, 2002) was a serial killer in Spotsylvania, Virginia, in 1996-

97. Born in Columbia, South Carolina to Joseph and Tess Ragin Evonitz, he was the oldest of three children. After high school, Evonitz joined the US Navy and served as a sonar technician. He received a Good Conduct Medal and was honorably discharged after eight years.

While still in the navy, in January 1987, Evonitz exposed himself and masturbated in front of a girl, age 15, in Orange Park, Florida. He was arrested when his ship returned to that port; he pleaded no contest and was sentenced to three years' probation.

Evonitz is suspected by investigators of an abduction and rape in 1994, and a rape in Massaponax, Virginia, in 1995. Sofia Silva, age 16, was abducted from her front yard in Spotsylvania County, Virginia and murdered on September 9, 1996. Her body was found in a creek in King George County about one month later.

Kristin Lisk, age 15, and her sister Kati Lisk, age 12, were abducted from their front yard on May 1, 1997. Their bodies were found in the South Anna River in Hanover County on May 6.

These three abductions and murders were some of the most publicized cases in Virginia history. Psychics were called in and more than 11,000 leads were investigated. Laboratories tested more than 400,000 DNA samples of convicted felons. A $150,000 reward was offered. After more than five years, there were still no suspects and few clues.

Then in late June 2002, a message was left on the Spotsylvania sheriff's hotline. It was from Charles Pickett, a case manager with the National Center for Missing and Exploited Children in Alexandria, Virginia. His message said, "I think I've found your boy." Computer data had linked Richard Marc Evonitz to the abduction and rape of a teenage South Carolina girl on June 24, 2002, and also linked Evonitz with the murders in Spotsylvania, Virginia.

Evonitz had served three years' probation after pleading no contest to a charge of lewd and lascivious behavior in the presence of a child in Florida in 1987. Police were looking for him after a South Carolina girl Kara Robinson, age 15, was abducted from a friend's yard in Columbia, South Carolina, on June 24, 2002. She was raped repeatedly during that evening. She managed to escape while her captor was sleeping and notified the police. Evonitz fled when he discovered she had escaped.

Police found Evonitz near the waterfront in Sarasota, Florida. When police surrounded him, they urged him to surrender, but he kept a pistol in his hand. A police dog that was released bit his leg several times. This cowardly murderer of young girls fatally shot himself.

Faba Jr., Ralph John (b. August 30, 1977) was convicted of murdering Angela Durling, age 16, in St. Augustine, Florida, in 2000. He confessed to this murder and was serving a 40-year sentence when he was charged with the murder of his girlfriend, Alicia Eakins, age 25. He led detectives to her body in the Ocala National Forest where she had lain for eight years. He has also been charged with the murder of his father in October 1999, whose death had originally been ruled a suicide. At that time, Faba Jr. told authorities that he had found his father hanging in the woods, cut him down, started CPR, and called 911. After entering his plea of no contest to the murders of Alicia Eakins and his own father, Faba Jr. was given two concurrent 25-year sentences, which will run consecutive to the 40-year sentence he is already serving for the murder of high school student, Angela Durling. He is currently housed at the Gulf Correctional Institute, Wewahitchka, Florida.

Falling, Christine (b. March 12, 1963) was born in Perry, Florida, to a father who was 65 years old and a mother who was only 16; the second child to this mother and father.

She was raised in poverty, was obese and dull-witted, and required medication to control epileptic seizures. As a child she murdered cats by dropping them from heights or strangling them to "test their nine lives." At age 14, she was married to a man in his 20s, but the marriage was wrought with domestic violence by Christine. Her marriage ended after just six weeks and Christine became a hypochondriac with over 50 visits to the hospital in a two-year period. Her ailments ranged from "red spots" to "vaginal bleeding" to "snakebites." Doctors found no treatable conditions. Since she was unemployable due to her appearance and being intellectual challenged, she babysat for neighbors and relatives to earn money.

In about 1980, 2-year-old Cassidy Johnson, whom Christine was babysitting, was rushed to a doctor's office in Blountsville. She was initially diagnosed with encephalitis, but died three days later. An autopsy found that her death was caused by blunt trauma to the skull. Christine told the authorities that little Cassidy had passed out and fallen from her crib.

Christine moved to Lakeland. Two months later, Jeffrey, age 4, suddenly stopped breathing, according to Christine who was babysitting. Three days later, while the family was away at Jeffrey's funeral, Joseph Spring, age 2 and cousin to Jeffrey, died in his crib while napping, according to the babysitter who just happened to be Christine Falling. Christine moved back to Perry and found a job housekeeping for William Swindle, age 77, who died on Christine's first day on the job.

A few days later, Christine accompanied her stepsister to the doctor's office for her 8-month-old niece, Jennifer Daniels, for the standard childhood vaccinations. Stopping by the market on the way home, the stepsister went into the grocery while Christine stayed in the car with the niece. The baby "just quit breathing" according to Christine. So far very little, if any, suspicion fell on Christine.

On July 2, 1982, Travis Coleman, just 10 weeks old, was under Christine's care when he died. The autopsy revealed internal ruptures caused by suffocation. Christine was brought to the police station for questioning. She confessed to killing three children by "smotheration" (pressing a blanket over their faces in response to the voices telling her "to kill the baby"). According to Christine, she, "Done it the way I had seen it done on TV, but I had my own way. No one could hear them scream."

Christine Falling was sentenced to a term of life imprisonment with no parole for at least 25 years. She became eligible for parole in November 2017, but her application was rejected by the Florida Parole Review Board. She remains behind bars at the Homestead Correctional Institute in Homestead, Florida. Her next parole hearing is scheduled for 2024.

Falls, Neal (September 24, 1969 – July 18, 2015) is a serial killer suspected by police of having murdered as many as 12 women in the states of California, Illinois, Kentucky, Nevada, New York, Ohio, Oregon, and Texas.

It is known that Falls tried to kill Heather Saul of Charleston, West Virginia, who was an "escort" he met online on backpage.com, a site often used to arrange sexual liaisons. Sometime during their encounter, things turned sour and Falls held Heather at gunpoint and tried to strangle her. She grabbed a rake and he put the gun down to get the rake away from her. Heather grabbed his gun and shot and killed him. Police were called and investigated. They found four sets of handcuffs on Falls' body and a list of names, ages, and phone numbers of six other women, apparently found on the Backpage website. Police notified the six women. In his car, they found what they called a "kill kit"— more handcuffs, a machete, knives, axes, a sledgehammer, a bulletproof vest, a gun, shovels, plastic bags, plastic tub full of towels, shovel, and bleach, along with clean white socks and underwear.

Officials in eight states are of the opinion that he may be responsible for the murders of the 12 women—Shasta Himelrick, Tameka Lynch, Wanda Lemons, Timberly Claytor, Loretta Joe Gates, and Terri Lynn Bills; plus these women missing from Chillicothe, Ohio: Jodi Marie Brewer, Misty Marie Saens, Lindsay Marie Harris, Tiffany Sayer, and Jessica Edith Foster. The Ohio Task Force in Chillicothe, Ohio presumes they have been murdered, but only four bodies have been found. The Ohio Task Force is investigating if Falls may be responsible for their disappearances. These murders are known as the *"Chillicothe Killer" – See separate article.*

Father Bluebeard aka **Pandy, Andras** (June 1, 1927 – December 22, 2013) was a serial killer in Brussels, Belgium, who murdered two wives and at least four of his eight children.

Pandy met his first wife, Ilona Sores, in 1957. They had three children—Agnes, born in 1958; Daniel, born in 1962; and Zoltan, born in 1966. The couple divorced in 1967 and Ilona moved out of the house, taking Daniel and Zoltan with her. Pandy began an incestuous relationship with his daughter, Agnes.

In the early 1970s, Pandy went to Hungary where he met his second wife, Edit Fintor, who at the time was married and had three children: Tunde, Timea, and Andrea. They married and Pandy, with his new family, moved back to Brussels, Belgium. They had two more children.

In 1984, Pandy began an incestuous relationship with his stepdaughter, Timea. Agnes found out about the relationship and tried to bludgeon Timea to death. Timea was able to escape and soon moved to Canada.

In 1986, Pandy's wife, Edit, and her daughter, Andrea, disappeared. Pandy claimed they had moved to Germany.

In 1988, his first wife, Ilona, and sons, Daniel and Zoltan, disappeared. Pandy told everyone that they had moved to France. His story changed and he claimed they had gone to South America. In 1990, Agnes was sent on vacation with the remaining children fathered by Pandy. Tunde disappeared in Belgium during this time. Pandy claimed he had thrown her out of the house.

In the early 1990s, Agnes reported to the police that several of her family members were missing and that she and her stepsisters had been raped by their father, but nothing was done by police at the time. In 1997, Andras Pandy's homes were searched, both in Belgium and Hungary, where authorities found teeth, bones, and other human remains.

On March 6, 2002, a court in Belgium convicted Andras Pandy of murdering six family members and dissolving their bodies in chemical drain cleaner. He was also convicted of raping two of his daughters. He was sentenced to life in prison.

Agnes, who admitted to murdering her mother, was found guilty of being an accomplice to five murders and one attempted murder.

There is some conjecture that the convicted man was not Andras Pandy, but actually the younger brother of the real Andras Pandy, who had died in Hungary in 1956.

Fautenberry, John Joseph (July 4, 1965 – July 14, 2009) was a traveling serial killer. Wherever John Fautenberry showed up, murder happened. In November 1990, he murdered a man in Oregon and stole $10,000. He left Oregon and traveled to New Jersey, where he murdered a man at a truck stop by shooting him in the head, and stole his wallet. He left New Jersey and traveled to Ohio, where he was picked up by Joseph William Daron while hitchhiking on I-275 (bypass around Cincinnati). Daron took Fautenberry to the intersection of I-275 and I-71, where Fautenberry thanked Daron by shooting him twice in the chest, killing him. Fautenberry dumped the body in Anderson Township, along the north bank of the Ohio River. He stole Daron's car, credit cards, cash, watch, and Bible. Fautenberry then drove back to Oregon and shot a woman twice in the back of her head. From Oregon, Fautenberry went to Juneau, Alaska, where he murdered an acquaintance in March 1991 by stabbing him 17 times.

John Fautenberry was arrested in Alaska and confessed to the murder in Juneau, as well as the other murders. He was convicted of Joseph Daron's murder in Ohio and sentenced to death. After years of appeals, he was finally executed by lethal injection on July 14, 2009, at the Southern Ohio Correctional Facility in Scioto County, Ohio.

Fayne, Lorenzo (b. 1971) is a confessed Illinois serial killer suspected of murders in Milwaukee, Wisconsin. Fayne was born and raised in Milwaukee. He began traveling back and forth between Milwaukee and East St. Louis, Illinois, to visit with his grandmother in 1989 when he turned 18.

In August 1994, Fayne was convicted of the 1989 beating death of a 6-year-old boy in East St. Louis, Illinois, and was serving a life sentence without the possibility of parole when he confessed to murdering four girls (also in East St. Louis and the neighboring town of Centreville). He was convicted of murdering Latondra Dean, age 14, in March 1992; strangling Fallon Flood, age 9, in July 1992; stabbing to death Glenda Jones, age 17, in June 1993; and stabbing to death Faith Davis, age 17, in July 1994.

Learning of Fayne's confession, Milwaukee Police Chief Arthur Jones ordered an investigation into any unsolved murders during 1989 and 1994 when Fayne could have been in Milwaukee. A search of the national DNA data base linked Fayne to the murder of Rita D. Scott, some 20 years before, whose body was found partially clothed in a pool of blood near a loading dock. Fayne is currently incarcerated at Menard Correctional Center in Menard, Illinois.

Feltner, Jeffrey Lynn (1962 – March 17, 1993) called a Florida TV station in July 1988, telling them that he was killing patients at a nursing home and that he was likely to kill again. The TV station contacted the police and they began an investigation which led them to Jeffrey Feltner. Feltner was questioned but denied any knowledge of the phone call or the murders and he was released.

The calls began again, and the caller claimed to have killed a certain patient, which was easily disproved. Feltner was arrested and found guilty of filing a false report. He served four months.

After his release he moved to Daytona Beach, where he worked at several nursing homes during the next year. The calls started again. This time the police knew who was making the calls and Feltner was arrested. The investigator found out that the calls were not false at all. Some of the patients had been cremated and were not available for autopsy, but one of the patients had not been cremated and his autopsy proved that he had been murdered.

Feltner was found guilty and given a life sentence. He died of AIDS on March 17, 1993.

Feminicides of the Cotton Field aka **Alvarez Cruz, Edgar Ernesto** (c. 1980), Granados **de la Paz, Jose Francisco** (b. 1979), and **Valles, Alejandro Delgado** (c. 1980) were serial killers in the years 1993 to 2003 of at least 14 women in Ciudad Juarez, Mexico. The victims were kidnapped, tortured, raped, and murdered. Some of the victims were mutilated during satanic rituals held by Alverez Cruz. At least one of the victims (Rosario "Chayito") was run over by Alverez Cruz in his 1980s Renault. The killers buried the bodies, or they were taken to vacant lots and dumped. Eight were buried on the cotton fields owned by Alvarez Cruz. Six were found in Mount Cerro Negro. Only seven of the women have been identified.

Oscar Maynez, Chief of State Forensics in Northern Chihuahua where the murders occurred, stated that he believed the murders of the women were committed by an organized group with significant resources. Of the more than 350 women who have disappeared since the early 1990s, at least 93 are very similar. The victims showed signs of torture, mutilation, and rape.

Edgar Ernesto Alvarez Cruz moved to Denver, Colorado with his wife and child in the late 1990s. They separated after two or three years. Pablo Arambula, who had been friends with Alverez Cruz since they were small children, moved into the apartment with him after his wife left.

Mexican authorities asked the US Marshals Service and the Immigration and Customs Enforcement (ICE) for help in locating Alvarez Cruz. He was arrested on West Nevada Place in southwest Denver on August 16, 2006. Jose Francisco Granados de la Paz was also arrested in the United States, but the location was not named. Francisco Granados told authorities that Alvarez was the alleged mastermind of at least 17 of the murders.

Nothing was found on the trial or sentences of these two men. *See separate article Dead Women of Juarez.*

Ferrari, Werner (b. December 29, 1946) was born to an 18-year-old single woman in Switzerland and subsequently placed in a children's home. He returned to his mother's care for a brief time when he was 12 years old, but he began setting fires and committing robberies and was sent back to the home. At the age of 19, he was placed in a psychiatric hospital and diagnosed with a paranoid schizoid personality disorder.

On August 6, 1971, Ferrari murdered a 10-year-old boy. He was sentenced to 10 years, but was released after eight years. Children subsequently began to disappear. At least 11 children from eight different cantons (states) disappeared between 1980 and 1989. Eight of the children's bodies have been found; three are still missing.

On June 8, 1995, Ferrari was convicted of five of the murders and sentenced to life imprisonment. On April 10, 2007, he was acquitted of one of the murders after a nationwide review process, but he remains in prison for the four others.

Fikackova, Marie

Fikackova, Marie (September 9, 1936 – April 13, 1961) was a nurse in a hospital in the town of Susice, Czechoslovakia who is believed by local police to be a serial killer of newborn babies.

She was born into a dysfunctional family. She married, but the union did not last and they divorced. In 1960, she was arrested and accused of murdering a newborn baby. She soon confessed to murdering 10 newborn babies since 1957. She beat the babies about the head, which caused them to die shortly afterward. She never offered a reason for this behavior. Since the hospital lacked procedures for finding these murders, they were discovered simply by chance. Fikackova was charged with only two murders since it was impossible to prove the other killings. No administrator or physician was ever held responsible for not finding the murders, no one was demoted, and the murders were kept secret for decades.

Marie Fikackova was convicted of the murders and sentenced to death. On April 13, 1961, she was hanged at Pankrac Prison in Prague.

Fischer, Joseph (1923 – December 1991) was a transient serial killer. He was arrested in Dutchess County, New York in 1979 and charged with the murder of his wife, Claudine

Eggers, who was 20 years his senior. He was simply tired of having her around. While in custody, Fischer confessed to an additional 32 murders during his travels around the country.

By 1979, investigators had enough solid evidence to connect him to the murders of Betty Joe Gibson, who was killed in Oklahoma, and Alaine Haperman and Veronica Tassielo, both teenagers, who were stabbed to death in Norwalk, Connecticut. He was arrested on July 2 and on May 16, 1980, he was sentenced to life in prison. His involvement in other murders remains unconfirmed.

Joseph Fischer died in prison of a heart attack in December 1991.

Fisher, Constance (c. 1930 – October 1973) murdered her six children by drowning. In March 1954, Fisher was hospitalized at the Augusta State Hospital after she drowned her three children, ages 6 years, 4 years, and 11 months. She was declared cured and released from the hospital in 1959. On June 30, 1966, she drowned three more of her children, ages 6 years, 4 years, and 9 months. She was found not guilty by reason of insanity and recommitted to the Augusta State Hospital.

On the night of October 1, 1973, Constance Fisher escaped from the hospital. Her drowned body was found a week later by duck hunters about seven miles from the hospital.

Fleury, Sergio Paranhos (May 19, 1933 – May 1, 1979) was a police deputy in Sao Paula, Brazil, during the military dictatorship (1960s –1970s). He was chief of D.O.P.S., Brazil's Department for Political and Social Order, as well as the main leader of a repression group known as the *Death Squadron,* and is famous for his cruel torture methods. He was directly responsible for the torture deaths of Jaoquim Ferreire and Eduardo Leite Collen. He was also responsible for the capture and death of guerrilla leader Carlos Marighella in 1969, the massacre at Lapa, and other tortures and murders of political activists and students. He was indicted and convicted of the crime of torture but never served any time. On May 1, 1979, he died mysteriously on his private boat. His body was not autopsied, and the cause of death is not known. It is said that he was murdered in revenge for his crimes against humanity.

Floyd, Cecil Henry (b. March 1941 – June 17, 2011) murdered five men and one woman in 1973-74 during the committing of robberies in Kansas, Nebraska, Indiana, and Florida. He was sentenced to life in Indiana and Nevada, and died of natural causes while in an Indiana prison.

Floyd, Charles (c. 1920) was a truck driver and serial killer. He was a life-long voyeur whose "peeping Tom" activities sometimes failed to satisfy his cravings and he resorted to rape and murder.

On July 10, 1942, the red-headed wife of William Brown, a Tulsa truck driver, who was within days of delivering a baby, was raped and murdered in their apartment on Tulsa's north side. The baby also died.

The next known attack was in December, when Clara Stewart and her daughter, Georgina Green, who were sharing an apartment while Georgina's husband served in the army, were bludgeoned to death and raped. Both women had red hair.

There were no known murders for about 2-1/2 years. On May 15, 1945, Panta Lou Niles, another redhead, was bludgeoned in her sleep and raped after death. The killer entered through the open bedroom window and was still there to answer the phone when a friend called Panta Lou on the phone to wake her for work. When a man answered the phone, the friend became concerned and called the police, but by the time they arrived the man was gone. Henry

Owens, a dull-witted drifter, was arrested on suspicion of murder. Owens had previously been arrested on sexual assault charges, but when he took a polygraph, the results were inconclusive. However, he was still in custody on July 1, 1948, when the killer struck again. Owens was released.

This time, the killer broke into an apartment, clubbed the mother, her 12-year-old daughter, and a young girl spending the night. A neighbor who heard the screams coming from the apartment called the police, but again they arrived too late. The killer was gone and three people were dead. Two blocks away, the killer broke into the apartment of Ruth Norton, another redhead, bludgeoned her to death and raped her. This time a neighbor saw the killer and described him to police stating that he looked like a "truck driver."

Authorities contacted local trucking companies with the description and one company thought that it sounded like Charles Floyd, who was known to have an obsession for redheads. Floyd had quit his job on July 2. His description was broadcast to nearby agencies and to neighboring states. Charles Floyd was arrested on November 22, 1949 in Dallas, Texas. Despite his claim of confusion, he was able to give detectives details of the crimes that only the police and the killer would know. Psychiatric evaluation confirmed his low IQ, which saved him from the electric chair. He was sent to a mental institution where he died a few years later.

Flying Nightmare/Butcher Baker aka **Hansen, Robert Christian** (February 15, 1939 – August 21, 2014) may be responsible for the deaths of at least 21 people near Anchorage, Alaska. Born and raised in Iowa, as a teenager he suffered from chronic acne and severe stuttering, and was frequently bullied at school. He joined the US Army Reserves, but was discharged after serving only one year. He married in the summer of 1960, but his wife divorced him when he was arrested for burning down a school bus garage in Pocahontas, Iowa. He was jailed several times for petty theft. In 1963, he married for the second time. He and his wife moved to Anchorage, Alaska, in 1967, where he was a local hunting champion and broke several records which were documented in the Pope & Young's *Book of World Hunting Records.* These records were removed after his conviction for murder.

It is believed by investigators that Hansen began his serial murders in 1979. His modus operandi would be to pick up a prostitute, pay her for her services, kidnap, torture, and rape her, tie her up, and fly her out to his Knik River Valley cabin in his private airplane. He would strip her naked, release her in a desolate location, and then stalk and kill her with his .223 caliber Ruger Mini-14 rifle or with his hunting knife.

His known victims are: Unidentified female, dubbed "Eklutna Annie", age teen to early 20s, found on July 21, 1980, on Eklutna Lake Road; Joanne Missina, age 24, whose body was also found in July 1980 at a gravel pit nearby Eklutna Lake Road; Andrea Altiery, who disappeared in 1981. No dates given when or if she was found.

On September 12, 1982, the body of Sherry Morrow, age 23, was found on the banks of the Knik River. She was last seen on November 17, 1981.

In June 1983, Cindy Paulson, age 17, was kidnapped and raped by Robert Hansen. She was the lucky one— she managed to escape. She told police that she had been offered $200 by Hansen to pose for pictures, but that Hansen kidnapped her, raped her, and sexually assaulted her with the wooden handle of a hammer. Hansen secured her hands with handcuffs and then put her in his plane. She managed to work one cuff loose and escape from the airplane's cockpit while Hansen was distracted loading supplies. She identified Hansen as her abductor and rapist.

On September 2, 1983, the body of Paula Goulding, age 17, was found on the banks of the Knik River. On April 24, 1984, Malai Larsen's body was found in the parking area by old Knik Bridge. The body of Sue Luna was also found on April 24 along the Knik River. DeLynn Frey's body was found on August 25, 1984, at Horseshoe Lake. On April 26, the body of Teresa Watson was found on the Kenai Peninsula. The body of Angela Feddern was found at Figure Eight Lake on the same day. The body of Tamara Pederson was found on April 29 about 1-1/2 miles from old Knik Bridge. Lisa Futrell's body was found on May 9, just south of old Knik Bridge.

Some serial killers collect trophies from their victims. Hansen was one of those. Police searched his house after his arrest and found his "trophy collection." They found a fish necklace that had been custom-made for Andrea Altiery. They also found jewelry items and identification belonging to other victims, newspaper clippings about the murders and several firearms, including the .223 caliber Ruger Mini-14 rifle used in some of the murders.

Robert Christian Hansen was sentenced to life plus 461 years. He was imprisoned at the Spring Creek Correctional Center in Seward, Alaska, until May 2014, when he was transferred to the Anchorage Correctional Complex because of health issues. He died on August 21, 2014 at Alaska Regional Hospital in Anchorage.

Fokin, Viktor Viktorovich (February 19, 1935 – 2003) aka *The Grandfather Ripper* was born in Novosibirsk, Soviet Union (modern-day Russia). He graduated from high school and was drafted into the Soviet Army. After his discharge from the army he began working at the Novosibirsk Semiconductor Devices Plant. In 1950, he married and had a family. After his wife died in 1988, he developed an insatiable desire for women. He began by dating respectable women, but soon began having sex with prostitutes, tramps, and alcoholics. By the mid-1990s, Fokin found himself to be impotent.

In April 1996, Fokin murdered for the first time. He is believed by Russian police to have murdered at least 10 women. The women he killed were between 18 and 55 years old, most had no specific place of residence, most were alcohol abusers and/or prostitutes. He chose single women and always asked if they had any relatives. The women he murdered were never identified. Some of the victims were picked up in the Railway Square. He took them to his home, raped them, and killed them. Some were strangled, some were drowned in the bathtub, and some were stabbed. He dismembered all of his victims and threw the remains in the garbage container.

His last victim was murdered on March 5, 2000. After dismembering the corpse, he threw the remains into a trash container on Timiryazev Street near his home. That day, a man found a bloody bag of sugar with human remains and took it to the police department. The area was put under surveillance. Hundreds of houses and thousands of apartments were searched. Fokin was detained in mid-March 2000 after his house was searched and police found a lot of female items. He confessed to the murders during the interrogation.

Fokin went on trial in May 2001 and was convicted of killing eight women in Lipetsk Oblast and Tambov Oblast between 1996 and 2000. On October 22, 2001 he was sentenced to 19 years in prison in a corrective labor colony and died two years later.

Folbigg, Kathleen Megan Donovan (b. June 14, 1967) was only 1 year and 7 months old when her father murdered her mother by stabbing her at least 24 times. Kathleen was made a ward of the state and placed into foster care. At the age of three, Kathleen's behavior of simulating sex play and masturbating concerned her caregivers. She was removed from the foster care home and sent to a children's home. Two months later she was sent to the foster care home of a couple who eventually were able to adopt her. Kathleen was not told of her mother's murder until 1984. She met Craig Gibson Folbigg in 1985, purchased a home in Newcastle, New South Wales, Australia and was married to Gibson in September 1987.

On February 1, 1989, Caleb Gibson Folbigg was born. He suffered from a mild case of laryngomalacia (loud breathing), which the doctor told his parents he would outgrow. On February 20, 1990 Kathleen put Caleb to sleep in his room next to his parents' room. Caleb stirred around midnight until about 2 a.m. Kathleen went into the baby's room several times and eventually smothered him. The death was attributed to SIDS (sudden infant death syndrome).

Patrick Allen Folbigg was born on June 3, 1990. His father remained home to help care for Patrick for the first three months after his birth. On October 17, 1990, Craig Gibson Folbigg was awakened by the sounds of his wife screaming and found her standing by Patrick's bed. He was not breathing. Craig tried to revive him with CPR (cardiopulmonary resuscitation). Patrick was taken to the hospital and survived, but he suffered from epilepsy and cortical blindness. On February 13, 1991, Craig received a call at work from Kathleen. She screamed, "It's happening again!" Patrick was dead. He had been smothered by his mother.

Sarah Kathleen was born on October 14, 1992, in the city of Maitland where the couple had moved after Patrick's death. On August 29, 1993, Sarah Kathleen was dead. She had been smothered by Kathleen.

Three years later, the couple moved to Singleton and on August 7, 1997, Laura Elizabeth Folbigg was born. On February 27, 1999, Laura Elizabeth was dead. She too had been smothered by her mother, Kathleen Megan Folbigg.

When Gibson Folbigg discovered Kathleen's diary, he was horrified at what he read. She had murdered their children. The diary detailed her killing spree which started in 1990 and ended in 1999 when all of her babies were gone.

On May 21, 2003, Kathleen Folbigg was found guilty of three counts of murder, one count of manslaughter, and one count of maliciously inflicting grievous bodily harm. She was sentenced to 40 years with a non-parole period of 30 years. In 2005, her sentence was reduced to 30 years in prison with a non-parole period of 25 years. She is being held in protective custody.

Foley, Robert (b. September 13, 1956) is a serial killer from Kentucky. After a day at a car auction, Robert Foley returned to his home where several adults and several children were already congregated. As the adults sat at the kitchen table drinking beer an argument broke out. Foley knocked Rodney Vaughn to the floor and shot him six times. Everyone left quickly except Rodney's brother, Lynn. Foley then shot Lynn in the back of the head and dumped both bodies in a local creek. Their bodies were found two days later. Foley was arrested and charged with capital murder. He was convicted and sentenced to death on September 23, 1993.

In 1994, Robert Foley was charged with the October 8, 1989, murders of Kim Bowerstock, Calvin Reynolds, Lillian Contino, and Jerry McMillan. Foley believed that Kim Bowerstock had reported to his parole officer that he was selling drugs. He found Kim in the company of the other three victims, grabbed her by the hair, and Reynolds came to her assistance. Foley shot Reynolds, and then shot Bowerstock, Contino, and McMillan. He shot Bowerstock a second time. He put the bodies in a septic tank and covered them with lime and cement. On April 27, 1994, Robert Foley was again sentenced to death. He is still awaiting execution at the Kentucky State Penitentiary in Eddyville, Kentucky.

Forces of Evil aka **Hance, William Henry** (c. 1952 – March 31, 1994) was a US soldier and a serial killer who murdered at least four women in and around military bases during 1977-78 in the states of Georgia and Indiana. At the same time as these murders were being committed, there was also a string of murders of several elderly white women by a perpetrator who was nicknamed the *Stocking Strangler*. These murders were committed by Carlton Michael Gary, another black man. *See separate article - Gary, Carlton Michael.*

In September 1977, the body of Karen Hickman, age 24 and an army private, was found at Fort Benning, Georgia. Hickman, who was white, was known to date black men and to frequent pubs where black men hung out.

The local chief of police received a letter written on United States Army stationery. The handwritten note was supposedly from a gang of seven white men who were holding a black woman hostage and would kill her if the *Stocking Strangler* was not apprehended. The writer of the letter referred to the seven white men as the "Forces of Evil". This letter was thought by police to be an effort to draw attention away from the murders at Fort Benning.

In April 1978, the body of Gail Jackson, age 21, was found. She had been murdered in March, weeks before the letter was sent to the police chief. A later letter made a ransom demand of $10,000 to keep Gail alive. The letters were followed by phone calls. Soon after the discovery of Gail Jackson's body, a phone call directed the authorities to a second body at a rifle range at Fort Benning. This was the body of Irene Thirkield, age 32. State investigators were searching bars frequented by blacks. They soon identified the killer as William Hance, who had been a Marine before joining the army. When confronted with the letters in his handwriting, voice recordings, and shoe prints from crime scenes, Hance quickly confessed to the murders of Gail

Jackson and Irene Thirkield. He also confessed to murdering Karen Hickman at Fort Benning in 1977.

Hance was tried and convicted by a court martial for this murder. He was also responsible for the murder of a young black woman at Fort Benjamin Harrison in Indiana. He was not charged with this murder. Hance was sentenced to death in a civilian court for the murder of Gail Jackson. He was executed in the electric chair by the State of Georgia on March 31, 1994.

Forest Park Killer aka **Reed, Todd Alan** (b. May 22, 1967) Three murdered women were found in a city park in Portland, Oregon. The women, found on May 7, May 8, and June 2, 1999, were in steep terrain off a dirt road along NW Saltzman Road. The women were identified as Lilla Fay Moler, age 28; Stephanie Lynn Russell, age 26; and Alexandria Nichole Ison, age 17. All three were from Portland and had similar facial features, were about the same height and weight, and had almost identical hair styles. They were all involved with heroin and two were involved in prostitution.

On July 7, Todd Alan Reed, age 32, was arrested by Portland police as he was leaving his place of employment in the middle of his night-shift job as a produce worker. He had received a telephone call from his girlfriend and he tried to leave immediately after that, but police got to him just as he was unlocking his bicycle.

In February 2001, Todd Alan Reed was sentenced to life without the possibility of parole.

Fornuto, Debbie (1955 – July 11, 2002) In Cook County, Illinois, all six of Debbie's babies died, one after the other between 1972 and 1987, and her estranged husband died from a single gunshot into his left temple as he slept on the couch. Four infants' deaths were attributed to SIDS (sudden infant death syndrome) by the medical examiner;

the other two were undetermined. Then an assistant medical examiner, Dr. Mary Jumbelic, discovered that two of the infants had undergone extensive testing that showed they had no medical problems before they died and police learned that Debbie was the only person at home at the time of each death.

Jumbelic issued new death certificates to show that the children were victims of homicide. However, Dr. J. Bruce Beckwith, a pediatric pathologist who had defined SIDS in 1969, said that it was more likely that Debbie's children had died from a breathing disorder. Faced with conflicting opinions by medical experts, prosecutors closed the case in July 1990. Prosecutors quietly reopened the investigation. Debbie had remarried and was living in Las Vegas when the case was reopened. She refused repeated offers for an interview. Her lawyer, Rick Halprin, said that Debbie denied killing her estranged husband or harming any of her children. She died in a vehicle accident in Las Vegas on July 11, 2002.

Forrest, Warren Leslie (b. 1949) appeared to be a normal 25-year-old, married and the father of two children, until October 2, 1974, when he was arrested for the kidnapping and sexual assault of a young woman. Forrest grew up in Vancouver, Washington and attended Vancouver schools. He then served in the US Army during the Vietnam conflict as a Specialist 5 Missile Crew Service gunner. After his discharge, he attended the North American School of Conservation in Newport Beach, California, and obtained a job with the Clark County Parks and Recreation Department (Washington), where he worked from January 1, 1971, to October 2, 1974. He drove a blue 1974 Ford van with Washington license plates.

On October 2, 1974, Forrest was arrested and charged with the kidnapping and sexual assault of a 20-year-old woman who disappeared on October 1. A man in a blue van stopped at the street corner where she was standing in downtown Portland. He told her he was working on a thesis for class work at Seattle University, and offered her money to pose for him. She got in the van and they drove to the Washington Park area of Portland. There he bound her with tape and drove her to Lacamas Park, where he sexually assaulted her and then shot her in the chest with darts from a .177 caliber dart pistol. He tied a rope around her neck and led her down a path and choked her unconscious. He stabbed her five times in the chest area. There he left her for dead, covered with brush and debris. He took all of her clothing and left the scene. She was not dead and was able to make her way to a public road over a two-hour period. Items used in kidnapping her and other women were found in a footlocker in Forrest's van and articles belonging to the 20-year-old were found in his home. The victim identified Forrest in a lineup. He pleaded not guilty by reason of insanity and was sentenced to commitment at Western States Mental Hospital in Steilacoom, Washington, based on the recommendations of three local psychiatrists. It was later revealed that he told his therapist that he had a total of 13 victims.

In 1979, Forrest was charged with the murder of Krista Kay Blake, age 19, who was last seen on July 11, 1974, getting into a blue van driven by a white male on a street in Vancouver. The blue van with Krista and the white male were seen in the area of Lewisville Park around the time of her disappearance. Her body was discovered, partially disrobed and missing her bra, in a shallow grave at Tukes Mountain. Her hands and feet were tied behind her with baling twine. Warren Leslie Forrest was found guilty of this murder and sentenced to life imprisonment. This was before mandatory sentencing laws, making him eligible for parole in 2014.

Forrest is also a suspect in the following murders/ attempted murders, but to date the evidence against him is not enough to convict him in a court of law:

On December 7, 1971, Jamie Grissim disappeared without a trace. At the time, she was considered a "runaway." Her body has never been found. Five months after she disappeared, her student ID and other of her belongings were found near Sunset Falls in Clark County. Later, the bodies of two women were found nearby.

On February 11, 1972, Barbara Ann Derry, age 18, was last seen hitchhiking along SR 14 east of Vancouver. Her body, also partially disrobed and missing her bra, was found under boards and other debris at the bottom of a silo at the Grist Mill Park in northern Clark County on March 29, 1972. Cause of death was a stab wound to the heart. Her identification was established through dental records.

On July 17, 1974, a 15-year-old girl who was a regular hitchhiker was seen being picked up by a white male in a blue van in the area of SR 502 east of Ridgefield, Washington. Her abductor held her at knife point and drove to Tukes Mountain. The van was parked at the gate to the park, where she was beaten. She was then taken into the woods and tied to a tree with baling twine (the same as was used on Krista Kay Blake). The perpetrator cut off her bra and used it as a gag. He then told the girl that he would come back later and left. The girl managed to chew through the baling twine and escaped. She hid until morning when she found an employee of the park. The abductor returned during the night and gathered up her bra and the twine used to bind her. His van was seen at the park during that time by two witnesses. The girl failed to positively identify her abductor in a police lineup.

On October 12, 1974, two bodies were found in shallow graves in the Dole Valley area of Clark County, Washington. One was the body of Carol Valenzuela, age 18, who had disappeared on August 2, 1974. Authorities later determined that she was a victim of the infamous Ted Bundy. The other female has yet to be identified. She was determined to be a white female, 17 – 23 years old, approximately 5 ft. 6 in. tall, 125 lbs., with long, dark brown hair.

On May 9, 1989, Gloria Nadine Knutson's body was found near Lacamas Lake. She had disappeared from downtown Vancouver on May 31, 1974.

Warren Leslie Forrest is currently incarcerated in the Washington State Penitentiary in Walla Walla, Washington. In 2017 he tried but failed to get parole.

Fowler, Bobby Jack (June 12, 1939 – May 15, 2006) was a serial rapist and suspected serial killer. Nothing was found on his early life. As an adult, he was a transient construction worker who travelled extensively across the United States and western Canada. It is known that he was an alcoholic and addicted to both "speed" and methamphetamine. Fowler could be a charmer, but his personality could change to violence in an instant. It is also known that he spent time in Arizona, Florida, Iowa, Louisiana, Oregon, South Carolina, and Texas, as well as British Columbia in Canada.

In 1969, Fowler was charged with the murder of a man and a woman in Texas, but due to lack of evidence, he was only convicted of discharging a firearm within the city limits. He has an extensive criminal record in the US including attempted murder, assault with a dangerous weapon, sexual assault, arson, and kidnapping. He is believed by investigators to have murdered between two and ten people.

Fowler was arrested in Oregon on June 28, 1995, after a woman reported to police that Fowler had tried to rape her at a local motel. She managed to escape by jumping out the window of the motel with a rope still tied to her ankle. On January 8, 1996, Fowler was convicted of kidnapping, attempted rape, sexual abuse, coercion, assault, and menacing. He was sentenced to a total of 195 months (16 years, 3 months) with the possibility of parole.

On May 15, 2006, Fowler died of lung cancer at Oregon State Penitentiary.

Since that time, Bobby Jack Fowler has been definitely linked to the murders in British Columbia. His DNA was found on the body of Colleen MacMillen, who was murdered in 1974. He is also suspected in the murders of Gale Weys and Pamela Darlington in 1973. The Royal Canadian Mounted Police believe he may have murdered as many as 10 victims in the *Canada Highway of Tears* murders.

For more information see article – "Canada Highway of Tears Murders"

Frampton, Morris (c. 1947) is a probable serial killer. On October 19, 1976, the body of Agnes Williams, age 48, was found beaten and strangled to death in West Seattle. Her skull had been fractured, but police had very little evidence. The case lay unsolved until 2006 when the new Cold Case Squad had DNA testing of evidence found on Agnes Williams' body. They found a match—Morris Frampton. Detectives Mike Ciesynski and Gregg Mixsell paid a visit to Frampton, who was housed in the state prison in Walla Walla, Washington. Five days later, Frampton called the detectives and said he was ready to talk. A few minutes after that, the detectives received a phone call from Agnes Williams' daughter inquiring about her mother's murder. She was not aware that they had DNA evidence to prove that Agnes Williams' murderer was Morris Frampton. After talking with Morris Frampton, they informed Williams' daughter that they had found her killer.

In August 1977, the body of Rosemary Stuart was found in the South Park Marina, Seattle, Washington. Frampton was charged with her death and attacking two other women in 1977. Morris Frampton was sentenced to death in 1978, but his life was spared on appeal.

Frankford Slasher aka **Christopher, Leonard** (b. December 9, 1951) was a serial killer in the Frankford neighborhood of Philadelphia during the same time period as two other serial killers, Gary Heidnik and Harrison Graham.

Christopher's killings stretched over a longer period of time: 1985 – 1990. Although he was convicted of only one murder, police suspect him of these eight other murders: Helen Patent, age 52, murdered on August 19, 1985; in 1986, Anna Carroll, age 68, murdered on January 3 and Suzanna Olszef, age 75, killed on December 25; in 1987, Jeanne Durkin, age 28, murdered on January 8; Catherine M. Jones, age 29, also murdered in January 1987; however, investigators have not definitely tied this murder to the *Frankford Slasher*. Margaret Vaughan, age 66, was murdered on November 11, 1988; Theresa Sciortino, age 30, was murdered on January 19, 1989; and Michelle Dehner, age 30 was murdered on September 6, 1990.

All of the victims were sexually assaulted and stabbed to death. Leonard Christopher was convicted of Carol Dowd's murder. Officially, the eight other murders remain unsolved.

Franklin, Joseph Paul

Franklin, Joseph Paul (April 13, 1950 – November 19, 2013) was an American serial killer who, in high school, was very interested in Evangelical Christianity, then turned to Nazism with memberships in the National Socialist White People's Party and the Ku Klux Klan.

Franklin was born James Clayton Vaughn to a poor family in Mobile, Alabama. In 1976 he changed his name to Joseph Paul in honor of Paul Joseph Goebbels, and Franklin in honor of Benjamin Franklin. He drifted up and down the east coast and through the midwest states, wreaking his brand of havoc as he went. He was a very organized killer who did not try to contact his victims, but killed them from a distance. He was a very proficient marksman with either his rifle or pistol in "cleansing the world" of what he felt were inferior people--Blacks and Jews—and especially mixed couples.

In September 1976, Franklin sprayed mace on an interracial couple he had followed down an alleyway. On July 29, 1977, he firebombed the Beth Shalom Synagogue in Chattanooga, Tennessee. On August 7, he shot and killed another interracial couple while fleeing a bank robbery in Madison, Wisconsin. On October 8, he hid in the tall grass behind the Brith Shalom Synagogue in Richmond Heights, Missouri, where he shot and killed one man and injured two others using a Remington 700 hunting rifle.

On March 6, 1978, he shot pornographer Larry Flynt and his lawyer in Lawrenceville, Georgia, which he says was his retaliation for Hustler (magazine) displaying interracial couples having sex. On July 29, he again hid in long grass by the Pizza Hut in Chattanooga where he used a 12-gauge shotgun to murder a black man and injure his white girlfriend.

On July 12, 1979, the manager of a Taco Bell in Doraville, Georgia was shot and killed through a window from a distance of about 150 yards. On August 18, Franklin murdered a black man at a Burger King in Falls Church, Virginia. On October 21, Franklin fired five shots from a distance of 100 yards to murder a mixed-race couple in Oklahoma City, Oklahoma. On December 5, he murdered a 15-year-old white prostitute with a shotgun because she told him she had black customers.

In January 1980, somewhere around the 10th, Franklin, with a long-distance rifle, murdered a black man, age 19, in Indianapolis, Indiana. On the 16th or 17th, he murdered another black man in Indianapolis with the same rifle from 150 yards away. By May, Franklin was in Wisconsin. He used a handgun to shoot a girl who was hitchhiking in Monroe County. On May 29, Franklin claimed he shot and seriously wounded Vernon Jordan, Jr., a civil rights activist, after seeing him with a white woman in Fort Wayne, Indiana. On June 8, Franklin was in Bond Hill (Cincinnati), Ohio, where he had waited for hours on an overpass looking for an interracial couple to shoot. He grew tired of waiting and instead murdered Darrel Lane, age 14, and Donte Evans, age 13, who were cousins. On June 15, Franklin was in Johnstown, Pennsylvania, where he shot and killed Arthur Smothers, age 22, and Kathleen Mikula, age 16, an interracial couple. On June 25, Franklin killed two hitchhikers, Nancy Santomero, age 19, and Vicki Durian, age 26, using a .44 caliber Ruger pistol in Pocahontas County, West Virginia. They had told him they were into race-mixing. On August 20, Franklin murdered two black men from 40 yards away while they were jogging with white women in Salt Lake City, Utah, using a Marlin Firearms lever-action rifle.

Joseph Paul Franklin was finally arrested in 1980. He has either been charged with or confessed to 20 murders, six aggravated assaults, 16 bank robberies and two bombings. Having been convicted of murder in several states where he received life sentences, he was finally convicted of the murder of the man in Richmond Heights, Missouri, and was sentenced to death and housed in the Potosi Correctional Center in Potosi, Missouri.

On November 19, 2013, Joseph Paul Franklin was executed by lethal injection by the State of Missouri.

Franklin, Ricky Levert (c. 1980) is suspected of being a serial killer by investigators in Jackson, Mississippi. In 1999, the bodies of five women were found near the house where Ricky Franklin lived. Finally in 2008, he was charged with the murder of one of the women, but the charge was dropped due to lack of evidence. In 2006, he was accused of stabbing a woman, but he was acquitted. In 2007, he was again acquitted of assaulting a woman.

Franklin was arrested in November 2009 and charged with kidnapping, sexual battery, rape, and assault of a woman in Jackson, Mississippi.

Authorities can tie him to at least 10 murders, but they cannot garner enough evidence to convict him. Witnesses claim that the police are "blowing them off" because they are considered "undesirables," "women of the streets," or "prostitutes."

Since 1992, he has been arrested at least 11 times on charges ranging from misdemeanors, assaults, rapes, and murders, but he has not been convicted due to reluctant witnesses and insufficient evidence to convict him. He has been acquitted or cases end in mistrials, and for the convictions he has served only a total of three years in jail.

Frankston Killer aka **Denyer, Paul Charles** (b. April 14, 1972) was an Australian serial killer who stalked and murdered three young women in 1993.

On June 11, Elizabeth Stevens, age 18, had just exited a bus when she was dragged to nearby Lloyd Park where Denyer slashed her throat and carved a criss-cross pattern into her chest.

In early July, Deborah Fream, age 22, left her 12-day-old baby at home with a friend in the early evening and went to buy milk. She left her car unlocked as she ran into the store. Denyer had climbed into the backseat during her absence. When she returned, he hijacked the car. Deborah was taken to Taylor's Road and her throat was savagely slashed.

On the same evening, Rosza Toth was attacked by Denyer while she was walking home from the Seaford railway station. Denyer dragged her toward the toilet block, but she managed to break free and notified police.

On July 30, Natalie Russell, age 17, was walking home from school and took a short-cut along a bicycle path through a park when she was attacked. Denyer dragged her through a large hole in a wire fence. She put up a fight, which angered her attacker. He slashed at her head and neck, brutally killing her.

In 1990, Sarah MacDiarmid disappeared from the Kananook railway station. The only evidence that a crime had been committed was a pool of blood next to her car, parked at the station. Her body has never been found. Denyer denied any involvement. Michelle Brown's murder was also looked into. Her body had been found naked, but was too decomposed to determine the cause of death.

Paul Denyer was arrested on March 31, 1994, and charged with three counts of murder and one count of abduction. He was given three consecutive life sentences with a non-parole period of 30 years.

Freeway Killers were a group of men who murdered together and singly. Those who murdered together were **William George Bonin** (January 8, 1947 – February 23, 1996), **Vernon Butts** (August 27, 1957 – January 11, 1981), **Gregory M. Miley** (c. 1960 – May 25, 2016), **James Michael Munro** (c. 1961), **William Ray Pugh** (c. 1962), and **Eric Marten Wijnaendts** (c. 1960).

Beginning in December 1972, there were more than 44 murders of young men and boys during the next 7-1/2 years in seven southern counties in California.

The arrest of **Patrick Kearney** in July 1977 solved at least 21 of the murders. *See separate article - Kearney, Patrick.*

The arrest of **Randy Kraft** aka the *Scorecard Killer* in 1983 solved 16 of these murders. *See separate article - Kraft, Randy Steven.*

In most of the murders, the modus operandi was strangulation, stabbing with knives and ice picks, and sadistic torture. According to authorities, 21 of the murders were probably committed by the same person or persons. The murders committed between 1972 and 1978, however, were probably not the work of those listed above, except for William Bonin, as they would have been too young.

When William Ray Pugh was arrested on June 10, 1980, he started confessing and named William Bonin as the killer.

William George Bonin had arrest convictions for kidnapping, sodomy, child molestation, and forcible oral sex in four separate attacks between November 1968 and January 1969. In 1980 he was arrested, charged with 16 murders, convicted, and sentenced to death. He was executed by lethal injection at San Quentin State Prison on February 23, 1996. *See separate article - Bonin, William George.*

Vernon Butts was charged with three counts of first-degree murder and 17 felonies including conspiracy, kidnapping, robbery, sodomy, oral sex, and sexual perversion. He tried several times to commit suicide. On January 11, 1981, he was finally successful. He hanged himself in his cell.

Gregory M. Miley was charged with first-degree murder and seven related felony counts. He was sentenced to 25 years to life for first-degree murder. He was attacked at Mule Creek State Prison, where he was being held, and died of his injuries on May 25, 2016. James Michael Munro was charged with one count of first-degree murder. He pleaded guilty to second-degree murder and was sentenced to 15 years to life. He came up for parole in 2014, but was denied after admitting in a telephone call that he had saved enough money to buy a van like the one he and Bonin had used and intended to continue Bonin's work once released.

William Ray Pugh was charged with voluntary manslaughter and sentenced to six years. He served five years at Mule Creek State Prison before being paroled.

Freight Train aka **Guatney, William** (February 14, 1922 – March 31, 1996) traveled around the United States in boxcars. He lived off the land and picked up odd jobs here and there. He was also a serial killer who murdered boys.

In September 1975, Jon Simpson, age 13, and Jacob Surber, age 12, went to the State Fair in Lincoln, Nebraska, but did not return. Their bodies were discovered several days later. Guatney was charged with this murder on August 22, 1979.

On August 1, 1976, Mark Helmig, age 9, disappeared from his home near Pekin, Illinois. His mummified body was discovered on August 24, 1976 in a boxcar. Four years earlier, Richard Griener, age 13, disappeared on January 17, 1972. He had left his home in Pekin about 4:00 p.m. to go sledding at a nearby park, less than 200 yards from where Mark Helmig disappeared. He never returned home. His body has never been found.

In 1978, Marty Lancaster, age 14, disappeared from his home in Normal, Illinois. No other information was found.

On May 20, 1979, Jack Hanrahan, age 12, disappeared from a local bowling alley in Topeka, Kansas, where he was playing pinball. Jack's body was found May 30, 1979, floating face-down in a creek in northern Osage County. A local Topeka man was charged and tried for this murder, but was found not guilty in 2000.

William Guatney was declared insane and committed to a mental hospital, where he died at the age of 74.

French, Anne aka **Shoebox Annie Mayer** and her son **French, William Donald** were career criminals who robbed and murdered at least seven people in Montana and Washington in the 1920s. Anne was sentenced to life in Washington as a habitual criminal in 1928. William was sentenced to five to ten years in Washington in 1928. Both died in prison.

Fry, Robert (b. August 18, 1973) was a serial killer in New Mexico. On November 29, 1996, Fry murdered Matthew Trecker, age 18, and Joseph Fleming, age 25. They were stabbed and their throats were slashed at a store in Farmington. Fry was sentenced to two terms of life in prison for these two murders.

On March 31, 1998, he murdered Donald Tsosie, age 40, by beating him to death with a shovel. Tsosie's body lay for almost a month at the bottom of a cliff south of Farmington before being discovered. Fry was sentenced to life in prison for this murder.

On June 9, 2000 he stabbed and bludgeoned Betty Lee, age 36, to death with a sledgehammer in San Juan County. Robert Fry was sentenced to die by lethal injection. In June 2019, his sentence was changed to life in prison by the New Mexico Supreme Court. He is currently housed at the Penitentiary of New Mexico, Santa Fe, New Mexico.

Fuhr, Christian Stephen (b. May 16, 1968) was a tree-trimmer, a cocaine user, and a serial killer in Columbus, Ohio. He served time in New York for possession of stolen property and was released in 1992 and came to Columbus about 1997. He chose white prostitutes between the ages of 29 and 36 as his victims, and their bodies were found within a half-mile radius of each other.

On November 7, 2001, the body of Kimberly Rodgers, age 29, the mother of two small children, was found partially nude in a cornfield off Groveport Road. She had been strangled to death. She worked as a cashier at a convenience store on the south side of Columbus and had been convicted of prostitution.

On November 18, the partially nude body of Shawna L. Sowers, age 30, was found at a construction site, about 30 yards from where Kimberly Rodgers' body had been found. She had also been strangled and her neck was broken. She also had a conviction of prostitution.

On November 24, Thanksgiving Day, the body of Lisa Crow, age 36, the mother of four children, was found behind a business on South High Street very near where the other two victims had been found. Although she had never been convicted of prostitution, several sources, including Lisa's mother, said she was involved in it.

The police connected Fuhr to the murders through a pickup truck, with a flat tire, located near the Ohio Wire Form and Spring Company on South High Street, where Crow's body was discovered. The truck had been loaned to Fuhr by his boss the day before Crow's body was found. Fuhr was interviewed several times by authorities. At his second interview, blood was taken for DNA testing. Finally, when he appeared for his third interview, he was arrested for the murders of Shawna Sowers and Lisa Crow.

Christian Stephen Fuhr was sentenced to two terms of life and has been designated a "violent sexual predator." He is currently serving his life sentences at Lebanon Correctional Institute in Lebanon, Ohio.

Fukiage, Sataro (February 1889 – September 28, 1926) was born in Shimogyō-ku, Kyoto, Japan, and was forced by his parents to go to work at age nine. His first experience with sex was at age 11 when he had sex with a girl about 17 years old. He murdered for the first time in 1906, an 11-year-old girl who was an acquaintance.

In 1901, he was arrested for theft. He used his time in prison to learn kana (symbolic writing of the Japanese language) and math. He was again arrested for theft a very short time after his release. He learned classical Chinese during his second stint in jail.

Arrested in 1906 for the rape and murder of a girl in Kinkaku-ji, Fukiage was in jail until 1922. During this period in jail, he studied the works of Confucius, Mencius, Socrates, Aristotle, and Nichiren. Upon his release in 1922, he was able to find a job, but was released due to his criminal record.

When he was arrested on July 28, 1924, police in Kyoto believed that between June 1923 and April 1924, Fukiage had raped and murdered six girls between the ages of 11 and 16. He confessed to 13 murders but later recanted. He was found guilty of the six murders and was sentenced to death on May 17, 1925. The sentence was upheld by the Supreme Court of Japan and Fukiage was hanged on September 28, 1926.

Fyfe, William Patrick (b. February 27, 1955) was born in Toronto, Ontario, Canada, and raised by an aunt. In 1958, they moved to Montreal, Quebec, where he grew up and became a handyman. He also became a serial killer.

The actual number of his victims may never be known, but he is suspected by Montreal investigators of being responsible for the murders of at least nine women, all between the ages of 45 and 62, except two; one was 26 and the other 37. All had been sexually assaulted and stabbed to death. He was tied to the murders by a fingerprint left on the door frame of Mary Glenn's house on December 15, 1999. DNA evidence tied William Patrick Fyfe to the other murders.

Fyfe was sentenced to life in prison. He is serving his time at a psychiatric hospital in Saskatchewan. Montreal police also consider Fyfe a suspect in the *Plumber* violent serial rapings in the 1980s in downtown Montreal. A book about his life, entitled, *The Killer Handyman William Patrick Fyfe,* was written by CL Swinney in 2015.

Gaidamachuk, Irina Viktorovna (b. 1972) was born in Nyagan, Khanty-Mansi Autonomous Okrug, Soviet Union. She became addicted to alcohol at an early age. In the early 1990s, she moved to Krasnoufimsk, Sverdlovsk Oblast, where she met and married Yuri. They had two children. Her alcoholism was so severe that Yuri refused to give her any money, knowing she would spend it on alcohol.

In 2002, Gaidamachuk came up with a brilliant idea. She posed as a social worker to gain access to the home of elderly women, whom she killed with an axe or hammer and robbed of whatever money she could find. She sometimes set fire to the victim's home in an effort to cover her tracks. After a while, the fires were linked together, but there were few leads. Most of the crimes were committed in Yekaterinburg, Serov, Achit, and Druzhinino.

Gaidamachuk attempted to kill an elderly woman in 2010, but the woman managed to escape. She reported the incident to the police and said that her assailant was a female, which was an important clue as the police had been looking for a male.

When Gaidamachuk murdered her last victim, she was seen by a neighbor as she left the scene and reported it to police. Gaidamachuk was quickly found and arrested. She confessed to the murders and said that she committed the murder-robberies to pay for vodka because her husband refused to give her any money.

Irina Gaidamachuk was charged with 17 counts of murder and one count of attempted murder. She was sentenced to 20 years in prison. Relatives of the victims were outraged at the short sentence, stating that she had received only one year per victim and that she should never be freed.

Gainesville Killers aka **Henry, William Glen** (b. May 3, 1970) and **Crockett, David Lynn** (b. May 1, 1969) On March 7, 1988, Tommy Matthews and Kenny Davis spotted a couple of teenagers (Henry and Crockett) in Gainesville,

Texas, around 10:00 a.m. looking around their father-in-law's car parked in the yard. When questioned, the teens said they were looking for a phone to use. Matthews and Davis told the boys there was no phone in the car and asked them to leave, which they did.

About an hour later, Deana Woodard returned to her trailer home about 200 yards from where Matthews and Davis had seen the teens. She was found stabbed to death and nearly decapitated with an axe. Her son, Cory, age 1, was left alone in the trailer. Among things that were stolen were Deana's guns. Her blue Thunderbird had also been stolen and driven 60 miles southeast before being abandoned.

Henry and Crockett's next known location was in Farmersville, Texas where they broke into the house of Cecil Morrison, age 85, and his son, Cecil Jr., age 62. For the next hour, they beat and tortured the two men before shooting them to death with Deana's guns. They stole a beige Chevrolet pickup truck from the Morrisons and drove it into a lake at about 9:00 p.m. They also threw Deana's guns in the lake.

They were next seen walking along a highway after crossing over into Arkansas. About 10:00 p.m., they stopped at a trailer in Saratoga, Arkansas, owned by Kenneth Olden to ask for help with their broken-down truck. Kenny left with the strangers in his 1983 Mustang, as witnessed by Kenny's girlfriend Brenda. Shortly after, the teens shot and killed Kenny Olden and stole his Mustang. They drove the car into a creek in Brown Springs, Oklahoma, and left their footprints in the mud near the car.

Police in Texas, Arkansas, and Oklahoma were left with only one clue: an earring was found in Cecil Morrison's truck. A young man came forward and claimed he had owned it but had given it to a boy named John Colwell. Colwell had lived about 200 yards from Deana Woodward, but the Colwell family had moved away about a month before the murders. Investigators contacted him and he said that he did not know what had happened to the earring.

Authorities did learn that two teens matching the killers' descriptions had been seen walking away from the Colwell home on the morning of the murders.

On February 1, 1990, William Glen Henry was arrested after his fingerprints matched those found in Kenneth Olden car. He soon confessed and named Davey Lynn Crockett as his accomplice. Crockett was arrested on February 10. He led investigators to where they had ditched Deana's car. The reason given for the murders—they were bored.

William Henry pleaded guilty to three counts of first-degree murder and was given two life sentences to be served consecutively. He is currently being held at the George Beto Unit, a maximum-security prison, in Tennessee Colony, Texas.

David Crockett pleaded guilty and was also given two life sentences. He is currently serving his sentences at Alfred Hughes Prison in Gatesville, Texas.

Gainesville Ripper aka **Rolling, Danny Harold** (May 26, 1954 – October 25, 2006) was a serial/mass killer who murdered three people in Shreveport, Louisiana in 1989 and five in Gainesville, Florida, in 1990. Rolling was born in Shreveport to James and Claudia Rolling. His father was a police officer who physically abused his wife, Danny, and Kevin, his younger brother. During one incident, Danny's father pinned him to the ground, handcuffed him, and had fellow officers take his son away. In his teen and young adult years, Rolling was arrested several times for robberies. In May 1990, he tried to kill his father during a family fight. His father lost an eye and an ear during the fight.

On November 4, 1989, Rolling broke into a home in Shreveport while the family was preparing dinner. He murdered William Grissom, age 55, his daughter, Julie, age 24, and his grandson, Sean, age 8. Julie's body was mutilated, cleaned, and posed. There were no arrests.

August 1990 found Rolling in Gainesville, Florida. On August 24, well after midnight, he broke into an apartment at the University of Florida shared by freshmen Sonja Larson, Christina Powell, and Tonya Wilson. Fortunately for Tonya, she was not home that night. Rolling saw Christina asleep on the couch and decided to see who else might be there. He found Sonja asleep in an upstairs bedroom. He first taped her mouth shut, then stabbed her to death. Rolling returned downstairs, found Christina still asleep on the couch, taped her mouth, and tied her hands behind her back. He cut off her clothes and then raped her. He forced her to lay face-down on the floor and killed her with five stabs to her back. He then posed the two girls in sexually provocative positions, which he had also done to the victim in Shreveport.

On August 25, Rolling broke into Christa Hoyt's apartment through the sliding glass door, but no one was there. He sat in a chair in the living room as he waited for someone to come home. Christa opened the door to her apartment and was surprised by Rolling, who put her in a chokehold. He taped her mouth, bound her hands together, led her into the bedroom, cut off her clothes, and raped her. He forced her to lay face-down and stabbed her to death— almost an exact duplicate of the murder of Christina Powell except that he decapitated Christa and put her head on a shelf facing her body.

News of the murders had caught the attention of the entire country. Students began staying and sleeping in groups, changing their routines; some even withdrew from the school and headed home.

On August 27, Rolling broke into another apartment through the sliding glass door shared by Manny Taboada and Tracy Paules, both 23 years old. He entered the bedroom where Manny was sleeping. Manny was a burly

200 pounder but lost the struggle with Rolling and was killed. Tracy heard the commotion and walked down the hall to Manny's bedroom, saw Rolling, and ran back to her bedroom and tried to barricade herself in the room. Still Rolling had little trouble getting into the room, taping her mouth and wrists, cutting off her clothes, and raping her. He then turned her face-down and stabbed her to death. She was posed the same as the other women, but he left Manny as he had died.

Four of his victims were female, petite, Caucasian, brunettes, and had brown eyes. Manny was just collateral damage, in the wrong place at the wrong time.

On September 7, 1990, Rolling was arrested for burglary in Ocala, Florida. Investigators determined that the tools he used in the burglary matched the marks left at his break-ins in the three apartments in Gainesville. Authorities in Shreveport, Louisiana, notified the authorities in Gainesville, Florida, that there were many similarities between their 1989 murders of the Grissoms and the murders of the students in Gainesville.

Investigators in Florida found where Rolling was camped in a wooded area near the apartment complexes where his victims lived and died. At the camp, they also found recordings of Rolling singing country songs he had composed, but more importantly, they found audio recordings alluding to the murders. In November 1991, Danny Harold Rolling was charged with the murders.

He was finally brought to trial in 1994 by Len Register, State Attorney, Alachua County, Florida. Rolling stated that his motive was to be a serial killer "super star" like Ted Bundy. Rolling unexpectedly pleaded guilty to all of the charges before the trial began. State Attorney Rod Smith presented the penalty phase for the prosecution. Rolling was sentenced to death on each count of murder. Shortly before his execution, Rolling confessed to the murders of the Grissom family. He was executed by lethal injection on October 25, 2006, at the Florida State Prison, Raiford, Florida.

Gallego Sex Slaves aka **Gallego, Gerald Armond** (July 17, 1946 – July 18, 2002) and **Gallego, Charlene Adell Williams** (b. October 10, 1956) were husband and wife serial killers in California and Nevada during the years 1978 – 1981. They kidnapped their victims and kept them for a period of time as sex slaves before murdering them.

Gerald Gallego's father was executed in 1955 in Mississippi's gas chamber for the murders of two policemen. Gerald was arrested in 1959, at the age of 13, for raping a 6-year-old girl. He was also arrested, some years later, for having sex with his teenage daughter.

On September 10, 1978, Rhonda Scheffler and Kippi Vaught were shopping at the Country Club Plaza in Sacramento when Charlene enticed them into the Gallegos' van. The girls were repeatedly raped that night. The following day they were taken to Sloughhouse, made to get out of the van and walk into a field where there was a ditch. Gerald hit Kippi with a tire iron, then turned and hit Rhonda. He then shot each in the head with a .25 caliber pistol, and saw Kippi move, so he shot her in the head three more times.

On June 24, 1979, at the Washoe County Fair (Nevada), Brenda Judd and Sandra Colley were lured into the Gallego van when the Gallegos promised to pay them for helping to deliver some leaflets. Charlene drove the van while Gerald repeatedly raped both girls. The girls were forced to perform sexual acts on each other. When the Gallegos grew tired of the girls, Gerald took Sandra to a dry creek bed and hit her with the shovel. He then beat Brenda to death. The girls were buried in a deep hole and a rock was placed on their grave. The girls were listed as runaways.

On April 2, 1980, Stacey Redican and Karen Chipman Twiggs were kidnapped from the Sunrise Mall in Citrus

Heights. The Gallegos sexually abused the girls and when they grew tired of this, they murdered them.

On June 7, 1980, the Gallegos were in Oregon on a short vacation when Gerald found his next victim, Linda Aguilar, who was pregnant at the time, walking down a highway going home from a local store. Even though she was 21 and too old to be Gerald's type, he decided he wanted her. She accepted his offer of a ride. After Gerald had raped the young woman, Charlene drove the van to an isolated area. Gerald struck Linda with a rock and strangled her while Charlene wandered aimlessly in the woods.

The Gallegos found their next victim on July 16, 1980, at a West Sacramento bar called the Sail Inn. They spent the day there drinking, stayed until closing time, and went to their van in the parking lot, but they did not leave. Virginia Mochel, the bartender, closed the bar and walked to the parking lot where she was forced into the Gallegos' van by Gerald using his .357 caliber pistol. This time, Gerald drove the van and they went to the Gallego home. Charlene went inside and watched television while Gerald raped Virginia. Charlene then drove while Gerald strangled Virginia to death. Her body was dumped close to Clarksburg. Virginia had two small children at home waiting for her. The following day was Gerald's 34th birthday.

On November 2, 1980, in the early morning, Gerald spotted a young couple, Craig Miller, and his fiancée, Mary Elizabeth Sowers, standing on the side of a street. He got out of the car and walked brazenly up to them, pointing his .25 caliber Beretta, and ordered them into the van. Friends of the couple saw the abduction and wrote down the van's license plate number. Arriving at a secluded area, Gerald ordered Craig out of the car and shot him in the back of his head. Gerald fired two more shots into the head of Craig Miller's lifeless body. Charlene drove them to their apartment, taking Mary with them. After raping Mary for several hours, Gerald ordered Charlene to drive them to a remote area where he ordered Mary out of the van and then shot her three times.

The couple was arrested shortly afterward, thanks to the friends of Craig Miller and Mary Elizabeth Sowers who had given the license plate number to the police. Sacramento investigators believe Gerald and Charlene Gallego were responsible for the murders of at least 10 people, most of them female teenagers, plus Linda Aguilar's unborn child, between 1978 and 1981.

In 1984, Gerald Gallego was convicted of the murders in Nevada. He received a sentence of death. His death sentence was overturned in 1999 and he won the right to a new trial. He was again convicted and sentenced to death. Charlene testified against him and pleaded guilty, and agreed to a sentence of 16 years and eight months in Nevada. She was released from the Nevada prison in July 1997.

Also in 1984, Gerald Gallego was convicted of the murders in California and sentenced to death. Again, Charlene testified against him in exchange for not being charged in California. Gerald Gallego died of rectal cancer on July 18, 2002 at the Nevada prison's medical center.

Gansu Ripper aka **Gao Chengyong** (November 10, 1964 – January 3, 2019) was a married man with two children, but he was a distant father, seeing his children only once a year during the Lunar New Year festival. Gao Chengyong was known as a quiet man and respectful of others. People who worked with him at a vocational school in Baiyin did not know him well and said he almost never talked about his past. It was a shock to all who knew him when he was arrested for killing 11 people in Baiyin, in Gansu Province, China, and Baotou in Inner Mongolia between 1988 and 2002.

Chengyong's victims were usually dressed in red. His first known victim was a 23-year-old woman killed in her home in Baiyin in 1988 by being stabbed 26 stab times.

In November of 1988, he raped and murdered Cui Jinping. He also cut off her hands and her breasts. These parts have never been found. The killings continued until 2002, when they stopped.

Forensic officers finally linked one man to all 11 killings. Police had gathered fingerprints, semen, and DNA samples, but did not tie them to Gao because he was not listed as living in Baiyin. They released a statement in 2004 about the killings and offered a reward of $30,000 for information leading to the arrest of the killer. When Chengyong's uncle was arrested for a minor crime in Baiyin, his DNA was collected and tested. The test showed that the uncle was related to the killer. The *Gansu Ripper* was finally arrested.

Gao Chengyong was found guilty of 11 murders and sentenced to death. He was executed by lethal injection on January 3, 2019.

Gargiulo, Michael Thomas (b. February 15, 1976) is a serial killer who may have murdered 10 women. He stands accused of murdering three women and attempting to murder a fourth.

Investigators believe that he stabbed his neighbor Tricia Pacaccio, age 18, to death on August 14, 1993. He was under watch by the police in Northfield Township (Chicago), Illinois. He then moved to Los Angeles to avoid this scrutiny.

Between 2001 and 2008, Gargiulo committed three murders. On February 21, 2001, Ashley Ellerin was stabbed 35 times in her home in Hollywood. On December 1, 2005, Gargiulo's neighbor, Maria Bruno, was stabbed 17 times and her breasts were cut off at her home in El Monte. On April 28, 2008, another neighbor of Gargiulo's, Michelle Murphy, fought off her attacker in her home in Santa Monica. Blood matching Gargiulo's DNA was found at the scene.

Gargiulo was arrested on June 6, 2008, by the Santa Monica Police Department. He has been charged with the murders of Ellerin and Bruno in California, as well as the murder of Pacaccio in Illinois. Michael Thomas Gargiulo was found guilty of the two murders in California. On October 18, 2019, after several hours of deliberation, a jury recommended the death penalty. In late February 2020, a judge postponed the expected sentencing amid defense claims that Gargiulo's initial trial was flawed.

Garrow, Robert F. (March 4, 1936 – September 11, 1978) shot and killed four people in Adirondack Park in New York State. He raped two of the victims. He was serving 25 years to life when he was shot and killed during a prison break on September 11, 1978.

Gas Man aka ***Sassak, Harald*** (1948 – August 21, 2013) was so-named because he posed as an employee of the gas plant to gain entry to his victims' homes in Vienna, Austria, between 1971 and 1972.

Sassak was the son of a bricklayer. He learned the plumber trade and served in the military at Lainz Hospital from 1966 to 1969 where he worked as an auxiliary. He was dismissed from the hospital when he did not produce a medical confirmation after suffering a case of jaundice. By 1971, Sassak was working at the gas plant as an equipment checker.

He only robbed the elderly and his modus operandi was to announce, "The gas man is here." He was then allowed entry into the house to check out their equipment. After he had completed his inspection, he presented the occupant of the home with a statement of the amount owed. The occupant would then go to where they kept their money and Sassak would knock them down, rob, and sometimes murder them. During his 11 known robberies, he murdered six women and one man, all aged 66 to 88 years. The man suffered 20 broken ribs, a shattered larynx, and multiple contusions. Sassak also injured six other elderly victims and raped an 83-year-old woman.

His victims described him as a chubby, nice man. The neighbor of one of his victims drew a composite sketch which led to Sassak's arrest and conviction. He was charged with seven murders, 11 robberies, and one rape. He was sentenced to life in prison. He died at a Lower Austrian nursing home after a prolonged illness on August 21, 2013.

Gatchina Psychopath aka **Smirnov, Vasily Alexandrovich** (November 30, 1947 – 1980) was born in Sopka, Tver Oblast, RSFSR (Russian Soviet Federative Socialist Republic), and was an only child. His father died when he was very young and his mother indulged him in every way possible, except that he was not allowed to talk with his peers and he was not permitted to attend dances or go to places where he could meet girls.

At the age of 18, he tried to rape his mother after hitting her on the head with a hammer, but she escaped. He served his obligation to the Soviet Army. After being discharged, he raped an elderly woman and was sent to prison, where he was raped by another inmate. His mother died while he was imprisoned.

The raped and brutally murdered body of Marina Koshkina, age 8, was found on the bank of the Izhora River on September 3, 1979. Her killer had driven a nail into her skull. Soon after, a boy's body was found at Silver Lake. He was identified as Andrei Lopatin. He had been raped and then stabbed to death. Smirnov was in the process of cutting off a piece of the body to use for food, but was frightened off by a man on a bicycle. Very soon after the murder, rumors were rampant of a vampire in the area who drank children's blood.

Smirnov did not always kill his rape victims and frequently was not reported to police due to the humiliation the victims felt after being violated. His next murder victim was an elderly woman who was considered rich. After raping her, he tore off her head and robbed her. He set fire to the home as he was leaving. Smirnov fled to Petergof, where he raped a pregnant girl, but she did not report it at the time. Tatyana Emshova, the mother of two and a teacher, came to Gatchina for a seminar. She was raped and murdered. A woman who had been raped by Smirnov contacted the investigators. She told of being raped on the very same day that Emshova was raped and murdered. Smirnov was identified as the perpetrator. Investigators went to Smirnov's house only to find a burned-out shell.

Smirnov attacked a group of children and managed to rape one girl. He was found and arrested shortly afterward. He talked freely of the rapes and murders, and confessed to a murder that had been classified as a traffic collision. The police and coroner had overlooked the nail that was driven into the woman's skull, which he had done to all of his victims. Vasily Smirnov was convicted of the five murders and sentenced to death. In 1980, he faced the firing squad.

Gavit, Seema Mohan (b. 1975) and her half-sister **Shinde, Renuka Kiran** (b. 1973) are killer sisters in Pune, state of Maharashtra, India, who kidnapped and murdered at least 13 babies and small children. They taught the children to pick pockets and used them to take the blame for their own crimes. When they became too problematic, the children were murdered. The sisters were arrested on November 19, 1996.

On June 29, 2001, Seema and Renuka were convicted of kidnapping 13 children and murdering six of them. They were given the death penalty, the first women in India to be sentenced to death. The Supreme Court confirmed the death penalty. In 2014, President Pranab Mukherjee rejected their pleas for mercy. No date has been established for their execution.

Genesee County Serial Slasher aka **Abuelazam, Elias** (b. August 29, 1976) was convicted of the August 2, 2010, murder of Arnold Minor, age 49, in Flint, Michigan.

Abuelazam, who is Israeli-Arab, is suspected of the racial serial killings of four African American men and 18 stabbings in the spring and summer of 2010 in Genesee County, Michigan; Leesburg, Virginia; and Toledo, Ohio. All of his victims were small-framed and thin. Abuelazam was 6 ft. 5 in. and weighed 280 pounds. He was not tried for any of these crimes since he was already serving a life sentence without the possibility of parole in Michigan for the murder of Arnold Minor. He is currently serving his sentence at the Gus Harrison Correctional Facility in Adrian, Michigan.

Gentleman Killer
Mazurkiewicz,
Wladyslaw

Gentleman Killer aka **Mazurkiewicz, Władysław** (January 31, 1911 – January 31, 1957) was a serial killer in Poland during the 1950s who supported his lavish lifestyle by robbing and murdering his victims. He was initially charged with 30 murders when he was arrested in the spring of 1956, but this was reduced to the murders of four women and two men, when he went to trial. He was convicted and sentenced to death on August 30, 1956. Wladyslaw Mazurkiewicz was hanged on January 31, 1956 at Montelupich Prison in Cracow, Poland.

George, Nolan Ray (b. May 6, 1943) is a serial killer whose murderous career began in the 1960s. His modus operandi was to lure his victims to dark and lonely places where he would rape and strangle them.

George spent 12 years in a Michigan prison for the 1969 murder of Francis Brown, age 23, who was pregnant at the time of her murder. He was sentenced to 40 – 60 years, but appeals and hung juries cut his sentence to just 12 years. He confessed to two more strangulation murders in exchange for a promise that he would not be prosecuted in those cases.

Within a year after being released from prison, in 1982 he murdered Cindy Rose Garland, age 22, in Hamilton, Ohio, where he then lived. He was charged with manslaughter and spent only eight years in an Ohio prison. He was released in 1992.

In 2011, George was arrested for the 1968 murder in Michigan of Gwendolyn Perry, age 36, thanks to Deborah Dixon, an investigative reporter for a local Cincinnati TV station; Detective Frank Smith, retired, of the Butler County, Ohio, Sheriff's Department; and a relentless task force of detectives from Ohio, Michigan, and Kentucky. Gwendolyn was found in a heavily thicketed area in Pontiac, Michigan on December 8, 1968. She had been strangled with her stockings tied around her neck. Nolan Ray George was found guilty of first-degree murder and on May 19, 2011, was sentenced to life in prison without the possibility of parole.

George remains a suspect in at least five homicides in Michigan, Kentucky, and Ohio. Three of the victims have been identified. August 5, 1967, Della May Miller was working her second day on the job at a restaurant in Covington, Kentucky. That was the last day she was seen alive. Eight days later, her body was found by squirrel hunters in Ludlow. She had been strangled with her own stockings. Nolan George lived a few blocks from the restaurant.

In January 1998, the body of Alana "Laney" Gwinner from Fairfield, Ohio, was found in the Ohio River. She had been strangled. Alana had last been seen on December 10, 1997.

November 13, 1982, the body of Tammy Lynn King, age 22, was found in a wooded area in Reily Township in Butler County, Ohio. She was last seen on October 25 as she was leaving her apartment. This murder was committed within three weeks of Cindy Rose Garland's murder.

Nolan Ray George is currently serving his life sentence at Lakeside Correctional Facility in Coldwater, Michigan.

Geralds Jr., Hubert (b. November 13, 1964) had the mental age of eight, but was a serial killer in Chicago's South Side during December 1994 through mid-June 1995. He might have continued killing, but his sister found a victim's decomposing body in a trash can near her home and called the police. Geralds confessed to the killings of six prostitutes, but claimed that they were the result of drug disputes.

Geralds was arrested on June 18, 1995. On November 13, 1997, his 33rd birthday, he was convicted on five counts of first-degree murder and one count of attempted murder. He was sentenced to life times five, plus 30 years for the attempted murder.

Gert aka **van Rooyen, Cornelius Gerhardus** (April 11, 1938 – January 15, 1990) was born in South Africa and was known as "Gert". South African Police Force believe he was part of a pedophile group, but have not fully investigated due to the fact that van Rooyen committed suicide on January 15, 1990 to avoid prosecution.

At the age of 16, he was sent to reform school for stealing a car to drive from Cape Town to Pretoria to visit his dying mother. He was convicted of stealing motor spares and clothing in 1960. After serving his time in prison, he seemed to live a more normal life. He married and fathered six children and earned a living as a building construction business along with his brothers.

It is believed by investigators in South Africa that he was the pedophile murderer of six young girls in 1988-89 in or near the city of Pretoria, South Africa. He also shot his adult lover (female). He shot and killed himself in 1990 to avoid arrest.

Van Rooyen abducted two girls, ages 10 and 13, took them to Harbeespoort Dam in 1979, hit them in the face, ordered them to remove their clothes and molested them. The girls were released the following day. Van Rooyen was arrested, convicted, and sentenced to four years. His wife divorced him in 1983 and he began dating Francina Johanna Hermina Haarhoff, better known as "Joey". Investigators believe that Joey was his accomplice as they vacationed at the beaches on the coast of KwaZulu Natal and the disappearances occurred during these vacation periods. They also believe that some of the victims may be buried on the beaches. It is believed the following girls are victims of van Rooyen.

Tracy-Lee Scott-Crossley, age 14, disappeared on August 1, 1988. She was seen getting into a Volkswagen Beetle outside the Cresta Shopping Centre in Johannesburg.

Fiona Harvey, age 12, disappeared from Pietermaritzburg on December 22, 1988. A white Ford pickup truck was used in her abduction. It was later linked to van Rooyen's building contractor business which was advertised on the truck.

Joan Horn, age 12, disappeared from Pretoria on June 7, 1989.

Janet Delport, age 16, disappeared in July 1989 from a shopping mall. A blond woman was seen abducting her. Janet was later found. She was very distressed but unharmed. Rosa Piel, age 9, disappeared of Alberton, Gauteng Province, a few weeks later. Odette Boucher, age 11, and Anne-Mari Wapenaar, age 12, disappeared of Kempton Park, Gauteng

Province disappeared on September 22, 1989. A letter from Anne-Mari to her mother was received on September 29 saying that she and Odette had run away to Durban with some boys. A week later, a letter to Odette's mother arrived even though it posted on the same day as Anne-Mari's letter. Yolanda Wessels, age 13, a niece of Joey's, disappeared on November 3, 1989.

Joan Booysen, age 16, was abducted in January 1990 by Joey in Church Square, Pretoria and taken to van Rooyen's home in Capital Park. She was handcuffed, drugged, sexually assaulted, and locked in a cupboard. She managed to escape and went to police. They placed van Rooyen's house under surveillance. He was identified by Joan as he drove past his house in the white Ford pick-up. Discovering that Joan had escaped, he killed Joey with a .22 revolver and then committed suicide on January 15, 1990.

Ghanam, Mohammed Elsayed (b. 1964) was an Egyptian tour guide who targeted foreign travelers arriving at Bangkok's Don Muang Airport in Thailand. The known murders occurred between August 17, 1998 and April 6, 1999. The killer waited at the airport and/or a hotel, offered his services, and then drove to an out-of-the-way place to rob his victims and stab them to death. The victims included Herbert Reiter, age 41, from Germany; Eric Berduc, age 32, and Jesus Benamard, no age given, from France; one man from Austria; one man from Iran; and one man from the United Arab Emirates.

Interpol repeatedly told the Bangkok police that the murders of these tourists could be linked, but Thai police failed to launch an investigation.

Ghanam was arrested on June 5, 1999, after the European Union Embassies confronted the Thai government about the murders with concern that there could be more murders than the six known. Nothing was found on his trial or sentence.

Gibbs, Charles (November 5, 1798 – April 25, 1831) aka *James D. Jeffers*, a native of Newport, Rhode Island, was a pirate in the 1820s who claimed to have murdered about 400 people. He would sign onto a small vessel as a crewman and then murder the crew and steal the vessel and the cargo. He was captured and convicted of mutiny and murder in 1831. He was first incarcerated at Bridewell Prison in London, England, then moved to Belle Vue Gaol in Manchester. He was eventually hanged on Ellis Island in the state of New York on April 25, 1831.

Gibbs, Janie Lou (December 25, 1932 – February 7, 2010) was a serial killer from Cordele, Georgia, who murdered for money.

Janie appeared to be a devoted wife and mother who volunteered at her church. On January 21, 1966, after eating a good meal prepared by Janie, her husband, Charles Clayton Gibbs, died suddenly. Doctors determined he died of liver disease. The people from Janie's church overwhelmed her with their caring and sympathy. She decided to give part of the insurance money she collected from her husband's death to her church to show her appreciation.

On August 29, 1966, Marvin Gibbs, her 13-year-old son, also died. According to doctors, it appeared that he had inherited the liver disease that had killed his father. Again the church came to Janie's side with caring and sympathy and again, she decided to give part of her son's insurance money to the church.

On January 23, 1967, her son, Melvin, age 16, died suddenly. Janie tithed 10% of the insurance money to her church. So far, she had collected $31,000 from the three deaths.

On October 28, 1967, her 1-month-old grandson, Ronnie, and son of Roger Gibbs, died. Then on December 24, 1967, her oldest son and father of Ronnie, Roger Ludean Gibbs, age 19, died.

This was the fifth death under mysterious circumstances, but no autopsies had been performed. However, upon Roger's demise, his wife demanded an autopsy of her husband. It found fatal levels of arsenic in his system. Autopsies were ordered for the rest of the family. Each was found to have been murdered by arsenic poisoning.

Janie admitted that she had killed her family members by feeding them rat poison. In 1968, she was found to be insane and housed in a state mental hospital until 1976 when she was found fit to stand trial. She was convicted of poisoning the five male members of her family and sentenced to five life sentences.

Due to Parkinson's disease, Janie Gibbs was released in April 1999 on a medical reprieve into the custody of her brother. She lived in a nursing home until her death on February 7, 2010.

Gifford, Bertha Alice Williams Graham (October 1871 – August 20, 1951) was born in Morse Mill, Missouri, one of ten children born to William Poindexter Williams and Matilda Lee Williams. She was first married to Henry Graham and they had one child, a daughter named Lila. Graham died and Bertha married Eugene Gifford. They had one child; a son named James.

Bertha was known for her cooking skills and caring for neighbors and relatives who became ill. In 1928, however, she was arrested and charged with three murders committed between 1900 and 1928. The bodies of Edward Brinley, Elmer Schamel, and Lloyd Schamel had been exhumed and found to contain large amounts of arsenic.

Gifford had played nurse for her sick neighbors and 17 people had died in her care. Five deaths were investigated, and the cause of death changed to murder. This raised questions about the additional 12 deaths.

Bertha went on trial for three of the murders and was found not guilty by reason of insanity. She was committed to the Missouri State Hospital No. 3, a psychiatric institution where she died in 1951.

Giggling Granny aka **Doss, Nannie** (November 4, 1905 – June 2, 1965) was a serial killer in the states of Alabama, North Carolina, Kansas, and Oklahoma. She confessed to murdering 11 people between 1927 and 1954. Born in Blue Mountain, Alabama, as Nancy Hazle to James and Lou Hazle, she was one of five children; she had one brother and three sisters. The Hazle children did not attend school very often because James Hazle forced them to work on the family farm. At age seven, Nancy hit her head on a metal bar when the train they were taking to visit relatives stopped suddenly. Afterward, she suffered severe headaches, blackouts, and depression. She would later blame this accident for her mental instability. Nancy and her sisters were forbidden to wear makeup or attractive clothing. They were also forbidden to go to dances and other social events.

With her father's approval, Nancy married Charlie Braggs after they had dated for only four months. Nancy was only 16 years old. Charles' unmarried mother lived with them and ruled the roost. The unhappy marriage produced four girls in just four years. Two of the girls died in 1927 of suspected food poisoning. Charles left, suspecting that Nancy had murdered them. They divorced the following year.

In 1929, Nancy met a man from Jacksonville through a lonely hearts column, Robert (Frank) Harrelson, who would become her second husband. The marriage lasted 16 years despite the fact that he was an alcoholic and had a record for assault. Melvina, Nancy Doss' oldest daughter, gave birth to a baby girl. Melvina told her sisters that she thought she had seen her mother, now known as Nannie, stick a hatpin into the baby's head. Nannie said the baby was dead and the doctor could not give a reason for the death. On July 7, 1945, Melvina's son, Robert, died while in Nannie's care. The cause of death was determined to be asphyxia from unknown causes. Two months later, Nannie collected $500 from the insurance policy she had taken out on Robert.

In 1945, celebrating the surrender of Japan which ended World War II, Harrelson was one who robustly celebrated and drank heavily. He raped Nannie; it was the last straw for this marriage. Working in her garden the follow day, Nannie discovered her husband's corn whiskey jar buried in the ground. She filled the jar with rat poison. Harrelson died an agonizing death that evening.

Nannie traveled to Lexington, North Carolina, where she met her third husband, Arlie Lanning, again through a lonely hearts column. They were married after only three days. Unbeknownst to Nannie, Lanning was also an alcoholic, as well as a womanizer. He died of suspected heart failure. The house the couple had lived in burned to the ground. It had been left to Lanning's sister. The insurance money, however, went to Nannie. Nannie went to live with her sister, Dovie, who was bedridden. Dovie died shortly after Nannie's arrival.

Nannie then met Richard L. Morton, soon to be her husband, of Emporia, Kansas through the Diamond Circle Club. While Morton was not an alcoholic, he was a womanizer. Nannie's mother, Louisa, came to live with them in January 1953, and died within a very short time. Morton died three months later.

In June 1953, Nannie met and married Samuel Doss of Tulsa, Oklahoma. In September, Samuel Doss was taken to the hospital suffering flu-like symptoms. He was diagnosed as having a severe digestive tract infection. He was treated and released on October 5. He died that evening. Nannie was in a rush to collect on the two insurance policies she had taken out on him. His sudden death alerted his doctor and an autopsy was performed, which revealed a huge amount of arsenic in his system. Nannie was arrested.

Nannie soon confessed to murdering four husbands; her mother, Louisa; her sister, Dovie; her grandson, Robert; and her mother-in-law, Arlie Lanning's mother. The trial centered on the death of Samuel Doss. Nannie pleaded guilty and on May 17, 1955, Nancy "Nannie" Doss was sentenced to life imprisonment. She was never charged with the other deaths. Nannie died of leukemia in the hospital ward of Oklahoma State Penitentiary on June 2, 1965.

Gilbert, Kristen Heather Strickland (b. November 13, 1967) grew up in a well-adjusted home in Fall River and Groton, Massachusetts. There were never any significant problems. So, what turned this supposedly "normal, well adjusted" girl into a serial killer? She did have one major flaw—she was the consummate liar.

Kristen Gilbert earned her registered nurse degree in 1988 from Greenfield Community College. That same year she was married to Glenn Gilbert. In 1989, she began working as a nurse at the Veterans Administration Medical Center in Northampton, MA. For the first year, things ran smoothly at the Veterans Hospital. She was rated as "highly skilled" on her job performance report with a notation that her actions during medical emergencies were extremely good.

After the birth of the Gilberts' son, Kristen Gilbert switched to the 4:00 p.m. to midnight shift. Other things changed also. Patients began to die at a rate triple those of the last three years. By 1993, Gilbert had developed a friendship with a newly hired security guard, James Perrault, who worked the 3:00 p.m. to 11:00 p.m. shift at the VA Hospital. He was called when there was a medical emergency on Gilbert's ward. By 1994, the relationship had become intimate. Perrault insisted that Gilbert leave her husband or the affair was over. She left her husband and children and moved into her own apartment. The relationship between Gilbert and Perrault blossomed.

Things at the hospital were changing too. There was talk between coworkers about the number of deaths that occurred on Gilbert's shift. There were always deaths at the hospital; many of the patients were old and had serious health problems, but now patients who had no history of heart problems were dying of cardiac arrest. Some of the nurses started monitoring drugs that could cause cardiac arrest. Epinephrine, normally used to treat a number of conditions including cardiac arrest, anaphylaxis, superficial bleeding, and severe allergic reactions, was continually coming up missing. An overdose of epinephrine can cause cardiac arrest. Nurses reported their suspicions to hospital authorities. Federal authorities quickly came to the conclusion that Kristen Gilbert was the common thread to most of the 350 deaths during her shift on Ward C. Gilbert was suspended during the investigation and immediately the death rate dropped to normal in Ward C.

In June 1996, Perrault decided to end his relationship with Gilbert. She tried to change his mind, but to no avail. On July 8, 1996, Gilbert overdosed on drugs and was admitted to a hospital psychiatric ward. She phoned Perrault continually. Finally she confessed to him that she had "killed those guys." Perrault told the federal grand jury of Gilbert's confession.

Gilbert purchased a toy that would change her voice. She called Perrault at the hospital and told him (in a man's voice) that there were three bombs planted in the hospital and that they were set to go off in two hours. All of the hospital's patients and employees were evacuated. The investigation resulted in Gilbert's arrest and conviction of the bomb threat. She was sentenced to 15 months in a federal prison.

During her trial, federal investigators were having the bodies exhumed of those men who were suspected of being Gilbert's victims. In 1998, Kristen Gilbert was indicted for the murder of four of her patients and the attempted murder of three others. She was found guilty and sentenced to life. She is currently housed at the Carswell Federal Medical Center, Ft. Worth, Texas.

Giles, Bernard Eugene (b. April 9, 1953) is a very disturbed sex offender who murdered four women in Brevard County, Florida, in 1973. He was also a practicing necrophile.

Giles confessed to killing five women in the Titusville area between September to November 1973. At his first trial, he was sentenced to life for the murder of Nancy Gerry, age 18, plus 15 years for the armed robbery and attempted rape of a Cocoa woman. His other victims were Paula Hamric, age 22, a waitress in Titusville; Carol Bennett, age 17, of Mimes; Sharon Wimer, age 14, of Titusville; and Kristi Melton, age 15, of Titusville. He was given four life sentences for these murders.

Giles was sent to a state hospital for treatment. He is presently incarcerated at Okeechobee Correctional Institution in Okeechobee, Florida. If he ever declared cured by state psychiatrists, he will begin serving his life sentences plus 15 years.

Gilham Park Strangler aka **Jackson, Ray Shawn** (b. August 28, 1967) raped and murdered six prostitutes in Kansas City, Missouri in 1989-90. He was sentenced to six consecutive life terms without the possibility of parole. He is serving his six life sentences at South Central Correctional Center at Licking, Missouri.

Gilligan, Amy Archer (October 31, 1873 – April 23, 1962) was born in Milton, Connecticut, the eighth of ten children. She opened a home for the elderly in 1901 in Windsor, Connecticut. She married five of the elderly men, then murdered them. But first, she made sure that they had a good amount of life insurance. At least four of the women living in her home for the elderly were also poisoned. They had changed their wills to make Amy Archer Gilligan their beneficiary. In November 1914, Amy Hosmer died. Her family demanded an autopsy which showed that she had been poisoned. Other bodies were exhumed and autopsied. It was found they also had been poisoned with either arsenic or strychnine. Gilligan was arrested in May 1916 and charged with only one count of murder. On June 18, 1917, Gilligan was found guilty and sentenced to life. She appealed and was granted a new trial in 1919. This time she pleaded insanity. She was transferred to the Connecticut Hospital for the Insane in Middletown, where she lived until her death on April 23, 1962.

Gillis, Sean Vincent (b. June 24, 1963) was born in Baton Rouge and raised in southern Louisiana. His mother described him as a good, happy kid who did well in school. His trouble with the law began in 1980, but it was only for minor offenses. By 1999, he was a serial killer who stalked, kidnapped, raped, murdered, and mutilated his eight victims. His reign of terror began in 1994 and continued until his arrest in 2004.

Gillis' first murder occurred on March 21, 1994. His claim is that he had only intended to rape 81-year-old Ann Bryan at a retirement home in Baton Rouge, but he became so frightened when she screamed that he slit her throat to quiet her, then stabbed her 50 times.

Katherine Ann Hall, age 29, was murdered on January 4, 1999. Her body was found later in January in southeastern East Baton Rouge Parish. In May 1999, Gillis began stalking Hardee Schmidt, age 52. Gillis claimed that he hit her with his car and knocked her into a ditch. He stopped, placed heavy-duty wire plastic wrap tightly around her neck, and forced her into his car. After raping and murdering her, he put her body in the trunk of his car and dumped it two days later.

Joyce Williams, age 36, was murdered on November 12, 1999; Lillian Robinson, age 52, was murdered in January 2000; and Marilyn Nevils, age 38, was murdered in October 2000.

These murders were not yet connected, and Gillis' presence remained unknown to the authorities. It took another serial killer to bring attention to Gillis' murders. Derrick Todd Lee was arrested on May 27, 2003, and linked to seven murders. Several murders could not be linked to Lee and an investigation was begun on these unsolved murders. Authorities now knew that they had at least two serial killers operating in Baton Rouge at the same time. Until then, they had not been aware that they had even one serial killer in their midst.

Johnnie Mae Williams, age 45, was murdered in October 2003. Derrick Todd Lee was in jail so this case could not be linked to him. Gillis' final murder was in February 2004, when he met Donna Bennett Johnston. She was raped, then strangled with a nylon rope. After her death, Gillis slashed her breasts, cut off her left nipple, gouged out a tattoo on her right thigh, and severed her left arm at the elbow. Tire tracks found near her body led the police to Gillis.

Sean Vincent Gillis was arrested on April 29, 2004. In 2007, he pleaded guilty to the second-degree murder of Joyce Williams. In July 2008, he was convicted of the murders of Katherine Hall, Johnnie Mae Williams, and Donna Bennett Johnston. He was sentenced to life in prison. He has been convicted of seven murders. He has not been charged with the murder of Lillian Robinson due to lack of evidence. He is currently incarcerated at the Louisiana State Prison in Angola, Louisiana, the largest prison in the United States.

Gilyard Jr., Lorenzo Jerome (b. May 24, 1950) was a trash company supervisor and a convicted serial killer in the Kansas City, Missouri, area. He was also convicted of molesting the 13-year-old daughter of a friend. He was suspected of five other rapes but was never charged due to lack of evidence.

Gilyard came from a family of people in trouble with the law. His father, Lorenzo Sr., was convicted of rape; his brother, Darryl, was convicted of a drug-related murder (serving a sentence of life without parole); and his sister, Patricia, was a prostitute convicted of the murder of a customer who served 10 years in prison.

All of Gilyard's victims were prostitutes, or thought to be. All were found dumped in secluded areas in and around Kansas City, Missouri, and most of the victims had cloth or paper stuffed into their mouths and ligature marks around their necks. All of the victims showed signs of a struggle, all were missing their shoes, and all showed distinct signs of sexual assault.

Gilyard was connected to the murder of Sheila Ingold, age 36, in 1987 through DNA tests. The DNA was used to connect him to 13 victims murdered between 1977 and 1989. Gilyard was charged with seven first-degree murders. His victims were Catherine M. Barry, age 34; Naomi M. Kelly, age 23; Ann Barnes, age 36; Kellie A. Ford, age 20; and Carmeline Hibbs, age 30. He was acquitted of the murder of Sheila Ingold, age 36, due to insufficient evidence.

He was tied to seven other murdered prostitutes but has not been charged. Lorenzo Gilyard Jr. was sentenced to life in prison for the murder of Sheila Ingold, without the possibility of parole.

Glamour Girl Slayer aka **Glatman, Harvey Murray** (December 10, 1927 – September 18, 1959) was born in the Bronx, New York, and raised in the state of Colorado. He showed

Glamour Girl Slayer
Glatman, Harvey
Murray

antisocial behavior traits and sadomasochistic sexual tendency as a small child.

At the age of 12, his parents noticed a red mark and swelling around his neck. When questioned, he told them that while he was in the bathtub, he put a rope around his neck, ran it through the tub drain, and pulled it as tight as he could against his neck. He said he achieved some kind of sexual pleasure while doing this. His mother took him to see their family physician, who said that he "would grow out of it."

By 1957, Glatman was in Los Angeles, California. He began hanging around modeling agencies looking for potential victims. He would offer them modeling jobs and tell them he would have to take their photos for their new portfolio. He would take them back to his apartment where he tied them up and sexually assaulted them while he was photographing them. Afterwards, he would dump their bodies in the desert. Two of his known victims that he met through trolling the modeling agencies were Judith Dull and Ruth Mercado. A third victim was Shirley Ann Bridgefore, who answered his lonely hearts ad in the newspaper.

Glatman was a suspect in the slaying of an unidentified woman in Boulder, Colorado, who was named "Boulder Jane Doe" in 1954. Some 55 years later, a woman came forward who thought the unidentified woman might be her long-lost sister. Mitotyping Technologies in State College, Pennsylvania, ran DNA tests from the sister and "Boulder Jane Doe". It was a match. She was Dorothy Gay Howard, age 18, from Phoenix, Arizona.

Glatman was arrested in 1958. A patrolman saw a man and woman struggling at the side of the road. He stopped and separated them. Glatman had been in the process of kidnapping his fourth victim in California. He willingly confessed to the three murders and led police to a toolbox where he kept the photos he had taken while he sexually assaulted and murdered his victims.

He was found guilty of two first-degree murders and sentenced to death. He asked the warden at San Quentin State Prison in California to do nothing to save his life. The warden did as he was asked and Glatman was executed in the gas chamber on September 18, 1959.

Goble, Sean Patrick (b. November 1, 1966) was a long-distance truck driver from Asheboro, North Carolina. Goble is 6 ft. 3 in. and weighs about 310 lbs. He was known as a gentle giant and a quiet man, but there is a side of this man that few know. He is a very, very scary man. He is a serial killer. His father was a rapist who preyed on little girls.

Goble's childhood was unhappy and unstable. He dropped out of high school after the eleventh grade and joined the army. He was married briefly and fathered a son. His sisters describe him as a big teddy bear of a man, sensitive, and a man who cares about people. This is the side of him that his friends and family knew. This story is about his other side, the side his family and friends knew nothing about.

Goble travelled the highways in his black Peterbilt 18-wheeler with the words, "The Wild One" boldly written across the cab of his truck. A string of murders followed the black truck, but until 1995 the police had not connected the murders. Most of the victims were prostitutes he picked up along his route. Once he was "serviced," the victim was smothered or strangled and dumped somewhere farther down the road, sometimes hundreds of miles from where she had been picked up.

In January 1995, the body of a woman was found dumped on a residential road close to exit 10 on I-81, north of Bristol, Virginia. Her right leg had been run over by a vehicle and from the tire marks left on it, it was obvious that the vehicle was an 18-wheeler. She was identified as Brenday Kay Hagy, age 45, from Bloomington, Indiana. A plastic bag was found at the scene. The bag was submitted for analysis and was found to contain a clear large thumbprint, probably belonging to a man. The bag was sent to AFIS (Automated Fingerprint Identification System), a database of about 30 states, but no match was found. It was then sent to the FBI, which has a massive fingerprint database that covers all criminals charged in federal crimes, all military service personnel, and states which are not part of AFIS, to see if they could tie the print to the killer.

One of the detectives, who answered the call of a body found, remembered an episode of the TV show *Unsolved Mysteries*. The story was about prostitute murders in the Midwest whose bodies had been dumped along the highways of several states. The details were the same as the murder they were now investigating. It was known that the killer was a truck driver who used the CB handle of "Stargazer". They believed that this woman had been the victim of this truck-driver serial killer. Investigators learned that there had been a black Peterbilt in the area. For three months, the investigation was intense. In the interim, two more women were found dumped along highways—one in Tennessee and one in North Carolina.

About three weeks after the discovery of the body on March 19, the detectives received a call from the FBI. They had made a match. The print belonged to Sean Patrick Goble, who had been arrested in West Memphis, Arkansas in September 1994 for reckless driving, resisting arrest, and creating a public disturbance with a prostitute. The detectives made a call to the West Memphis police and learned that Goble was employed as a truck driver by Rocky Road Express near Winston-Salem, North Carolina, and that his truck was a black Peterbilt.

The investigation moved to the Rocky Road Express. The company told investigators that Patrick was due to return to the terminal later that night. In the meantime, Goble's travel logs showed that he had been in the area of each of the three murders. Goble rolled in the next morning of April 13, 1995 and was arrested without incident. While Detective Wilson accompanied Goble to Winston-Salem, Detective Sheets stayed at the Rocky Road Express see if there was any evidence to be found in Goble's truck. He found a purse belonging to Rebecca Hanes.

After his arrest, Goble confessed to murdering Brenda Kay Hagy, the woman found near Bristol, Virginia. He also confessed to killing Alice Rebecca Hanes, age 36, from Ohio, whose body was found in Kingsport, Tennessee, on March 19, and to the murder of a woman found in Guilford County, North Carolina, on I-40 in February. This woman was later identified as Sherry Tew Mansur, age 34, of Clearwater, Florida.

An investigation of Goble's home near Asheboro, North Carolina, revealed a collection of women's shoes and panties. It appeared to be a trophy collection, as is done by many serial killers.

On December 15, 1995, Sean Patrick Goble was sentenced to two consecutive life terms in Tennessee. He was arrested on September 24, 1996, for a capital murder in Baldwin County, Alabama. He is being held at the Northeast Correctional Complex in Mountain City, Tennessee.

There are numerous unsolved murders in at least seven states with similar abduction, murder, and dumping characteristics—New York, Pennsylvania, Ohio, Indiana, North Carolina, Tennessee, and Virginia—but they have not as yet been linked to Sean Patrick Goble.

Godfather of Matamoros/El Padrino de Matamoros aka **Constanzo, Adolfo de Jesus** (November 1, 1962 – May 6, 1989) was a serial killer, drug dealer, and cult leader in Mexico.

Born in Miami, Florida, to a Cuban immigrant who was only 15 at the time, Constanzo spent the first 10 years of his life in Puerto Rico. He was baptized Catholic and served as an altar boy. His mother practiced a dark ritualistic religion known as *Palo Mayombe**, which had a strong influence on the young Constanzo. The family returned to Miami in 1972 and Adolfo Constanzo's stepfather died soon after the move. His mother soon remarried, and the new stepfather was involved in *Palo Mayombe* and drug dealing.

Constanzo and his mother were arrested many times for theft, vandalism, and shoplifting, all minor crimes. He graduated from high school and entered prep school from which he was expelled (reason not known). He foretold of the attempted assassination of US President Ronald Reagan in 1981, which led his mother to believe that he had psychic powers. In his teens, a priest (Palero) taught Constanzo the skills of being a Palero and drug dealing.

In 1983, Constanzo lived in Mexico City and supported himself as a tarot card reader. Constanzo pledged himself to Kadiempembe, his religion's version of Satan. He recruited **Martin Quintana Rodriguez** and **Omar Chewe Orea Ochoa** to be his servants, lovers, and disciples. He soon became a *Palo Mayombe* Palero, having under his command drug dealers, musicians and some police officers. He was based in Matamoros on the US – Mexico border at a place called Rancho Santa Elena. There they sold drugs, held religious ceremonies, and did pretty much anything he wanted to do. By 1987, he was offering human sacrifices.

The downfall of the cult and Adolpho Constanzo began when 21-year-old Mark J. Kilroy, a US citizen and student from the University of Texas, was abducted and murdered while he was on spring break. In 1989, under severe pressure from Texas authorities to locate Kilroy, the local police stumbled upon Constanzo's religious sanctuary at Matamoros during an unrelated drug investigation. After the arrest of several members of the cult, it was discovered that they were responsible for Kilroy's murder. His body had been dismembered and burned. More members were found and arrested.

Finally, on May 6, 1989, Constanzo and four of his followers were located in a dilapidated apartment in Mexico City. Constanzo did not want to go to jail and ordered one of his followers to shoot him and Martin Quintana Rodriguez. They were found dead by police. **Sara Maria Aldrete** aka *La Madrina,* **Omar Orea Ochoa**, and **Alvaro de Leon Valdez** were arrested and charged with the murder of Constanzo and Rodriguez. They were also charged with 13 counts of murder for the deaths at Rancho Santa Elena, plus other charges of drug-trafficking, criminal association, and cover-up.

At Rancho Santa Elena, at least 15 bodies were unearthed. Also found on that site were 21 blood-soaked sticks, 14 horseshoes, railroad spikes, a roasted turtle, animal corpses, and the rotting remains of human organs and blood. A cross was erected by local peasants and everything that could be burned, was burned. A *curandero,* or white witch, was hired by Mexican federal police to perform an exorcism at Constanzo's temple of human sacrifice at Rancho Santa Elena. The ranch stood abandoned for a year after the exorcism. It is now owned by the Mexican government, which tried to hire workers to harvest the corn and sorghum in the fields, but no one was willing to work there, so the crops withered and rotted where they were. *See separate article - Godmother (La Madrina).*

*Palo Mayombe is said to be the world's most powerful and feared form of black magic. Its origin was in the African Congo and it was integrated as part of the Santeria religion. It came to the western world during the slave trade to Cuba and Puerto Rico in the 1500s. Today it is found in Central America, Brazil, and Mexico. The main difference between Palo Mayombe and Santeria is Santeria uses the forces of light and Palo Mayombe uses the forces of darkness to achieve goals and magic spells. The individuals who practice Palo Mayombe, *called Palero, practice extremely* *strong and powerful black magic. It is believed that some practice human sacrifice.*

Godmother (La Madrina) aka **Aldrete Villareal, Sara Maria** (b. September 6, 1964) headed a drug smuggling group and, along with Adolfo Constanzo, was the leader of a human sacrifice cult in Matamoros, Tamualipas, Mexico. She also became a serial killer under the direction of Constanzo (*Godfather of Matamoros*).

Sara Maria was born in Matamoros, Tamaulipas, Mexico. Although still living in Matamoros, she attended high school in Brownsville, Texas. She was a good student. She studied physical education at Texas Southmost College and planned to attend a university where she could earn a teaching certificate in physical education, but then she met the Godfather.

She engaged in the rituals which were a combination of Santeria, Aztec warrior ritual, and *Palo Mayombe*. Soon, Constanzo made her the Godmother. Drug dealers were sexually assaulted, murdered, and mutilated for use in their rituals. The body parts were cooked in a large pot called an *nganga* (religious receptacle).

Their downfall came when they kidnapped Mark J. Kilroy when he was on spring break in Matamoros from the University of Texas. The site of their religious rituals, Rancho Sant Elena, was discovered on the outskirts of Matamoros by Mexican officials in their hunt for Kilroy.

Aldrete was convicted of criminal association in 1990 and sentenced to six years in prison. In her second trial, she was charged with several of the murders and was sentenced to 30 years. If she is ever released from the Mexican prison, American authorities will extradite her to the US and prosecute her for the murder of Mark Kilroy. *See separate article - Godfather of Matamoros.*

Goebbels, Peter (b. 1961) worked five days a week on an assembly line. The weekends were his free time to do what he wanted. Many believe he worked some weekends too—as a serial killer.

On Saturday, July 6, 1985, a teenage boy came upon a couple grappling in an alley in the Lichterfelde neighborhood of West Berlin. Thinking it to be just a lovers' quarrel, he passed on by. Later the body of Marion Bormann, age 17, was found raped and murdered by strangulation. The boy went to the police and gave them a description of the suspect. Homicide detectives were studying the files of similar murders. They found three more cases very similar to the Bormann rape and murder.

On Sunday, August 26, 1984, the body of Helga Kousdoefer, age 22, was found. She had been raped and strangled in the Lichterfelde area. On Sunday, March 24, 1985, the body of Liselotte Mohn, age 19, was found in the same area and she too had been raped and strangled. On Saturday, June 1, 1985, the body of Karola Eisenstein, age 20, was found raped and murdered in the same area.

There was one more case, but this victim was not murdered. The attack took place in the same general area as the murders, only this one occurred on a Wednesday in mid-July of 1984. The perpetrator had been scared away by the appearance of pedestrians; however, he dropped his identification card at the scene. The name on the card was Peter Goebbels. There was a problem—Goebbels worked during the week and only had weekends off. However, during further investigation, authorities found that the plant where Goebbels worked had been closed on that particular Wednesday for the retooling of the machinery.

Goebbels was convicted of the rape and given a one-year suspended sentence. But this is not the end of the story. Detectives put Goebbels in a lineup for the teenager who was a witness in the Bormann case. He selected Goebbels as the person he had seen fighting with the 17-year-old girl.

Goebbels confessed to Bormann's murder, but denied his involvement in the other cases. He was convicted of this murder and sentenced to life in prison. Police continue to seek evidence linking him to the other three cases.

Gohl, Billy (February 6, 1873 – March 3, 1927) was a union official at the Sailor's Union of the Pacific located in Aberdeen, Washington. He was also a serial killer for many years and is suspected by Aberdeen investigators of committing at least 41 murders.

Before becoming a union official, Gohl worked as a bartender. He is suspected of murdering countless migrant workers whose bodies washed ashore in Grays Harbor during his tenure as a bartender.

As a union official, Gohl was usually on duty alone. Sailors arriving in the port of Aberdeen would visit the Sailor's Union building first where they would collect their mail and put some of their pay into savings. Gohl would ask if the sailors had any family or friends in the area, then ask about money and valuables. Those who had no family or friends in the area and who supplied information as to their money and valuables became his targets. The building was ideally suited for his scheme. It would supply the victims and was located on the Wishkah River. Gohl would shoot the sailor in the union building, take his money and any valuables he could find, then dispose of the body by throwing it into the Wishkah River behind the building, and the body would later be found in the harbor.

His downfall was his accomplice in one of the murders. John Klingenberg tried to jump ship in Mexico and was arrested and brought back to Aberdeen. Klingenberg testified in court to seeing Gohl alone with a sailor, Charles Hatberg, shortly before Hatberg's body was found in the harbor. Gohl was convicted for the Hatberg murder and for the murder of John Hoffman, a witness to the Hatberg murder. He was shot and wounded by Gohl on the night of the Hatberg murder, but the next day he was killed by Klingenberg, who was sentenced to 20 years.

Billy Gohl was transferred to an asylum for the criminally insane. He died there on March 3, 1927.

Golden State Killer/East Area Rapist/Original Nightstalker/Goleta Murders is suspected by California investigators to have committed as many as 50 rapes and 13 murders between 1976 and 1986 in the California counties of Sacramento and Contra Costa. DNA has linked the rapist to six murders between March 1980 and May 1986. Similarities in additional area murders have brought the number to 12. Between June 18, 1976 and July 5, 1979, he is known to have raped at least 50 women in east Sacramento where he was dubbed the East Area Rapist. The rapist is known to have prowled and burglarized homes during the day, then return at night to commit his rapes and murders. At night he wore a ski mask, gloves, and dark clothing with long sleeves, and either sneakers or military-style boots. He gained entry by prying open sliding-glass doors with a screwdriver. He was described as white, 40s to early 50s, possibly with a bull tattoo on one of his hands. In the early stages of the case, he was called the *Original Nightstalker.*

On October 1, 1979, at a home in Goleta, a couple was tied up by an intruder. When the intruder left the room in search of things to steal, the couple made attempts to escape and the woman screamed. Their neighbor, who was an FBI agent, heard the scream and chased the perpetrator, who fled on foot and abandoned a knife. This attack was later linked to the murders that occurred on December 30 by a shoeprint and the same roll of twine used to bind the victims.

On December 30, Dr. Robert Offerman, age 44, and Debra Alexander Manning, age 35, were found shot to death in Offerman's condominium in Goleta. Offerman apparently lunged at the attacker as his bindings were being tied. Neighbors heard the shots but ignored them. The killer also broke into an adjoining residence, but it was vacant. He then stole a bicycle at another nearby residence. It was found abandoned a short distance from the crime scene.

On March 13, 1980, Lyman Smith, age 43, and Charlene Smith 33, were murdered in their home in Ventura. They were bludgeoned to death with a log from their fireplace and bound with a cord from the drapes. Their wrists were tied with an unusual Chinese knot known as the diamond knot.

On August 19, 1980, Patrice Harrington, age 27, and Keith Harrington, age 24, were found bludgeoned to death in their home in a gated community in Dana Point. There was evidence that they had been bound at their wrists and ankles, but no ligatures were found. The murder weapon was apparently taken by the killer.

On February 6, 1981, Manuela Witthuhn, age 28, was found bludgeoned to death in her home in Irvine. The body showed signs of being bound, but the ligatures were not found, nor was the weapon. A couple of items were missing from the house and the police found their television in the backyard.

On July 27, 1981, Cheri Domingo, age 35, and Gregory Sanchez, age 27, were also found bludgeoned to death in their home in Goleta. Sanchez had been shot, but not bound.

On May 4, 1986, Janelle Lisa Cruz, age 18, was found bludgeoned to death in her home in Irvine. The other members of the family were vacationing in Mexico.

There were suspects:

Brett Glasby (October 21, 1961 – February 2, 1982) was an alleged drug dealer and gangbanger in Goleta. However, he was killed in 1982, prior to the murder of Janelle Cruz.

Paul Schneider (c. 1962) was a high-ranking member of the Aryan Brotherhood prison gang who was living in Orange County during the time of the murders of the Harringtons, Manuela Witthuhn, and Janelle Cruz. DNA cleared him of the murders.

Joe Alsip was a business partner of Lyman Smith who was murdered, along with his wife, on March 13, 1980. Alsip was arraigned for the murder of the Smiths in 1982, but the charges were later dropped.

In June 2016, a new search was begun for this killer.

April 24, 2018, **Joseph James DeAngelo** (b. November 8, 1945) was arrested at his home in Citrus Heights, about 16 miles from Sacramento, California. A discarded DNA sample from DeAngelo matched the DNA found at crime scenes of the *Golden State Killer*. DeAngelo is suspected of 13 murders and kidnappings, 45 rapes, and more than 120 burglaries in some 10 California counties. He appeared in court on April 27 and was charged with two murders. He was denied bail.

DeAngelo cannot be charged with the rapes or burglaries because the statute of limitations has expired for those crimes. He can, however, be charged with the murders and kidnappings.

Joseph James DeAngelo will be tried on multiple murder charges. Prosecutors in six counties filed an amended felony complaint in Sacramento Superior Court to combine the previous cases against DeAngelo in those counties, which include 13 counts of murder with special circumstances, including murder committed during the course of a burglary and rape. Also made 13 new charges of kidnapping to commit robbery using a firearm and a knife during those alleged crimes. On April 10, 2019, prosecutors announced that they would seek the death penalty. On March 4, 2020, DeAngelo pleaded guilty if the death penalty were taken off the table. In response, the Sacramento County District Attorney's Office said they wished to continue seeking the death penalty. As of this writing, the case was still in progress.

Golden Years Killer in 1996 in Richmond, Virginia, was the work of **Burchart, Leslie Leon** (1949 – August 1,

2002) who was known to be a homeless schizophrenic who was off his medications during this six-month killing spree. There was no evidence to tie him to the murders, just his confessions. He knew things that only the killer and police would know.

He was called the *Golden Years Killer* because he stalked and murdered older women in the West End. He confessed to murdering four women: Mamie Verlander, Lucille Boyd, Elizabeth Siebert, and Jane Foster; and three homeless men. He also confessed to killing a woman at Kensington Gardens. He said that the woman was lying in bed with an oxygen mask; he removed the oxygen mask and watched her suffocate, then left the room. He also confessed to killing a homeless man behind a grocery store on West Broad. He said, "He was just like me, he was suffering. I took my shirt off, put it around his neck, and choked him." Police said that these deaths were not publicized and Burchart knew very specific details of both deaths.

Leslie Leon Burchart pleaded guilty to the seven murders. He was sentenced to four life terms plus 105 years, which he served at the Wallens Ridge State Prison in Wise County, Virginia. On July 30 he was transported to the Lonesome Pine Hospital with an unspecified illness. He died two days later.

Gomes da Rocha, Tiago Henrique (b. February 4, 1988) a former security guard, was a prolific serial killer in the city of Goiania, state of Goias, Brazil. He has confessed to murdering at least 39 people between 2011 and October 2014. Gomes da Rocha claims to have had a good childhood until he was 11 years old, when a neighbor sexually assaulted him. He claims this led to murderous urges which he could not control. He targeted homeless people, women, and homosexuals.

His first victim was a man, the first of 17 males he would murder. He killed 15 women in seven months in 2014. They ranged in age from 14 to 29. He was arrested on October 16, 2014, by a special police team that was investigating the murders. During the search of his mother's house, where he lived, authorities found a .38 caliber pistol and a motorbike with fake license plates. He had stolen the .38 caliber pistol when he worked at a private security firm. As he confessed to the murders, he referred to his victims as numbers (1 – 39), accurately described the locations of each murder and his emotions during the murder, but he could not remember the victims' faces. He shot his victims from a motorbike while wearing a helmet which covered most of his face. He shouted "robbery" before shooting them, but he never took anything from them. He is also being investigated for more than 90 robberies of shops, pharmacies, and lottery outlets.

The only victims publicly identified are Barbara Costa, age 14; Diego Martins Mendes, age 16; Beatriz Moura, age 23; Janaina Souza, age 24; Aleandro Santos Miranda, age 35; Ana Maria Duarte, age 26, Valdivino Ribeiro, age 56; Wanessa Filipe; and Ana Gomes, his last victim.

In May 2016, Gomes da Rocha was convicted of 11 murders and sentenced to 25 years in prison.

Gomez, Lloyd (1923 – October 16, 1953) was a hobo and a farm laborer from Mexico who "rode the rails" and murdered other hoboes because, "I had to eat and I needed money to do it." Gomez had a police record dating back some 15 years.

Investigators believe Gomez may have murdered nine men between 1949 – 1951. In 1950, Warren Cunningham, age 42, who was a cook, was shot to death near Sacramento on November 11; and Earl Franklin Woods, age 50, was murdered near Mojave on November 19.

In 1951, John Doe (No. 1), age about 50, was beaten to death in Stockton on June 9; George Jones, age 69, was clubbed to death in Merced on June 22; and a man named Arvid, age 40, was murdered at Roseville on July 18; and,

Roy Chester Hanson, a cook, was murdered August 16 at Ben Ali, north of Sacramento.

Three more bodies have been found but their death dates could not be established—

Elmer Cushman was killed in a railroad car en route from Oakland to Stockton; John Doe (No. 2), about age 50, was killed at Marysville; and John Doe (No. 3) murdered in Oroville, date unknown, maybe a Native American.

Gomez stated that the total of the money he had killed for amounted to about $62. The most he got from any victim was $24 and the least was a nickel. All of these deaths are verified by police records and newspaper accounts.

Lloyd Gomez was convicted of killing Warren Hood Cunningham on November 11, 1950, near Sacramento, California. He was sentenced to death in California's gas chamber and executed on October 16, 1953.

Goncalvez Gallareta, Pablo Jose (b. March 6, 1970) was born in Bilbao, Spain to Hamlet Goncalvez, a diplomat representing Uruguay in Spain. At the age of nine, Pablo moved with his family to the Carrasco neighborhood in the capital city of Montevideo. Pablo attended Stella Maris School (a primary school) and completed his studies at a public high school. He studied economic sciences at the University of the Republic.

In the early morning hours of New Year's Day 1992, Ana Luisa Miller Sichero, age 26, was suffocated and discarded on the beach at Solymar. The killer left his tie wrapped around her neck.

On September 20, 1992, after leaving a disco spot in Montevideo, Andrea Castro, age 15, was found manually suffocated. Again the killer left a tie wound around the neck of the murdered girl.

Maria Victoria Williams, age 22, disappeared on February 8, 1992, while waiting for the bus to take her to work. She was lured into Goncalvez Gallareta's house when he came running to her asking for help with his grandmother who was very ill and had suffered a sudden attack. As soon as they entered the house, he asked that she call for emergency help. When the girl turned to place the call, she was struck from behind and then murdered when he placed a plastic bag over her head. He again left his tie wound around her neck.

Pablo Jose Goncalvez Gallareta was arrested and charged with the three murders. His guilt was confirmed when he took the investigators to the place where he had discarded Ana Luisa Miller Sichero's body.

Goncalvez Gallareta was convicted of the murders and was sentenced to 30 years in prison. He was released on June 23, 2016, having completed his sentence.

Gong Runbo (1972 – December 31, 2006) was a serial killer in the city of Jiamusi in the northeast province of Heilongjiang Province, China. In October 1996, Gong Runbo was sentenced to eight years for raping a young girl. He was released in 2004.

Between March 2005 and February 2006, he molested five children, ages 12 and 13. He also lured, molested, and murdered six children between the ages of 9 and 16.

Gong Runbo was arrested on February 28, 2006, when a boy he had abducted escaped from his apartment and called the police. Police, who captured Gong in a nearby Internet café, found four decomposing bodies, children's clothes, and a rocking horse made from the remains of the murdered children in his apartment. Gong was convicted of the murders and sentenced to death. He was executed on December 31, 2006.

Gonzalez, Alberto aka **Artieda, Ramiro** (September 4, 1889 – July 3, 1939) was a Bolivian serial killer. Artieda's first murder was fratricide—he murdered his brother so that he could inherit the family estate and marry his 18-year-old fiancée. From the beginning, Artieda was the chief suspect in his brother's murder, but investigators could not find conclusive proof that it was Ramiro who committed the murder. His fiancée felt she could not marry someone who was suspected of murder, so she jilted him. Artieda left his home country and traveled to the United States, where he worked as an actor. It is not known if he started his killing of young girls while in America, but it is known that upon his return to Bolivia, a series of mysterious stranglings began.

The first was the death of Margarita Rios in a deserted building in the city of Cochabamba. The second was Luisita Toranza in Oruro. Then in La Paz, the capital city of Bolivia, Rosalino Villavencio was murdered after being lured to an apartment by a man claiming to be a film company executive (a role played expertly by Artieda). Next, Teresa Ardiales was murdered at the Villa Montes on the Pilcamayo River. Maria Perez became his next victim when a visiting professor (again played by Artieda) made an appearance at her college at Cucre and murdered her in one of the classrooms in November 1937. Mariana Aramayo walked into the church at Potosi with a "monk." Her strangled body was found hidden behind the altar. Artieda's final victim was Julia Caceres who was murdered in a deserted house in La Paz on December 8, 1938. This time, Artieda was playing the role of a "travelling salesman."

All of the women were 18 years old and bore a striking resemblance to Artieda's former girlfriend. Ramiro claimed that he intended to kill as many 18-year-old girls who looked like his faithless girlfriend as possible. Whatever the reason, Artieda was tried and convicted of the seven murders and sentenced to death. On July 3, 1939, he faced the firing squad in the courtyard of Cochabamba Prison.

Gonzalez Escamilla, Martin (b. 1953) was arrested in November 1998 and charged with the kidnapping of Olivia

Perez Estrada, age 54, in Austin, Travis County, Texas. She had been reported missing by her family on October 29, 1998.

On January 28, 1999, police identified remains, found about three years earlier, as those of Gonzalez's wife, Sylvia Garcia Gonzalez, age 45, who had died from blows to the head. They were able to make the identification by using DNA from the body found in September 1995 in East Austin and comparing it with the DNA from the dried saliva found on envelopes of the letters Sylvia had mailed to her family in Mexico.

Gonzalez was also a suspect in the disappearance of Erica S. Perez, age estimated to be in mid 30s, who worked for Gonzalez on a few temporary jobs, and who police had listed as missing in December 1997; and Maria Gladys Flores, age 53, who was reported missing by Martin Gonzalez in May 1998.

Sylvia Garcia Gonzalez was married to Martin Gonzalez in May 1994 in Monclova, Mexico. Martin moved to Austin in late 1994 and Sylvia followed him to Austin in March 1995. She telephoned her daughter in Monclova almost daily. The last call received by her daughter was on June 8, 1995, and by coincidence, the day she received the last letter from her mother.

Maria Gladys Flores, age 53, was a native of Panama who had moved to Austin in 1994 with two of her children. She met Martin Gonzalez in 1998 and was soon living with him. She worked two jobs and was forced to give all of her money to Gonzalez. She was last seen when she left work on May 20, 1998, with Gonzalez. On November 22, 1999, her remains were found in a field in southeast Austin. The medical examiner stated that her cause of death was at least 15 blunt force blows to the head and face which could have been made by a hammer.

Olivia Estrada, age 54, met Gonzalez at a dance hall in 1998. Estrada grew frightened of Gonzalez because of his violent temper. Her family urged her to get a restraining order. On October 29, 1998, Estrada's daughter called the police to report that her mother had not answered her telephone for two days and family members went to her house to find it unoccupied. Police found that the hall carpet in Olivia's house was soaked with water and blood splatters were found on the doorframe in a bedroom, in the hall, and on the kitchen door. They found blood and one of Olivia's rings on the carport. On October 18, 1999, her skeletal remains were found in a field in Bastrop County, east of Austin. The medical examiner said the skull showed evidence of blunt force trauma to the forehead and she had been shot in the back of the head.

Martin Escamilla Gonzalez was charged in the deaths of Sylvia Garcia Gonzalez, Maria Gladys Flores, and Olivia Perez Estrada. He denied knowing either Sylvia Garcia Gonzalez or Maria Gladys Flores. He was found guilty and was sentenced to life in prison. He is currently at the H. H. Coffield Unit, in Tennessee Colony, Texas.

Goodin, Anthony (b. 1965) is a suspected serial killer in Georgia, Florida, and Alabama. Goodin was arrested in July 1987 in Columbus, Indiana, on charges of assault and the attempted robbery of his girlfriend, and an earlier charge of trespassing. On December 11, 1987, Goodin was indicted for the murder of Marlin Carpenter in Valdosta, Georgia. He waived extradition to Georgia and on June 11, 1988, he was convicted of first-degree murder and sentenced to life imprisonment.

Goodin had been living "on the road" since 1984 and was known to have travelled through Alabama, Florida, and Georgia before venturing to the Midwest. He is suspected by police in those states of the murders of several others in Florence, Alabama, and Lowndes County, Georgia, plus an open case in Florida.

Goodman, Keith Eugene (b. 1959), **Holland, Tracy Lynn** (b. 1968) and **Mead, Jon Christopher** (b. 1967) murdered four holdup victims in 1989-90 in New York and Mississippi. In 1990, Goodman was sentenced to life plus 20 years in New York. In 1991, Mead was sentenced to life plus 20 years in New York. Holland turned state's evidence. Goodman and Mead were convicted of murder in Mississippi and sentenced to life. As of August 30, 2011, they are both still in prison in Mississippi. No further information was found on Tracy Lynn Holland.

Gore, David (August 21, 1953 – April 12, 2012) and **Waterfield, Fred** (b. September 29, 1952) were born and raised in Florida. They could not have been more alike if they were brothers, but they were cousins. They both enjoyed violent sex and they were serial killers.

Their first attempts at abducting and raping women were pretty much fiascos. They followed a female motorist and Fred flattened her tires with a rifle, but the woman jumped out of her car and escaped on foot. Their next attempt was to follow a woman from Vero Beach to Miami, but when she parked on a busy street in Miami, they gave up.

In early 1981, Gore worked for his father in a citrus grove during the day and by night he patrolled the streets with a badge as an auxiliary sheriff's deputy. Waterfield recognized the possibilities of using the badge to stop women travelling alone and offered to pay Gore $1,000 for each pretty girl he could supply him.

In February, Gore found Ying Hua Ling, age 17, just alighting from a school bus and using his badge got her into his car. He drove her to her home, and "arrested" her mother. He handcuffed the mother and daughter together. He phoned Waterfield in Orlando to tell him of his captives and his location. While awaiting his cousin's arrival, Gore raped both women. When Waterfield arrived, he told Gore that the mother was too old and tied her up in such a way that she choked herself to death while trying to get free. Waterfield then raped and murdered the daughter and paid Gore just $400. David Gore was left with the chore of disposing of the bodies.

On July 15, Gore made a trip to Round Island Park in search of the blonde his cousin had requested. He saw Judith Daley, age 35, and decided she was the one. He first disabled her car, then acted "the Good Samaritan" and offered to take her to the nearest telephone (this was 1981, long before anyone had a cell phone). She entered his pickup and was immediately faced with a pistol being held by "the Good Samaritan". Gore handcuffed Judith and telephoned Waterfield. Waterfield gave Gore a check for $1500 when they were done with their victim. Gore told officials, two years later, that he had "fed her to the alligators" in a swamp west of I-95.

Later in July, a man reported that a deputy had stopped his teenage daughter on a rural highway and attempted to hold her for questioning. She escaped. Gore was stripped of his badge and fired from the Sheriff's Department. He was arrested several days later when police found him hiding in the back of a woman's car in Vero Beach. He was armed with a pistol, handcuffs, and a police scanner. He was tried and convicted him of armed trespass and was sentenced to five years. He was paroled in March 1983.

Now back home, Gore and Waterfield resumed their "hunting women" activities. On May 20, 1983, a prostitute slipped away from them even though she was being held at gunpoint. On May 21, they picked up two girls hitchhiking, Barbara Byer and Angelica Lavallee, both 14 years old. Gore and Waterfield took turns raping them before Gore shot the girls to death. Barbara Byer was dismembered and buried in a shallow grave. Angelica Lavallee was dumped in a canal.

On July 26, police responded to a report of a nude man firing shots at a naked girl on a residential street in Vero

Beach. Surrounding the house owned by relatives of Gore, they found a car in the driveway with blood dripping from the trunk. They found the body of Lynn Elliott, age 17, dead from a shot to the head. Gore surrendered peacefully and directed the police officers to the attic where he had a 14-year-old girl tied to the rafters. She told police that she and Lynn Elliott were thumbing rides when Gore and another man offered them a ride. Immediately upon entering the vehicle, one of the men flashed a pistol and they were taken to this house (where they were found) and they were stripped naked and raped repeatedly. Elliott managed to get free and escaped on foot with Gore in hot pursuit firing the pistol. Gore hit her with a shot, and she fell dead. The other man had left the house in the interim.

Gore was taken to police headquarters where he confessed to the crimes committed with his cousin, Fred Waterfield. Both men were convicted of their crimes. Gore was sentenced to death and Waterfield was sentenced to two life sentences to run consecutively, with a minimum of 50 years to be served before being considered for parole.

After spending 28 years on death row, Gore was finally executed by lethal injection at the Florida State Prison in Starke, Florida, on April 12, 2012.

Gorilla Killer
Nelson, Earle
Leonard

Gorilla Killer aka **Nelson, Earle Leonard** (May 12, 1897 – January 13, 1928) was a serial killer in the early 20th century in the states of California and Oregon, the upper Midwest, and into Canada. After his mother and father both died of syphilis, before he was two years old, he was sent to be raised by his maternal grandmother. About eight years later he was hit by a streetcar while riding his bicycle. He remained unconscious for six days and after he awoke, he suffered from frequent headaches and loss of memory and his behavior became erratic.

In 1915, Nelson broke into a cabin he thought was abandoned and was sentenced to two years. Upon his release, he joined the United States Navy, but was committed to the Napa State Mental Hospital due to his odd and erratic behavior. He escaped three times. The hospital stopped trying to find him after his third escape and he began committing sex crimes. In 1921, he attempted to molest Mary Summers, age 12, but he was caught when Mary began screaming. He was again sent to the Napa State Mental Hospital. He again tried several times to escape and succeeded at least once but was captured and returned to the mental hospital. He was released in 1925. His killings began shortly afterward.

By February 1926, he was living in a boarding house and had two landladies, Clara Newmann and Laura Beal. On February 20, he murdered Clara Newmann. Two weeks later, he murdered Laura Beal. He often pretended to study his Bible in their presence to keep them at ease. After he killed them, he engaged in necrophilia. He then hid their bodies under the nearest bed.

On Jun 9, 1927, Lola Cowen, age 14, was selling paper flowers on the street to help her family when she met Nelson. He somehow lured her to his room at the boarding house, where he raped, mutilated, and murdered her. He slept with Lola under his bed for three nights, despite the fact that he had mutilated her in a similar fashion of *Jack the Ripper,* with their throats slashed and abdomens mutilated.

On the following day, June 10, Nelson somehow managed to get inside the home of Emily Patterson, age 27, as she was cleaning house. Nelson raped her and then strangled her. He hid her body under the bed, as was his habit. When Emily's husband arrived home, he found Emily missing, and knelt by the bed to pray for her safe return. During the prayer, he discovered his wife's body under the bed.

By being on the move constantly and using aliases, Nelson stayed ahead of authorities for 18 months. Police were hampered by the fact that serial killing was relatively unknown at that time. There were several men arrested for the murders here and there, which further confused the authorities.

Nelson was arrested twice in Canada. On June 15, 1927, in Wakopa, Manitoba, he was arrested for the murders of Lola Cowan and Emily Patterson. At the time of his arrest, Nelson claimed his name was Virgil Wilson. He escaped that evening and hopped the same train that members of the Winnipeg Police were traveling on. They captured him and he was arrested again at Crystal City, Manitoba, by the police when the train arrived there. During the complex investigation, Nelson was linked to at least 22 murders between February 20, 1926, and June 10, 1927.

Earle Nelson was tried and convicted of the murders of Lola Cowan and Emily Patterson and was sentenced to death. He was hanged at the Vaughan Street Jail, Winnipeg, Manitoba, Canada at 7:30 a.m. on January 13, 1928.

Gorton, Jeffrey Wayne (b. November 1, 1962) is currently in prison in Michigan for the murders of Margarette Eby and Nancy Ludwig. He is a suspect in other rapes and murders.

Margaret Eby, age 55, was a music professor and former provost at the University of Michigan-Flint. Her body was found in her home on November 9, 1986. She had been raped and nearly decapitated. Nancy Ludwig, age 41, from Minnetonka, Minnesota, was a flight attendant for Northwest Airlines. She was staying at the Hilton Airport Inn near Detroit Metropolitan Airport after a flight from Las Vegas, Nevada. Her body was found on February 18, 1991. She had been tied up, raped, and had her throat slashed. Injuries to her body suggest that she put up a fight against her assailant. A witness had seen a man loading burgundy colored airline-style luggage into a bronze or brown Chevrolet Monte Carlo on the night of the murder. Police found a 1982 gold Monte Carlo near the Detroit Metropolitan Airport and found luggage similar to that used by Northwest Airlines employees. Police collected DNA from the scene of the murder, but at that time they did not have a DNA database to compare it to.

In the summer of 2001, a forensic specialist for the Michigan Police matched semen in Margaret Eby's killing to that found in the Ludwig murder. A fingerprint left at the scene of the Eby murder was matched to Gorton.

In the meantime, Gorton had come under police scrutiny. On February 7, 2002, a police officer was able to pick up a drinking cup Gorton had discarded; it was used in testing his DNA. The DNA matched the DNA found at the scenes of the Eby and Ludwig murders. Gorton was arrested on February 9 and charged with the murder of Margarette Eby. On February 11, he was charged with Nancy Ludwig's murder.

A search of Gorton's house revealed at least 800 pairs of women's underwear, labeled with dates and places. According to the assistant prosecutor of Wayne County, "There were a lot of things here that are very disturbing. Investigators would be remiss if they didn't do follow-ups."

Homicide investigators in Orange County, Florida have been in contact with the Michigan authorities about the disappearance of a 14-year-old girl, Vickie Wills, who vanished in April 1983. At the time, Gorton was a sprinkling-service employee living near Orlando. In May of that year, Gorton broke into a house and stole a woman's underwear. He was convicted and sent to prison. He was released in 1985 and moved to Michigan.

Jeffrey Gorton was convicted of the murder of Nancy Ludwig and sentenced to life in prison. He pleaded no contest to Margarette Eby's murder and was sentenced to life in prison. He is currently serving his sentence at Saginaw Correctional Facility in Freeland, MI.

Gorton is suspected by investigators of a murder in 1983 and murders in 1986 and 1991. He is only accounted for from mid-1983 to 1985.

Gosnell, Kermit Barron (b. February 9, 1941) was a physician who owned and operated the Women's Medical Society Clinic in Philadelphia, Pennsylvania, where hundreds, possibly thousands, of abortions were performed.

He was charged with eight murders but convicted of only three murders—three babies were born alive and killed by cutting the infant's spine with scissors—and one charge of involuntary manslaughter—one mother died due to complications of the abortion.

Gosnell was also convicted of 21 felony counts of illegal "late-term" abortions and 211 counts of violating the 24-hour informed consent law.

After his conviction, in 2013 he waived the right to appeal his conviction in return for the prosecutors not seeking the death penalty. He was sentenced to life in prison without the possibility of parole. He is incarcerated at State Correctional Institution—Huntingdon, a close-security correctional facility, located near Huntingdon, Pennsylvania. A book about him, entitled *Gosnell: The Untold Story of America's Most Prolific Serial Killer,* was published in 2017.

Graham, Harrison (b. October 9, 1959) aka *Marty* was a mentally retarded drug abuser who lived in a slum district of Philadelphia called Frankford, Pennsylvania, where he rented a third floor two-room apartment. Frankford was also home to serial killers Gary Heidnik and Leonard Christopher, both convicted of murders committed during the time period of 1986-87.

In 1987, Graham was evicted from his apartment because of the horrific smells coming from it. Before he left, he nailed up the bedroom door claiming he left some of his property there and would return for it. When he never came back, authorities broke down the door to find seven bodies, all in various stages of decomposition. Only two bodies could be identified, and one was his former girlfriend. They had all been murdered in 1986-87.

On August 17, 1987, Graham turned himself in to police, and admitted strangling all of the women while having sex with them. He also admitted to having sex with them after their deaths. He was charged with seven counts of murder and seven counts of abuse of a corpse. He was sentenced to life on the murder charges plus seven sentences of death (in an effort to prevent him from ever being released). He is imprisoned at State Correctional Institution – Coal Township near Shamokin, Pennsylvania.

Granny Killer aka **Glover, John Wayne** (November 26, 1932 – September 9, 2005) was a serial killer in Australia during the years 1989-90. Glover was born to a working-class family in Wolver Hampton, England. By 1947, he had been arrested for petty crimes, such as stealing clothing and handbags. He joined the British Army but was discharged when authorities became aware of his criminal record. In 1956, he moved to Australia and settled in Melbourne.

Glover had trouble with establishing relationships with older women, first his mother, then his mother-in-law after he married and lived in Mosman, Sydney, with his in-laws. Glover had continued his criminal ways in Australia. He was convicted of larceny in Victoria, a stealing charge in New South Wales, and in Melbourne was convicted on two counts of assaulting women, two counts of indecent assault, one count of assault causing bodily harm, and another four counts of larceny for which he received a three-year *Good Behavior Bond**.

Glover was a volunteer at the Senior Citizens Society. On January 11, 1989, Margaret Todhunter, age 84, was walking down a local street and was seen by Glover in his car. He parked the car, walked over to the woman, punched her in the face, stole her purse which contained $209, and then went to the RSL Club (support organization for men and women who have served or are serving in the Australian Defense Force) and spent Mrs. Todhunter's money. She was only injured in the attack. On June 6, 1989, a 77-year-old woman was molested at the Wesley Gardens Retirement Village. On June 24, 1989, at the Caroline Chisholm Nursing Home,ome Glover raised the dress of an elderly patient and fondled her buttocks and in a neighboring room, he slid his hand down the front of a patient's gown and stroked her breasts. On August 8, 1989, Glover assaulted an elderly woman on a back street of Sydney's upper North Shore. On October 18, 1989, Glover followed an 86-year-old widow to her retirement village where he attacked her and rammed her face into a brick wall before taking her purse. These were just the attacks that were reported.

There is nothing to indicate that Glover began killing before 1989. He murdered for the first time when he was 52 years old, old for a first-time serial killer.

On March 1, 1989, Glover saw Gwendoline Mitchelhill walking down the street. He got a hammer from his car, put it under his belt, and followed Ms. Mitchelhill to her apartment building. He hit her on the back of the head and continued to hit her on the head and body, then he grabbed her purse and fled. The purse contained $100. Two schoolboys found Ms. Mitchelhill, but she died shortly afterward.

On May 9, 1989, Lady Ashton, age 84 and widow of Sir William Ashton, was walking along Military Road when she was seen by Glover. The man followed her into the foyer of her apartment and attacked her with his hammer. He dragged her into an alcove and began hitting her head on the pavement. When she was unconscious, Glover removed her pantyhose and strangled her with them. He then placed her shoes and walking stick at her feet and left with her purse. Again he went to the RSL Club and spent the $100 he found in Lady Ashton's purse. The pantyhose found around Lady Ashton's throat were tied so tightly that they were cutting into her neck. No sign of semen was found during the autopsy.

On November 2, 1989, Glover met an elderly woman on a quiet backstreet and helped her carry her groceries to her home. She invited him for a cup of tea, but he declined and left. He came upon another elderly woman, Margaret Pahud, and attacked her from behind. He hit her with a blunt instrument on the back of the head and again on the side of her head when she fell. Glover left with her purse which contained $300 that he spent at the RSL Club.

On November 3, 1989, Glover murdered Olive Cleveland, age 81. He struck up a conversation with Ms. Cleveland who was sitting on a bench at the Wesley Gardens Retirement Village. Ms. Cleveland grew uncomfortable with Glover and got up to walk to the main building. Glover grabbed her from behind and forced her down a ramp to a secluded area. He hit her repeatedly and pushed her into the concrete. He removed her pantyhose and strangled her with them. He found $60 in her purse and fled with it.

The state government was offering a reward of $200,000 for information leading to the arrest and conviction of the *Granny Killer.*

On November 23, 1989, Glover spotted Muriel Falconer, age 93, returning home from shopping. He grabbed his gloves and hammer, and followed Ms. Falconer to her home. He moved up behind her and she could not hear him as she was partially deaf and blind. He put his hand over her mouth as she opened the door. Glover hit her repeatedly on the head and neck with the hammer. She fell to the floor and Glover began to remove her pantyhose, which helped to revive the woman. He promptly hit her several more times and then proceeded to strangle her with her pantyhose. He found $100 in her house.

The state government increased the reward to $250,000.

On January 11, 1990, Glover visited the Greenwich Hospital and entered the palliative care ward. In the four-bed ward, he approached Daisy Roberts, asked if she was losing any body heat, pulled up her nightgown and touched her in an inappropriate way. She screamed for help. A nurse approached Glover, but he fled. She was able to get the license number of his car and called police. Members of the hospital staff identified Glover from a photograph. This incident was not connected to the murders and the *Granny Killer* task force was not told of this incident for three weeks. The task force then contacted Glover and he agreed to be interviewed at the station the following day. Glover did not show up for the interview, so the authorities contacted his wife and she told them that Glover had attempted suicide and was at the Royal North Shore Hospital. The police went to the hospital, but Glover refused to be interviewed. A staff member handed the police a note written by Glover on a piece of business paper for the Four 'n' Twenty Pies (for whom Glover worked) that contained the phrase, "No more grannies . . . grannies," and, "Essie (Glover's mother-in-law) started it." Police now believed that Glover was the *Granny Killer* but had no evidence to prove it.

Glover was interviewed concerning the assaults at the nursing homes and he denied all of them. They did not ask about any of the murders since they did not have any evidence and did not want to let him know that he was a suspect. They did, however, put him under police surveillance. Glover suspected he was being followed and was very careful. He would drive around a block more than once and even drove the wrong way up one-way streets.

On March 19, 1990, Joan Sinclair was murdered in her home. She and Glover had a platonic relationship. The police watched as Glover was admitted to her home at about

10:00 a.m. By 1:00 p.m., Glover was still in the house. By 5:00 p.m. the police became concerned and got permission to enter the house at 6:00 p.m. They first knocked on the door to check for barking dogs, then went around back and saw through the rear door a hammer lying in a pool of dry blood. At this point the police entered the house and found Sinclair's body. Her head was battered and wrapped in blood-soaked towels. She was naked from the waist down and her pantyhose were tied around her neck. There was evidence of rape, but Glover would later deny that he raped her. They found Glover unconscious in the bathtub filled with water. He said he had swallowed a handful of Valium with a bottle of Vat 69 (a scotch blended whiskey), slashed his left wrist, and lay in the tub waiting to die.

At his trial, which began on March 28, 1990, Glover pleaded not guilty on the grounds of diminished responsibility. Regardless of his plea, he was found guilty and sentenced to life. On September 9, 2005, John Wayne Glover hanged himself in his cell at Lithgow Prison.

Days before Glover's suicide, he handed a sketch to his last outside visitor. The sketch is of a park in which Glover pointed out two palm trees. In the middle of the palm tree on the right, he had drawn the number "nine" between leaves and branches. This number "nine" is thought to be the number of murders Glover committed, or the number of unsolved murders he committed that he had not been connected with. This number may include Emmie May Anderson, age 78, murdered on October 19, 1961; Irene Kiddle, age 61, murdered on March 22, 1963; Elsie Boyes, age 63, murdered on June 3, 1967; Christina Yankos, age 63, murdered on April 9, 1968; Florence Broadhurst, age 78, murdered on October 16, 1977; Josephine McDonald, age 72, murdered on August 29, 1984; and Wanda Amundsen, age 83, murdered on November 21, 1986.

* A Good Behavior Bond is an order of the court that requires one to be of good behavior for a specified period of

time. The court will impose conditions that must be obeyed during the term of the Good Behavior Bond.

Granny Killer aka **Kaprat III, Edward Bernard** (1964 – April 20, 1995) was a machinist as well as a rapist and murderer of five elderly women in Hernando County, Florida in 1991 – 1993. After killing them, he set fire to their houses. He also beat a man to death. He confessed to the murders of four of the women and was sentenced to death, but before the sentence could be carried out, he was murdered in prison on April 20, 1995.

Grant, Gary Gene (c. 1953) is a serial killer who confessed to the sex-slayings of 6-year-old Bradley Lyons and Scott Andrews and two teenage girls, in the 1970s in Renton, Washington. The body of Carol Erickson, age 19, was found in December 1969. The body of Joanne Zulauf, age 17, was found in September 1970. The boys' bodies were discovered in April 1971. All of the victims had been stabbed, strangled, or both, and dumped in the wooded area of Honey Creek Ravine near a Renton trailer park where Grant lived with his parents. With the help of Explorer Scouts, the knife used in the slayings was found and traced to 19-year-old Gary Gene Grant. He was convicted of four murders and was given four life sentences to be served consecutively. He is currently housed at the Monroe Corrections Complex in Monroe, Washington.

Gray, Dana Sue Armbrust (b. December 6, 1957) was a nurse and an expert skydiver who excelled at both windsurfing and golf. She was also a serial killer in California.

On February 14, 1994, Norma Davis, age 86, was murdered in her home. She was found two days later with a knife still in her neck and a fillet knife in her chest. Gray knew Norma and had shared her home at one time. Davis is thought to be Dana Sue Gray's first victim, but due to lack of evidence, Gray has never been charged with her murder.

On February 28, June Roberts, age 66, was murdered. Gray visited with June on that day, asking to borrow a book. Gray unplugged the phone (both cords) while June was searching for the book. She used the handset cord (the curly one) to strangle June Roberts. Gray took two of June's credit cards and went on a shopping spree at an upscale shopping area in Temecula.

On March 10, Dorinda Hawkins, age 57, was working alone at an antique store, when Gray came in, supposedly to buy a frame for a photo of her deceased mother. Gray strangled her with a telephone cord, took money from her purse and from the cash register, and went on another shopping spree again with June Roberts' credit card. Dorinda Hawkins survived the assault and was able to give a description of her attacker.

On March 16, Gray murdered Dora Beebe, age 87. She gained entry by knocking on her door and asking for directions. Gray went inside to "look at a map" and murdered Dora. She then used Dora Beebe's credit card to go on another shopping spree.

Gray's shopping sprees were her downfall. Her description was supplied by various merchants where she had used the credit cards. She had spent so much money on June Roberts' card that the credit card company called the Roberts family to alert them of the massive spending. When the detectives interviewed the merchants where Roberts' credit card had been used, they learned that the killer had recently dyed her hair and had a little boy named "Jason". Detectives had stayed in touch with Jeri Armbrust, who was married to Dana's father and was the ex-daughter-in-law of Norma Davis. Jeri had stayed in touch with Norma and at one time was a suspect in her murder. Upon hearing the description, Jeri told detectives that she believed the suspect was her stepdaughter, Dana Sue Gray, who had recently dyed her hair and whose boyfriend had a son named Jason. Gray was arrested later that day.

Dana Sue Gray pleaded insanity on all counts. However, after a witness claimed to have seen Gray at Roberts' house on the day of her murder, she changed her plea to guilty of robbing and murdering two women and the attempted murder of a third to avoid the death penalty. She was sentenced to life without parole. She is presently incarcerated in the California Women's Prison in Chowchilla, California.

Gray, Marvin Gayle (August 7, 1954 – July 23, 2013) was born in Princeton, a rural community in Caldwell County, Kentucky. He was the seventh of ten children. He suffered panic attacks starting at the age of four and took drugs to control them. At the age of 11, his panic attacks stopped after his father died of a heart attack and his behavior changed—but not for the good. At age 12 he was arrested for infiltrating into foreign property and theft and sent to a juvenile offenders' institute.

His time in the institution was spent being sexually violated and humiliated consistently. Gray learned self-defense and had feeling of rage, hatred towards elders and those representing the law. He was released in 1968. On the first day back in school, he was expelled for carrying deadly weapons and threatening school officials.

He was arrested in 1971 and was sentenced to five years for robbery, burglary, illegal possession of weapons, and the threat of murder. While imprisoned at the Kentucky State Prison, he began powerlifting, developed an addiction for tattoos, and became an ardent supporter of white supremacy. When he was released in 1975, he was a force to be reckoned with at 6 ft. 2 in. and 220 lbs. He moved to Denver and got a job at the O'Neal Hotel.

Gray and his friend, **William Felder**, were arrested in the summer of 1975 for assaulting a police officer, James Datsman. Officer Datsman had been investigating the murder of Joseph Didier who had been killed early that day in the vicinity of the hotel. When Officer Datsman found them near the crime scene, Gray and Felder shot Datsman. Feldman was convicted of shooting Datsman and received 20 years. Gray was convicted only of theft and complicity and received 4 years.

At the end of 1977, David Cook, another inmate, was found beaten and strangled to death in his cell. Gray was named as the offender by several inmates but they changed their testimonies. Gray was never charged with the murder.

Released in 1978, he met Sheila Olsbrook and they had a son born in 1979. Olsbrook was beaten often by Gray until he was arrested in 1979 along with William Purdue, for stealing a car. He and two other inmates, William Purdue and Jerry Keller, escaped. After hijacking a van, the two quarreled and Gray beat Keller to death and disposed of the body. Gray went to Denver where he was identified as a prison escapee and was arrested. Although blood was found in the van and on a screwdriver in the van, he was never charged with Keller's murder. Purdue had also disappeared, and investigators suspected that Gray had killed him. Purdue's body was never found.

Sent back to prison, he escaped again and was arrested on August 11, 1982. He met Joleen Sue Gardner in Denver on September 1. She refused to have sex with him, so he stabbed her 14 times. He was arrested and convicted in 1984 and was given a sentence of 16 years. In 1986, he was charged with raping a cellmate, but was not convicted due to lack of evidence. He was released in 1991. He was, according to his parole, to find a job, was to report to his probation officer, prohibited from leaving the limits of the state of Colorado or moving closer to places where children and adolescents congregate. Two days after his release, he left on a bus for Paducah, Kentucky. His relatives were afraid of him and police told them to be vigilant. The family given $200 by police and Marvin was returned to Colorado by bus.

He managed to have odd jobs, but in 1992 he was arrested for burglary. Due to the severity of the murder of Joleen Sue Gardner and violating the conditions of his parole, he was given life imprisonment. In November 1992, Gray was charged with the murder of another prisoner, Daniel Green, who was an informant in a drug case.

Transferred to another prison, On July 19, 1993, Gray beat and raped cellmate Gary Hilton. With a week he had beaten and raped James Mervyn. He was then transferred to the Colorado State Penitentiary, a special high-security prison.

Beginning in the year 2000, Gray suddenly began confessing to murders law enforcement was aware that he had committed. By December of that year, he had confessed to 23 murders. By March 2001, he had confessed to 31 murders. He said he committed his first murder 1971; that he was the person who killed Joseph Didier; he had committed seven murders in the states of Nebraska, Tennessee, Iowa, Kentucky and Illinois; and he murdered Purdue by stabbing him in the neck with a screwdriver.

By the time he was finished confessing, he had claimed to have murdered more than 40 people. Police claim that results of polygraph tests have tentatively confirmed his involvement in more than 20 murders. He was incarcerated at the Colorado Territorial Correctional Facility in Canon City, Colorado. He died of heart failure on July 23, 2013.

Gray, Ronald Adrin (b. August 14, 1965) was born in Cochran, Georgia and raised in Miami, Florida. He joined the US Army in 1984. In 1986, he was assigned to Fort Bragg in North Carolina. His arrival coincided with the beginning of a reign of terror that gripped the area.

On April 29, 1986, Linda Coats, age 24, was raped and killed by a single shot to the head. She was attending the university and was enrolled in the Army's ROTC program. She was expecting to receive her commission during that week.

A few days later, the body of Teresa Utley, a Fayetteville prostitute, was found. She had been abducted, stripped naked, beaten, raped, and then knifed to death by her assailant.

On November 16, two women were abducted at gunpoint by a black man who raped them both and threatened to kill them. Neither woman reported the assault to the police. One of the women and her boyfriend later spotted Gray in the neighborhood and the woman was certain that he was the man who had raped her.

November 22, another woman from Fayetteville was raped and her assailant slashed her face and body and left her for dead. On the same night, a female soldier was attacked. Both women survived their attacks. Less than a week later, another female soldier was raped and stabbed.

December 12, Tammy Wilson, age 18 and the wife of a soldier, was abducted from her home. Her husband discovered her naked body several hours later in a nearby wooded area. She had been raped and shot at point blank range.

December 15, Sergeant Michael Clay was called home to inspect the smoking ruins of his mobile home in Fayetteville. His wife, Private Laura Lee Vickery-Clay, was missing. Her body was found some five weeks later in nearby woods. She had been raped, sodomized, and murdered.

On January 3, another female soldier, Private Mary Ann Lang Nameth, age 20, was attacked, but she survived.

On January 7, Kimberly Ruggles, age 23, a cab driver in the city of Fayetteville, was dispatched to pick up a "Ron" at Ronald Gray's address. Her cab was found abandoned on a city street. She had been abducted, raped, and beaten. Her assailant had murdered her by slitting her throat. Hearing of this latest murder, the two women who had been attacked on November 16 reported their rapes. One of them identified the suspect to the police.

After a six-month investigation, Ronald Gray was arrested and charged with 23 felonies, including two counts of first-degree murder.

November 7, 1987, Gray pleaded guilty to all charges in Fayetteville and was sentenced to three consecutive terms of life and five concurrent terms of life.

Ronald Gray was also tried by a military court. He was convicted of 14 charges, including two counts of premeditated murder (Ruggles and Vickery-Clay), attempted premeditated murder of Nameth, three rapes, two robberies, and two counts of forcible sodomy. He was found guilty and on April 12, 1988, he was unanimously sentenced to death. He was also given a Dishonorable Discharge, forfeiture of all pay and allowances, and reduction to the rank of Private E-1. He could not be executed until the president, as the Commander-In-Chief of the United States Armed Forces, approved the death sentence.

President George W. Bush approved Gray's execution on July 28, 2008. Gray is the first service member to be sentenced to death since 1957. His execution was scheduled for December 10, 2008; however, on November 26, 2008, a federal judge granted Gray a stay of execution to allow time for further appeals. On January 26, 2012, the US Army Court of Criminal Appeals denied his appeal. On November 13, 2017, the US Court of Appeals for the Air Force denied Gray's Writ of Error Coram Nobis with prejudice for lack of jurisdiction. On June 28, 2018, the US Supreme Court declined to hear Gray's case, without giving a reason why.

Great Basin Serial Killer aka **Eaton, Dale Wayne** (b. February 10, 1945) is believed by law enforcement to be responsible for nine murders in Idaho, Utah, Wyoming, and Nevada that occurred between 1983 and 1997. The women, between the ages of 18 and 35, were violently attacked and murdered. Their bodies were dumped along remote highways. Most of the victims were either shot or strangled and all were beaten around the head and face. Five of the victims have not been identified. The Great Basin is an area of 184,427 square miles in the western US that encompasses parts of Oregon, California, Idaho, Nevada, Wyoming, and Utah.

On August 15, 1997, a couple found the body of Tonya Teske, age 18, beside the southbound on-ramp to US Highway 20 near Ucon, in eastern Idaho. She is thought by investigators to be a victim of the Great Basin Serial Killer.

July 24, 1997, was the last day anyone saw Amy Wroe Bechtel, age 24. She left her apartment in Lander, Wyoming, to run errands and was last seen at a photo shop about 2:30 p.m. It is believed that from the photo shop she drove to the Shoshone National Forest to check out the course of a 10K race her gym was planning. When her husband arrived at home at about 4:30 p.m., she had not returned. Later in the evening, he checked with neighbors and alerted police that his wife was missing. Her white Toyota station wagon was found on a dirt road in the Shoshone Forest. Amy's body has not been found.

Two other murder victims were found in the Casper, Wyoming, area and may be the work of the Great Basin Serial Killer. The women were walking alone, and their bodies were dumped along highways, one along I-25, north of Casper 347, Wyoming.

Lisa Marie Kimmell was visiting a friend in Denver, Colorado and left there on March 25, 1988, to pick up her boyfriend in Cody, Wyoming and then continue on to her parents' home in Billings, Montana. Records of the Wyoming State Highway Patrol show that she was stopped for speeding in Douglas, Wyoming. She never arrived in Cody. Her body was found floating in the North Platt River near Casper on April 2, 1988, by two fishermen.

Her autopsy revealed that she had been bound, beaten, and raped, and that she had probably died on March 31. This meant that her captor and killer had kept her for at least six days. Her black 1988 Honda CR-X with a Montana license plate bearing "LIL MISS" was not found. On October 13, 1988, a note was left on her grave:

"Lisa –
There are'nt (sic) words to say how much you're missed the pain never leaves
it's so hard without you
you'll always be alive in me.
Your death is my painful loss but Heaven's sweet gain.
Love always,
Stringfellow Hawke"

"Stringfellow Hawke" was a character in the US television program *Airwolf*. The association of the killer to this character is not known.

In the summer of 2002, investigators researching cold cases came across Lisa Kimmell's rape kit and submitted semen for DNA testing. Entering it into the law enforcement CODIS database, they got a hit showing that it was from Dale Wayne Eaton, age 57, of Moneta, Wyoming, who was currently incarcerated in Englewood Federal Prison at Littleton, Colorado on an unrelated weapons charge. Witnesses who lived next door to Eaton reported that they had seen him digging a large hole on his property around the time of Lisa's murder. The property was about an hour's drive from where Lisa had last been seen alive. The Honda CRX was unearthed and still had the license plate "LIL MISS" attached. Neighbors gave investigators letters that Eaton had written to them and it was determined that he was the one who had left the note at Lisa's grave.

Dale Wayne Eaton was charged with eight crimes related to the Kimmell case, including first-degree premeditated murder, aggravated kidnapping, aggravated robbery, first-degree sexual assault, and second-degree sexual assault. He was tried and convicted of all charges and sentenced to death on March 20, 2004. He was scheduled to be executed in February 2010, but he received a stay. In 2001, he murdered his cellmate Carl Palmer.

In 1994, the US Supreme Court ruled that the death penalty shall not be carried out upon a person who has mental retardation. The Court did not specify a number, but of the states that carry this stipulation in their laws, the IQ cut-off ranges from 60 to 70, with most stating that the cutoff is an IQ of 70. Eaton's lawyers are now trying to establish that he is a person with mental retardation. According to records, Dale Wayne Eaton has an IQ measured in the 80s to 90 range.

Eaton's execution was once again stayed in 2014. In February 2020, he asked the US Supreme Court to review his case, indicating that his mental capacity had previously not been properly determined. He remains for the moment at the Wyoming Medium Correctional Institute in Torrington, Wyoming.

Green Man
Desalvo, Albert
Henry

Green Man/The Measuring Man aka **DeSalvo, Albert Henry** (September 3, 1931 – November 25, 1973) was a serial rapist in Boston, Massachusetts. He is included here because in 2013, his DNA was definitely tied to the murder of Mary Sullivan, the *Boston Strangler's* last victim and is believed by Boston authorities to be responsible for all of the murders by the *Boston Strangler.*

In the early 1960s, *The Green Man/The Measuring Man*, Albert DeSalvo, gained entry into women's apartments posing as a building maintenance worker who was to make some repair in their apartment or as a representative of a modeling agency and wanted to measure them for possible modeling jobs. He tied his victims to the bed and sexually assaulted them, sometimes leaving hurriedly saying, "I'm sorry." After his arrest, many women identified him as the man who had assaulted them. DeSalvo was sentenced to life in prison.

In February 1967, DeSalvo escaped from the Bridgewater State Hospital with two other inmates. A note addressed to the superintendent, found on his bunk, stated that he had escaped to focus attention on the conditions in the hospital and his own situation. The next day, he surrendered to his attorney in Lynn, Massachusetts.

It is said that he originally confessed to being the *Boston Strangler* to fellow inmate George Nassar (himself a suspect of being the *Boston Strangler)*. There is also the case for more than one strangler/murderer. Between June 14, 1952 and August 30, 1962, the women murdered were between the ages of 55 and 85. Between December 5, 1962 and January 4, 1964, five of the women murdered were between the ages of 19 and 23; one was 56 and one was 69. Albert DeSalvo was never charged with any of the murders of the *Boston Strangler,* or any other murder.

On November 25, 1973, DeSalvo was found in the prison infirmary stabbed to death. In July 2013, DNA found at the scene of Mary Sullivan's rape and murder matched the DNA provided by DeSalvo's nephew. *See Boston Strangler in the Unsolved Serial Killer Cases section in Book 4.*

Green River Killer aka **Ridgway, Gary Leon** (b. February 18, 1949) was born in Salt Lake City, Utah. He has two brothers and was raised in the McMicken Heights neighborhood of Seattle/Tacoma, Washington. He has an I.Q. of 82, which is low intelligence, and his performance in school was poor. His classmates described him as congenial but forgettable. When he was 16, he stabbed a

6-year-old boy, who survived the attack. Ridgway walked away laughing and said, "I always wondered what it would be like to kill someone." He joined the navy while in high school, was sent to Vietnam after graduation, and worked on a supply ship. He was married three times, the first two ending in divorce. He had a son with his second wife.

In early 1982, young women and girls, mostly prostitutes, began to disappear. On January 21, 1982, the first body was found in a field near Federal Way, eight miles south of Seattle. Another body was found in the Green River on July 15, 1982. The body count rapidly increased throughout the rest of 1982 and continued through 1983 and into 1984. By this time, the body count was 33. By the year 2000, the body count totaled 87. Five bodies have been located since the year 2000, and there are still eight women who disappeared, but have never been found. The killer sometimes contaminated the area with gum, cigarettes, and written material belonging to others in an effort to confuse the investigation. Some of the first bodies were dumped in wooded areas around the Green River, hence the name, *The Green River Killer.* Two of the victims' bodies were taken to the Portland, Oregon, area to try to throw off the investigators. The victims were often left in clusters and usually nude. Sometimes they were posed. Because most of the remains were only skeletons when found, nine are still unidentified. All of these murder victims may or may not be the victims of Gary Ridgway. Some of the unidentified may actually be victims listed as not found.

Gary Ridgway became a suspect in 1984 when one of the victims' boyfriend reported that he last saw her getting into a pickup identified as belonging to Ridgway. Ridgway told the police he did not know the woman and a police investigator in Des Moines, Washington, who knew him, cleared him as a suspect. However, police in the Seattle/Tacoma area still suspected him. Later that year, Ridgway passed a polygraph test. In 1987, his house was searched by police and they took a saliva sample. This was years before reliable DNA testing was able to link that saliva sample to DNA taken from the bodies of three of the earlier victims.

On November 30, 2001, Gary Ridgway was arrested as he left the Kenworth Truck Company where he worked as a spray painter. He was charged with seven murders. He pleaded not guilty, but realizing they had DNA evidence which could positively tie him to these murders, and he could possibly be sentenced to death, he began cooperating. He confessed to 42 of the 48 murders, and six other murders not on the list. As part of the plea agreement, he led authorities to the remains of four more victims. In various interviews with authorities, he claimed to have murdered 65 women; later he admitted to 71 victims and admitted to having sex with them prior to their murders. He also admitted to having sex with the earlier victims' bodies after they were murdered but claimed to have started to bury his victims so he could not commit necrophilia. He murdered them by choking them with his arm, but because he would have wounds from the earlier victims' struggle to stay alive, he began using a garrote. He also told investigators that he targeted prostitutes and runaways as they were easy to pick up and the prostitutes because he "hated most of them."

On November 5, 2003, Gary Ridgway faced the court, and as the clerk read each of the 48 charges of murder, he answered, very stoically, "Guilty." The court sentenced Ridgway to 48 consecutive life sentences without the possibility of parole. The plea agreement provided that he would plead guilty to any and all future cases (in King County) where his confession could be corroborated by reliable evidence. Rebecca "Becky" Marrero's remains were found on December 21, 2010. Ridgway was charged with her murder, pleaded guilty, and was given another sentence of life imprisonment.

The following 49 victims are the women and girls that Gary Ridgway admitted to murdering and for which he was charged:

Wendy Coffield, age 16, was reported missing from her foster home on July 8, 1982. Her naked body was found on July 15 in the Green River near the PD&J Meat Company by an employee while he was taking a break outside to smoke a cigar. A description of the tattoos found on her body was published in the newspaper. A local tattoo artist recognized the descriptions and identified the girl as Wendy Coffield.

Gisele Ann Lovvorn, age 17, was last seen on July 17, 1982, near Pacific Highway South. Two months later, her remains were found in the woods near an apple tree in Des Moines Creek Park, south of Seattle-Tacoma International Airport on September 25, 1982.

Debra Lynn Bonner, age 23, was last seen on July 25, 1982, on the Pacific Highway South near the Sea-Tac International Airport. Her body was discovered on August 12, 1982, in the Green River near Kent.

Marcia Fay Chapman, age 31, was last seen on August 1, 1982, when she left her home to go work the Sea-Tac strip. She was found August 15, 1982, in the Green River by a man rafting down the river.

Cynthia Jean Hinds, age 17, was last seen on August 11, 1982, at a convenience store near the Sea-Tac Strip. Her body was also found on August 15, 1982, in the Green River, only a few feet from Marcia Chapman's body.

Opal Charmaine Mills, age 16, called her parents from Angle Lake Park on August 12, 1982, at a public phone booth. She was never heard from again. Detectives investigating the discovery of the bodies of Cynthia Hinds and Marcia Chapman found Opal Mills' body on the banks of the Green River on August 15, 1982, near Kent.

Terry Rene Milligan, age 16, was last seen on Pacific Highway South on August 29, 1982. Her remains were found April 1, 1984, off Star Lake Road in south King County.

Mary Bridget Meehan, age 18, was seven months pregnant when she disappeared on September 15, 1982, from the Sea-Tac Strip. Her remains were found on November 13, 1983, partially buried near South 192nd Street and 27th Avenue South.

Debra Lorraine Estes, age 15, was a runaway who was last seen on September 20, 1982, on Pacific Highway South. Her body was found by workers digging holes for a playground at a Federal Way apartment complex on May 30, 1988.

Linda Jane Rule, age 16, was last seen on September 26, 1982 in Seattle. Her remains were found in a shallow depression outside Northwest Hospital on May 30, 1988.

Denise Darcel Bush, age 23, was last seen on October 8, 1982, when she left her apartment to buy cigarettes. Some of her skeletal remains were found June 12, 1985, in a wooded area of Tigard, Oregon. Her skull was found in Tukwila, a southern suburb of Seattle, on February 10, 1990.

Shawnda Lee Summers, age 16, went missing on October 9, 1982, near Yesler Way in Seattle. Her body was found August 11, 1983, north of Sea-Tac International Airport.

Shirley Marie Sherrill, age 18, went missing between October 20-22, 1982, in Seattle's Chinatown International District. Her remains were found on June 14, 1985, in Tigard, Oregon, near where Denise Bush's body was found.

Rebecca R. Marrero, age 20, was last seen leaving the Western Six Motel on December 3, 1982. Her remains were found on December 21, 2010, in the vicinity of where the remains of Marie Malvar were found in 2003. **

Colleen Renee Brockman, age 15, disappeared on Christmas Eve 1982. Her family last saw her on December 23, 1982. Her remains were found on May 26, 1984, near Sumner, Pierce County.

Sandra Denise Major, age 20, also disappeared on Christmas Eve 1982. Her remains were found in the Mountain View Cemetery in Auburn, Washington, about 30 miles southeast of Seattle on Dec. 30, 1985, but were not identified until June 2012.

Alma Ann Smith, age 18, was last seen on March 3, 1983. She was working the area at Pacific Highway South and 188th Street, which was in the heart of the prostitution zone where Gary Ridgway prowled. Her remains were found on April 2, 1984, at the Star Lake Road site.

Delores LaVerne Williams, age 17, went missing between March 8 – 14, 1983. She was last seen along Pacific Highway South. Her remains were recovered on March 31, 1984, just off Star Lake Road.

Gail Lynn Mathews, age 23, disappeared on April 10, 1983. She was last seen by her boyfriend, Curt, who saw her sitting in a tan or blue pickup truck with spots of primer paint. Her body was found on September 18, 1983.

Andrea M. Childers, age 19, disappeared on April 14, 1983. Her body was discovered on October 11, 1989.

Sandra Kay Gabbert, age 17, quit school in the 11th grade and became involved in prostitution. On April 17, 1983, she went back to the motel to give her boyfriend/pimp $70 and told him she was going back out "to try to catch a few more dates." Her body was found on April 1, 1984, at the Star Lake Road dump site.

Kimi-Kai Pitsor, age 16, was last seen in downtown Seattle on April 17, 1983. Her body was found on December 15, 1983, just outside of Mountain View Cemetery near the place two other victims were found.

Marie M. Malvar, age 18, was standing on the corner with her boyfriend/pimp, Bobby Woods, on April 30, 1983, when a pickup truck stopped, and Marie got in. Bobby and Marie's father looked for Marie for days. Bobby Woods identified the pickup truck as the one he saw parked in a driveway of a rundown ranch house and called the police.

Marie's remains were found on September 26, 2003, with information provided by Ridgway.**

Carol Ann Christensen, age 21, was last seen on May 3, 1983, when she walked out of the Barn Door Tavern, where she worked on Pacific Avenue South. She planned to return for her evening shift. Her body was found on May 8, 1983, by a family hunting for mushrooms in a wooded area of Maple Valley.

Martina Theresa Authorlee, age 18, was last seen on May 15, 1983 at the Public Safety Building in downtown Seattle, where she had just been released from jail on a prostitution arrest. Her body was found on November 14, 1984, 10 miles east of Enumclaw by two hunters.

Cheryl Lee Wims, age 18, disappeared on May 23, 1983, from the central district of Seattle. Her remains were found on March 22, 1984, just north of the Sea-Tac International Airport.

Yvonne "Shelly" Antosh, age 19, went missing on May 31, 1983, from the Ben Carol Motel. Her body was recovered on October 15, 1983, just off Highway 18, near I-90.

Carrie Ann Rois, age 15, was a frequent runaway. She disappeared between May 31 and June 13, 1983. She frequented the area around South 144th Street and Pacific Highway South. Her body was found on March 10, 1985, just off Star Lake Road, in the general area where five other victims had been found.

Constance Elizabeth Naon, age 19, went missing on June 8, 1983, after she had told her boyfriend that she was picking up her paycheck from work and would see him in about 20 minutes. Her body was found on October 27, 1983, just south of the Sea-Tac International Airport, near the area where three other bodies had been found.

Kelly Marie Ware, age 22, was last seen on July 18, 1983, in the Central District of Seattle. Her body was found on October 29, 1983, just south of the Sea-Tac International Airport, where three other bodies have been found.

Tina Marie Thompson, age 21, disappeared on July 25, 1983, and was found on April 2, 1984, in a green garbage bag.

April Dawn Buttram, age 16, disappeared on August 18, 1983 and was found on August 30, 2003. Ridgway provided the information of her whereabouts to investigators.

Debbie May Abernathy, age 26, went missing on September 5, 1983 and her body was found on March 31, 1984.

Tracy Ann Winston, age 19, disappeared on September 12, 1983. Her body, minus the skull, was found on March 27, 1986, near Kent's Cottonwood Park. The skull was found in November 2005, near Tiger Mountain, miles away from where the body was found.

Maureen Sue Feeney, age 19, went missing on September 28, 1983 and her body was found on May 2, 1986.

Mary Sue Bello, age 25, disappeared on October 11, 1983. Her body was found on October 12, 1984.

Pammy Annette Avent, age 15, was last seen on October 26, 1983. Ridgway led investigators to her body near the city of Enumclaw and only 40 feet from SR 410 on August 16, 2003.

Delise Louise "Missy" Plager, age 22, was last seen on October 30, 1983, at a Halloween party. Her body was found on February 14, 1984.

Kimberly L. Nelson aka Tina Tomson, age 21, was last seen on November 1, 1983, on the Pacific Highway South. Her partial skeletal remains were found just off I-90 near Exit 38 on June 14, 1986, about 35 miles east of Seattle near where two other victims had been found.

Lisa Yates, age 19, was last known to be going to Rainier Avenue in Seattle on December 23, 1983. Her remains were found on March 13, 1984, along Interstate 90, along with two other victims near North Bend, 35 miles east of Seattle.

Mary Exzetta West, age 16, disappeared February 6, 1984, from South Seattle. Her remains were found on September 8, 1985 in Seward Park.

Cindy Anne Smith, age 17, disappeared on March 21, 1984 from Pacific Highway South. Her skeleton was found on June 27, 1987 near Auburn.

Patricia Michelle Barczak, age 19, went missing on October 17, 1986, in Auburn. She was last seen getting on a Metro bus. Her body was found in February 1993 off Highway 18 near Seattle International Raceway.

Roberta Joseph "Bobbie Joe" Hayes, age 20, disappeared on February 7, 1987 in rural King County. Her body was found on September 11, 1991, off Highway 410, near five other victims.

Marta Kalas Reeves, age 36, disappeared on March 5, 1990 in rural King County. She was found September 20, 1990, eight miles east of Enumclaw off Highway 410. Reeves was believed to have disappeared from Seattle, where she had been arrested twice for prostitution.

Patricia Yellowrobe, age 38, disappeared in January 1998. Her remains were found on August 5, 1998.

Unidentified White Female (known as Jane Doe B-10), age 12 – 18, died prior to May 1983. Remains were found on March 21, 1984.

Unidentified White Female (known as Jane Doe B-17), age 14 – 18, died between December 1980 and January 1984. Remains were found on January 2, 1986.

Unidentified Female (known as Jane Doe B-20), age 13 – 24, died between 1973 and 1993. Remains were found on August 2003.

Ridgway was formally charged with Marrero's murder on February 11, 2011. On February 18, 2011, he entered a guilty plea and the court added a 49th life sentence to his existing 48.

The agreement between the Courts of King County, Washington, and Gary Leon Ridgway states that he would plead guilty to any additional charges of murder in King County and receive a life sentence without the possibility of parole. This plea agreement applies only to murders committed within King County. This leaves open the possibility of a death sentence if he is tried and convicted of murder in any other county in Washington, or anywhere else in the United States.

Gary Ridgway is a suspect in as many as 76 other murders because the victims disappeared from areas he frequented, were strangled to death, and/or their bodies were left in areas close to areas where Ridgway disposed of other bodies.

** Marrero's murder was not included in the original 48. Her skull was found on December 21, 2010 by hikers near the West Valley Highway in Auburn, Washington, very near to where the remains of Marie Malvar were found in 2003.

Green, Ricky Lee (December 27, 1960 – October 8, 1997) was a radiator repairman. He was also a serial killer in Texas during 1985-86. Green's childhood was not a happy one. He was subjected to physical and mental abuse by his father and sexual abuse by his grandfather. Green married Mary Francis when he was 24, but the marriage was short-lived. Mary arrived home one night to find Ricky drunk. He threatened her with a knife and raped her. She grabbed her belongings at first opportunity and left permanently. Shortly thereafter, Ricky Green met **Sharon Dollar** and moved in with her. Theirs was a life of booze and sex. They married in 1980.

On a night when Sharon was out of town, Ricky Green invited Jeffrey Davis, a teenager whom Green had met before, to hang out with him. They went riding around. Davis made a pass at Green and Green got mad and beat him. Green continued to beat him while driving and finally pulled into a secluded spot where he killed Davis by beating and mutilating him with a knife.

His next victim was a woman hitchhiker. He picked her up and asked if she would like to take a shower and clean up somewhat. The woman, who told Green her name was Montana, went with him to the house and showered. Green joined her in the shower and had sex with her. They picked up Sharon from her job and then the three went back to the house to have three-way sex, but Montana refused. She was tied to the bed and sexually assaulted by both Sharon and Green. Afterward, Sharon got a knife from the kitchen and stabbed Montana. Green obtained another knife and stabbed her several times, but she was still alive. He left and came back with a large hammer with which he proceeded to bash her in the head several times. They dumped her in a secluded area, after first having sex in the bathroom where Montana lay dead.

Green met a woman named Sandra Bailey in a club he visited frequently. He took her back to the house, but Sandra wanted to leave when she saw Sharon was home. The couple did to her what they had done to Montana and then disposed of her body in a secluded area.

Green met Steven Fefferman in a parking lot frequented by homosexuals. They went to Fefferman's house. After showering, Green suggested that he tie Fefferman up for sex and they would take turns being tied up and having sex. Ricky went first. He tied Fefferman up, then drew his knife and proceeded to stab him again and again, telling Fefferman how much he hated homosexuals. Fefferman was still alive, so Green went to the kitchen for a larger knife. He stabbed Fefferman in the throat and then cut him from sternum to scrotum. Green took some money and left.

The marriage began to deteriorate, and Sharon finally left. One night, Green found his house surrounded by police. He was arrested for the murder of Steven Fefferman. Sharon had been talking to the police.

Ricky Lee Green was found guilty of the four murders. He was given three life sentences for the murders of

Montana, Jeffrey Davis, and Sandra Bailey. For the murder of Steven Fefferman, Green was sentenced to death. Sharon Dollar Green was given probation in exchange for her testimony against Ricky.

On October 9, 1997, Green was executed by lethal injection in Huntsville, Texas.

Greenawalt, Randy (February 24, 1949 – January 23, 1997) and **Tison, Gary** (1936 – August 1978) met in prison. Randy Greenawalt was serving a life sentence for the murder of a trucker in 1974. Gary Tison was serving a life sentence for the murder of a prison guard.

On July 30, 1978, Tison's son Ricky, age 18, came to visit at the state prison in Florence. Shortly, his other two sons, Raymond, age 19, and Donald, age 20, arrived carrying a basket of food (and a shotgun). When they entered the lobby, one of the boys drew out the shotgun, covered the guards, and demanded his father's release. Randy Greenawalt had disabled the prison telephones and alarm system. Greenawalt and Tison were released. They left the prison so casually, the tower guards mistook them for visitors leaving after their visit with loved ones.

The following day, Marine Sgt. John Lyons, age 24, travelling with his wife, their infant son, and 16-year old niece, made the mistake of stopping in the desert to help stranded motorists. It cost him his life, plus the lives of his wife, son, and niece. He had offered help to Greenawalt and the Tisons.

The authorities scoured the countryside for the killers and established a roadblock near Tison's hometown of Casa Grande in Arizona. They saw a silver van approaching and the van slowed. A blast of gunfire from the van scattered the officers, and the van blew past. There was another roadblock five miles farther down the road. This time the deputies were ready. They killed Donald Tison with their first shots. The standoff lasted for half an hour. Greenawalt and the two Tison boys surrendered because they ran out of ammunition. Gary Tison escaped on foot out into the desert. His bloated and decomposed body was found the last week of August near the tiny town of Chuichu, Arizona.

Authorities discovered that the van belonged to newlyweds James and Margene Judge from Colorado. Their bodies have never been found, but Greenawalt and the Tisons were charged with their murders.

Randy Greenawalt was sentenced to death. Ricky and Raymond Tison were also sentenced to death. However, on appeal, due to the fact that they were under 20 years of age at the time of the murders, their sentences were reduced to life.

After 19 years of litigation, Randy Greenawalt was executed by lethal injection on January 23, 1997.

Grim Maniac aka **Dudin, Nikolai Arkadievich** (b. December 22, 1973) was born to Arkady Dudin and his wife, in the village of Mikhalkovo, USSR. Arkady was an abusive father who taught Nikolai to hunt and butcher his kill at a very young age. Nikolai killed his father when he was 13 years and 11 months old. Because he was under the age of 14, he was not executed, as was the punishment for murder at that time. He was sentenced to seven years. While imprisoned, he was constantly in trouble—trying to organize a riot and escape, attempting to kill another prisoner, and other infractions—and ended up serving 12 years.

On February 15, 2002, a drunken Nikolai murdered a woman by striking her in the head and breaking the skull at the base, killing her. He claimed he was going to rob her. Later on the same day, he murdered two girls at a sewing shop. He tried to get acquainted with the girls, but they were not interested, so he stabbed them. One he stabbed 28 times and the other girl was stabbed 32 times.

On the night of May 1, 2002, he murdered a woman whose body was not found until after Dudin was arrested in July. On May 8, again he was drunk when he murdered Andrei Polozov with a sawed-off shotgun. He then murdered Andrei's wife with the shotgun and stabbed to death their 11-year-old daughter. Two days later, he committed another triple murder. He also committed a double murder later in the month.

Nikolai Dudin was arrested on July 17, 2002, during an attempted murder. In his confession he said that he killed those who humiliated his dignity. In December 2003, he was sentenced to life in prison. He is incarcerated at the White Swan Prison, home to 260 men convicted of murder, living under one of the strictest prison regimes in Russia.

Grim Sleeper aka **Franklin Jr., Lonnie David** (August 30, 1952 – March 28, 2020) was arrested on July 7, 2010, and charged with 16 murders, one attempted murder, and special circumstances of multiple murders which began in 1985. In the mid-1980s the Los Angeles Sheriff's Department was investigating the *Southside Slayer* who had murdered several women. They did not realize that they had more than one serial killer in their midst. Once they realized this, there was the problem of linking the murders. Louis Craine and Daniel Lee Siebert were arrested and each charged with two murders. Ivan Hill and Michael Hughes were charged with one murder each.

The murder of Debra Jackson, age 29, on August 10, 1985, was the first by a different killer. The murders continued: August 12, 1986, Henrietta Wright, age 34; August 14, 1986, Thomas Steele (Franklin has not been charged with this murder because there was no DNA to test); January 10, 1987, Barbara Ware, age 23; April 15, 1987, Bernita Sparks; November 1, 1987, Mary Lowe, age 26; January 30, 1988, Lachrica Jefferson, age 22; September 11, 1988, Alice Monique Alexander; March 19,

2002, Princess Berthomieux, age 15; July 11, 2003; Valeria McCorvey, age 35; and on January 1, 2007, Janecia Peters, age 25. These murders had a different modus operandi. The killer was using a .25 caliber gun. All of the victims were shot with the same gun and 10 were tied to Franklin through DNA tests. All of the victims were dumped outdoors, a few miles from Los Angeles.

Mayor Antonio Villaraigosa and Police Chief William Bratton never released any information concerning the work of this serial killer. They never issued a press release, nor did they warn the South Los Angeles community of his existence.

In September 2007, the *LA Weekly*, an alternate Los Angeles newspaper, was the first to break the news of the "800 Task Force" that was investigating the murders dating back some 23 years.

There was also an unnamed survivor who gave a very thorough description of her attacker and his vehicle. When the police searched Franklin's home, they found over 1,000 photos of women, mostly nude. They also found video tapes and photos dating back some 30 years. One hundred and eighty of the photos of women had never been identified. These were released to the public and are possibly more victims. The photos are mainly African American women, from teenagers to middle age and older, some appearing conscious and some unconscious (or dead).

Lonnie David Franklin Jr.'s trial began in March 2016. On May 5, 2016, Franklin was found guilty of 10 murders. On August 10, 2016, he was sentenced to death. On March 28, 2020, he was found dead in his cell at San Quentin State Prison in California. Cause of death was not immediately clear, but there were no signs of trauma.

Grimson, Allan (b. 1958) joined the Royal British Navy in 1978, served aboard the *HMS Illustrious,* and was stationed at HMNB (Her Majesty's Naval Base) Portsmouth where he taught fire-fighting techniques. By November 1997, he had reached the rank of Petty Officer.

One night in December 1997, Grimson was out drinking with Nicholas Wright, an 18-year-old on leave from the *HMS Edinburgh*, when they were seen leaving a Portsmouth nightclub together. According to Grimson, they went to Grimson's flat where he tried to kiss Wright. Wright became very upset and Grimson first punched him and then hit him several times with a baseball bat. He then cut Wright's throat and put his body into the bathtub. Sometime later, Grimson left the body on the A272 road near Cheriton, Hampshire, England. Grimson was questioned by police but lied to try to stay out of trouble with authorities.

In December 1998, one year later and the exact same date of Wright's murder, Grimson met up with Sion Jenkins, age 20, at Joanna's, a nightclub in Portsmouth. Jenkins worked as a bartender in the Hogs Head Pub in Portsmouth, where he originally met Grimson. On this night, Jenkins got drunk and they went back to Grimson's flat. Grimson forced Jenkins to have sex with him by hitting and threatening him. In the morning when Jenkins wanted to leave, Grimson wanted to experience the feeling he'd had when he murdered Nicholas Wright. Grimson bound Jenkins in the bathtub and beat him to death with the baseball bat. Grimson put him in his vehicle and drove out to the A32 road at West Tisted, where he left the body.

In 2001, Grimson was tried and convicted of killing both Wright and Jenkins. The judge recommended a term of 22 years and that he never be released. This term of imprisonment was increased to 25 years by the Home Secretary. In 2008, the time he spent in remand reduced his sentence by three years, taking it back to the original sentence recommended by the judge.

Allan Grimson is suspected of more killings, according to authorities. There is a 12- month period between the murders. Was Nicholas Wright the first murder? Did he kill before 1997? Is he responsible for the disappearance of Simon Parkes who went missing while his ship, the *HMS Illustrious*, was docked at Gibraltar? Grimson and Parkes were both stationed on the *HMS Illustrious* at the same time and witnesses say they saw the two together on the night Parkes disappeared. Police speculate that Grimson killed on the 12th of December each year and there could be as many as 20 unidentified murders committed by him.

Grissom, Richard (b. 1960) was a rapist and murderer of three women whom he abducted from their homes in 1989. Joan A. Butler, age 24, was abducted from her home in Overland Park; Theresa Brown, age 22, and Christine Rusch, age 22, were abducted from Lenexa, Kansas. Grissom was also a suspect in the murder of Terri Maness, a girl in Wichita whom he had dated. He was never charged with her death.

In the mid-1960s, Grissom murdered a woman in Lansing, but due to the fact he was only 16 years old at the time, he was tried as a juvenile and served only three years.

Grissom was convicted of three counts of kidnapping and first-degree murder and on November 20, 1990, he was sentenced to life without the possibility of parole. He is currently housed at the El Dorado Correctional Facility in El Dorado, Kansas. The bodies of his victims have not been found.

Groblersdal Serial Killer aka **Madiba, Petrus** (b. 1984) is a man from the Limpopo Province, South Africa, who murdered eight women and a baby. Madiba was serving a 35-year sentence in prison for murdering a woman in November 2011. Authorities believe that Madiba lured the women away with the promise of jobs. He claims that all but two of the women were his girlfriends and accused them of cheating on him or stealing his money. Families of the victims deny that Madiba had a romantic interest in the women.

On April 8, 2012, a woman's body was found in the bushes in Groblersdal, Limpopo Province, South Africa. She was wearing a brown T-shirt and black tights. In June, the body of Monica Mohlahlo of Masakaneng village was found at Krokodilsdrift Farm in Groblersdal. Madiba has been positively linked to the death of Monica Mohlahlo. In July, another woman's body was found, burned beyond recognition, in the bushes in Groblersdal. In addition to the charge of the murder of Monica Mohlahlo, Madiba is also accused of murdering by strangulation Portia Moela, Thandi Masegela Majola, Mapule Maria Matlala, Phologo Mokwena, Lebo Mokwena, Mankgele Peggy, Gloria Mamodupi Pookgwadi Moshitoa, and Dinah Lekola (eight women and a 2-year-old girl who was being carried by her mother).

Madiba apologized to the families of his victims, saying that he was sorry he had taken their loved ones away. He was sentenced to life in prison on October 17, 2013.

Grossi, Cayetano Domingo (1854 – April 6, 1900) was born in Italy and died in Buenos Aires, Argentina. He was Argentina's first serial killer, having murdered at least five of his newborn babies. The babies were the result of his violation of his stepdaughters, Clara and Catalina.

On May 29, 1896, a bag was found containing the arm of a newborn baby. An inspection of the area was ordered by the police. In the trash inspected at the scene, they found a newborn's shattered skull, both legs, and the other arm. Police kept this area under surveillance and later in the day one of the trucks yielded the baby's body. No evidence was found to lead investigators to the person responsible.

On May 5, 1898, the body of a newborn was found with a shattered skull. The body was in an advanced state of decomposition. Signs of first and second-degree burns were on the arms and neck. An autopsy revealed that the baby had lived four days after being burned and had died of severe compression of the neck. The body was wrapped in black burlap used in car repairs. A man named Carretero was interviewed and stated that he had seen the remains, but was afraid of being accused of being the killer and had decided not to report it to the police. Investigators discovered the remains of cigarettes and anise grains. Knowing that Spanish and Calabrian (from the southwest part of Italy) people carried anise grains, they narrowed their search to these people, and further narrowed it by the quality and condition of the cloth used.

Police staked out the area and watched those who used it to dispose of their "garbage." They noticed one family who were very obviously poor and were at the dump site frequently: the mother, Rosa Ponce de Nicola; her spouse, Cayetano Domingo Grossi; her daughters, Clara and Catalina; and three younger children. Neighbors told police that Grossi had intimate relations with his stepdaughters. They also told police that Clara had been pregnant but a few days later, it was obvious that she had delivered the baby. During the search of the room where the family lived, they found a tin containing the body of a newborn wrapped in rags.

Rosa and her daughter Clara confessed that Clara had had two children with Grossi, who denied having sex with his stepdaughters. He blamed boyfriends for the pregnancies. He later confessed to murdering the first baby found in 1896 and to incinerating several others. During later interviews, Grossi confessed to having one child with Catalina and four with Clara.

Rosa, Clara, and Catalina accepted their responsibility in concealing the crimes and were each sentenced to three years. Catalina's sentence was later changed to two years.

Cayetano Domingo Grossi was convicted of the murders of the babies and sentenced to death. On the day of his execution, his children entered the prison chapel. His oldest son showed no emotion; his youngest son, who was only six years old, did not approach his father and pulled away when Cayetano tried to hug him. His daughter, Teresita, cried and resisted his offer to hug her.

On April 6, 1900, Grossi was executed by firing squad.

Groves, Vincent Darrell (April 19, 1954 – October 31, 1996) was a serial rapist and murderer on the streets of Denver, Colorado, during the years 1978-88, with a five-year respite from 1982 – 1987. Groves was in prison at that time for the murder of a woman in 1981. The murders resumed when he was paroled in 1987 and stopped when he was again arrested on September 1, 1988.

Groves' victims of choice were prostitutes who would not be missed immediately, are easy prey, and for whom the general public attitude was "nobody cares." Investigators in Denver suspect he may be responsible for the murders of as many as 20 prostitutes whose bodies were found dumped in out-of-the-way places. Denver police and investigators of the metro area suspect Vincent Groves.

Investigators believe Groves is responsible for at least 14 murders that occurred during the same time period.

Groves was initially suspected in the murders of Karolyn Walker, whose body was found on July 5, 1987, and Robin Nelson, whose body was found on June 12, 1988. It was determined that Robin died of an accidental overdose and he was cleared in Karolyn's death.

Vincent Groves was arrested on September 1, 1988. He was found guilty of the first-degree murder of Juanita "Becky" Lovato and sentenced to life without parole. He was also found guilty of the second-degree murder of Diane Montoya Mancera and sentenced to 20 years. He died in prison on October 31, 1996.

Guangzhou Ripper aka **Li Wenxian** (1952 – December 18, 1996) was the serial killer who opened the eyes of the Red Chinese government to the fact they had a serial killer in their country. This came about in March 1992, when the mutilated body of a young woman floated ashore in Hong Kong, then a British colony. The young woman was cut open from her throat to her groin, and her fingers cut off. Authorities determined that the body had washed from the mainland of China to Hong Kong. It was now known that a savage killer was violating and mutilating Chinese mainland women. Until that day, China theorized that serial killers were the product of decadent Western capitalism and could not exist in the Peoples Republic of China. This woman was actually the seventh known victim of the *Guangzhou Ripper.*

The first known victim turned up in Guangzhou in February 1991. By the end of August, there were five more dead young women who had been raped, murdered, mutilated, dismembered, stuffed into burlap rice bags, and dumped on rubbish heaps. Chinese authorities, in their reluctance to admit to the existence of a serial killer, were very slow in solving the case. By November 1996, a total of 13 women had been murdered. If not for a woman who survived the brutal attempt on her life, the killer may never have been caught. The woman was able to identify her attacker as Li Wenxian, a construction worker who had moved to Guangzhou in 1991, just before the killings began. Li Wenxian was getting revenge against prostitutes after one of them cheated him of money, so he claimed. He was sentenced to death in November 1996 and duly executed.

Gufler, Max (January 5, 1918 – 1966) suffered a serious head injury when he was nine years old and afterward was plagued with violence. During his World War II service as an ambulance driver, he was again injured in his head by shrapnel. Returning home after the war, he found work as a bookseller in the town of St. Polten in Austria. He also sold pornographic photos from his father-in-law's kiosk. They were later arrested and sent to prison.

After Gufler's release from prison, the killings began. Between 1946 and 1958, Gufler murdered at least four women and is suspected by Austrian investigators of as many as 18.

He was arrested on November 1, 1958, and charged with seven murders, but was convicted of only four murders and two attempted murders. Gufler was sentenced to life in prison in May 1961. He died in 1966 at Stein Prison in Krems an der Donau, Austria.

Guimaraes, Edson Izidoro (b. 1957) was a nursing assistant in Brazil and a serial killer. He worked as a nurse in the Salgado Filho Hospital in Rio de Janeiro. In 1999, he was seen filling a syringe with potassium chloride and injecting a comatose patient. The patient died almost instantly. Guimaraes was reported to police and it was learned that during his shift, his ward had a higher death rate than other wards. He was arrested and confessed to five murders. He is suspected by Rio de Janeiro investigators of murdering at least 131 patients between January 1 and May 4, 1999, yet was never charged in any other case.

He was convicted on February 21, 2000, of four of the murders and sentenced to 76 years in prison.

Gunness, Belle Sorenson (November 11, 1859 – April 28, 1908) was born and raised in Norway. In about 1878, she took service for a wealthy farmer and served for three years to pay for her passage to America. After she had completed her servitude, she found work as a servant for which she was being paid. In 1884, she met and married Mads Ditlev Anton Sorenson in Chicago, Illinois and they opened a confectionery store. Within the first year, the business was failing and mysteriously burned down. The Sorensons collected the insurance and bought a house.

They reportedly had four children, but two of them died in infancy from colitis, which has the same symptoms as many poisons—nausea, fever, diarrhea, lower abdominal pain, and cramping. Again, the Sorensons collected insurance. On July 30, 1900, Mads Sorenson died, remarkably on the very day that his two insurance policies overlapped. Sorenson's family demanded that an inquest be held. There is no documentation available that proves this was done. Belle collected about $8,500 (about $215,000 in today's dollar). She bought a farm near La Porte, Indiana, which at one time had been a brothel for the rich from Chicago. The brothel included a jetty, a boathouse, and an expansive carriage house to accommodate the clients' needs. Shortly after Belle purchased the farm, both the boathouse and the carriage house burned to the ground. Again, she collected on her misfortune.

On April 1, 1902, Belle married Peter Gunness, a widower also from Norway, who was living in La Porte. One week later, Peter's infant daughter died while alone in the house with Belle. In December 1902, Peter had a tragic accident. It seems that he was working alone in a shed when part of a sausage-grinding machine fell from a shelf, crushing his head, killing him instantly. Peter's brother came and claimed Peter's other daughter before she, too, had an "accident." Belle collected about $3,000 for her husband's death. The district coroner reviewed the case and convened a coroner's jury. Jenny, believed to be an adopted daughter of Belle, was overheard telling a fellow classmate, "My mama killed my papa. She hit him with a meat cleaver and he died. Don't tell a soul." Jenny testified before the coroner's jury that she never said that to anyone. Belle Gunness was pregnant at the time, apparently swaying the jury. She was released and no charges were brought.

Jennie disappeared in 1906 and Belle told, if anyone asked, that she had sent Jennie to a Lutheran College in Los Angeles. Some years later, Jennie's body was found buried on the farm.

Belle began placing advertisements in the Chicago daily newspapers, and in other large Midwestern city newspapers, for a gentleman of equal means with a view of marriage and joining their fortunes. Several men responded. John Moe arrived, bringing with him over $1,000 to pay off Belle's mortgage. He soon disappeared. George Anderson, an immigrant from Norway, arrived and Belle raised the issue of her mortgage. Anderson agreed to pay it off if they wed. That night he awoke to find Belle standing over him with a strange look on her face. He fled the farm.

More suitors arrived, but none left. Belle began ordering large trunks. The delivery man, Clyde Sturgis, told how the heavyset Belle would lift the trunks to her shoulder and carry them into the house.

An elderly widower from Iola, Wisconsin, was last seen at a savings bank on April 6, 1907. He mortgaged his Wisconsin land, signed over the deed, and obtained several thousand dollars in return. His sons inquired to Belle about their father, but she promptly replied that she had never seen him. Other middle-aged men disappeared while visiting Belle's farm. In December 1907, Andrew Helgelien arrived from Aberdeen, South Dakota, bringing with him a check for $2,900, his life savings. He and Belle went to the savings bank in La Porte to deposit the check. Helgelien was not seen again. Within the next week, Belle deposited $500 at the savings bank on one visit and $700 on a second visit. Helgelien's brother inquired about Andrew, but Belle said she thought that he may have gone to Norway to visit relatives.

During this time, Ray Lamphere, Belle's hired hand, began making trouble for Belle and her suitors. Belle finally fired him on February 3, 1908, went to the courthouse to declare that Lamphere was not in his right mind and was a menace to the public. She convinced the authorities to hold a sanity hearing, which they did. They declared that Lamphere was sane and released him. Belle later claimed that Lamphere returned to the farm and argued with her, and he posed a threat to her family. He was arrested for trespassing.

Joe Maxon, Lamphere's replacement, awoke in his room on the second floor of the Gunness home to the smell of smoke. The hallway outside his door was a wall of flames. He yelled for Belle and the children but got no response. He leapt from his second-story window and barely survived the fire. By the time the firemen arrived, the house was a pile of smoking ruins. The floors had collapsed, and they found four bodies in the basement. Lamphere was quickly a suspect. When told about the fire, he denied starting it. A young man said he had been watching the Gunness place and that he saw Lamphere running down the road from the Gunness house shortly before he saw the fire. He further stated that Lamphere found him hiding behind the bushes and threatened to kill him if he didn't leave immediately. Lamphere was arrested and charged with arson and murder.

One of the bodies found after the fire was the charred remains of a woman who had been beheaded, but neighbors and friends of Belle stated that they were not her remains. Belle stood 5 ft. 8 in. or taller and weighed around 200 lbs. This body found was of a woman who was about 5 ft. 3 in. and weighed approximately 150 lbs. After further examination of the internal organs, Dr. J. Meyers reported that the woman had been poisoned with strychnine. The local dentist said that if the teeth had been located, he could definitely ascertain if it was Belle. Louis Schultz was hired to build a sluice and began sifting the debris. The sluice was used mainly to separate body parts from the soil. A piece of bridgework was found, and the dentist identified it as belonging to Belle. The coroner stated that the female body was that of Belle Gunness.

Helgelien's brother arrived in La Porte and told the sheriff that he believed that his brother had been murdered by Belle Gunness, and the new hired hand, Joe Maxon, told the sheriff that he had been asked by Belle to fill in some holes where rubbish had been buried. The sheriff took a dozen men to the farm and they began digging in that area. On May 3, 1908, they found the body of Jennie Olson. They also found the bodies of two small unidentified children, then Andrew Helgelien, then one body after another. When the digging was over, they had unearthed the remains of more than 40 people, mostly men, with several children and women.

Ray Lamphere was tried for murder and arson. He pleaded guilty to arson but denied having murdered Gunness and her three children. He based this on the fact that the woman's body found in the basement was not Belle Gunness. He was convicted of arson but acquitted of murder. He died of tuberculosis on December 30, 1909.

On January 14, 1910, the Reverend E. A. Schell came forward with a confession from Ray Lamphere made on his death bed. The confession told of Gunness' murders and that she was still alive. He had helped Gunness bury many of her victims. Gunness' method of murder was to cook the suitor a large meal, drug his coffee, and when he passed out, hit him in the head with a meat cleaver. She would then take the body to the basement where she would dissect it, bundle the parts together, and bury it in the hog pen and the grounds about the house—the source of the depressions that Joe Maxon filled at Belle's request. The body found in the basement after the fire was that of a woman from Chicago whom Gunness had "hired" to be her housekeeper. Belle disposed of the woman's head by throwing it into a swamp. Belle was supposed to meet with Lamphere and they would leave together, but Belle never arrived at the rendezvous spot.

Belle Gunness was reportedly sighted in places across the US, cities like Chicago, San Francisco, New York, and Los Angeles, plus many other places. In 1931, she was reportedly living in a town in Mississippi. The banks in La Porte admitted that Belle had withdrawn most of her funds within days before the fire; her death has never been officially confirmed.

Gunning, James D. (b. April 15, 1971) was a Pennsylvania auto mechanic and a suspected serial killer. He was arrested on charges of aggravated assault on May 2, 1999, in Hamilton Township, New Jersey after a woman, wearing only her underwear, escaped from his parked truck and ran toward police. She told the police that Gunning had tried to strangle her. Police found clothesline in Gunning's truck. On June 9, the charge was changed to attempted murder. He was convicted of those charges and sentenced. He is currently at the South Wood State Prison in New Jersey. He is a suspect in at least 10 murders: three in New York, two in Philadelphia and five in New Jersey.

Haapooja, Matti (September 16, 1845 – January 8, 1895) was a serial killer in Finland and Siberia. His actual number of victims is not known. He was convicted of two murders and was scheduled for a third murder trial when he committed suicide. Police had linked him to at least seven other murders, but those were committed in Siberia and were poorly documented.

Heikki Antinpoika Impponen, a farmer and drinking friend, was stabbed to death by Haapooja on December 6, 1867, during a drunken brawl. He was convicted and sentenced to 12 years in prison at Turku. While serving this sentence, he managed to escape four times and was free for months at a time. As a result of his escapes and thievery, he was sentenced to life in prison in 1874. He petitioned the court to change his sentence to an exile in Siberia. He was sent to Omsk Oblast in 1880. In Omsk, he killed a man in 1886 and was exiled to East Siberia. In 1889, he escaped from Siberia and returned to Finland. On October 8, 1890, he murdered prostitute Maria Jemina Salo. Haapooja was captured in Provo about two days later. He hoped that he would be sent back to Siberia, but that was not to be. The court sent him back to the prison at Turku. During an escape attempt on October 10, 1894, he stabbed to death prison guard Juho Rosted and wounded two others. When he realized that he could not escape he attempted to commit suicide by stabbing himself but was unsuccessful. Recovered from his self-inflicted stabbing wound, he hanged himself in his cell on January 8, 1895. His skeleton was kept at the Museum of Crime in Vantaa until he was finally buried in Ylistaro in 1995.

Haddouche, Jacquy (February 19, 1964 – October 23, 2010) was born in France to Algerian parents, mother Djouber Azzouz and father Ahmed Haddouche. Jacquy was the third of 12 children. Ahmed Haddouche had served in the French Army during the Algerian war. In 1962 he moved his family to France, where he found work at the local Lockheed factory, but he lost his job after he became an alcoholic and was very violent.

Jacquy attended George Sand College and was thought to be intelligent, but he was unstable, aggressive, impulsive, intolerant, and manipulative. His father committed suicide in front of Jacquy, and Jacquy was splashed with his father's blood as the man fell on him. He quit school and became a delinquent and substance abuser. He began having serious problems with law enforcement—rape, robbery, burglary, counterfeiting, fraud, and aggravated theft.

On the evening of November 30, 1992, Haddouche met Gilles Canette, a depressed and divorced French teacher.

Canette asked Haddouche to join him in his apartment. Two students of Canette's stopped to talk with him and observed Haddouche in the apartment. They left about an hour later. Haddouche spent the rest of the evening at the apartment, where he poisoned Canette with an antidepressant and cyamemazine and then, to make sure that he was dead, he suffocated him.

A short time later, Gilles Canette's credit card was used at an ATM, which was out of character for Canette who never used his card at ATMs. He always went inside to the bank counter whenever he needed money. Early the following morning, Haddouche went to the teenagers' home and warned them to deny seeing him at Canette's apartment on the previous night. Canette's nude body was found that same morning by the cleaning lady. In searching the apartment, investigators found Haddouche's fingerprint on a bottle of strawberry syrup. Haddouche admitted he had been in Canette's apartment, but not on the night of the murder. He claimed he was in Paris with his girlfriend, Cloe, who substantiated his claim.

Haddouche was taken into custody on December 13, 1993, but he was released due to lack of enough evidence to convict him.

In May 1995, Haddouche met Francine C., who was with a group of friends at a bar in Beauvais, France. Francine was director in a medical/educational institute. Haddouche became friends with the group. About a month later, Haddouche went to Francine's home and knocked, but she refused to allow him in. He kept knocking so hard that she finally relented and let him in. She offered him some coffee, which he drank before forcing her into her room where he raped her and left.

In June 2002, he reconnected with Isabelle, a woman he had met about 10 years earlier. One evening, a drunk Haddouche raped Isabelle and struck her in the face in the presence of her daughter. The following day, Haddouche called Isabelle, feigning heart problems and claiming he was dying, and asked her to bring him some medicine. Upon her arrival, he raped her again.

On June 20, Haddouche forced his way into Léo Capon's studio. He attacked and killed Léo, after which he searched and stole whatever he could find of any value. When her daughter, Daniele, arrived at the Capon apartment, she found her mother's body on the floor of the bathroom beaten and disfigured. Her autopsy showed that she had choked to death on her own blood.

On July 4, Haddouche tried to rape a woman named Liliane D., who was the owner of a bar in Boulogne-sur-Mer but was not successful.

On July 15, Haddouche met Sylvain Rome at a bar; they left together to go to Rome's house and stopped at the Superette to buy drinks. Later in the evening, Haddouche poisoned Rome with Bromazepam and then stabbed him. He stole his checkbook and mobile phone, plus his identity papers and keys to the apartment. Rome was found by his father about two weeks later. A facial composite was made from the descriptions given by the bartender and a customer, Lucien Florent, at the bar.

In late August, Haddouche seduced Nathalie, who received RMI (a form of welfare in France) after introducing himself as a doctor at the hospital center of Beauvais. About a week later, he drugged Nathalie and stole her bank card and her RMI.

On September 13, Liliane Michaud, age 82 and using a walker, was attacked upon returning to her apartment from the supermarket. Haddouche stole her wallet. When investigators heard the description of her attacker, they positively identified Jacquy Haddouche. A warrant was issued for his arrest.

On October 2, Haddouche tried to break into a building by breaking a window, but the security guard alerted police and he was arrested. He gave his name as Said Haddouche, but passing his fingerprints into the automated fingerprint file, they learned that he was Jacquy, not Said, and he was wanted for murder in Beauvais.

On December 3, 2002, Haddouche was charged with the murder of Leo Capon, but Haddouche denied it. Objects taken from the Capon home were found in Haddouche's home. Phone records showed that Haddouche's phone was detected by the cell tower covering the area of Sylvain Rome's home on the date of his murder and both the bartender and Lucien Florent immediately identified Jacquy Haddouche.

Haddouche was sentenced to sentenced to eight years in prison for the attack on Liliane Michaud; 30 years in prison with a 20-year lock-in period for the murder of Sylvain Rome; and life in prison with a 22-year lock-up period with 20 years of mandatory care and treatment for the murders of Gilles Canette and Léo Capon, and the 1995 rape of Francine C.

Jacquy Haddouche appealed his conviction for the murder of Gilles Canette and the rape of Francine C. His appeal was denied, and he was again sentenced to life in prison with a 22-year lock-in period.

On October 23, 2010, Jacquy Haddouche died from a cerebral hemorrhage at Fresnes Prison in the Val-de-Marne.

Hadi, Abdelaâli (1962 – December 25, 2006) was a serial killer in the southwestern city of Taroudant, Morocco, during the early 2000s. He murdered at least nine children after sexually abusing them. The children were all between the ages of 13 and 16. They were all mutilated and were found in plastic bags in the city of Taroudant. The death dates were estimated to be from two or three months to three years old. Hadi was charged with premeditated serial assassinations, torture, violence, rape of minors, kidnapping, and sequestration of minors.

Abdelaâli Hadi was convicted of all the crimes and sentenced to death on December 2, 2004. He was executed by hanging on December 25, 2006.

Hae-sun, Kim (May 6, 1969 – December 24, 2001) was born in North Jeolla Province Gochang County, South Korea. Between October 25 and December 19, 2000, Kim murdered three local minors.

The body of Jung Hye-in, age 11, was found by her best friend on October 25, 2000, about 150 meters from where she was last seen. She had been strangled and semen was found on her body.

On December 19, Kim saw a high school girl returning home, but she sensed something was not right and hurriedly left the area. Later the same day, Park Hong-sun, age 12 and in junior high school, and his sister, Park Eun-mi, age 15 and a high school student, disappeared as they walked home after school.

Hong-sun's body was found about 300 meters from his home. He was covered with a shawl and had a yellow fabric wrapped around his neck. The bra and panties of a female were found nearby. They had been cut into pieces.

Eun-mi's body was found about 500 meters from where Hong-sun's body was found. Her skirt had been pulled up and over her face, her arms and legs were tied to a tree with her stockings and some cords, her left foot was bare, and her right foot had been buried in the ground. Her killer had stuffed her gloves in her mouth, stabbed her in the neck, legs, chest, and vagina, and made 15 cm (6 – 7 inch) cuts on her thighs. Some of the missing pieces were found in front of Kim Hae-sun's house. He was arrested the day after the murders and admitted to eating some of the pieces he had cut off.

On July 11, 2001, Kim Hae-sun was sentenced to death for the rapes and murders. His appeal to the Supreme Court was dismissed on September 27 and on December 24, 2001, he was executed.

Haerm, Dr. Teet (b. 1953) was the Senior Police Medical Examiner in Stockholm, Sweden, and one of the world's most respected pathologists. Along with **Dr. Thomas Lars Allgen,** a family doctor and dermatologist, he was suspected of being a serial killer by Stockholm investigators. Between 1982 and 1987, they allegedly lured at least six women, some of whom were prostitutes, to the city morgue where they were tortured, mutilated, and murdered. After the murders, they allegedly practiced cannibalism, blood drinking, and necrophilia.

Katrina de Costa was the first to be murdered. Her body was found on July 19, 1984. Annika Mors was found in Hagensten Park on July 26, 1984. Kristine Cravache was found under a bridge leading to the suburb of Sollentuna on August 1, 1984.

The bodies of Lena Grans and Cats Falk were found in March 1985 in a car sunk at Hamarby Dock. Lena Bofors disappeared after talking with the police. She told them that the killings were done by a team and she thought she knew who they were. Her body was never found. Lota Svenson also disappeared. Her body was never found.

Tazugu Toyonaga, a Japanese student, was found in Copenhagen, Denmark, on January 7, 1986. She had been tortured, mutilated, and strangled, as were all of the other victims.

The police reinterviewed more than 600 streetwalkers/prostitutes. Their description was of a boyish-looking, well-dressed young man who drove a white Volkswagen Rabbit. One of the women told of being beaten by the man who drove the VW Rabbit; he then drove her home, as if nothing had happened. The quick-thinking woman made notes of the attacker's appearance and clothing, as well as the license number of the VW Rabbit. The police were shocked when the name of the owner of the car turned out to be none other than their own medical examiner, Dr. Teet Haerm.

Authorities did a thorough background check and put the doctor under heavy surveillance. His wife's death came to light. She had been found hanging from the end of her bed by Dr. Haerm, and the woman he moved in with not long after his wife's death suffered the same fate. Police confiscated copies of the medical journal, *The Lancet*, and in it they found that the good doctor had published studies of his own crimes.

In 1987, Dr. Thomas Allgen was arrested for abusing his daughter. His daughter also told of being at the scene of Katrina de Costa's murder. Even though only two years old at the time, the detail was so convincing the child was believed. At first Allgen denied the charges, but finally pleaded guilty to the incest charge and to his part in the de Costa murder. Dr. Haerm was also arrested and charged with the murder of seven prostitutes, his wife, and the Japanese student in Copenhagen. In January 1988 both Haerm and Allgen were put on trial and convicted, but the trial was overturned on a technicality by the Swedish Supreme Court.

Both men were retried in May 1988, and acquitted. On May 23, 1989, the Swedish authority rescinded the doctors' right to work due to a medical-negligence assessment, and the ruling was upheld in a 1991 appeal.

Hagedorn, Hans Erwin (January 30, 1952 – September 15, 1972) was a pedophile in Eberswalde, Germany, about 50 miles northeast of Berlin.

On May 31, 1969, Henry and Mario Specht disappeared while riding their bicycles in the forest near Eberswalde. Henry's body was found the next day. His throat had been cut. A woodcutter found Mario's body and his bicycle 13 days later. Mario had been stabbed in the heart.

On September 10, 1971, Ronald Winkler, age 10, was running through an open meadow when Hagedorn appeared. Ronald's body was found the next day. Traces of fibers were left at the scene of the murder, but the police could make nothing of them.

In early November 1971, Andreas, age 12, and his mother were skiing through the woods when they met Hagedorn. His mother gave Andreas permission to go with Hagedorn and the man later sexually molested Andreas. Andreas identified him from a passport photograph and Hagedorn was arrested on November 12, 1971.

Hans Erwin Hagedorn was convicted of the three murders and sentenced to death in May 1972. He was executed by firing squad on September 15, 1972, the last civilian to be executed in Germany.

Hahn, Anna Marie (July 7, 1906 – December 7, 1938) was born in Bavaria, Germany, the youngest of 12 children. Her birth name was Filser. She claimed to have had an affair with a Viennese physician and became pregnant. After her son, Oscar, was born, Anna Marie was sent to America and her son remained with Anna Marie's parents. While in Cincinnati, Ohio, she met and married Philip Hahn in 1930. Anna Marie brought her son, Oscar, to Ohio to live with her husband and her. Anna Marie developed a serious gambling habit; to support this habit she began poisoning and robbing elderly men and women in Cincinnati's German community.

It is believed that Anna Marie's first victim was Ernst Kohler, who died on May 6, 1933. She had befriended him and he, in turn, left her a house in his will.

Albert Parker, age 72, died soon after Anna Marie began caring for him. She borrowed $1,000 from Parker and signed an I.O.U. After his death, the I.O.U. could not be found.

Jacob Wagner, age 78, was her next patient and victim. He died on June 3, 1937, and left "his beloved niece," Anna Marie Hahn, a sum of $17,000.

George Gsellman, age 67, was her next victim. She was paid $15,000 "for her service" before his death on July 6, 1937. In mid-summer 1937, Anna Marie and her son traveled with Georg Obendoerfer to Colorado Springs, Colorado. Obendoerfer became ill while still on the train. He died on August 1, 1937. An autopsy was ordered and revealed high levels of arsenic in Obendoerfer's body. Authorities ordered exhumations of Hahn's two previous clients. Their autopsies revealed that they also had been poisoned.

Anna Marie Hahn was arrested and subsequently convicted of murder. She was sentenced to death in Ohio's electric chair. Anna Marie Hahn paid her debt to society on December 7, 1938. She had professed her innocence up to the time of her execution. Her 20-page confession was discovered in her cell shortly after her death.

Haifa Killer aka **Bonner, Nicolai** (b. 1973) was born and raised in Moldova, formerly part of the Soviet Union. Because his wife was Jewish, he was eligible to immigrate to Israel. He and his wife moved to Haifa, Israel in 2000. His wife soon died of tuberculosis. In 2005, he murdered four homeless people by beating them to death and then set fire to their bodies. Evidence gathered by investigators proved that the murders had been committed by the same person. They linked them to Bonner and he was soon arrested. He went on trial in 2007 for four murders and was convicted. On May 6, 2007, he was sentenced to four consecutive terms of life imprisonment.

Haigh, Paul Steven (b. September 5, 1957) is an Australian serial killer responsible for the murders of seven people in the late 1970s. He was paroled from prison in 1978 where he had served time for a string of armed robberies. Within two weeks, he had committed two armed robberies and murdered two people: Evelyn Adams, age 58, was murdered when Haigh robbed the Tatts Lotto Agency and Bruno Cingolani, age 45 and the father of two, was murdered when Haigh robbed his pizza shop.

Haigh became very paranoid and in 1979, he began killing people whom he thought knew too much about his crimes. He murdered Wayne Keith Smith, age 27, his former associate; Sheryle Gardner, age 31, who was Haigh's former girlfriend, and her son Danny Mitchell, age 10; his girlfriend, Lisa Brearley, age 19, by stabbing her 157 times after he had allowed another man to rape her at knifepoint; and a convicted sex offender, Donald George Hatherley.

Haigh claims he helped Hatherley commit suicide by putting the noose around his neck, kicking away a cupboard that he was standing on, and pushing down on Hatherley's shoulders.

He was convicted of all seven murders and sentenced to six life sentences without parole. On April 19, 2001, he won the right to have his sentence reviewed. The appeal was rejected on December 13, 2012.

Haley, Kevin Bernard (b. 1964) and **Haley, Reginald Jerome** (b. 1960) were brothers and a killing team in Los Angeles, California. They did everything together including drugs, women, burglaries, rapes, and murders.

On April 30, 1983, Isabel Burton, age 90, was beaten to death by the Haleys, who then looted and ransacked her home. The following year in April, they beat, raped, and murdered D. Robinoff, age 78, in her Los Angeles apartment. On May 12, the brothers tried to abduct Willa Gerber, but she managed to escape. On May 17, Jodie Samuels, age 15, was shot to death as she ran to catch her school bus.

The brothers then reverted back to victimizing and murdering older women. On June 28, Laverne Stolzy, age 56, was raped and murdered. The next victims were Elizabeth Burns, age 79, whom they beat to death, and

Elizabeth Karp, age 89, who was strangled to death. In August, the brothers murdered T. Okauchi, age 88, by beating her to death in her home. On September 27, Dolores Clement was raped and murdered in her home.

On October 11, 1984, the brothers Haley were arrested and quickly confessed. They provided graphic details of previously unreported rapes.

The brothers were charged with the murders, plus robbery, kidnapping, rape, and sodomy. In 1987, Reginald Haley was convicted on a total of 20 counts and sentenced to 60 years plus one term of life imprisonment. Kevin Haley was convicted on charges of murder, rape, sodomy, robbery, and burglary. He was sentenced to death.

The brothers are in the California prison system, but no longer together. Kevin is serving his sentence at San Quentin State Prison in San Quentin, and Reginald is currently at California Health Care Facility at Stockton.

Halliday, Eliza Margaret "Lizzie" (c. 1859 – June 28, 1918) born in County Antrim, Ireland, her family moved to the state of New York when Lizzie was a young girl. She became a serial killer in the 1890s, killing at least four people according to investigators.

Lizzie Halliday was married at least six times: four in Pennsylvania—1879 Charles Hopkins (they had a son); 1881 Artemus Brewer, a pensioner; c. 1883 Hiram Parkinson; c. 1886 George Smith, a war veteran; one in Vermont. c. 1887 Charles Playstel; and one in New York 1889 Paul Halliday.

In 1888, Lizzie Halliday was working at a saloon in Philadelphia, where she found the McQuillan family, who had been her neighbors in Ireland. She set up a shop, but it burned down. Halliday was convicted of setting the fire for the insurance money. She was sentenced to two years in prison.

Lizzie was soon married to Paul Halliday, who said that their marriage was tainted by "Lizzie's spells of insanity." While she was still married to Halliday, Lizzie eloped with a neighbor, stealing a team of horses to take them to Newburgh, New York. She was acquitted of stealing the horses on the grounds of insanity and was sent to an asylum. She convinced Paul Halliday to get her released from the asylum.

After being released from the asylum in May 1893, she went back to the Halliday farm and burned it down, along with a barn and a nearby mill. One of Paul Halliday's sons was killed in the fire. Soon after, Paul Halliday disappeared. Lizzie told neighbors that he had gone to a nearby town to do some masonry work. The neighbors were suspicious and searched the property. They found two bodies under a haystack in the barn but did not find Paul. The bodies were identified as Margaret and Sarah McQuillan, the wife and daughter of the family she had found in Philadelphia. They had been shot to death. Lizzie was arrested. A few days later, authorities found Paul Halliday's body under the floorboards of the house. Lizzie was charged with the murders of Margaret McQuillan, Sarah McQuillan, and her husband, Paul Halliday.

On June 21, 1894, Lizzie Halliday was convicted of the murders of Margaret McQuillan and Sarah Jane McQuillan. She was sentenced to death in the electric chair. Her sentence was later commuted to life in a mental institution after she was declared insane by a medical commission. She was sent to the Matteawan State Hospital for the Criminally Insane. While there, she murdered nurse Nellie Wickes in 1906, stabbing her more than 200 times with a pair of scissors.

Lizzie Halliday died on June 28, 1918.

Hamamatsu Deaf Killer *aka* **Nakamura, Seisaku** (c. 1924 – June 19, 1944) was a serial killer in the state of Shizuoka, Japan, while in his teens and was executed at age

19. Nakamura was born deaf, but was intelligent, achieving high marks in school. However, he was not treated well by his family, was a social misfit, and enjoyed watching movies where Japanese men used swords to assassinate people.

At the age of 14, he attempted to rape two women, but they resisted and he stabbed them to death.

On August 18, 1941, Nakamura stabbed to death one woman and injured another woman. On September 27, 1941, he murdered his brother and injured his father, sister, his brother's wife, and his brother's child. All were stabbed.

On August 20, 1942, he stabbed to death a couple, as well as their son and one daughter; he attempted to rape the other daughter. Due to World War II, information about his crimes is scarce. His family knew he was responsible for the murders but did not report him because they were afraid of him. He was arrested on October 12, 1942. His father committed suicide on November 11. Nakamura was convicted of nine murders and sentenced to death. He was executed by hanging on June 19, 1944.

Hammer Killer aka **Poehlke, Norbert** (c. 1951 – October 22, 1985) was a Chief Inspector for 14 years in Stuttgart, Germany. After his suicide on October 22, 1985, investigators discovered that he was a serial killer.

Siegfried Pfitzer, age 47, was found a quarter mile from his car in a rest stop in Marbach, West Germany, on May 3, 1984. He had been shot in the head. His car was linked to a bank robbery earlier in Erbstetten. The robber smashed the teller window and took what money he could reach through the window.

Eugene Wethey, age 37, was found shot dead at a rest stop near Grossbottwar on December 21, 1984. His car was used in a bank robbery a week later in Cleebron. The robber had wielded a sledgehammer.

Wilfried Scheider, age 26, was shot and killed in a parking lot in Beilstein-Schmidhausen on July 22, 1985. He had been shot with a Walther P5 pistol, a weapon commonly used by police. His car was found in Spiegelberg at the scene of a bank robbery.

Anti-terrorist Police were searching a Ludwigsburg railway station for bombs on September 29, 1985, when they found a police uniform in one of the lockers which they traced back to Norbert Poehlke. He told investigators that he left it there for a quick change for a family member's funeral, causing a great deal of suspicion for the investigators. On October 14, Poehlke requested some sick leave time. Authorities went to his home a few days later to question him about the robberies and murders. When he did not answer and they feared Poehlke had fled, they entered the house to find Poehlke's wife dead in the bathroom and his son, Adrian, dead in his bedroom. They had both been shot. Poehlke was not there.

On October 23, Poehlke's body and the body of his son, Gabriel, were found shot to death in his car near Brindisi, Italy. It was clearly a murder-suicide. It was confirmed that Poehlke's pistol was used in all the murders.

Hammer Killer of Frankfurt aka **Gatter, Arthur** (1940 – December 12, 1990) was born in Ravensburg, Germany. He was a loner who suffered from anxiety and showed signs of mental health problems; by the 1990s, he was in a world of madness. He reported that a dark force had taken his victims to the park so he could kill them.

Beginning on February 2, 1990, Gatter murdered six homeless people and two homosexuals in the city parks of Frankfort, Germany. His weapon was a hammer which he carried in a plastic bag in his armpit. He searched the park benches where the homeless people slept. He would watch them for a period of time until he was sure he could murder them without being seen.

43-year-old Hans-Peter "Peterchen" S. was found by a security guard in Weißfrauenstraße about 5:00 a.m. on

February 2, 1990. Kurt Helmut H. was found on February 7, but he was not a homeless person. He had fatal injuries made by a hammer. Helmut R., a tramp, was found with severe head injuries about 5:40 a.m. on April 2, at the bus stop at Rechneigrabenstraße.

Two victims were found on April 3 near the Eschenheimer plant. Another man named Helmut R. was murdered on April 9 in Ostzeil. Hans-Peter M., age 46, was found about 7:30 a.m. on May 4. Engelbert G., age 60, and Nicola Z., age 42, were found about 50 meters apart on May 5 within 24 hours of finding Hans-Peter M.

At this point police tried to catch the killer by using surveillance; however, the diffused lights in the parks and the camera technology at that time did not give enough detail to point the finger at anyone. They also put up additional shelters and left the subway shelters open, so the homeless would not have to sleep on the park benches. Life-sized dolls placed on the benches with officers hiding nearby did not bring any favorable results.

Anderson S. followed a man into the bush, expecting to have sex with him on May 20, but this was not to be. He was stabbed but managed to survive and fled. He collapsed on a park bench where he was then killed by the man with the knife.

On May 22, Heinrich O. became Gatter's last victim. A person who lived nearby witnessed the murder and alerted the police. Gatter was arrested within 12 minutes of the murder.

Before he could be taken to court on December 12, 1990, Arthur Gatter hanged himself with a gauze bandage.

Hampton Roads Killer aka **Jackson, Elton Manning** (b. 1956) is suspected of murdering at least 12 gay men in and around the Norfolk, Virginia, area between 1987 and 1996 and dumping their bodies in the Chesapeake/ Portsmouth area. Jackson was arrested in May 1997 and charged with the murder of Andrew D. Smith in July 1996. Smith's body was found on the shoulder of a dead-end road in the Deep Creek section of Chesapeake. DNA testing showed that Jackson and Smith had sex just hours before Smith was murdered. Smith's blood, along with the blood of Reginald Joyner, was found in Jackson's bed. Joyner is a known victim of the *Hampton Roads Killer.*

Jackson was convicted of murdering Andrew D. Smith and sentenced to life in prison on October 27, 1998. He is currently housed at the River North Correctional Center at Independence, Virginia.

The FBI has confirmed that all 12 of the killings bear a similar modus operandi that marks them as being the work of one serial killer. Most of the victims were strangled to death, their nude bodies dumped along isolated and wooded paths and trails. There have been no similar killings in the area since Jackson's arrest in May 1997, which does boost the validity that Elton Manning Jackson is indeed the serial killer. All of the victims were found nude, except one. Ten of the victims were strangled. The others were too decomposed to determine their cause of death. Officially, the *Hampton Roads Killer* case remains unsolved.

On September 5, 2000, Jackson appealed his conviction of first-degree murder, but the judgment of the trial court was affirmed.

Hampton, Kevin L. (b. 1962) is a serial killer who murdered three women in Terre Haute, Indiana, in the early 2000s.

Dianna Lehman, age 18, was found murdered in her home in Terre Haute on May 19, 2000. She had been strangled to death.

Timothy Bailey, an associate of Hampton's, told police that he and Hampton picked up Tanette "Toni" Dickison, age 18, at her home on or about November 28, 2004, and they both had sex with her. Bailey said that Dickison was alive when he last saw her. Dickison's body was found in a private pond in Clay County on November 30.

On February 10, 2005, the partially decomposed body of Cassie M. Harris, age 48, was found in a creek near the Novelis plant in Vigo County. The autopsy showed that Harris had died approximately two months earlier. Dickison and Harris knew each other and had disappeared the same night.

Kevin Hampton was convicted of the murder of Dianna Lehman, plus charges of rape and criminal deviate conduct in 2006 and sentenced to 85 years in prison.

In 2007, Hampton was convicted of the murders of Tanette Dickison and Cassie Harris and was sentenced to 65 years imprisonment for each charge, which would begin upon completion of serving 40 years for an unrelated dealing cocaine conviction, then an 85-year sentence for a separate murder conviction of Dianna Lehman in 2000.

Hanebuth, Jasper (1607 – February 4, 1643) was born near Hanover, Germany, to Hans Hanebuth, a cotter (farm laborer or tenant occupying a cottage in return for labor) in Groß-Buchholz. Jasper became a mercenary during the Thirty Years' War, after which he became a robber and murderer. He was described as being very rude and had tantrums which everyone feared.

Hanebuth preyed mainly on those in Eilenriede, the forest near the area which is now the Hanover Zoo. He had at least two accomplices, namely **Caspar Reusche** and **Hanschen von Rode**. He usually shot his victims from afar without knowing if they had anything worth stealing. His victims included his own wife.

He was hired as a horse dealer, but that did not last very long as he was arrested on November 14, 1652, for horse theft. During the repeated threats of torture by his captors, he confessed to 10 thefts and 19 murders. On February

3, 1653, he was sentenced "to be judged by the breaking wheel by his limbs from life to death."

On February 4, 1653, Jasper Hanebuth was executed in front of a stone gate on the breaking wheel.

Hanks, John Norris (b. 1947) was a serial killer believed to be responsible for at least eight known murders in the San Francisco area in the late 1970s and early 1980s.

In 1966, Hanks stabbed his sister-in-law to death. He was convicted of second-degree murder and served 5-1/2 years. In early 1977, he was arrested and questioned about the murder of Patricia Ann Crawford, age 22. Charges were dismissed. On June 21, 1980, the body of Arnetta Oakes, age 30, was found in a creek bed near San Jose. Hanks was questioned again but was not charged. Three years later, police had enough evidence to arrest him and convict him. In 1986, John Norris Hanks was sentenced to life in prison without the possibility of parole for the murder of Arnetta Oaks. He is housed at Mule Creek State Prison in Ione, California.

Hanni, Johannes-Andreas (1957 – November 6, 1982) was born in Estonia to a family of devout Baptists and was treated badly by his parents, particularly his father who was a minister. Over the years, Hanni learned to hate his father. As a juvenile, he had quite a lengthy police record and spent a great deal of the time in prisons and reformatories. On December 11, 1981, he married Pille Toomla, who drove a trolley. His span of murders began on March 5, 1982 and ended with his arrest on October 2, 1982.

Eimar Vibo, a sailor, was stabbed to death on March 5 on Valdeku Street in Nomme. Hanni cut out part of one of his thighs and took it home with him to cook and "had wished to try eating human flesh for a long time." On May 23, 1982, in Johvi, Ivan Sivitsky, age 75, of Belarus was stabbed to death by Hanni. Hanni cut off his genitals, hoping to use them as a dildo.

In July 1982, Hanni raped and killed Yevgenia Koltsova, a middle-aged female vagrant who was picking raspberries in the forest.

Hanni and his wife made plans to murder a random taxi driver, which they did on September 2, 1982 in Tallinn. They attacked taxi driver Alari Kivi with a knife. Kivi fought back and survived but had serious injuries. Johannes-Andreas Hanni was arrested on October 2, 1982 and charged with the three murders. Toomla was arrested and charged with accessory to murder. Hanni hanged himself in prison before he could be sentenced. Toomla was convicted and spent about 12 years in Harku Women's Prison. When she was released, she changed her name and moved to Finland.

Happy Face Killer aka **Jesperson, Keith Hunter** (b. April 6, 1955) was born in Chilliwack, British Columbia, Canada, and became an American serial killer.

As a young boy, Jesperson tortured and murdered small animals. He captured birds, cats, and dogs around the trailer park where he lived. He would beat the animals and then strangle them to death. He and his friend, Martin, got into trouble together. Jesperson says that many times he was punished for things that Martin had done. In retaliation, when he was just 10 years old, he attacked Martin and beat him savagely until he was stopped by his father. In another incident, while a group of boys were swimming in a lake, one of the boys held him under water until he blacked out. Later at the public pool, Jesperson attempted to drown the boy, but a lifeguard pulled him away.

Jesperson never dated in school, never went to a dance or prom. After high school, he entered into a relationship with Rose Hucke and married her in 1975. The couple had three children. After several years, Rose suspected that Keith was having affairs while he was on the road as a truck driver.

Tensions grew, and in 1989, Rose packed up hers and the children's belongings and drove 200 miles to live with her parents in Spokane, Washington. She and Jesperson divorced in 1990.

Jesperson dreamed of being a Royal Canadian Mounted Policeman. At the age of 35, he stood 6 ft. 6 in. and weighed about 240 pounds; he began working toward this goal. An injury suffered while training ended this dream. He went to work as an interstate truck driver after relocating to Cheney, Washington. This afforded him the opportunity to kill, be miles away by the time the body was found, and not be a suspect.

On January 23, 1990, he met Taunja Bennett at a bar and later invited her to his house. After sex, they got into an argument and he brutally beat her and strangled her to death. Her body was found a few days later, but there were no suspects.

After this murder, Jesperson decided he was not getting the attention he deserved for this murder and he wrote a confession on the bathroom wall of a truck stop, signing it with a smiley face. In April 1990, at a shopping center parking lot in Mt. Shasta, California, he was approached by a woman carrying a baby. The woman was very intoxicated, but she and the baby wound up in Jesperson's car. During their conversation, Jesperson revealed a lot about himself. They drove to an isolated area and during oral sex, the woman stopped and asked to be driven home. Jesperson forced her to finish the oral sex and then tried to break her neck, which he could not do. He took the woman and baby back to the shopping center. The woman filed charges and told investigators all she knew about Jesperson. He was arrested at gunpoint soon after. After being questioned he was uncuffed and told to go speak to a detective with the Shasta Police Department. His version of events evidently was more convincing than the woman's and he was released. A charge of sexual assault was filed against him. When he did not show up for his court date, a felony warrant was issued, and he was arrested in Iowa at a weigh station. Shasta County's warrant was weak, so the charge was reduced to a misdemeanor and the cost of extradition was not worth it.

On August 30, 1992, the body of a woman was found near Blythe, California. She had been raped and strangled. She was not identified and was referred to as Jane Doe. Jesperson later told the police her name was Claudia.

In September 1992, Cynthia Lyn Rose's body was found in Turlock, California. Jesperson claimed that she jumped into his truck uninvited at a truck stop while he slept.

The first week of November 1992, Laurie Ann Pentland was strangled to death. Jesperson said that she had attempted to double her fee after having sex with him. She threatened to call the police, so he strangled her.

Still feeling he was not getting the attention he wanted, he wrote letters to media outlets, including *The Oregonian,* and police departments confessing the murders and signed each with a smiley face. Phil Sanford, the journalist working the serial killer story for *The Oregonian*, dubbed this killer *The Happy Face Killer*.

In July 1993, a woman's body was found in Santa Nella, California. She has not been identified. She was first thought to have died from a drug overdose, but upon closer examination, the coroner determined she had been strangled.

On September 14, 1994, a woman's body was discovered in Crestview, Florida. She was not identified, but Jesperson said that her name was Susanne.

In January 1995, Jesperson agreed to take Angela Surbrize from Spokane, Washington to Indiana in his truck. About a week later in Wyoming, Surbrize began to nag Jesperson to hurry up because she was anxious to see her boyfriend. Jesperson raped and strangled her. He strapped her body to the undercarriage of his truck and dragged her,

"Face down to grind off her face and prints." She was found months later after Jesperson gave details of her location to the police.

By February 1995, Jesperson decided that Julie Ann Winningham, his girlfriend, was only interested in him for his money. On March 10, 1995, Jesperson strangled her to death. She was the only victim Jesperson had a link to. The police questioned Jesperson about Julie Winningham's murder, but they had no grounds to arrest him. Jesperson thought he would be arrested for her murder and tried to commit suicide twice but failed. He turned himself in to police and began revealing details of other murders. He was arrested on March 30, 1995, for Julie Winningham's murder.

Jesperson claimed to have murdered as many as 160 women, but only eight murders were confirmed. These murders were committed in California, Florida, Nebraska, Oregon, Washington, and Wyoming.

Jesperson is currently serving three consecutive life sentences in the Oregon State Penitentiary in Salem, Oregon. In October 1995 in the state of Washington, Jesperson was sentenced to life for Julie Winningham's murder; this sentence is to be served consecutively after his life sentences in Oregon. In June 1998, the State of Wyoming convicted him of the murder of Angela Surbrize in Laramie County and Jesperson was given another life sentence, which is to be served consecutively after his life sentences in Oregon and Washington.

In 2008, Jesperson's daughter, Melissa G. Moore, published a book about her father entitled *Shattered Silence: the Untold Story of the Daughter of a Serial Killer.*

Harding, Donald Eugene (March 1, 1949 – April 6, 1992) was a serial killer who murdered at least seven people between 1979 and 1980. Harding escaped from an Arkansas jail on September 17, 1979, by sawing his way out. Over the next few weeks, he tried to rob a prostitute in Chicago on September 27, but failed; robbed a steakhouse of $83,000 (cash and jewelry) and pistol whipped a patron in Omaha, Nebraska on September 30; and held up a bank for an unknown amount in Knoxville, Tennessee, on October 23.

Nothing was heard of Harding in November, but beginning on December 11, he kidnapped and robbed the B. R. Baker family in Dallas, Texas; on December 18, he used a phony badge of a security guard to enter Ronald Svetgoff's room at a motel in Waco, Texas, then tied and gagged him before stealing his car; December 24, he tied up Clayton Hall and his wife, plus another couple and then robbed them in Dallas, Texas; and on December 31, he tied and gagged Phillip Buss in his room at a hotel in Salt Lake City before robbing him and stealing his car.

January 3, 1980, Harding tied up and gagged Charles Dickerson before robbing him and stealing his car at a motel in South Lake Tahoe, California. Dickerson's body was found under the bed where he had died of asphyxiation. On January 5, using a .25 caliber pistol to gain entry, Harding tied up Frank Palmer with cord and neckties at his apartment in Sacramento, California, and stole his car and credit card.

On January 6, using the ruse of wanting to rent an apartment from Lyle and Margaret Murphy in Bakersfield, California, Harding stole money and their car. Also on January 6, after stealing from the Murphys, he forced Joseph Wohlers and his uncle, Robert Stoick, into the hotel room at gunpoint in Los Angeles, and hogtied them before stealing their credit cards, luggage, and car. January 10, he murdered Gerald Huth, a businessman from Minnesota, and stole his car on US 101 near Paso Robles, California.

January 21, he kidnapped and robbed Shirley Land and four others in the optometry clinic of Shirley's husband in San Diego, California. January 25, he tied Allan Gage's hands and feet using the adhesive tape from Gage's colostomy bag and robbed him in his room at a Phoenix, Arizona, motel. Gage suffocated on the sock stuffed in his mouth. On January 25, again using a fake security guard badge, Harding gained entry into the room shared by Robert Wise and Martin Concannon at a motel in Tucson, Arizona, hogtied the two men, and shot them in the head and chest at close range. Harding took various articles from each man and stole Concannon's car. Harding was arrested in Flagstaff, Arizona, at approximately 8:00 p.m. on January 26, 1980, while driving Concannon's car.

Donald Eugene Harding was convicted of the murders of Robert Wise and Martin Concannon on April 27, 1982, and sentenced to death. On April 6, 1992, he was executed in Arizona's gas chamber.

Harding's ashes were mistakenly sent to a John Harding in Oregon, who does have a relative by that name, but it was not this one. Thinking that the ashes belonged to his estranged biological father, he spread them in the most serene places in Oregon and Alaska, only to find that they were not the ashes of his biological father, but those of a monster.

Harris, DeWayne Lee (c. 1964) is a serial killer of at least three prostitute/transient women in Seattle, King County, Washington.

On September 12, 1997, the body of Denise Marie Harris, age 42, was found; on January 10, 1998, the body of Olivia Smiths, age 27, was found; and on February 1, 1998, the body of Antoinette Jones, age 34, was found. All three had been bound with shoelaces. Two had been strangled and the third had had her throat slashed. Two were found in "The Jungle", an area of undeveloped land under Interstates 5 and 90 that is frequented by the homeless. One of the bodies was found in a stairwell of a building nearby.

DeWayne Lee Harris was arrested for the murders. During the trial, Harris shouted obscenities, threw objects, and shoved chairs. He was finally strapped to a restraining chair. When the guilty verdict was read, Harris dropped his head and laughed. He was sentenced to 94 years and 5 months in prison.

Harris, Michael Darnell (b. March 7, 1963) is a convicted serial killer serving four life sentences for the murders of four elderly women in the cities of Lansing, Ann Arbor, and Ypsilanti, Michigan, in the years 1981 and 1982. In 2015, DNA testing was ordered, and someone else's DNA was found at the scene of Ula Curdy's rape and murder. But it was not to be. Additional testing of DNA from the crime scene did identify Harris as being at the scene. He is serving his life sentences at the Muskegon Correctional Facility in Michigan. In October 2018, he sought a retrial, but in June 2017, the request was denied by an Ingham County Circuit Court judge.

Harris, Ralph (b. July 11, 1972) was a serial killer in Chicago, Illinois. In 1992, authorities believe he committed four murders, before he was convicted of a 1991 armed robbery and sentenced to seven years. He was released on January 20, 1995, and within a month he was raping and robbing women at gunpoint. The six men he is known to have murdered are Thomas Hodges, Jimmie Bramlett, David Ford, William Patterson, Eric Watkins, and James Williamson. Most of Harris' victims were older men.

In 1995 he was charged and convicted of six murders, 13 armed robberies, and six sexual assaults. He was initially sentenced to death. The death sentence has been commuted to life. Harris is currently at the Pontiac Correctional Institute in Pontiac, Illinois. It is believed he murdered two more men in 1995. He has not been charged with these murders.

Harrison, Lester (b. 1933) was a known thief and had been convicted on various charges including larceny, attempted armed robbery, unlawful use of a weapon, battery, and indecent exposure. No one linked him to the grisly homicides committed around Grant Park in downtown Chicago.

On September 5, 1972, Judith Bettely was found beaten to death near Grant Park's band shell. In late July 1973, Irene Koutros was stabbed to death in the underground garage at Grant Park. On August 3, 1973, Lee Wilson was stabbed to death in the park. On August 13, 1973, Judith Ott, age 28, was stabbed to death in a park restroom. Seeing a black man sprinting from the restroom, David Ott, Judith's husband, gave chase and tackled Harrison, unaware that his wife had been murdered.

Lester Harrison was arrested and confessed to four of the Grant Park murders. He denied any involvement in the murder of Irene Koutros. Authorities sought to link him to the death of Elizabeth Dawson, who was found in August 1972 in a building next door to where Lester Harrison lived, but were unsuccessful. At his trial, Harrison was acquitted on the grounds of insanity, but authorities were not willing to set this "lust killer" free. They used a little-used law to confine him while he remained a menace to society. By this time, Harrison claimed to be a quadriplegic and his attorneys petitioned for his release from state custody, describing him as "harmless." Guards at Belleville State Hospital, where Harrison was housed, testified that Harrison was capable of raising his arms, that he spoke incessantly of sexual activity, and that he was visibly aroused when certain nurses were nearby. The petition to release him was withdrawn on August 11, 1986.

Harwell, Joseph (b. April 14, 1960) was already serving a life sentence for the 1997 murder of Teresa Vincon in Columbus, Ohio, when he was charged with the deaths in

Cleveland of Mary Thomas in 1989 and Tondilear Harge in 1996. He pleaded guilty in February 2012 to two counts each of involuntary manslaughter and abduction. He was sentenced to life. He will be eligible for parole in 2047. He is currently housed at the Allen Correctional Institute in Lima, Ohio.

Hayes, James Michael (b. 1955) is a suspected serial killer. He is currently serving a sentence of life without parole for the murder of Regina Quarles on August 25, 1978. Her body was found three days later along Highway 69 south near Branscomb Apartments in Tuscaloosa, Alabama. Hayes was convicted of attempting to rape and murder two women several months earlier and was sentenced to 20 years for each count, to be served consecutively.

Hayes is also a suspect in the murder of Teresa Carol White, age 18, whose body was found in the Lake Nicole area near Northport, Alabama, in April 1978. The case has never been solved. Hayes denies killing her.

The Tuscaloosa County District Attorney said, "I'm absolutely convinced he's a serial killer."

Heidi Killer aka **Holst, Thomas** (b. April 1, 1966) was a serial killer in the city of Hamburg, Germany. Between 1987 and 1990, Holst raped, tortured, and dismembered three women.

On November 25, 1987, Andrea Grube-Nagel, age 21, was walking to her parents' house from the Rissen train station and was forced into Holst's car when he threatened her with a knife. Her body was found on November 27 in Kaltenkirchen.

On February 11, 1988, Petra Maaßen, age 28, was also forced into Holst's car when he threatened her with a knife. Her mutilated body was found the following day in a field in Bargfeld-Stegen.

Lara Holz, age 22, missed her bus and climbed into Holst's car when he offered her a ride on November 27, 1989. Her body was found on December 2, 1989.

Examined by psychiatrists and therapists, Thomas Holst has been diagnosed as being unresponsive to treatment and extreme recidivism (most likely to repeat criminal offenses). He is serving three life sentences and is in solitary confinement in a psychiatric hospital.

Heidnik, Gary M. (November 22, 1943 – July 6, 1999) was a murderer of at least two women in Philadelphia, Pennsylvania. He is included here because of the heinous crimes committed that led to the murders. Between 1986 and 1987, Heidnik kidnapped six women and held them captive in the basement of his house in Philadelphia. He dug a four-foot deep pit that he used as solitary confinement when one of the captives disobeyed. The captives were all African American women and they were beaten, abused, and tortured at the hands of Gary Heidnik. The victims were encouraged to "rat" on each other to earn better treatment. Heidnik also forced the women to beat each other.

Heidnik used electric shock as one means of torture. One day, he forced two of his victims, who were bound with chains, to go into the pit. He ordered two of the other women to fill the hole with water. He then stuck a stripped extension cord to the women's chains. Deborah Dudley was electrocuted. Heidnik disposed of her body in a park in New Jersey.

His captives were Josefina Rivera, age 25, kidnapped on November 26, 1986; Sandra Lindsay, age 24, kidnapped on December 3, 1986, and murdered by starvation, torture, and untreated fever; Lisa Thomas, age 19, kidnapped on December 23, 1986; Deborah Dudley, age 23, kidnapped on January 2, 1987 and murdered by electrocution on March 22, 1987; Jacqueline Askins, age 17, kidnapped on January

18, 1987; and Agnes Adams, age 24, kidnapped on March 23, 1987.

Sandra Lindsay, one of his captives, died in February 1987. Heidnik dismembered her body, wrapped the arms and legs, marked them as "dog food," and put them in the freezer. He cooked her ribs in the oven and her head in a pot on the stove. Police answered complaints from neighbors of a very bad odor coming from Heidnik's house. The police left after Heidnik told them he had tried to cook meat that had gone bad.

On November 25, 1986, Heidnik kidnapped Agnes Adams with the help of Josefina Rivera, his first victim. Rivera convinced him to allow Adams a visit with her family. He drove as far as a gas station within a block of her house. Adams walked to her home and instantly called 911. They were not convinced of her story and asked her to repeat it. She told the story again and they were convinced. They saw chafing on her leg from the chains that held her captive. Heidnik was arrested where he sat in his vehicle waiting for Agnes Adams to return.

Heidnik was convicted of two murders and sentenced to death on July 1, 1988. He was executed by lethal injection on July 6, 1999 at State Correctional Institution Rockview in Centre County, Pennsylvania.

Hein, Jurgen (b. 1939) was born in Berlin, Germany to an alcoholic father and mentally retarded mother. He was the oldest of eight children. He left home when he became of age, was married in Berlin and fathered two children, but found this marriage was as bad as his parents'. On March 3, 1967, Hein strangled his wife to death after an argument. He was convicted of manslaughter and sentenced to eight years in prison. He was released early on November 24, 1972.

On April 4, 1973, Sonja Kleber, age 6, disappeared on her way home from school. She was found that night in a wooded park, unconscious, but alive. She was naked and hemorrhaging from her vagina. She was able to give police a good description of her attacker. She led police to the building where she was attacked. They arrested Jurgen Hein. He confessed and was sentenced to an additional 10 years (he still had three years to serve on his original sentence). He was released in mid-July 1985 and moved to Baden-Baden, West Germany, just a few miles from Strasbourg, France.

Shortly after his move, he met Elvira Kaszuba, age 50, and invited her to have dinner with him that evening. They soon became lovers. On November 6, Hein cooked their dinner. After dinner he killed Elvira and disemboweled her with a hunting knife. He stuffed her body in a closet.

On November 6, the son of Theresia Hoog, age 55, reported her missing from the home they shared. He tried calling her closest friend, Elvira Kaszuba, but got no answer. He also told police that his mother's car was missing. She had gone to a local clinic for rheumatism treatments on the evening of November 10, and a nurse at the clinic verified that she had seen her there. However, the nurse said she left before her treatment because she was called away by a man, who was described to authorities. Her car was not in the clinic parking lot. A composite sketch was made of the man and given to all officers.

The car was found outside an apartment house by a traffic officer. As the officer made his way to a call box to report the car found, he saw a man resembling the suspect sketch exiting one of the apartments. Jurgen Hein, the man matching the sketch, was arrested. When authorities searched his apartment, they found Mrs. Hoog alive, but nude and bloody, her wrists and ankles tied to the bed. She had been tortured with the hunting knife also found on the bed. She told police that she had been lured away from the clinic when the man told her that her friend, Elvira Kaszuba, had been seriously injured in an accident. Police then went to Elvira's home and found her body in the closet. She too had been mutilated. They went to find the apartment manager, but what they found was her body, also stripped and slashed, in her bathroom. She had been murdered 11 days before.

Hein confessed to his crimes. He was convicted and sentenced to two consecutive life terms on June 27, 1986.

Hembree, Dannie Robbie (b. 1962) is a suspected serial killer in Gaston County, North Carolina. He was convicted of the 2009 murder of Heather Catterton, age 17, and sentenced to death. During his trial for the 2009 murder of Randi Dean Saldana, age 30, he alleged a sexual relationship with the assistant district attorney, and the trial was thrown out of court. He is currently incarcerated at the Central Prison in Raleigh, North Carolina.

Henyansyah, Very Idham (b. February 1, 1978) aka *Ryan* was a serial killer in Jakarta, Indonesia, during 2006 – 2008. When apprehended in 2008, he confessed to killing 11 people. Most of his nine victims were homosexual, like he was. He said he killed them because the way they "came on" to him was humiliating and degrading. He said he murdered Nanik Kistanti, age 28, because she tried to seduce him and her 3-year-old daughter, Silvia Ramadhani, because she was a witness. Except for the last, all of the victims were buried in his parents' backyard. The body of Heri Santosa, age 34, was found at the side of a road in Jakarta cut into seven pieces and skewered with a crowbar.

Henyansyah's other victims include Agustinus Fitri Setyawan, age 28; M. Zainul Abidin alias Zaki, age 27; Muhammed Aksoni, age 28; Guruh Setyo Pramono, age 27; Grady Gland Adam, age 24; Muhammad Asrori, no age given; and Vincentius Yudhy Priyano, age 30.

Henyansyah was sentenced to death on April 6, 2009, and is awaiting execution at Kesambi Penitentiary in Cirebon, West Java, Indonesia.

Hernandez, Cayetano (c. 1940 – 1963) and **Hernandez, Santos** (c. 1940 – 1963), petty criminals, came to the small town of Yerba Buena, Mexico, and formed a cult in 1963. **Solis, Magdalena** aka the *High Priestess of Blood*, and her brother, **Solis, Eleazar** were asked to join the cult and the villagers were told that Magdalena was the reincarnation of an Inca goddess.

Magdalena and Eleazar came from a poverty-stricken dysfunctional family. She worked as a prostitute from an early age, with her brother Eleazar as her pimp, until her association with the Hernandez brothers.

The Hernandez brothers claimed to be prophets and high priests of the "powerful and exiled Inca gods" and demanded worship and tribute from the people of this small community in the Mexican state of Nuevo León, in exchange for treasure hidden in caves near the village. The community was a village of about 50 mostly impoverished and illiterate inhabitants. They did not realize that the Inca were not part of Mexican history and accepted that the Hernandez brothers were indeed Inca prophets. Magdalena soon took over the cult. She and the others tired of the orgies and demanded human sacrifice. The one sacrificed was always a dissenting member of the cult. Blood was collected in a cup mixed with chicken or other animal blood (from animal sacrifices). The victims, both human and animal, were left to bleed to death. These sacrifices went on for four weeks and reached the point of dissecting the heart of a victim who was still alive.

In May of 1963, Sebastian Guerrero, age 14, came upon the caves where the cult was practicing their beliefs. He ran over 25 km (15.53 miles) to the town of Villa Gran, the nearest police station, and reported what he had seen to the police. He referred to the perpetrators as vampires. The following morning, Investigator Luis Martinez took the boy back to the village and Guerrero took Martinez to the place where he had seen the "vampires." Martinez and Guerrero were never seen alive again.

On May 31, 1963, police and the army were dispatched to the village of Yerba Buena. Eleazar and Magdalena Solis were arrested for possession of marijuana. Santos Hernandez was shot by police while resisting arrest. Cayetano Hernandez was killed by a member of the cult. During the investigation, the mutilated bodies of Sebastian Guerrero and Luis Martinez were found near the farm where the Solises had been arrested. They also found the dismembered bodies of at least six other persons near the caves. Many members of the cult were shot during the shootout with police. Those who were arrested were sentenced to 30 years in prison.

In June 1963, Magdalena and Eleazar Solis were each sentenced to 50 years in prison for the murders of Gerrero and Martinez. Authorities were unable to prosecute them for the other murders because the cult members refused to testify against them.

Herrington, Michael Lee (b. 1943) was the son of a Kansas City policeman and a mother who beat him often with a belt. By 1966, he was living and working in Milwaukee, Wisconsin. He was married, and he and his wife were expecting their first child.

On September 1, 1966, a 34-year-old woman was driving to work when she was pulled over (by means of a ruse) and slashed with a knife. The assailant fled when she began to scream.

Just two days later, Julia Beckwith, age 10, was beaten, raped, and stabbed to death on a vacant lot in the city. Herrington was questioned, but then released.

In early October, Sherryl Thompson's partially nude body was found by her brother behind a Catholic church. She had been stabbed at least 22 times.

On November 4, the body of Diane Olkwitz, age 19, was found at the factory where she worked in Menominee, Wisconsin. She had been stabbed more than 100 times.

In mid-November, a man with a knife slashed Kathleen Dreyer, age 11, and escaped in a 1957 Chevrolet. A neighbor saw the car at a nearby gas station and summoned the police. Herrington was arrested. He confessed to the murders of Julia Beckwith and Sherryl Thompson, plus the attack on Kathleen Dreyer.

Herrington was convicted on July 7, 1967, and sentenced to two consecutive life terms for the murders plus 30 years for attempted murder.

Hertogs, Jacobus Dirk (December 16, 1949 – July 19, 2015) aka *Koos* is a convicted Netherlands serial killer. He is responsible for the rapes and deaths of:

Tialda Visser, age 12, who disappeared on May 11, 1979. She had gone to her ballet classes at the Royal Conservatory and failed to return home. Her body was found four days later. Her cause of death was not determined.

On April 3, 1980, Emy den Boer disappeared on her way to the Academie voor Lichamelijke Opvoeding in The Hague from her home in Schiedam. Her body was found by a hiker in the forest near Nistelrode. She had been shot in the head and abdomen.

Edith Post, age 11, disappeared on September 29, 1980, during school when she left class to get some material from a closet in the hallway. She did not return to the classroom. Three days later, her body was found in the dunes of Wassenaar. She had been beaten to death.

A call was received by police from an anonymous caller who told them that Edith had bitten her murderer, and the bouncer at De Nachtegaal nightclub had a severe bite wound on his little finger. The bouncer, Jacobus Dirk Hertogs, was arrested. Traces of blood were found during the investigation of his home. The blood was determined to be from Tialda Visser and Emy den Boer.

Koos Hertogs was convicted and sentenced to life in prison. He died in prison in Vught, Netherlands, on July 19, 2015.

Hicks, James Rodney (b. April 17, 1951) was arrested in 1983 for the murder of his wife, Jennie, who disappeared in 1977. He spent six years of a ten-year sentence in prison for this murder. The search for Jerilyn Towers, who disappeared in 1982 in Newport, Maine, prompted the investigation into the disappearance of Hicks' wife, Jennie, resulting in his arrest and conviction. At the time, police did not have sufficient evidence to charge Hicks with Towers' disappearance.

After his release from prison, Hicks obtained a job at the Twin City Motel in Brewer, Maine. There he met Lynn Willette, also an employee. They moved in together after a short time. Lynn disappeared in 1996. Authorities were not able to discover enough evidence to charge him with this murder. Even though he has not been charged with their murders, Maine authorities consider him a serial killer.

By the year 2000, Hicks was living in Levelland, Texas, with his new wife, Brandie. Hicks was arrested and accused of holding a Lubbock woman at gunpoint, forcing her to drink cough syrup, and attempting to rob her. When Hicks was sentenced to 55 years in prison, he asked to cut a deal with authorities in Maine in exchange for telling them where the three missing women were buried. Authorities located the remains of Hicks' three victims after digging for two days around his place in Etna and at several roadside sites in Aroostook County.

James Hicks was sentenced to life in prison. He is incarcerated at the Maine State Prison in Warren, Maine.

Hidaka, Hiroaki (April 1962 – December 25, 2006) was a serial killer in Japan. He had been an excellent student but failed to gain admission to the University of Tsukuba, his college of choice. He instead entered Fukuoka University, but dropped out. He began to borrow money, drank too much, and frequented the local prostitutes.

In 1989, he moved to Hiroshima and found work as a taxi driver. He married and they had a daughter in 1993. Then his wife entered a mental hospital.

In 1996, between April and September Hidaka robbed and murdered four women, including a girl who was only 16. He was arrested on September 21, 1996.

On February 9, 2000, the Hiroshima Court sentenced Hidaka to death. He did not appeal. On December 25, 2006, Hiroaki Hidaka was executed by hanging.

Highwayman Serial Killer aka **Chauke, Elias** (c. 1962) was a serial killer in Pretoria, Gauteng Province, South Africa in 2002. He was found guilty of raping, robbing, and then murdering five women in October and November 2002.

His first known murder was an unidentified woman whose decomposed body was found on October 7, 2002, in Rooihuiskraal. Her naked body was found under a car seat cover.

On October 8, Confidence Ramonyathi was in Pretoria looking for work. Her half-naked body was found nine days later in the Waterkloof Heights area.

On November 12, another unidentified woman's body was found near R21 in Monument Park.

On November 13, Grany Lekala went to Pretoria to look for work. Her body was found covered by a blanket the following day at Highveld Park in Centurion. Her blouse had been used to strangle her and was still wound around her neck.

Joyce Kabini, a friend of Grany Lekala, testified at Chaulke's trial that he had approached her, asking if she was looking for a job and gave her his cell phone number. She had given that cell phone number to Grany.

Beauty Ditshego was in Pretoria on November 14 to do some shopping. Her body was found the next day in Newlands.

Chauke was convicted of murdering the five women, robbing three, and raping one. He was sentenced by the Pretoria High Court to six terms of life in prison, plus an additional 52 years.

Hill, Dr. John (1931 – September 24, 1972) was a prominent plastic surgeon in Houston, Texas, and is suspected of being a serial killer by Houston investigators. His wife, Joan Robinson Hill, was the daughter of Ash Robinson, a Texas oil millionaire. Joan died on March 19, 1969. Hill was charged with her murder for withholding medical attention. He is also suspected by the investigators of murder in the deaths of his first wife, his father, his brother, and a fellow physician.

Hill went on trial in February 1971, but a mistrial was declared. Before a second trial could be held, Dr. John Hill was shot to death at the door of his River Oaks mansion. The killer, Bobby Wayne Vandiver, was shot to death by police in Longview, Texas. Lilla Paulus and Marcia McKittrick were convicted of arranging the murder, at the request of Ash Robinson. Robinson was never charged.

Hill, Walter (1935 – May 2, 1997) was freed from prison in 1961 after serving 10 years for second-degree murder. He was later convicted of kidnapping and sentenced to 14 years. While serving his time in an Atlanta, Georgia, prison he was convicted of murdering a fellow inmate. He was released from prison in 1975.

On January 7, 1977, Hill murdered Willie Mae Hammock, age 60, grandmother and legally adopted mother of 13-year-old Toni; John Tatum, age 36, step-son of Willie Mae; and John's wife Lois Jean Tatum, age 34, in the Booker Heights community of Jefferson County, Alabama. The three were shot in the head after Willie Mae told Walter Hill, who at the time was 42 years old, that she would not give Hill permission to marry her daughter, Toni.

In February 1980, Walter Hill was convicted of the triple murder and sentenced to death. On May 2, 1997, after spending more than 17 years on death row, he was executed in the electric chair at Holman Correctional Facility near Mobile, Alabama.

Hilley, Audrey Marie (June 4, 1933 – February 26, 1987) was a serial killer of family members. A native of Anniston, Alabama, Audrey apparently had a normal childhood and was married at the age of 18. After the birth of her second daughter, marital problems began when she experienced a radical change in her personality and showed resentment toward her baby daughter, Carol. Audrey's husband, Frank Hilley, died in 1975 and his death was attributed to cancer. In 1977, Audrey's mother, Lucille Frazier, passed away and her death was also attributed to cancer. In 1979, daughter Carol became gravely ill and lingered on the brink of death for several weeks, but doctors were able to save her. In November of that year, Carrie Hilley, mother-in-law to Audrey, died after a long illness.

Authorities were already suspicious of Audrey. Doctors had discovered abnormal amounts of arsenic in Carol's blood during her illness. They began further investigations into the deaths of the other family members who had recently passed on. On October 25, 1979, Audrey was charged with attempted murder of her daughter and arrested. She posted her bond of $14,000 and disappeared. Audrey Hilley became "Robbi Hannon" and soon was living with John Homan in

Marlow, New Hampshire. They were married in May 1981. Within 6 weeks, "Robbi" was living in Texas where she telephoned Homan occasionally as herself (Robbi) and as her twin, "Teri Martin". They reconciled briefly in 1982, then "Robbi" left for Florida where she faked her own death (as Robbi). She then went back to Homan in New Hampshire as "Teri" to console her "brother-in-law". Very shortly, "Teri" moved on to Vermont. Authorities found her behavior suspicious, determined that she was Audrey Marie Hilley, and arrested her in January 1983 for the murder of her husband, Frank Hilley, and for the attempted murder of her daughter. Audrey Hilley was sentenced to life for her husband's murder, plus 20 years for the attempted murder of her daughter, Carol.

Audrey was granted a three-day furlough on February 19, 1987 from the Wetumpka, Alabama, women's prison and did not return. During a winter storm on February 26, she was found on the porch of a home in Anniston, soaked and spattered with mud. She was suffering from severe hypothermia and fading in and out of consciousness. Police identified her from wanted posters. Audrey Marie Hilley suffered a heart attack on the way to the hospital and died. She was buried next to the husband she had poisoned.

Hillside Stranglers aka **Bianchi, Kenneth Alessio** (b. May 22, 1951) and his cousin, **Buono Jr., Angelo** (October 5, 1934 – September 21, 2002) were serial killers in Los Angeles during 1977-78.

Bianchi was born in Rochester, New York to a prostitute who gave him up for adoption. He was adopted when he was three months old by Frances Scioliono and Nicholas Bianchi of Rochester. According to his adoptive mother, he was a deeply troubled child. Although he was above average in intelligence, he was an underachiever and had a quick temper. He married his high school sweetheart in 1971, but she left him eight months later. He had quite a few menial jobs. His last one was as a security guard at a jewelry store, giving him the opportunity to steal valuables which he gave to girlfriends or prostitutes to buy their loyalty. It was during this time that he became a suspect in the *Alphabet Murders* (1971 – 1973) in New York State. He moved to Los Angeles in 1975 where he met his cousin, Angelo Buono Jr.

Buono was also born in Rochester, New York to first generation Italian Americans. Buono had a long criminal history before teaming up with Bianchi, with a record ranging from failure to pay child support to grand theft auto, assault and rape.

Bianchi and Buono cruised around Los Angeles using fake badges to persuade girls that they were "undercover" cops. In the beginning, they worked as pimps, but by 1977, they had escalated to murder. Beginning on October 17, 1977, they would order a girl into their "unmarked police car" and drive them to their home where she would be tortured and murdered. Both Bianchi and Buono would sexually abuse their victim before strangling her. They also experimented with other methods of killing. By February 16, 1978, they had tortured, sexually abused, raped, and murdered 10 girls, ranging in age from 12 to 28.

Bianchi had applied for a job with the Los Angeles Police Department during this time of torturing and killing girls and women. He had actually taken several ride-alongs while they were searching for the *Hillside Stranglers*.

After botching their 11th torture/murder, Bianchi told Buono about applying for the police job and the ride-alongs. He also said that he was currently being questioned about the strangler case. Buono flew into a rage and threatened to kill Bianchi if he did not flee to Bellingham, Washington, to join his girlfriend and son who were living there. In May 1978, Bianchi moved to Bellingham. He was able to secure a job as a security officer. While guarding a house on January 11, 1979, he lured two young women, students at Western

Washington University, into the house. He forced the first girl down the stairs and strangled her. He then forced the second girl down the stairs and strangled her. He left many clues and the police apprehended him the following day. His California driver's license led to a background check that linked him to the addresses of two of the victims of the *Hillside Stranglers.*

Hillside Strangler victims were Yolanda Washington, age 19, murdered on October 17, 1977; Judith Ann Miller, age 15, murdered October 31; Lissa Kastin, age 21, murdered November 6; Jane King, age 28, murdered November 10; Delores Cepeda, age 12, murdered November 13; Sonja Johnson, age 14, murdered November 13; Kristin Weckler, age 20, murdered November 20; Lauren Wagner, age 18, murdered November 29; Kimberley Martin, age 17, murdered December 9; and Cindy Lee Hudspeth, age 20, murdered February 16, 1978.

At his trial, Bianchi pleaded not guilty by reason of insanity. He claimed that one of his other personalities, "Steve Walker", had committed his crimes. Bianchi was so convincing that he even persuaded several expert psychiatrists that he did indeed suffer from multiple personality disorder. However, investigators brought in their own psychiatrist, namely Martin Orne. When Dr. Orne told Bianchi that in genuine cases of multiple personality disorder, there tends to be more than one other personality, Bianchi immediately created another one named "Billy". Investigators discovered that the name "Steve Walker" was a student whose identity Bianchi had attempted to steal so he could practice psychology. Investigators found many books in Bianchi's home on modern psychology which helped him in faking the disorder. Since the insanity defense was shot down, Bianchi offered to testify against Buono in hopes of getting a lesser sentence. But Bianchi was very uncooperative and self-contradictory, hoping to avoid being the ultimate cause of Buono's conviction. His efforts failed.

Buono was convicted on nine counts of first-degree murder and sentenced to life imprisonment without the possibility of parole. On September 21, 2002, Buono died of a heart attack in his cell at Calipatria State Prison in California.

While awaiting trial, Bianchi began a relationship with Veronica Compton, a woman he met while in prison. She testified for the defense, telling false tales about the crimes. She was later arrested, convicted, and imprisoned for attempting to strangle a woman she had lured to a motel in an attempt to have authorities believe that the *Hillside Stranglers* were still on the loose. Bianchi had given her some semen to use to make it appear that the attack was done by the *Hillside Stranglers*. This ploy did not work either.

Bianchi pleaded guilty to five of the ten California murders and was sentenced to life. He is serving his sentence at Walla Walla Prison in Washington. He will be eligible to apply for parole in 2025.

Hilton, Gary Michael (b. November 22, 1946) was born in Atlanta, Georgia and moved with his family to Hialeah, Florida in 1958. In 1959, at the age of 13, he shot his stepfather who would not press charges. His mother would not allow him back into the house until the start of school at Miami Springs Junior High. In 1961, he lived with Dawn and Mark Jeffers when for an unknown reason his mother again would not allow him in the house. He left school apparently during the 12th grade and joined the US Army. He served time in Germany, where he earned his GED and married Ursula, who returned with him to the US. They evidently divorced, and he married a woman named Sue in DeKalb County, Georgia, in 1969. They divorced in 1971. Hilton was married two more times, each of these marriages lasting from seven to nine months.

After the army, employment information is sketchy. Hilton held a chauffeur license in the state of Florida for a couple of years and from 1997 to about 2007 he sold siding for Insulated Wall Systems for John Tabor. There were also several arrests—DUI, arson, drugs, theft, solicitation, and carrying a weapon without a license—but never spent any time in jail. He was always given probation.

On December 7, 2005, Rossana Miliani, age 26, was hiking near Bryson City, North Carolina. A witness told investigators that Miliani seemed very nervous, and was with an older man, who was probably in his 60s, while they were in her store. They bought only clothes and the man mentioned that he was a traveling preacher. Hilton stole her bank card and tried to use it. Miliani disappeared and her body has not been found.

On October 21, 2007, John, age 80, and Irene Bryant, age 84, left their home in Hendersonville, North Carolina, to go hiking in the Pisgah National Forest and had the misfortune of meeting Gary Michael Hilton. Irene Bryant's body was found on November 9 a short distance from the couple's car. Irene had died of multiple blows to the head. John's remains were found on February 2, 2008, in the Nantahala National Forest. He had been shot in the head.

On November 21, 2007, Michael Scot Louis, age 27, was reported missing. His decapitated and mutilated body was found in three separate garbage bags at Tomoka State Park near Ormond Beach, Florida, on December 6. As of this writing, Hilton has not been charged with Louis' death.

On December 1, 2007, Cheryl Hodges Dunlap, age 46, was reported missing by a friend when she failed to attend church that Sunday morning. Her body was found on December 14 in the Apalachicola National Forest. She had been decapitated and her hands removed. Authorities believe that her killer tried to burn her head and hands. On January 1, 2008, Meredith Emerson, age 24, was abducted and later murdered in the Dawson Forest Wildlife Management Area in the north Georgia mountains. She was hiking when Hilton attacked her with a knife. She fought him and screamed while he was trying to subdue her. He took her credit card and asked Meredith for the pin number, but she kept giving him the wrong number. Hilton said he got very mad and killed her. Hilton told authorities that she fought him for four days before he killed and decapitated her. She is the only known victim who was raped.

Gary Michael Hilton was indicted for the murder of Meredith Emerson on February 1, 2008. He said he would plead guilty if the courts would take the death penalty off the table and he would show them where to find her body. He was sentenced to life in prison on February 15, 2010.

On February 29, 2008, Hilton was charged with the murder of Cheryl Hodges Dunlap. He was convicted and on April 21, 2011, he was sentenced to death. He is currently at Florida State Prison, Raiford, Florida, on death row.

On June 21, 2011, Hilton was charged with the murders of John and Irene Bryant, found guilty and sentenced to four life sentences.

Hinton, Ronald (b. September 17, 1972) is a serial killer currently serving three life sentences without the possibility of parole in Stateville Correctional Institute in Joliet, Illinois.

In December 1996, he murdered Felecia Mullins, age 17, after she told Hinton that she was going to tell his wife about their affair. In August 1998, Kerry Lea Gagnier, age 36, was raped and murdered during a home invasion. In February 1999, Merceda Ares, age 31, was raped and murdered during a home invasion.

A local TV station broadcast a photo of a man at an ATM machine trying to use Merceda Ares' bank card. Hinton's third-grade daughter told her teacher that she had seen her daddy on TV, resulting in Hinton's arrest and confession to all three murders.

Hippopotamus aka **Ryakhovsky, Sergei** (December 29, 1962 – January 21, 2005) was a serial killer in the Moscow area between 1988 and 1993. Ryakhovsky was born in the Saltykovka area of Balashikha, Moscow Oblast, about one kilometer east of Moscow. He grew to 6 ft. 6 in. tall and weighed 280 lbs. At 20 years of age, he said that he began to feel an irresistible desire for intimacy with an elderly woman. He made several attempts to rape elderly women until he was arrested and sentenced to 4 years for "hooliganism."

It is known that between 1988 and 1993, he murdered homosexuals and prostitutes claiming it was part of his personal mission to "cleanse" society. His methods of killing were stabbing or strangulation with his bare hands or with a rope. After killing his victim, he then mutilated the body, mainly in the genital area. He practiced necrophilia on some of his victims. Ryakhovsky murdered a 78-year-old man in 1993 and cut off his head. He returned the next day and cut off one of the man's legs. He killed a 65-year-old woman and ruptured her abdomen with a pyrotechnical device. He murdered a 16-year-old boy by hanging, disemboweled him, and then cut off his head. Most of his victims were over 40 to 50 years of age, with three being over the age of 60 and only one under the age of 18.

At a crime scene, investigators found a shack with a noose hanging from the ceiling. Believing it was the site of the next murder, they set up an ambush. On April 13, 1993, Ryakhovsky went to the shack and was arrested by police. Despite his size, he offered no resistance. He confessed to the murders and stated that they were not planned but were the result of sudden impulse, except the murders of the three homosexuals in Izmailovsky Park, which were planned. After psychiatrists evaluated Ryakhovsky and found him to be sane, competent to stand trial and fully responsible for his actions, he stopped cooperating and rescinded his confessions.

The "Hippopotamus" was sentenced to death by firing squad in July 1995, but it was not to be. In July 1995, a moratorium was imposed on executions and his sentence of death was commuted to life imprisonment in Solikamsk, Perm Oblast, a maximum-security penal colony. After serving almost 10 years in prison, Sergei Ryakhovsky died on January 21, 2005, from tuberculosis.

Hitch-Hike Murderer aka **Jackson, Anthony J.** (b. 1939) was a spree/serial killer in the state of Massachusetts in the early 1970s who preyed on "targets of opportunity," in this case female hitchhikers.

On September 13, 1972, Kathleen Randall, age 18, was last seen thumbing rides near the campus of Boston University where she had enrolled the preceding week. Her body was found two weeks later in rural New Hampshire. She had been raped and strangled.

Debra Stevens, age 19, was raped and strangled; her body was found within 50 yards of her home in Lynn on September 15, just two days after Kathleen Randall had disappeared.

Ellen Reich, age 19 and a sophomore at Emerson College, was a habitual hitchhiker. Ellen lived in the Back Bay area off campus. She was strangled and stabbed several times. Her body was found nailed inside the closet of an abandoned house in Boston's Roxbury district on November 14.

On November 27, Sandra Ehramjian, age 21, disappeared on her way to a dentist's appointment. Her body was found the following day in a culvert in suburban Brockton. She had been strangled.

Damaris Synge Gillespie, age 22 and an honor student, vanished two days later while hitchhiking to Boston. Her parents received a telephone call demanding a ransom of $25,000, but their daughter was not returned unharmed.

On December 26, Anthony Jackson, age 33, was arrested following a high-speed chase and shootout with Cambridge police. He was charged with assault with a deadly weapon, operating an automobile to endanger, and illegal possession of firearms. On February 3, 1973, he was charged with Damaris Synge Gillespie's murder. The blood-soaked Cadillac he was driving was thought to be the scene of the Gillespie murder. He was sentenced to life in prison.

He was never charged with any of the other murders, but authorities became aware that the co-ed murders stopped when Jackson was arrested.

Ho-Sun, Kang (b. October 10, 1969) is a serial killer in South Korea. His murders were all committed in Ansan, Gyeonggi Province in the years 2006 – 2008. He met most of his victims in karaoke bars or at isolated places such as a bus stop.

Bae, age 45, who worked at a karaoke bar, was murdered on December 14, 2006; Park, age 37, also worked at a karaoke bar, was murdered on December 24; Park, age 52, an office worker, was murdered on January 3, 2007; Kim, age 37, worked at a karaoke bar and was murdered on January 7; Yeon, age 20, a university student, was murdered on January 7; Kim, age 48, a housewife, was murdered on November 9, 2008; an unnamed university student was murdered on December 19.

Ho-Sun's fourth wife and mother-in-law were killed in a house fire in 2005. He is suspected of setting the fire.

He was arrested in 2009 and confessed to 10 murders. He was found guilty of rape, murder, and arson. He was sentenced to death on April 22, 2009, although moratorium of the death sentence in South Korea has been in place since 1997.

More remains have been found and are being identified by DNA testing.

Hobbs, Steven (c. 1977) was arrested in early October 2011 and charged with the murder of two known prostitutes and the assault of four others in Harris County, Texas. Hobbs is married and the father of two teenage sons. He stands 6 ft. 4 in., weighs over 300 pounds, and worked as a security guard.

On September 22, 2011, a Pasadena, Texas, motorcycle policeman pulled over on Red Bluff Road to clock the speed of passing motorists. He discovered the badly decomposed body of Wanda Trombley, age 57, who had disappeared from northeast Houston, and had been missing since July. Her body was found within 30 feet of the entrance to where Hobbs worked as a security guard.

The investigators questioned prostitutes in the area where Trombley's body had been found. A woman*, age 43, told investigators that a very large white man with "reddish-blond hair and thick eyeglasses" had picked her up and was supposed to take her to a motel for sex, but he took her to a desolate location in Houston and sexually assaulted her at gunpoint, handcuffed her arms and feet, and beat her with something like a broom or mop handle. She said that he had on a security uniform. She identified Hobbs when shown several photos of men in security uniforms and said she was "absolutely certain" he was her attacker. Two other prostitutes said that they were also assaulted by a very large white man in a security uniform fitting the same description.

Hobbs was charged with the aggravated assault in June 2011 of Danielle Perfitt, age 28, and the 2010 aggravated assault of Sandra Gunter, age 33.

Investigators had the DNA tested of all the security guards who worked at the business near where Wanda Trombley's body had been found. Steven Hobbs's DNA matched the evidence taken from two murders that had taken place in Harris County, but outside Pasadena. Hobbs was charged with the murder of Patricia Pyatt, age 38, whose body was found on November 19, 2002, beneath a bridge along the Beaumont Highway. He was also charged with sexual assault of another woman* that same year. In addition, he has been charged with the murder of Sarah Sanford, age 48. Her body was found in October 2010 in a wooded area about five miles from Hobbs' home.

Steven Hobbs is currently in the Harris County, Texas, jail awaiting trial scheduled for July 25, 2020.

The identity of this woman is being protected.

Hoch, Johann Otto (1862 – February 23, 1906) is the most famous alias of the German-born suspected serial killer, John Schmidt. He was also a bigamist. He married his first wife, Annie Hock, in Austria in 1881.

They came to New York in 1883. Annie, an invalid, died several years later. The year 1888 was the beginning of Hoch's marathon of marriages and alleged murders.

Over the next 17 years, he married at least 45 women in places like New York, Williamsburg and Buffalo, New York; Chicago and Joliet, Illinois; Milwaukee, Wisconsin; Wheeling, West Virginia; San Francisco, California; Cincinnati and Dayton, Ohio; Norfolk, Virginia; St. Louis, Missouri; Hammond and Argos, Indiana; and Philadelphia, Pennsylvania. Of these marriages, it is alleged that he murdered 19 wives. Those he did not murder were swindled out of their money or property and Hoch disappeared to do the same thing to some other woman.

Finally, in 1905, Johann Otto Hoch was arrested for the murder of Marie Walcker (wife number 40-something) in Chicago on January 12, 1905. He was found guilty and sentenced to death on June 23, 1905. On February 23, 1906, Hoch was hanged.

Hodges, Willie James (b. June 19, 1960) originally from Epps, Alabama, is a serial killer in the states of Florida, Alabama, and Ohio.

On November 26, 2001, Winnie Johnson, age 66, was shot to death in her home during a daytime burglary in

Gainesville, Alabama. On December 19, 2001, Patricia Belanger, age 58, was beaten to death with a hammer in her home in Pensacola, Florida. On March 19, 2003, Laverne Jansen, age 81, was raped and stabbed to death in her home in Price Hill (Cincinnati), Ohio.

Willie James Hodges was arrested in September 2004, in Escambia County, Florida, and charged with the murder of Patricia Belanger. When investigators learned that Hodges was from Sumter County, Alabama, they contacted Sumter County authorities and made the connection to the murder of Winnie Johnson of Gainesville. He was charged with her murder. Cincinnati police, upon learning of Hodges arrest, had evidence to tie Hodges to the murder of Laverne Jansen and he was once again charged.

On September 12, 2009, Willie James Hodges was sentenced to death by Judge Terry Terrell of Escambia County, Florida. Since he was sentenced to death in Florida, authorities in both Ohio and Alabama have said that further trials would be fruitless and a waste of taxpayers' money to try him in those states as well. He is currently on death row at the Union Correctional Institute in Raiford, Florida.

Högel, Niels (b. December 30, 1976) was born in Wilhelmshaven, Lower Saxony, Germany. He worked as a nurse at clinics in Oldenburg and Delmenhorst between 1999 and 2005.

Högel was arrested in 2005 after he was caught in the act of injecting a patient with ajmaline (an antiarrhythmic medication). In 2008, he was convicted of attempted murder and sentenced to 7-1/2 years in prison.

After his trial, a woman came forward and told police that her mother had died at a clinic where Högel worked and was suspicious of her mother's death. This prompted another investigation and Högel then admitted to giving about 90 unauthorized injections; at least 30 of these patients died.

Högel was convicted of six murders and sentenced to life in prison.

The investigation was ongoing and in October 2014, 200 suspicious deaths had been identified. In Germany, Poland, and Turkey, more than 130 bodies were exhumed. On August 28, 2017, police announced that Högel was responsible for the deaths of at least 90 patients, including the six deaths for which he had been convicted. By November 2017, the suspicious deaths had been revised to 106.

In January 2018, Högel was charged with 97 murders. It had been learned that Högel had used five different drugs—ajmaline, sotalol, lidocaine, amiodarone, and calcium chloride. Overdoses of these medications result in cardiac arrhythmia and a drop in blood pressure, causing a rapid decline in already-ill patients.

Högel was found guilty on 85 separate murder charges and not guilty on 15 others. On June 6, 2019, the court in Oldenburg sentenced him to life in prison.

Hofmann, Kuno (b. 1931) was so severely beaten by his alcoholic father as a child that he became deaf and mute. After being imprisoned for nine years for theft, he grew obsessed with the occult sciences and read about Satanism and black magic, particularly the rituals involving necrophilia and vampirism. He was a grave robber, necrophiliac, and serial killer in Germany in the 1970s.

Hofmann, who became known as the *Vampire of Nuremberg*, exhumed at least five bodies, ate some of the decaying flesh, and attempted to have sex with the female corpses. He eventually turned to murder. He shot and killed at least three females, drank their blood, and molested the dead bodies. He was arrested after he was surprised by a witness who caught him in the act of kissing a cadaver. He shot at the witness and missed. The witness gave authorities a description. Hoffman was arrested and through an interpreter, confessed to his crimes. His defense pleaded insanity, but the court decided otherwise and sentenced him to life in prison.

Hog Trail Murderer aka **Conahan, Daniel** (b. May 11, 1954) is a convicted murderer and suspected serial killer of more than a dozen, mostly homosexual men, in Charlotte County, Florida.

Shortly after his birth in Charlotte, North Carolina, Conahan's family moved to Punta Gorda, Florida. By his high school years, he realized he was homosexual, and his parents sent him to a psychiatrist, but that did not change him. He enlisted in the navy in 1977. He was discharged in 1978 for homosexual behavior. He had been stationed at the Great Lakes Naval Station in Illinois, and after his discharge he stayed in Chicago for 13 years before moving back to Punta Gorda in 1993. He enrolled at Charlotte Vocational-Technical Center and in 1995 he graduated at the top of his class as a licensed practical nurse. He then worked at Charlotte Regional Medical Center in Punta Gorda.

On February 1, 1994, a corpse was found in Punta Gorda. The body had been mutilated and had lain outside for several weeks. There were rope burns on the skin and the genitalia had been removed. The body was never identified.

On January 1, 1996, a dog in North Port brought home a male human skull. The decomposing remains were found and reconstructed. It was determined that the genitalia had been cut out, similar to the 1994 murder. This body was also never identified.

On March 7, 1996, another mutilated body of a man was found in North Port. He had been murdered about 10 days earlier. In June 1999 he was identified as John William Melaragno.

On April 17, 1996, another man's skull was found in Charlotte County. In searching the area, the rest of the body was found and later identified as Kenneth Lee Smith. They also found the remains of a second body, a man who had been raped, murdered, and mutilated within the last 24 – 36 hours. He was identified as Richard Allen Montgomery.

In May 1996, during the police investigation, a few people directed police toward Daniel Conahan. One of these was a man who had escaped from Conahan when Conahan's car got stuck while driving down a dirt road. With this information, the police also linked Conahan to a 1994 incident in Fort Myers where Stanley Burden had been tied to a tree and nearly strangled. Burden survived and still had rope burn scars two years later. On July 3, 1996, Daniel Conahan was arrested and taken to Lee County where he was charged with the attempted murder of Stanley Burden. In February 1995, he was charged with Richard Allen Montgomery's murder. While Conahan awaited trial, on May 22, 1997, another skeleton was found in Charlotte County. In March of the following year, the remains were identified, through DNA, as William Charles Patten who had disappeared in 1993.

In August 1999, Conahan waived his right to a jury trial. He was found guilty of the first-degree attempted murder of Stanley Burden and was sentenced to death on December 10. He is currently in prison at Union Correctional Institution in Raiford, Florida.

Since Conahan's sentencing, several more bodies have been discovered in Charlotte County with similarities to his murders: one in 2000, two in 2001, and one in 2002. On March 23, 2007, eight skulls and other skeletal remains were found in a wooded area in Fort Myers. This find was first thought to have a connection with a now-closed funeral home, but the attention was soon again on Conahan. Stanley Burden had been attacked within a mile of the site where the skeletons were found. Forensics estimated that the bodies had been dumped between 1980 and 2000—Conahan lived in Chicago from the late 1970s until 1993. Two were later identified as men who had disappeared in 1995. *Also see Fort Myers Unsolved Murders*

Hohenberger, Robert Carl (b. 1948) was an ex-convict and a California sheriff's deputy. He fled California after abducting and raping four females. He was also linked to the abduction, rape, and murder of five teenagers in Morgan City, Louisiana, in 1978. Two of the victims were dumped in a septic tank. The body of one victim, Leah Rodermund, has never been found.

Hohenberger was located in Tacoma, Washington. During the struggle with a Tacoma police officer in June 1978 his gun went off, killing him. His death leaves a number of unanswered questions; one in particular: "Where is Leah Rodermund?"

Holiday Murderer aka **Schmidt, Ulrich** (c. 1950) so-named since he murdered most of his victims on holidays, raped eight women, killing five of them between 1978 – 1989 in Germany. He was sentenced to life imprisonment.

Holloway Strangler aka **Bromwich, Tony King** (c. 1965) as he was known in Britain, murdered seven women and is believed to have killed four young women on Costa del Sol, in Spain, as the *Costa Killer*. The name on his birth certificate is Anthony "Tony" Bromwich; in Spain he used the name Tony King.

In 2003, Sonia Carabantes, age 17, was beaten into semi-consciousness near Mijas by King, who then drove her to a rural area, sexually assaulted her, and murdered her by strangulation. Five days later, her body was found partially buried under rocks. On November 15, 2005, Tony King was sentenced to 23 years for the murder, eight years for assault, and five years for kidnapping Sonia. He was also ordered to pay £200,000 compensation to her parents.

King is facing a second trial for the murder of Rocio Wanninkhof, age 19, in October 1999 near her home in Fuengirola. Her throat had been cut and she had been stabbed 21 times. Detectives in Spain are talking to King about the disappearance of Maria Fernandez, age 18, near her home in Motril, Granada, in August 2000. Police in Spain believe King committed two other murders, rapes and other violent sexual attacks.

During the investigation of the murders in Spain in 2003, it was found that King's fingerprints matched those of the *Holloway Strangler* in Britain. In 1986, Tony Bromwich, age 19, was sentenced to 10 years for beating and sexually assaulting five women. After he was released, he changed his surname to King and moved to Costa del Sol, Spain, in 1997. Authorities in Britain believe the man using the name of Tony King slipped back into Britain several times after moving to Spain since his fingerprints match those of the *Holloway Strangler.*

British authorities want to question him about the disappearances of Elizabeth Chau, age 19, in 1999; Lola Shenkoya, age 27, who disappeared from Ealing, West London, in 2000; the murder of Sara Marie Cameron, age 23, whose body was found on Good Friday in 2000 about 100 yards from her flat in Earsdon, Northumbria; and the murder of Milly Fowler, age 13, in March 2002, plus several other murders. British authorities will question him after his trial for the murder of Rocio Wanninkhof. Tony King Bromwich was found guilty at his trial in December 2006 and sentenced to 55 years in prison.

Holman, George was a serial arsonist and serial killer in the San Francisco area in 1944. He set 11 fires which claimed at least 22 lives and injured at least 27 other people. He was sentenced to 22 consecutive life terms.

Holmes, H. H. (May 16, 1861 May 7, 1896) was born Herman Webster Mudgett in Gilmanton, New Hampshire, but is better known by his alias of H. H. (Henry Howard) Holmes. He was one of the first documented serial killers

Holmes, H. H.
Mudgett, Herman

in America. He graduated in 1884 from the University of Michigan Medical School under his birth name, Herman Mudgett. During his time at the medical school, he stole bodies from the school laboratory and took out insurance policies on each of them. He then disfigured the corpses, claimed that the people were killed in accidents, and collected the insurance money. He moved to Chicago after graduation to pursue a career in pharmaceuticals, but he made many shady deals in businesses, real estate, and promotions under the name H. H. Holmes. On July 4, 1878, he married Clara Lovering and they had a son, Robert Lovering Mudgett, born February 3, 1880. He married a second time in 1886 to Myrta Belknap without divorcing Clara, and they had a daughter, Lucy Theodate Holmes, born on July 4, 1889. He married his third wife, Georgina Yoke, in 1894, and also had a relationship with the wife of an employee. This woman, Julia Smythe, became one of his victims.

Holmes got a job at Dr. E. S. Holton's drugstore. The doctor was battling cancer and his wife was running the store. Holmes persuaded her to sell him the store. The woman was allowed to live in the apartment above the drug store even after the demise of her husband. After her husband died, Mrs. Holton disappeared. Holmes told everyone that she was visiting relatives in California and had grown to love it so decided to stay there.

Holmes bought the property across from the drug store and built a three-story "castle" there. He opened it as a hotel for the World's Columbian Exposition in 1893. The ground floor was the home of Holmes' relocated drugstore and various other shops. The upper floors contained Holmes' office and was a maze of more than one hundred rooms with no windows, doors that opened up to brick walls, doors that could only open from the outside, stairways that went nowhere, plus a myriad of other strange constructions. His employees, mostly female, were required to take out life insurance policies; Holmes would pay the premiums and he was the beneficiary. Employees and guests were tortured and killed; some by suffocation in an air-tight bank vault; some were asphyxiated in gas-filled soundproof bedrooms; some were poisoned; and some were subjected to unimaginable horrors before their deaths. The bodies were dropped to the basement by means of a chute especially built for this purpose. They were then dissected, stripped of flesh, made into skeleton models, and sold to medical schools. Some were cremated, others placed in lime pits, and some put into one of the two furnaces to be cremated.

After the World's Fair, Holmes left Chicago and moved to Fort Worth where he had "inherited" property from two sisters who were railroad heiresses and had both been engaged to Holmes, and both murdered by Holmes. He began construction of another "castle" but decided that law enforcement in Texas was not for him. He gave up the project and moved around the United States and Canada. During this more-or-less year-long period, the only murders attributed to him were those of a business associate and three of his children. While serving time in the St. Louis jail in 1894 for a horse swindle, he and **Marion Hedgepeth**, a convicted train robber, came up with a plan to defraud an insurance company by taking out insurance on himself (Holmes) and then faking his own death. Hedgepeth was promised $500 for his part in the plan. The plan failed because the insurance company became suspicious and refused to pay.

Holmes then made a plan with his associate, **Benjamin Pitezel**, who would fake his own death so that his wife would collect $10,000 and split it with Holmes and a crooked lawyer Hedgepeth had found. Holmes was to find a cadaver to play the role of Pitezel. Pitezel was to set himself up as an inventor named B. F. Berry and then be killed and disfigured in a lab explosion. Holmes found his cadaver—he murdered Pitezel and convinced Mrs. Pitezel that her husband was alive and well, and hiding in South America. They collected on the insurance policy. Afraid that the Pitezel children might expose him, he also convinced Mrs. Pitezel to allow her three middle children to accompany him on his travels. The bodies of the two girls, Alice and Nellie, were found in Toronto, Ontario, Canada. The boy, Howard Pitezel, was murdered with drugs, his body dismembered and burned in the fireplace of a cottage Holmes had rented in Indianapolis, Indiana. The teeth and bones were discovered in the chimney.

In 1894, police got a tip from Marion Hedgepeth about H. H. Holmes. Holmes had not paid Hedgepeth for his finding of a crooked lawyer. Holmes was tracked down by the Pinkertons and arrested in Boston, Massachusetts, on November 17, 1894. It appeared that Holmes was about to flee the country. A custodian of the "castle" in Chicago told authorities that he was never allowed to clean the upper floors. Police began an investigation and found evidence of torture and murder, and Holmes' convenient way of disposing of corpses. A mysterious fire destroyed the building on August 19, 1895.

Although Holmes was charged with only 27 murders, the numbers are estimated to be between 20 and 100+.

Holmes was convicted of the 27 murders in Chicago, Indianapolis, and Toronto, plus six attempted murders. He was convicted and sentenced to death. Herman Webster Mudgett *aka* H. H. Holmes was hanged on May 7, 1896 at Moyamensing Prison in Philadelphia, Pennsylvania.

Honka, Fritz (July 31, 1935 – October 19, 1998) was a German serial killer who murdered at least four prostitutes in Hamburg's Red Light district between 1970 and 1975.

Being short in stature, 5 ft. 5 in., he preferred women who were shorter. He also preferred them toothless due to his proclivity of preferring oral sex to traditional intercourse.

He murdered four aging prostitutes and, disposal being a problem due to his size and laziness, he kept the bodies in his flat. When neighbors complained of the stench, he doused the apartment with cheap deodorant. He fortified himself with alcohol.

On July 15, 1975, there was a fire at the house and the mummified remains of his victims were found by firemen. Honka was not present at the time but was arrested when he returned from his shift as a night watchman. He told investigators that he had killed the women because they mocked his preference for oral sex. Honka was sentenced to life in prison, but he was released in 1993. He spent his remaining years in a home for the aged under the name Peter Jensen. He died on October 19, 1998, in a hospital in Langenhorn, Hamburg.

Hooijmaijers, Frans (d. August 20, 2006) was a nursing home attendant in the Netherlands whom investigators believe may have killed as many as 264 patients with insulin in the 1960s. He was sentenced to 18 years and was barred from nursing for 23 years. He was released in 1987, and died on August 20, 2006 of natural causes in Kerkrade, Netherlands.

Hopewell, Raymont (b. 1971) had a history of arrests for burglary, theft, drug possession, and other non-violent crimes in Baltimore, Maryland. He was arrested for the August 21, 2005, murder of Carlton Crawford, age 82, a deaf man whom he beat and then strangled to death.

In January 2006, Hopewell was charged with the 1999 rape and murder of Constance Wills, age 61; the November 2002 rape and murder of Sarah Shannon, age 88; the May 2005 murder of Sadie Mack, age 78; and the August 2005 rape and murder of Lydia Wingfield, age 78. DNA evidence linked Hopewell to all five of the murders, plus the rape of a woman who survived his attack. Most of the victims had a connection to Hopewell or his family.

Hopewell was convicted of the murders and sentenced to life in prison. He is serving his sentence at the North Branch Correctional Institute, Cumberland, Maryland.

Hopf, Karl (March 26, 1863 – March 23, 1914) was a pharmacist by trade and a serial killer who murdered his father, his first wife, an illegitimate child, and his daughter, Elsa, in the early 1900s. His motive was collecting the life insurance of his victims. He was named the beneficiary on each policy.

When his third wife became ill soon after their marriage, she went to the Deaconess Hospital in Frankfurt where toxicology specialist, Dr. Rossman, recognized the symptoms of poisoning and consulted with Georg Popp, who was a forensic physician. Hopf's home was searched and the investigators found large amounts of highly concentrated poisons—arsenic and digitalis—plus live cultures of typhoid and cholera bacilli.

Hopf was arrested on April 14, 1913. He was found guilty and sentenced to death on January 19, 1914. In the courtyard of the Royal Prison Pregesheim, Karl Hopf was guillotined on March 23, 1914.

Horton, Wayne Donald (January 26, 1950 – January 3, 2010) was a native of Las Vegas who possessed an explosive temper and a penchant for pulling the trigger. He murdered four people between 1972 and 1976.

On February 4, 1973, the skeletal remains and skull of a "Jane Doe" were found in the desert. She had been picked up by Wayne Horton at a liquor store in 1972, beaten to death with a jack handle, and dumped where she was found.

She had objected to Wayne smoking marijuana while he was driving.

On May 12, 1975, Horton tried to rob Edward Buccieri, age 52, a shift boss at Caesar's Palace. Horton shot him in the head five times because he had called Horton "dirty names."

In November 1975 Horton tried to rob William Tinnell, a Las Vegas cab driver, who was on his knees begging for mercy when Horton also shot him five times in the head.

Horton was in jail in Las Vegas awaiting trial on charges of rape, robbery, and kidnapping, when he and two cellmates fatally stabbed Calvin Brinson, age 19. On June 5, 1976, Wayne Donald Horton pleaded guilty to the murders of Buccieri and Tinnell. He was sentenced to two consecutive terms of life imprisonment with the possibility of parole. He made the claim that there were several more people he was going to kill if he could.

On August 3, 1976, he pleaded guilty to the murders of Calvin Brinson and the "Jane Doe" found in the desert. He was sentenced to two more life sentences without the possibility of parole. He was transferred to San Quentin Prison in San Quentin, California, so he would be permanently out of touch with the inmates he had vowed to murder. Horton died in prison on January 3, 2010, of natural causes.

Howell, William Devin

Howell, William Devin (b. February 11, 1970) is currently in prison at Garner Correctional Institution in Newtown, Connecticut, for the murder of Nilsa Arizmendi, age 33, who was last seen alive on July 25, 2003, climbing into Howell's van and whose body has never been found. He is now a suspect in the murders of seven women whose bodies were found buried behind the Hartford Road Plaza mall. Three of the victims were found in 2007 and have been identified as Diane Cusack, age 53, of New Britain was out of contact with her family and was never reported missing. Authorities believe she disappeared in 2003.

Joyvaline Martinez, age 23, was last seen in October 2003. She was unemployed and reportedly living with her mother.

Mary Jane Menard, age 40, of New Britain was a substance abuse counselor and also disappeared in October 2003.

Authorities have returned to the site annually, but no more bodies had been found until a specially trained dog from the FBI helped locate the new victims. Testing on the remains determined they were the remains of four individuals. The only remains to be identified were those of Melanie Ruth Camilini, age 29, of Seymour was last seen in Waterbury in the company of two men. Her mother reported her missing in April 2003.

On September 8, 2017, Howell pleaded guilty to the six remaining murder charges. Howell is also a suspect in the Route 8 murders. *See article "The Route 8 Killer."*

True crime author Anne K. Howard has penned a biographical true crime novel about him, entitled *His Garden: Conversations with a Serial Killer.*

Hoyt, Waneta Ethel (May 13, 1946 – August 13, 1998) was a serial killer of defenseless babies. Between 1965 and 1971, only one of the babies born to Waneta and her husband, Tim Hoyt, lived past the age of two years and three months. Three of them were murdered before they were three months old.

Waneta dropped out of high school in the 10th grade to marry Tim Hoyt. On October 11, 1964, their first son, Eric, was born. At the age of three months and nine days, he died on January 26, 1965. James was born on May 31, 1966 and died on September 26, 1968 at the age of two years, three months and 26 days. Julie was born on July 19, 1968 and died on September 5, 1968 less than two months old, one month and 17 days. Molly was born on March 18, 1970 and at the age of two months and 19 days, she died on June 5, 1970. Noah born on May 9, 1971, the last of the Hoyt children, was just two months and 19 days old when he died on July 18, 1971. Their deaths were attributed to SIDS (sudden infant death syndrome).

Molly and Noah were the subjects of SIDS pediatric research conducted by Dr. Alfred Steinschneider. Waneta confessed in 1994 that she had smothered the babies to quiet their crying. She recanted this confession during her trial. She was convicted and sentenced to 75 years. Waneta Hoyt died of pancreatic cancer on August 13, 1998, at Bedford Hill Correctional Facility for Women in Bedford Hills, New York.

Hu Wanlin (b. December 12, 1949) may be one of the most prolific medical serial killers in the world. He was arrested January 18, 1999 in Shangqiu, Henan Province, China, on suspicion of killing 146 people.

Hu Wanlin had been imprisoned in the 1980s and while in prison opened a medical practice. Upon his release he continued to practice medicine. His "treatments" were believed by investigators to have resulted in the deaths of at least 146 people. The treatments contained high amounts of sodium sulphate (sodium salt of sulfuric acid), which is poisonous in large doses.

On October 1, 2000, Hu Wanlin was convicted of practicing medicine without a license and sentenced to 15 years in prison, suspension of voting rights for five years and a fine of 150,000 Yuan (about $25,000 US). He was released in 2014 and media soon reported that he was responsible for the death of a 22-year-old student attending one of his "health retreats." He has not been charged with this murder as of this writing.

Huang Yong (November 18, 1974 – December 26, 2003) was born in Henan Province China. He became a serial killer because, "I've always wanted to be an assassin since I was a kid, but I never had the chance."

In 2000, Huang began to lure boys to his house by offering to recommend them for good well-paying jobs, offering to pay for their schooling, or to take them on sightseeing trips. The plan worked. He lured at least 17 boys to his apartment where he drugged, raped, and strangled them with a rope between September 2001 and 2003.

In November 2003, Zhang Liang, age 16, went to the police and told them that Huang had invited him to his apartment and offered him a job, but when he got there Huang tried to strangle him and he went unconscious three times. When he regained consciousness, Huang told him, "I've killed at least 25 people. You're number 26." Liang managed to escape. The police did not believe him at first, but he finally convinced them that the story was true. They went to Huang's apartment and arrested him.

Huang Yong was convicted of 17 murders and sentenced to death on December 9, 2003. On December 26, 2003, he was executed by firing squad.

Hughes, John Matthew (b. December 6, 1975) is currently serving a life sentence for the robbery and murder in August 2008 of David Durben of Zanesville, Ohio, who was stabbed to death. After killing Durben, he stole a 9mm handgun and other weapons. The 9mm linked him to the murder of a trucker, Valentin Kirilchuk, age 39, of Springfield, Missouri, at a rest area on I-29 near Dearborn, Missouri on September 8, 2008. Kirilchuk was approached by **Dana K. Tutor**, Hughes' accomplice, and told him she needed $100. Kirilchuk went into the rest area's building where Hughes forced him at gunpoint into the men's bathroom. Hughes attempted to rob Kirilchuk, but Kirilchuk fought back. Hughes shot Kirilchuk once in the head with the 9mm and took Kirilchuk's cell phone and wallet containing about $200. He and Dana fled the area in a white 2003 Chevrolet Trailblazer and were later arrested in York County, Nebraska. Hughes was charged with driving while intoxicated. During the arrest, it was discovered the state of Ohio had a warrant for Hughes' arrest. He was extradited back to Ohio and convicted of the 2008 murder of David Durben.

John Hughes was found guilty of first-degree murder and first-degree robbery and sentenced to life in prison. He is incarcerated at the Southern Ohio Correctional Facility in Lucasville, Ohio. Dana Tutor was charged with second-degree murder and second-degree robbery. She is currently serving time in Mississippi on two counts of forgery.

Hughes, Michael Hubert (b. 1956) is a serial killer who murdered six women and one girl in Los Angeles County, California in the late 1980s and early 1990s.

On January 22, 1986, Yvonne Coleman, age 15, was murdered and her body found in a park in Inglewood. On May 26, 1986, the body of Verna Williams, age 36, was found in a stairwell. Deborah Jackson aka Harriet McKinley, age 30, was found on December 1, 1987. The body of Theresa Ballard, age 26, was found in Jesse Owens County Park in Los Angeles on September 23, 1992.

Brenda Bradley, age 38 and a niece of former Los Angeles mayor Tom Bradley, was found in an alley in Culver City on October 5, 1992. On June 25, 1993, the body of Deborah Jackson, age 32, was found. The body of Terri Myles, age 33, was found in an alley in Culver City on November 8, 1993. Jamille Harrington aka Jamie Harrington, age 29, was found in an alley in Culver City on November 14,

1993. Authorities believe they are not the only victims of this serial killer.

Michael Hughes, a security guard, was arrested in December 1993 in Culver City and charged with the murders of Teresa Ballard, Brenda Bradley, Terri Myles, and Jamie Harrington. He was convicted of these murders and sentenced to life without the possibility of parole.

He was also charged with sexually assaulting and the strangulation deaths of Yvonne Coleman, Verna Williams, and Deborah Jackson on July 3, 2008. He was convicted of these murders and was sentenced to death in June 2012. He is currently on death row at San Quentin State Prison.

Huntsman, Megan (b. 1975) is a mother in Utah who has pleaded guilty to murdering six of her newborn babies between the years 1996 – 2006, in Pleasant Grove, Utah County, Utah.

Megan and her husband, Darren West, were separated. West was cleaning out the garage when he discovered the body of what appeared to be a newborn infant. He called police, who got a search warrant and discovered the bodies of six more newborns in boxes in the garage, each in a plastic bag and wrapped either in a towel or a shirt. West, who had recently been released from prison, is believed to be the father of all of the babies.

Megan Huntsman was arrested on April 13, 2014, and charged with the suffocation or strangulation deaths of only six of the babies, because she told them that one baby had not been alive when born. She was held on $6 million bond, $1 million for each baby. She pleaded guilty on February 12, 2015 and in April, Megan Huntsman was sentenced to life in prison. She is currently serving her sentence at the Utah State Prison, Timpanogos, Utah. She will be eligible for parole in 2064, when she will be 89 years old.

Husereau, Philip (d. February 18, 1988) was a sadomasicist who murdered five girlfriends in 1983-84 in Nevada and New York. The method of murder was strangulation and beating. On February 18, 1988, he died during autoerotic asphyxia. Husereau's sister told police the day following his death how he had killed his last five girlfriends.

Huskey, Thomas Dee aka *Zoo Man* (b. August 20, 1960) is a convicted rapist who is suspected by investigators of being a serial killer in the state of Tennessee. He was nicknamed *Zoo Man* by local prostitutes because he liked to have sex by the Knoxville Zoo, where he was once an elephant trainer. He is believed to have strangled to death Patricia Rose Anderson, Patricia Ann Johnson, Darlene Smith, and Susan East Stone during the years 1991 and 1992. He went on trial for these murders, but it was declared a mistrial.

In 1996 Huskey was convicted of four counts of rape involving four other women and sentenced to 66 years. He is currently serving his sentence at South Central Correctional Center at Clifton, Tennessee

Hutchinson, Lewis (1733 – March 16, 1773) was born in Scotland and moved to Jamaica in the 1760s to manage an estate named Edinburgh Castle. He had legal possession of the estate, although how he obtained it is not known. It is thought that he studied medicine while in Scotland.

Travelers began to disappear shortly after Hutchinson took possession of the estate. Edinburgh Castle was the only inhabited area for miles in any direction and frequently travelers would stop and rest at the estate. Hutchinson murdered for sport and he did not care who or what the travelers' nationality, shape, color of skin, size, religion, sex, income, or reason for traveling through this area.

It was said that he would shoot lone travelers, feed on their flow of blood, and dismember them. He was known to invite guests to his castle and entertain them before murdering them. His slaves would then toss the remains into a cotton tree or a sinkhole. The sinkhole became known at Hutchinson's Hole.

His slaves told tales of their terrible treatment and the gruesome details of the murders. He was feared by all and was allowed to roam free until he shot John Calendar, a British soldier, when he tried to capture Hutchinson. After he shot Calendar, Hutchinson went to Old Harbour and boarded a ship. The Royal Navy caught him before he could escape.

While searching his home, more than 43 watches and a large amount of clothing were found. Lewis Hutchinson was tried and found guilty of many murders, although the exact number is not known. He was hanged in Spanish Town Square on March 16, 1773.

During the trial, Hutchinson's slaves told that he had two accomplices in some of the murders, **James Walker** and **Roger Maddix**. They were later convicted and sentenced to death for helping in the murder of William Lickley, a farmer, and Timothy Cronin, the schoolmaster.

Huttenkloas aka **Annink, Klaas** (June 18, 1710 – September 13, 1775) was a serial killer in Twenthe, Netherlands. It was reported that his wife, **Aarne Spanjers**, and son, **Jannes**, helped in the robberies and murders. They were suspected of murdering numerous people.

In 1774, a merchant from Hanover had a family member who disappeared and was later found murdered. Annink was arrested, along with his wife. They were convicted, sentenced to death, and executed on September 13, 1775.

Hyatt, Terry Alvin (b. March 28, 1957) was a habitual criminal since he was first arrested in 1976. By mid-April 1979, he had graduated to murder.

On April 14, 1979, Harriett Delaney Simmons left her job on Capital Boulevard in Raleigh, North Carolina, around 1:00 a.m. to drive to Nashville, Tennessee, to visit a friend. She told her children she would not arrive in Nashville until 7:00 or 8:00 a.m. When she had not called by 10:30 a.m., they phoned the residence of their mother's friend in Nashville and were told that Harriett not yet arrived. The family called the police and informed them that their mother was missing.

When there had been no news concerning Simmons disappearance, on April 20, Ronald Wayne Dement, a good friend of the family, decided to drive along the route that Harriett Simmons would have taken. He found Harriett's car at a rest stop on Interstate 40, west of Statesville. Her suitcase and thermos were still in the car, but her keys and purse were missing. A search was made of the surrounding area but nothing more was found. Almost a year later, a skull and skeleton were found in a wooded area near the Pisgah National Forest on Highway 151 near Chandler in Western North Carolina. A search of the surrounding area produced more bones, clothing, jewelry, a set of car keys, and other personal effects that were proven to belong to Simmons. Dental records were used to identify the remains as those of Harriett Simmons. The autopsy revealed that she had suffered multiple stab wounds on the left side of the chest, which would have punctured the heart, lungs, and other organs.

On August 25, 1979, Dean and Sue Helms were looking out the window admiring the view of the French Broad River when they saw what appeared to be a body lying in their driveway. It was indeed a body and was identified as Betty Sue McConnell. She had telephoned her mother that after work she was going to meet a friend at the bowling alley in

Asheville. When found, she was soaking wet, her chest was covered with blood, her skin very light, and she was gasping for breath. She was able to tell the Helmses, that, "I was stabbed and thrown into the river," and that, "I was picked up at work by two men." A search was made of the area between the Helmses' home and the river approximately 50 feet away. Betty's sunglasses were found on the bank of the river, along with an area of bloodstains in the grass and a trail of blood leading from the river to the Helmses' driveway. Her car was found in the river with a scrape on the driver's side and that window rolled down. The autopsy showed that she had received five stab wounds on the left chest and the wound below the collarbone went through the upper lobe of the lung, perforating the pulmonary artery, causing her death. She also had a cloudy material in the vaginal vault which later proved to be semen.

On August 13, 1998, Jerry Harmon went to the Buncombe County Sheriff's Department to talk to Captain Pat Hefner. Harmon, who was known for being a heavy drinker, and was then drunk, told Captain Hefner and other officers the details of the rape and murder of Betty Sue McConnell. He had been in the truck with Hyatt when they saw McConnell at a traffic light and Hyatt made an obscene gesture to her. When the light changed, she took off and Hyatt positioned his truck directly behind the woman's car and drove into the back of McConnell's car, forcing her off the road. Hyatt ran to the car, opened the door, and forced the woman into the passenger seat. He told Harmon to follow him. They pulled off the road in an isolated area, Hyatt told the woman that they were going to have sex with her and then let her go. Hyatt raped the woman and then took the woman down to the river, stabbed her, and threw her into the river. He told Harmon what he had done. They left the area in the two vehicles and drove to another location where Hyatt drove McConnell's car into the river and left. After telling of the murder, Harmon dropped a bombshell. He told Hefner and the others that Dean Helms knew all about the McConnell murder.

In October 1998, Agent R. Timothy Shook, of the state Bureau of Investigation, and Detective Anne Benjamin, of the Buncombe County Sheriff's Department, went to Helms to talk with him. He told the officers that he was glad to see them and he had been praying about it. He told the two officers that in 1979 he and Hyatt were driving from Greensboro to Asheville when they kidnapped a woman from a rest area. She was having car troubles and they offered to drive her to a place to get the part for her car. She willingly got into their van and they drove up to a dirt road outside of Chandler, stopped on the dirt road, and Hyatt raped the woman. Hyatt then took the woman into the woods and Helms remained in the van. He heard the woman screaming. About 30 minutes later, Hyatt arrived back at the van and Helms noticed the blood on Hyatt's shirt. He told Helms that the woman had taken off walking. Agent Shook believed that this was very similar to the Harriet Simmons case.

There was also the murder of Jessi Ann Jones who disappeared in 1987. After finishing her job at Harris Teeter Supermarket on July 8, 1987, she was waiting for her boyfriend to pick her up. She disappeared on that night. Two days later her naked body was found about a mile away with her throat cut.

Terry Alvin Hyatt was arrested in May 1999 and charged with first-degree kidnapping, robbery with a dangerous weapon, first-degree rape, and first-degree murder in the cases of Harriett Delaney Simmons and Betty Sue McConnell. He pleaded guilty and was sentenced to death.

In 2004, Hyatt was tried for Jessi Anne Jones' murder. He was convicted and sentenced to life in prison. He appealed for a new hearing and on July 21, 2009, his request was denied.

He is currently housed on death row at Central Prison, Raleigh, North Carolina.

I-5 Killer aka **Woodfield, Randall Brent** (b. December 26, 1950) was a professional football player for the Green Bay Packers in 1974 who was cut from the team after several arrests for indecent exposure. Woodfield was also a serial killer who may have murdered as many as 44 people during the period between October 9, 1980 and February 15, 1981 in Washington, Oregon, and California.

Born into an upper-middle-class family, Woodfield began displaying sexually dysfunctional behavior during junior high school, especially exposing himself. He was arrested during his high school years for indecent exposure, and his parents forced him to attend therapy, his football coaches concealed the incident, and he continued to play football for the school. When he graduated high school, his juvenile criminal record was expunged.

After being cut from the Green Bay Packers football team, he began a series of robberies and sexual assaults at knifepoint in Portland, Oregon. During 1980 and 1981, Woodfield committed murders down the coast in Washington, Oregon, and California.

The first known murder was on October 9, 1980, of Cherie Ayers, a woman he had known since grade school. Woodfield raped and murdered her in her apartment on SW Ninth Place in downtown Portland. Her body was discovered by her fiancé on October 11. Knowing that Woodfield and Cherie had kept in touch by letters, Ayers family told authorities that they should check out Randy Woodfield. He was interviewed but refused to take a polygraph test.

On November 27, 1980, Woodfield went to the north Portland home of Darcey Renee Fix whom he had known in college and who was the girlfriend of Douglas Keith Altig, whom he also had known from college. Doug was at the apartment with Darcey. When they were found, they were both bound and had been shot execution-style. Darcey's 32-caliber revolver was missing. Due to Woodfield's acquaintance with Darcey, Woodfield was interviewed but police did not have any concrete evidence against him, so he was free to go.

Woodfield continued his trips on I-5 committing robberies and murders as he traveled—on January 8, he robbed the Vancouver, Washington, gas station that he had robbed in December, plus he made the female attendant expose her breasts; January 11, he robbed a market in Eugene, Oregon; January 12, he shot and wounded a female clerk at a grocery in Sutherlin, Oregon; January 14, he invaded a home and forced the two girls to take off all of their clothes and then sexually assaulted them; January 18, he entered an office building in Salem, Oregon, sexually assaulted and murdered Shari Hull, sexually assaulted Beth Wilmot and attempted to murder her, but failed.

During the following week, the killer committed robberies in Eugene, Medford, and Grants Pass, Oregon. In Grants Pass, Woodfield assaulted a customer and a clerk.

In Mountain Gate, California, the bodies of Donna Eckard and her daughter, age 14, were found in their home on February 3, 1981. Both had been shot several times in the head and sodomized.

Also on February 3, in Redding, California, a female clerk was kidnapped from the store where she worked. She was raped and sodomized. The next day, Woodfield committed the exact same crimes in Yreka, California, as well as robbing a motel in Ashland, Oregon that night.

On February 9, the killer held up a fabric store and then sexually molested the clerk and her customer in Corvallis, Oregon. Robberies in Vancouver, Olympia, and Bellevue, Washington were committed by a man fitting the description of the *I-5 Killer/Bandit*. He also raped three women at the Olympia and Bellevue sites.

In celebration of Valentine's Day, Woodfield planned to be in Portland, Oregon so he made plans to have a party at the downtown Marriott Hotel and invited friends and acquaintances from college. No guests showed up, so Woodfield drove to the home of Julie Reitz, age 18, in Beaverton, Oregon. Woodfield knew her from his time working as a bouncer at a bar in Portland named The Faucet. He arrived at her place about 2:00 a.m. on the morning of February 5. About 4:00 a.m. he raped Julie and then he shot her in the head, killing her.

By late February, investigators were focused on Woodfield being their killer. He had committed crimes in Eugene on February 18 and 21, and an assault in Corvallis on February 25.

Woodfield was picked up and taken to the police department in Salem, Oregon, for questioning. He had been positively identified by Lisa Garcia in a photo lineup. They obtained a search warrant for Woodfield's apartment in Springfield, Oregon. The investigators found a spent .32 shell casing inside a racquetball bag and tape that matched the tape used to bind his victims.

On March 7, 1981, Woodfield was arrested after being positively identified by several of the victims of the I-5 Killer/Bandit. On March 16, he was indicted for murder, rape, sodomy, attempted kidnapping, armed robbery, and illegal possession of firearms.

In the summer of 1981, Woodfield was tried first in Salem for the murder of Shari Hull, plus charges of sodomy and the attempted murder of Beth Wilmot who testified against Woodfield in the trial. The prosecutor was Chris Van Dyke, son of actor Dick Van Dyke. The jury found him guilty on all charges and he was sentenced to life in prison plus 90 years.

In October 1981, Woodfield was tried in Benton County, Washington for charges of sodomy and illegal possession of weapons. He was found guilty and sentenced to an additional 35 years. He is serving his sentence at the Oregon State Penitentiary in Salem, Oregon.

Although Woodfield has been connected to as many as 44 homicides by investigators, he has not been tried for any of the other charges due to the prosecution not having enough evidence to convict him.

The *I-5 Strangler* aka **Kibbe, Roger Reece** (b. May 21, 1939) was a serial killer who found his victims along the freeways in the area of Sacramento, California. Kibbe's modus operandi was to abduct his victims, tie them up, silence them with duct tape, cut off their clothes, and then rape and strangle them to death. He also cut off most of the victims' hair to remove the duct tape.

Lora Heedick, age 20, a known prostitute, was last seen by her boyfriend on April 21, 1986, getting into a car with a white man in his 50s. Her body was found on September 6, 1986, near Highway 12 and I-5 near the city of Lodi. Barbara Ann Scott, age 29, was kidnapped in Pittsburg on July 3, 1986. She was raped, murdered, and dumped at Lone Tree Golf Course in Contra Costa County. Stephanie Brown, age 19, went to pick up her roommate who needed a ride home from a bar, but she took a wrong turn and got on I-5. Her car was found at Hood Franklin Road. Her body was found July 15, 1986 off Highway 12. In 2003, DNA linked her murder to Kibbe.

Charmaine Sabrah, age 26, was last seen on August 17, 1986, when her car broke down on I-5 and she was picked up by a man in a car offering to help. Also on August 17, Katherine Kelly Quinones, age 25, was abducted near Thornton. Darcie Frankenpohl, age 17, ran away from her Seattle home and was working as a prostitute when she was abducted in West Sacramento. Her body was found near Echo Summit in Eldorado County.

Lou Ellen Burleigh, age 21, was murdered on September 11, 1977. Her body was found in June 2011, with Kibbe's help.

On May 10, 1991, Roger Kibbe was sentenced to 25 years to life for the murder of Darcie Frankenpohl. On November 5, 2009, he was sentenced to an additional six life sentences for the murders of Lou Ellen Burleigh, Lora Heedick, Barbara Ann Scott, Stephanie Brown, Charmaine Sabrah, and Katherine Kelly Quinones. He is currently housed at the Pleasant Valley State Prison in Coalinga, California.

Illinois Cannibal Murders/The Chicago Rippers was a group of at least four serial killers—**Gecht, Robin** (b. November 30, 1953), **Kokoraleis, Andrew** (c. 1961 – March 17, 1999), **Kokoraleis, Tommy** (b. July 10, 1960), and **Spreitzer, Edward** (b. January 5, 1961). The killings were originally called *Jack the Ripper* killings by the media.

On May 23, 1981, Linda Sutton, age 28, was kidnapped from Elmhurst, a Chicago suburb. Her mutilated body was found 10 days later in a field in Villa Park. Her left breast was missing.

Almost a year passed before another young woman disappeared. On May 15, 1982, Lorraine Borowski, age 21, was supposed to open the real estate office where she worked. When other employees arrived, they found the office locked. Lorraine's shoes and contents from her purse were strewn about outside the door. Five months passed before her remains were found in a cemetery south of Villa Park on October 10.

On May 29, Shui Mak was reported missing from Hanover Park. Her mutilated body was recovered at Barrington on September 30.

On June 13, Angel York, a prostitute, was picked up by a "John" driving a van. She was handcuffed and one of her breasts was slashed before she was dumped, still alive, on a roadside. Her description of her attacker led the police nowhere.

On August 28, Sandra Delaware, a teenage prostitute, was found stabbed and strangled to death on the banks of the Chicago River. Her left breast had been almost completely severed.

Another woman was found in a Chicago alley in almost identical condition on September 8. She was identified as Rose Davis, age 31.

On September 22, Carole Pappas, wife of Chicago Cubs pitcher Milt Pappas, disappeared from a department store in Wheaton, Illinois. She was gone for almost three years before her body was found in a car in a pond south of Wheaton on August 9, 1987.

On October 6, Beverly Washington, a 20-year-old prostitute, was found nude and savaged beside a railroad track in Chicago. Her left breast had been severed and the right was deeply slashed, but she was still alive and emergency treatment saved her life. Hours later, drug dealer Rafael Torado was killed, and a male companion was wounded when a van cruised by and riddled the phone booth they were using with shots from a rifle.

On October 20, Robin Gecht, age 18, was arrested and charged with the assault on Beverly Washington. He was also suspected of slashing prostitute Cynthia Smith. Gecht was believed to be involved in the *Ripper* killings, but authorities had no proof at that time. Gecht made bail on October 26.

Police learned that Gecht was one of four men who had rented rooms at a motel in Villa Park several months before Linda Sutton was murdered nearby. The manager remembered them and said that they had been some kind of cultists. The Kokoraleis brothers left a forwarding address when they left. Police found Tommy Kokoraleis at home. They did not like his answers to their questions and took him "downtown." He failed a polygraph test, cracked under interrogation, and admitted to the torture of women with knives and ice picks in Gecht's upstairs bedroom. The women were also gang-raped and then sacrificed to Satan by the members of the tiny cult; namely, Gecht, the Kokoraleis brothers, and Spreitzer. The breasts were severed with a thin-wire garrote and each member took "communion" by eating a piece of it before the remainder was consigned to Gecht's trophy box. Police had heard enough.

Police were armed with search warrants and arrest warrants and on November 5, Robin Gecht, Ed Spreitzer, Tommy Kokoraleis, and Andrew Kokoraleis were arrested and jailed, each under a $1 million bond. Authorities speculated that the *Chicago Rippers* had murdered at least 18 women during the 18-month rampage.

In late 1983, Robin Gecht confessed to the attack on Beverly Washington and was sentenced to 120 years. He is currently serving his sentence at Menard Correctional Center at Chester, Illinois.

On April 2, 1984, Ed Spreitzer pleaded guilty to four counts of murder (Rose Davis, Sandra Delaware, Shui Mak, and Rafael Torado) and was sentenced to life on each count. On March 20, 1986, he was convicted of the murder of Linda Sutton and was sentenced to death. Spreitzer is currently at Stateville Correctional Center at Joliet, Illinois.

On September 7, 1984, Tommy Kokoraleis was sentenced to life imprisonment for the murder of Lorraine Borowski. He was released from prison on March 26, 2019.

On February 11, 1985, Andrew Kokoraleis received the death sentence for the murder of Rose Davis. In 1999, Governor George Ryan suspended all Illinois executions with one exception. Andrew Kokoraleis was executed by lethal injection on March 17, 1999. He was the last person to be executed in the state of Illinois.

Incubus aka **Adams, Jeff** is a serial killer in San Gabriel, California. In 1988, he tortured three wealthy housewives to death. He raped them, put chopsticks in their ears and objects in their vagina and anus, and packed their mouth and throat with dog feces causing them to suffocate. All three of the women were married to rich men. They received letters describing exactly how they would be murdered, and the letters were signed "Incubus".

Adams was found guilty and sentenced to life.

India's Youngest Serial Killer aka **Sada, Amarjeet** (b. 1998) was only eight years old when he committed his first murder. He may be the youngest serial killer in the world. Amardeep was born to an impoverished family in Begusaray, Bihar, India. They later lived in Musahri, where his father was a laborer at Manavpur.

He murdered his sister who was only eight months old and a cousin who was about six months old in 2006. These two murders were not reported to the police because it was considered "a family matter."

A neighbor's child named Khushboo was left at the village primary school while her mother did her household chores. When the mother returned, the baby was gone. The villagers confronted Amardeep and he allegedly confessed to the murder saying, "I killed her by beating her with a brick." He led them to the place where he had attempted to bury her in a shallow grave. He then confessed to the murders of his sister and cousin.

He was arrested and questioned. He stated that he took the children to the fields and hit them with a stone and killed them. He smiled a lot while questioned and asked for biscuits. He was charged with murder.

Young Sada was examined by psychiatrists. Some said that he was a sadist who found joy in hurting others. One stated that he suffered from a "conduct disorder." Another explained that, "He did not know what is right and what is wrong." He was placed in a juvenile home without any contact with other children. It has since been reported that his condition can be controlled by medication and that he is living "free" under an assumed name.

Industrial Maniac aka **Trijueiro, Marcos Antunes** (b. May 29, 1978) was married three times and fathered five children. He is accused of raping and murdering at least five women in the years 2009-10 in the metropolitan area of Bel Horizonte, Brazil.

All of his victims had some of the same physical description—thin, with a dark complexion and long dark hair. Each of them had their cell phones taken by the killer. This was a mistake because he was traced to the victims by their cell phones.

The half-naked body of Ana Carolina Assuncao, age 25, was found on April 16, 2009 in the back of her car in the Joao Pinheiro neighborhood with her son, age 1, asleep in her lap. Maria Helena Lopes Aguiar, age 48, was murdered in September in the California neighborhood of Bel Horizonte, Brazil. Edna Cordeiro, age 35, was found murdered in November on a road in Nova Lima. Trijueiro is also suspected by police of murdering Natalia Cristina de Almeida Paiva, age 27, a student at the university, who went missing in October 2009. She was buried in the Public Cemetery of Ribeirao das Neves.

When arrested in the Linda neighborhood, Trijueiro had the cell phones of four of his victims, and his wife had the fifth one.

Marcos Antunes Trijueiro was sentenced to 30 years, the maximum time allowable in Brazil.

Infante Jimenez, Rudolph (b. 1963) and **Villeda, Anna Maria Ruiz** (b. 1971) lured at least eight young women with employment offers, then sexually molested and murdered them in 1991 in Matamoros, Mexico. They were arrested on October 21, 1991, convicted in 1993, and each given a sentence of 40 years.

Ingle, Phillip Lee (August 7, 1961 – September 22, 1995) murdered two couples in Rutherford County and Gaston County, North Carolina, in 1991.

On the night of July 28, 1991, Ingle went to the home of Fred Davis, age 68, and his wife, Margaret, age 67. He had once rented a trailer from them and told others that he liked them. But this night he entered their home uninvited and beat both of them to death with an ax handle.

He climbed through a bedroom window at the home of E.Z. Willis, age 70, and his wife, Sarah, age 67, about the middle of September. He beat them to death with a tire iron.

There seemed to be no motive. Ingle did not murder these people to rob them, or hold them hostage, or for revenge, or to commit a sex crime. He admitted these murders to a friend and told him that he enjoyed watching people die in agony. He was found guilty of first-degree murder and sentenced to death by the court on February 19, 1993. After he was sent to prison, he told a counselor that he thought the victims were devils with red eyes, horns, and tails, and he was doing God's work. On September 22, 1995, as he was being taken to the death chamber to be executed by lethal injection at Central Prison, he shouted, "I'm going to heaven!"

Inmon, William N. (b. June 1, 1988) walked into the police station in Springerville, Arizona, in 2009 and told the police chief that cops from out of town were in his jurisdiction. The other police from nearby St. Johns were investigating the murder of Ricky Flores, age 16, of St. Johns. Within hours, Inmon had confessed to the vigilante killings of three, including the murder of Flores and about his plans to kill more "undesirables." He said that he killed Flores because he wanted to get Flores off drugs but was not able to. He also admitted to shooting and killing William "Stoney" McCarragher, age 72, because Inmon said that McCarragher had touched him inappropriately in 2007. He told authorities that he had also shot and killed Daniel Achten, age 60, because Achten had shot his dog and generally mistreated people.

Inmon was charged with three counts of murder. Four others have been arrested for their parts in the three murders. In a plea agreement, Inmon pleaded guilty and was sentenced to 21 years for each of the three murders which are to run concurrently, and to one year and six months for abandon/conceal of a dead body on each charge and are to run consecutively.

Insurance Killer aka **Basson, Pierre Corneille Faculys** (c. 1880 – January 22, 1906) is known as South Africa's first serial killer. As a young boy, Basson began torturing and killing animals. In 1892, he viciously attacked another boy with a knife. He had no more known incidents until shortly after his father's death, when he took out a life insurance policy on his younger brother, Jasper. On February 3, 1903, he invited Jasper to go fishing with him. As he was returning home alone, he told several other fishermen on their way to the beach that his brother had been swept off the rocks by a huge wave and he was unable to save him. Jasper's body was never found. The insurance company refused to pay on Jasper's policy, so Pierre Basson cooked up other insurance schemes, murdered the people insured, and collected on the policies. His scheme was to give people loans on the condition that they take out an insurance policy and name him as the beneficiary to insure that he would get his money back even if "something should happen to them.» He also was eventually paid on his brother's policy after filing suit against the insurance company. It is believed he killed eight or nine people. Pierre Basson committed suicide on January 22, 1906, when police were closing in on him after getting some very good leads.

Interstate Killer/Highway Killer aka **Eyler, Larry William** (December 21, 1952 – March 6, 1994) was born to an alcoholic father, George Eyler, and Shirley Kennedy Eyler in Crawfordsville, Indiana. The father was known to physically and emotionally abuse his wife and children. His parents separated when Larry was about two and his mother struggled to support the family of four children. She often worked two jobs and the children with left with family, friends, babysitters, and foster care. Larry, the youngest of the four children, was bullied in school and often his sister, Theresa, confronted the bullies. Larry began to have erratic behavior and his mother placed him in a home for troublesome boys. There he was given a psychological evaluation which revealed him to be of average intelligence, suffering from severe insecurity, and having extreme fear of separation and abandonment. He was placed in a boys' home in Fort Wayne for a period of six months, then returned to his mother. As he grew into puberty, he realized he was homosexual and struggled with self-hatred over his sexual feelings. He dated girls occasionally, but none became physical. He failed to graduate from high school and was a house painter by trade in Indianapolis, Indiana. He later earned his General Educational Development certificate. He was good looking, had a hot temper and was violent during sex acts.

His first known murder was on October 3, 1982. Delvoyd Baker, age 14, was found strangled and dumped on the side of a road north of Indianapolis, Indiana. Steven Crockett, age 19, was found on October 23 outside Lowell, Indiana. He had been stabbed 32 times. Robert Foley's body was found in a field outside Joliet, Illinois, on November 6. On Christmas Day, the body of John Johnson, age 25, was found in a field outside of Belshaw, Indiana. The body of John Roach, age 21, was found on December 28 along Interstate 70 in Putnam County, Indiana. Steve Agan, age

23, was also found on December 28 north of Newport, Indiana.

The next known murder was that of Edgar Underkofler, age 27, whose body was found on March 4, 1983 in Danville, Illinois. Gustavo Herrera, age 28, was found murdered in Lake Forest, Illinois on April 8. On April 15, also in Lake Forest, the body of Ervin Dwayne Gibson, age 16, was found. Eighteen-year-old Jimmy T. Roberts' body was found in Cook County, Illinois, on May 9. An unidentified body was discovered in Ford, Illinois on July 2. The body of Ralph Calise, age 28, was found on August 31 in a field near Lake Forest, Illinois. He had been stabbed 17 times and had been dead less than 12 hours. On October 4, 1983, the dismembered body of Derrick Hansen, age 14, was found in Kenosha, Wisconsin. An unidentified body was found near Rensselaer, Indiana on October 15.

On October 18, four bodies were discovered in Newton County. One had been decapitated. One of the bodies was identified as Michael Bouer, age 22, and another as John Bartlett, age 19. Twenty-nine-year-old Jay Reynolds' body was found on March 22, 1983, off US25 about 10 miles north of Richmond, Kentucky. On December 5, an unidentified body was found near Effingham, Illinois.

On May 7, 1984, the body of David M. Block, age 22, was found in Lake Forest, Illinois. The dismembered body of Danny Bridges, age 15, was found in eight separate bags by the janitor of the apartment where both Eyler and Bridges lived. The janitor was led there by his dog. Eyler was arrested and charged with the murder of Danny Bridges.

Larry William Eyler was found guilty of murdering Bridges and sentenced to death by lethal injection. Eyler told authorities that he was ready to confess and provide more information on the murders if he was given a fixed sentenced of 60 years instead of the death penalty. The state refused, but Eyler avoided the death penalty by passing away on March 6, 1994, from an AIDS-related disease.

Kathleen Zellner, Eyler's attorney, held a news conference on March 8, 1994, and released a written confession by Larry Eyler that he murdered 21 people. The confession could not be released until after Eyler's death due to attorney-client privilege.

Ionosyan, Vladimir (c. 1938 – February 1, 1964) was an unemployed actor and **Dmitrieva, Alevtina** (c. 1940) was a former ballerina who posed as meter readers in Moscow to gain entry into homes for the purpose of robbing the occupants. The home intrusions soon turned to murder. On January 16, Ionosyan and Dmitrieva were arrested. Ionosyan was charged with the axe murders of two boys and a woman in downtown Moscow. He was also linked to two similar killings in a suburb of Moscow. After a three-day trial, Ionosyan was sentenced to death on January 31, 1964. He was executed by firing squad the following day. Dmitrieva was charged as his accomplice and sentenced to 15 years in prison.

Italian Rivera Serial Killer aka **Bilancia, Donato** (b. July 10, 1951) is an Italian serial killer also known as the *Monster of Liguria*. He was a chronic bed wetter until age 10 or 12 and his mother shamed him by putting his mattress on the balcony for all of the neighbors to see. His aunt would pull down his underwear to show his cousins his underdeveloped penis. Bilancia quit high school and worked at various menial jobs. His early crimes included stealing a motor scooter and stealing a truck loaded with Christmas sweets. He spent time in prison for robbery and armed robbery in Italy and France. Other than these crimes, there is no history of violence before age 47.

Bilancia had become a compulsive gambler. In October 1997, he strangled a friend who lured him into a rigged card game, and he lost £185,000. At the time, his death was thought to be from a heart attack. Bilancia shot and killed the game's operator and his wife. He said that these were revenge killings. He then emptied their safe. He made no attempt to hide the bodies. Also in October he followed a jeweler home to rob him. He shot both the jeweler and his wife, and emptied their safe.

He subsequently robbed a money changer, then murdered him. Later in 1997, he killed a night watchman simply because he did not like him. Next, he murdered two prostitutes, one Albanian and the other Russian. He then killed another money changer, shot him multiple times, and emptied the safe.

In March 1998, he tried to murder a transsexual prostitute (after receiving oral sex at gunpoint) and did kill two night watchmen when they interrupted them. The prostitute survived and later testified against him. Next in line were two more prostitutes, a Nigerian and a Ukrainian. Bilancia assaulted and robbed an Italian prostitute but did not kill her.

On April 12, 1998, on a train to Venice he followed a woman into the toilet, shot her in the head, and stole her train ticket. On April 18, on a train to San Remo, again he followed a woman into the toilet, shot her behind the ear, and then masturbated.

Bilancia's last murder was of a service station attendant where he filled his car up with gas. He then cleaned out the day's receipts of about 2 million lira (approx. $1,750 US).

Based on a description of a black Mercedes given by a prostitute, the police considered Bilancia a major suspect and followed him for about 10 days. They were able to collect his DNA from cigarette butts and a coffee cup which he had discarded. It matched DNA they had found at the crime scenes.

Bilancia was arrested on May 6, 1998. During his interrogation, he confessed to 17 murders on the Italian Riviera, which included a gas station attendant, two goldsmiths, two money changers, two women in train lavatories, three security guards, four prostitutes, an underworld gambling figure and his wife, as well as a fellow gambler.

On April 12, 2000, Donato Bilancia was convicted and sentenced to 13 terms of life imprisonment with no possibility of parole. He is said to be a model prisoner.

Jablonski, Phillip Carl (January 3, 1946 – December 27, 2019) is a serial killer responsible for the deaths of five women in California and Utah between 1978 and 1991.

Jablonski joined the military after graduating from high school. He married Alice McGowan, his high school girlfriend, in 1968 after his return from overseas. He became sexually violent and she left him after a short marriage.

He met Jane Sanders in November 1968 and raped her on their first date, but she did not report it. She soon became pregnant and they moved to California. They were never married. By then Jablonski had left the military. He became increasingly violent during sex and Jane left him in 1972.

He met and married Melinda Kimball in the mid-1970s, murdered her in Palm Springs in 1978, and was sent to prison. On June 16, 1982, Jablonski married Carol Spadoni, age 38, while he was serving his sentence for his wife's murder. They met when Carol answered a newspaper ad.

Jablonksi was released from prison for good behavior in 1990. On April 22, 1991, he murdered Fathyma Vann, age 38, in Indio. Her body was sexually mutilated, she was shot to death, and found in the desert. There were other mutilations including the removal of her eyes and ears. The words "I love Jesus" were carved into her back. The following day, April 23, Jablonski murdered his wife, Carol, and her mother, Eva Inge Peterson, age 72, in their home in Burlingame, California. Both women were shot to death and sexually mutilated.

Margie Rogers, age 58, was murdered by Jablonski during a robbery in Grand County, Utah, on April 27. Jablonski robbed her of $158. He was captured the following day at a rest stop in Kansas.

Jablonski was sentenced to death for the three murders in California. His sentence was upheld by the California Supreme Court in January 2006. On December 27, 2019, he died in his cell at San Quentin State Prison.

Jackal aka **Jackson, Robert John "Robin"** (September 27, 1948 – May 30, 1998) During the years 1973 to 1991, Jackson may have murdered as many as 100 people in his participation in the conflict in Northern Ireland. Even if he did not "pull the trigger" himself, Jackson has definitely been tied to the murders of at least 50 people.

Jackson was a Northern Irish loyalist who held the rank of brigadier in the UVF (Ulster Volunteer Force), a paramilitary group. He is believed to have committed a series of killings, mainly against Catholic civilians. He has never been tried nor convicted of any of the killings attributed to him.

October 28, 1973, Jackson allegedly went to the home of Patrick Campbell, a Catholic trade unionist, and shot him to death in the doorway of his home.

May 17, 1974, it is alleged that Jackson led one of the teams in the Dublin car bombings, killing 26 people. Later, a member of the UVF explained that, "The UVF wanted the Catholics across the border in the Republic of Ireland to suffer as Protestants in Northern Ireland had suffered the intense bombing waged by the Provisional IRA."

January 10, 1975, gunmen kicked down the front door of the "safe house" where John Francis Green, a senior IRA (Irish Republican Army) member was staying near Castleblayney, County Monaghan. They found Green alone in the living room and shot him six times in the head at close range. Jackson is alleged to have participated.

April 27, 1975, three Catholic civilians at a social club in Bleary, County Armagh, were murdered by the UVF. It is alleged that Jackson either planned the killings or actually took part in the attack.

July 27, 1973, William Henry Wilson "Billy" Hanna was a high-ranking Ulster loyalist. He founded and led the Mid-Ulster Brigade of the UVF. Hanna was shot twice in the head, once in the temple, and once in the back of his head, execution style. He was allegedly murdered by Jackson, who took over command of the Mid-Ulster Brigade.

July 31, 1975, Jackson is alleged to have participated in the Miami Show Band massacre at Buskhill, County Down, killing band members Brian McCoy, Fran O'Toole, and Tony Geraghty and wounding Stephen Travers and Des McAlea. A bomb had been planted in the band's minibus which prematurely detonated, killing two members of the UVF. The vehicle was ripped in half and the band members were then gunned down by the surviving UVF men.

August 22, 1975, a gun and bomb attack at McGleenan's bar was carried out by the UVF killing John McGleenan and Patrick Hughes, and injuring Thomas Morris. Morris died six days later.

October 23, 1975, Peter McKearney and his wife, Jenny, were murdered in their home in Moy, County Tyrone. Peter was shot at least 14 and as many as 18 times. Jenny was shot 11 times.

On December 19, 1975, a car bomb exploded outside Kay's Tavern in Dundalk, County Louth, killing Jack Rooney and Hughie Watters. It is alleged that Jackson led the group responsible for the bombing. Jackson was never identified by any eyewitness as being at or in the vicinity of the bombing.

January 4, 1976, it is alleged that Jackson organized the attacks against the O'Dowd and Reavey families. It is also alleged that he shot to death Joseph O'Dowd and his two nephews, Barry and Declan, at a family celebration in Ballydougan, County Armagh. Three masked men entered the Reaveys' home through an unlocked door, where the three brothers were watching television. The gunmen, carrying 9mm submachine guns, a 9mm Lugar pistol and a .455 caliber Webley revolver, opened fire killing John, age 24, and Brian, age 22. Anthony was badly wounded. He died of a brain hemorrhage on January 30. Both families were Catholic.

April 19, 1977, two men knocked on the door of William Strathearn, a Catholic chemist, in Ahoghill, County Antrim. Strathearn was shot twice and killed. It is alleged by John Weir, a member of the UVF, that Jackson shot Strathearn while he and Billy McCaughey waited in Weir's car.

In March 1991, according to Weir, Jackson reportedly made his last killings. Eileen Duffy and Catriona Rennie, both teenagers, and Brian Frizzell were shot to death at a mobile shop in Craigavon, County Armagh. Weir contradicted himself in his affidavit by saying that although Jackson was aware that the killings were to take place, he was not at the scene of the crime. It has been suggested that the attack was organized by Jackson.

"Robin" Jackson's only conviction was in 1979 after he was arrested on October 16. A .22 pistol, a .38 revolver, a magazine, 13 rounds of ammunition, and hoods were found in his possession. He was sent to Crumlin Road Prison in Belfast to await trial. On January 20, 1981, he was sentenced to seven years in prison. He was released on May 12, 1983.

In the early 1990s Jackson handed over the command of the Mid-Ulster UVF to Billy Wright, also known as *Rat King*.

It has been said that "Robin" Jackson was "a hired gun, a professional assassin. He killed people for a living. The state not only knew what he was doing, its servants encouraged him to kill its political opponents and protected him."

On May 30, 1998, Robert John "Robin" Jackson, aka *The Jackal,* died of lung cancer at his home in Donaghcloney, County Down, Northern Ireland.

Jackson, Calvin (b. March 5, 1948) was a small-time thief turned serial killer who stole to feed his narcotic habit. The Park Plaza Hotel on West 77th catered to middle-aged and older women with fixed incomes. It was a flea-bag type hotel but home to those who could afford nothing better.

The rapes and murders began on April 10, 1973, when Theresa Jordan, age 39, was found raped and suffocated in her tiny room. Her small apartment had been thoroughly trashed.

On July 19, Kate Lewisohn, age 65, was found murdered—tied to her bed, raped, strangled, and her skull bashed in. Her apartment had been looted.

The police lost interest after several months and there were no more rapes or murders at the Park Plaza Hotel, until the following year. Mable Hartmeyer, age 60, was found dead on April 24, 1974, but her death was overlooked after being attributed to arteriosclerosis. Authorities had a closer look and found that the victim had been raped and strangled. Various and assorted items were missing from her room.

On April 28, Yvetta Vishnefsky, age 79, was found raped, bound with her own nylon stockings, and a butcher knife plunged to the hilt in her back. Items were missing from her room including clothing and jewelry, plus a portable television set.

The killings continued into summer. On June 8, Winifred Miller, age 47, was found strangled, raped, and robbed. On June 19, Blanche Vincent was raped and suffocated. Her cause of death was initially attributed to alcoholism but was later changed to murder. On July 1, Martha Carpenter, age 69, was raped and suffocated. On August 30, Eleanor Platt, age 64, was also raped, suffocated, and robbed.

In every case, the person responsible for the murders had stolen radios, televisions, and other items which could be "hocked" or sold.

On September 12, 1974, the killer maybe thinking that the Park Plaza Hotel was "too hot," moved his killing one block away. Pauline Spanierman, age 59, was found dead in her apartment. She had been raped and strangled, and her television was missing. A neighbor told police that she had seen a man on the fire escape carrying a TV at about 3 a.m.

Investigators began a door-to-door search. In Calvin Jackson's flat, they found the missing television. Jackson was a known junkie-mugger who had a long list of arrests for robbery and assault. They also accounted for the killer's "winter vacation" in 1973-74. Jackson had been in jail for burglary and felonious robbery, which had been bargained down to a misdemeanor.

Calvin Jackson confessed to all nine murders, telling investigators that his crimes were all committed to support his habit. Jackson was sentenced to 18 consecutive terms of life in prison. He is currently serving his sentences at the Elmira Correctional Facility in Elmira, New York.

Jackson, Charles (February 12, 1937 – February 2002) was a serial killer who murdered at least eight people between 1975 and 1982, in the San Francisco, California, area. He was in Folsom Prison serving a life sentence for the 1982 rape and murder of Joan Stewart in the Montclair neighborhood of Oakland, when he died in February 2002 before he could be held accountable for the other seven murders.

Jackson was an illiterate high school dropout. He was convicted of his first felony in 1953. Between 1953 and 1982, he was in prison for burglary, rape, assault, and child molestation. The murders were committed during those periods when he was on parole. Jackson drove an old pick-up truck and would go door-to-door looking for handiwork and yard work. When he found a woman alone and she opened the door, he raped and stabbed her to death.

One month after he died, DNA expert Rockne Harmon, a senior deputy district attorney for Alameda County, said that DNA collected at five crime scenes tied Jackson to the following deaths: Sonya Higginbotham was raped and stabbed to death in her home in Oakland in June 1975; Ann Johnson, age 25, was raped and stabbed to death in her Montclair home in August 1975; Henry Vila and his wife, Edith, were stabbed to death and Edith was raped in their Albany Hill home during a night-time burglary in November 1981; Betty Jo Grunzweig was stabbed to death in her home in the Trestle Glen neighborhood in Oakland in December 1981; and Gail Leslie Slocum was stabbed to death in the yard of her home in Rockridge District of Oakland just four days after Betty Jo Grunzweig.

In September 2005, it was announced that Charles Jackson's DNA linked him to the rape and murder of Cynthia Waxman, age 11, on April 22, 1978. Cynthia was with her cousin playing with a kitten in a field in Moraga. Her cousin left to go get some cat food for the kitten and when she returned, Cynthia was gone. Her body was found in nearby brush several hours later.

Jackson, Vickie Dawn (b. 1966) was a nurse at Nocona General Hospital in Nocona, Texas, some 45 miles east of Wichita Falls. She had dreamed of becoming a nurse since she was a small girl.

Fellow nurses and supervisors praised her work. Suddenly Vickie became angered by her patients. Patients who came to the hospital with minor ailments such as a sore toe, diarrhea, or dementia, and who were about to be released, began to die. Vickie was injecting them with mivacurium chloride (a neuromuscular blocking agent—a paralyzing drug). The investigation found she had murdered at least 10 patients. She was arrested and charged with the 10 deaths which occurred during the years 2000-01.

Vickie pleaded no contest, waived her right to appeal, and was sentenced to life in prison. She is serving her life sentence at the Christina Melton Crain Unit (for women) of the Texas Department of Prisons in Gatesville, Texas.

Jacksonville Serial Killer aka **Durousseau, Paul** (b. August 11, 1970) was a taxi driver in the city of Jacksonville, Florida. He is also a serial killer of at least nine women. He was born in Beaumont, Texas. Nothing is known of his childhood. In November 1992, he enlisted in the US Army and was stationed in Germany where he met Natoca, the woman who would become his wife. They married in 1995 in Las Vegas. In 1996, they were transferred to Fort Benning, Georgia. In 1997, Durousseau was found in possession of stolen goods. In January 1999, he was found guilty of the charges at a court martial hearing and was dishonorably discharged from the army.

The couple then moved to Natoca's hometown of Jacksonville, Florida. Durousseau had trouble finding and keeping jobs, until he was hired as a school bus driver and an animal control officer in 2001. In 2003, he was hired by the Gator City Taxi Company who failed to check his background. It is believed that he may have used his taxi as a contact for his victims.

On September 7, 1997, the nude body of Tracy Habersham, age 26, was found at Fort Benning. She had been missing for about 48 hours. She had been raped and strangled to death with a cord. Durousseau was not a suspect but later DNA would provide the link.

On July 26, 1999, Tyresa Mack, age 24, was raped and murdered in her Eastside Jacksonville apartment. Durousseau was seen leaving her apartment carrying a TV.

In 2001, he was arrested and convicted of raping a young woman in Jacksonville. He spent 30 days in jail and was on probation for two years.

On December 19, 2002, the body of Nicole L. Williams, age 18, was found in a ditch in Jacksonville. Her body was wrapped in a blue blanket. She had been reported missing two days before.

On January 1, 2003, the body of Nikia Kilpatrick, age 19, was found by family members when they went to check on her since they had not heard from her for several days. She had been raped and strangled with a cord two days before. Her small sons, ages 11 months and two years, were alive but malnourished. Nikia was about six months pregnant at the time of her murder.

Just eight days later, Shawanda Denise McCalister, age 20, was raped and strangled to death in her Jacksonville apartment. She was also pregnant at the time of her murder. This was the same day that Durousseau started driving a taxi for Gator City Taxi.

On February 5, the bodies of Jovanna Jefferson, age 17, and Surita Cohen, age 19, were found in a ditch next to a construction site on New Kings Road in Jacksonville. It was determined that Jovanna had been murdered about January 20 and Surita had been murdered around January 30. Witnesses recalled seeing the victims with a taxi driver fitting Durousseau's description.

On June 17, 2003, Paul Durousseau was arrested and charged with five counts of murder. On December 13, 2007, he was sentenced to die by lethal injection for the murder of Tyresa Mack. In January 2017, his death sentence was overturned by the Florida Supreme Court. As of this writing, Durousseau is housed at Union Correctional Institution, Raiford, Florida.

Jaishankar, M. (1977 – February 27, 2018) was a notorious criminal in India in the years of 2008 through 2011. He sometimes had an accomplice, **P. Mohan Selvam**, in the rapes and murders he committed.

Jaishankar was the son of Maarimuttu and lived in the village Kanniyanpatti of Salem District, Tamil Nadu, India. He was a truck driver by trade and married with three daughters when he committed his first crime on July 3, 2009. He attempted to rape and murder P. Shyamala, age 45, in Perandahalli. He raped and murdered 12 women and raped another six by mid-August 2009.

On August 23, 2009, Jaishankar kidnapped then raped (several times) before he murdered M. Jayamani, age 39, who was a police constable. She was stationed at the Kangeyamall All Women Police Station and was on temporary duty during the visit of M. K. Stalin, the Deputy Chief Minister. Her body was recovered on September 19.

On September 10, 2009, Jaishankar and P. Mohan Selvam were arrested and charged with the murder of K. Thangammal Ponnaya. However, they were acquitted on these charges in 2014 due to insufficient evidence gathered by investigators.

Jaishankar was taken by police to Dharmapuri for a murder trial on March 17, 2011. Constables M. Chinnasamy and Rajavelu were assigned to take the prisoner back to Coimbatore. Somehow, Jaishankar managed to escape about 9:30 p.m. at the Salem bus stand and traveled to Karnataka. Constable Chinnasamy shot himself on March 19.

Over the next month, Jaishankar raped and murdered six women in Bellary. He also murdered a man and a child in Dharmapuri. Investigators traced his mobile phone to Delhi, then to Mumbai in May 2011. A special team was formed to find and arrest him.

They put up wanted posters all over Karnataka and Tamil Nadu. By May 4, driving a stolen motorcycle, Jaishankar had reached the Elagi village in Karnataka. A local woman, Chandrakala Hotagi, was working alone in a field when she was approached by Jaishankar asking for food and water. He tried to rape her but she screamed, sounding the alarm that she was in trouble. Her husband, Prakash Hotagi, and other villagers came to her rescue. They caught Jaishankar and took him to the Zalaki police station. They handed him over to the Chitradurga Police.

Jaishankar was held at the Parappana Agrahara Central Jail in Bangalore. He was tried and convicted and sentenced to 27 years in prison. After returning from a court appearance in Tumkur, he pretended to be ill and was taken to the prison hospital. Somehow he had managed to get a duplicate key to allow him to escape the prison (wearing a police uniform) by scaling a 20-foot wall, walking across a 15-foot wall, and scaling the 30-foot high compound wall, fracturing one of his legs in the process. He then crossed the electric fence (it was not turned on that particular night). Three wardens, two jailors, and six security guards were suspended following the escape.

A red alert was issued to all police stations in Karnataka and a ₹500,000 reward (approx. $6,700 US) was announced for any information leading to his arrest. The police printed wanted posters and 75,000 pamphlets with profiles of Jaishankar in five different languages and distributed them across Tamil Nadu, Andhra Pradesh, Kerala, and Maharashtra. A police informant managed to find Jaishankar. He lured the fugitive to a dilapidated building with the promise of a motorbike to facilitate his escape out of the city. Instead of the motorbike, he found police who arrested him. He was sent to Bengaluru Central Prison in Bangalore and was placed in a high-security cell with CCTV 24/7 monitoring and lights that were never turned off.

On February 25, 2018, Jaishankar tried again to escape but failed. He was put in solitary confinement where on February 27, he slit his own throat using a shaving blade he had obtained from the barber the day before. He was found in a pool of blood. He was moved to Victoria Hospital where he was pronounced deceased at 5:10 a.m.

James, Eugene H. (1918 – August 12, 1949) was released on "Christmas Parole" in December 1947 after serving 7-1/2 years in prison for stabbing several Baltimore women. In June 1948, he raped and robbed a housewife; 12 days later he murdered an 11-year-old girl; and nine days after that he murdered another 11-year-old girl. He was convicted and sentenced to death. He was executed by hanging in Maryland on August 12, 1949, although apparently the noose did not do the job and guards had to pull his legs to get him into a position to strangle to death.

Japanese Sex Murders aka **Unnamed 16-year-old Male** (c. 1950) was born to a Japanese mother and a black American soldier who was killed in the Korean War. The boy's mother then married another American and moved to the US, leaving behind her mixed-blood son with relatives. He was bullied and shunned by other children for being a "half-breed". He grew up undisciplined and had a police record which began when he was in junior high school.

He felt that every young woman laughed at him and he soon learned to despise them. Between December 1966 and January 1967, he raped and murdered three victims. He was arrested on January 27, 1967. He told detectives, "I hate my hair and skin." Nothing was found on his trial or punishment.

Jeanneret, Marie (January 13, 1836 – 1884) was born in Locle, canton of Neuchâtel, Switzerland. She poisoned seven patients and her employer in 1866-67 in Lausanne, Switzerland. She was arrested on June 28, 1868. On November 26 she was convicted and given a life sentence. She died in prison in 1884.

Jeffries the Monster aka **Jeffries, Mark** (c. 1780 – May 4, 1826) was born in Dorset, England and became a bushranger during the 19th century in Van Diemen's Land (now Tasmania, Australia). He was also a serial killer and cannibal.

Jeffries was originally from Scotland where he had been granted a reprieve from a death sentence since he was willing to act as an executioner and scourger. After a period of time, he was transported to Van Diemen's Land. Trained in acts of cruelty as executioner and scourger, he took to the bush where he could practice his new-found skill. For a brief period, he ran with Matthew Brady's gang. He was thrown out of the gang because Brady said he was a "de-humanized monster" and he molested women. Jefferies is known to have murdered and cannibalized at least four adults during his escape from Macquarie Harbour with several accomplices. It is known that he later ate one of the escapees. In one incident, Jeffries attacked a homestead, kidnapped the mother, father and 5-month-old baby. He urged the woman who was carrying the baby to move more quickly. He would not allow the father to carry the child. When the baby started crying, Jeffries took the baby by its legs and smashed its head against a tree. The father rushed at Jeffries in a rage and Jeffries shot the man dead.

Captured in 1825, Mark Jeffries was hanged on May 4, 1826, along with Matthew Brady and three other bushrangers (robbers), at the old Hobart Town Gaol on the infamous six-man scaffold. Brady complained bitterly at being hanged alongside such poor company as Mark Jeffries and the other bushrangers.

Jégado, Hélène (June 17, 1803 – February 26, 1852) was a domestic servant in France who is believed to have murdered as many as 36 people over a period of 18 years. Her weapon was arsenic.

Between June 28 and October 3, 1833, it is believed that she murdered seven members of the household where she was employed by Father François Le Drogo in the village of Guern. She murdered the priest, his mother and father, and her own sister, Anne Jégado, who was visiting. These deaths followed closely on the cholera epidemic of 1832 and the deaths were attributed to natural causes.

Jégado returned to the rectory of Bubry, where she had previously worked with her two aunts. Three more people died there over a three-month period, including one of her aunts. She then went to Locminé and boarded with Marie-Jeanne Leboucher. Shortly afterward Leboucher and her daughter died, and the son fell ill, but survived. A widow by the name of Lorey offered Jégado a room. Lorey died shortly after eating some soup that Jégado had made for her.

In May 1835, she was in the employ of Madame Toussaint. Four more people died. To date, seventeen people had died under the care of Helene Jégado. Jégado then was employed as a servant in a convent in Auray, but she was dismissed after several incidents of vandalism and sacrilege. Following that, she worked as a cook in many other households in Auray, Pontivy, Lorient, and Port-Louis, but stayed only a short time at each, as someone would become ill or die.

Most of her victims showed symptoms of being poisoned by arsenic, but none was ever found in her possession. Jégado was also a thief who was caught stealing at several places where she worked.

In 1850, she went to work for Théophile Bidard, who was a law professor at the University of Rennes. Rose Tessier, one of the other servants, fell ill and died. Jégado was taking care of her. Another servant, Rosalie Sarrazin, became ill and died in 1851. The same doctors tended to her as had tended to Rose Tessier. They were suspicious of the deaths of both women and convinced the relatives to permit an autopsy. Jégado announced her innocence before she was asked anything about the deaths. She was arrested on July 1, 1851.

She was linked to 23 deaths by poisoning between 1833 and 1841. However, they were beyond France's ten-year limit for prosecution. Jégado's trial began on December 6, 1851, but she was only accused of three murders, three attempted murders, and 11 thefts due to French laws of permissible evidence and statute of limitations. She consistently denied even knowing what arsenic was. Jégado was found guilty and sentenced to death. On February 26, 1852, Helene Jégado was guillotined in front of a large crowd on the Champ-de-Mars in Rennes.

Jenkins, James Gilbert (1834 – 1864) was a robber and murderer who claimed 18 victims between 1840 and 1864 in Missouri, Texas, Iowa, and California. He was hanged in California in 1864.

Jennings, Wilbur Lee (1941 – February 11, 2014) and **Johnson, Alvin** were serial killers in California in the early 1980s.

Wilbur Jennings was convicted of the murders of Karen Robinson, age 21; Jacqueline Frazier, age 26; Linda Johnson, age 28; and Olga Cannon, age 23. All were murdered by drowning or blows to the head in Fresno County, California. Jennings, who was dubbed the *Ditchbank Murderer,* was sentenced to death in 1986.

In 2008, a 25-year-old murder was solved, and authorities know where the suspects are—

Wilbur Jennings is on death row in California for murdering four other women and Alvin Johnson is in a Utah prison serving time for rape and murder. The victim was Clarice Reinke, age 76, who was raped and murdered in her rural home in 1983. DNA tied the murder to Wilbur Jennings and Alvin Johnson.

Wilbur Jennings died of natural causes on February 11, 2014 while in the Sacramento County Jail awaiting trial for the 1981 murder of Debra Chandler, age 17, whose beaten remains were found near a water-filled roadside ditch about 15 miles from Sacramento.

Nothing was found concerning a trial of Alvin Johnson for the murder of Clarice Reinke.

Jerome Romano Porrovecchio aka **Kinney, James Allen** (b. September 11, 1949) is a serial killer who is known to have murdered in the states of Washington, Michigan, and Iowa in 1997-98. Authorities in the states of Minnesota, Idaho, and Oregon are still looking at him for unsolved homicides of young women while he was known to have been in their areas.

Kinney had traveled across the US since the 1980s, staying at Veterans Administration hospitals and homeless shelters throughout the country and living off disability checks.

Authorities in Michigan are looking at Kinney for the murder of Billie Jo Watson, who was last seen alive on the night of November 30, 1997, in Grand Rapids. Four days after her body was found, Kinney left Grand Rapids on a one-way bus ticket for Iowa. He left behind a business started with another man and all of his personal belongings.

In 1998, Keri Lynne Sherlock, age 20, from Braintree, Massachusetts, disappeared while visiting relatives in Bellingham, Washington. Her raped and mutilated body was found two days later. A vehicle abandoned near her body had papers in it identifying its owner as Kinney and listing his address in Grand Rapids, where he had lived for about two years.

He is wanted for questioning in the murder in 1998 of a young white woman in Des Moines, Iowa. He is also a suspect in several other murders.

James Allen Kinney was arrested in 2001, after a tip was called into *America's Most Wanted,* which had aired a segment about him, and placed him in North Carolina. He was sent back to Washington to stand trial for Keri Lynn Sherlock's murder. Kinney was sentenced to life without the possibility of parole. He is serving his sentence at the Washington State Penitentiary, Walla Walla, Washington.

Jesse Sitting Crow aka **Glaze, Billy Richard** (July 13, 1944 – December 22, 2015) is a serial killer in the state of Minnesota and suspected of murdering at least 50 women in various western states.

Billy Glaze was arrested on August 31, 1987, in New Mexico for drunk driving, a violation of his parole on a charge of rape in 1974. The arresting officer found a bloody shirt, crowbar, and nightstick in the truck he was driving. Eventually, hair samples from the crowbar would be used to convict him.

Glaze had become a suspect in the murders of three Native American women in the Minneapolis area of Minnesota after a waitress talked to police and the police talked to Glaze's girlfriend. The girlfriend gave police information that directed their attention to looking for Glaze in New Mexico.

Billy Richard Glaze was charged with three counts of first-degree murder and three counts of second-degree murder in the 1986-87 deaths of Kathleen Bullman, age 19; Angeline Whitebird-Sweet, age 26; and Angela Green, age 21. He was found guilty and sentenced to three terms of life imprisonment.

Billy Glaze died in prison of lung cancer on December 22, 2015.

Jesus Killer aka **Maketta, Jimmy** (b. May 1964) was a serial killer in the township of Philippi just outside Cape Town, South Africa, in 2005. He was so-called because he had the word "Jesus" tattooed on his upper lip. As a child, he often fought with others, set fires, ran away from home, and was involved in acts of bestiality.

Maketta stalked his victims by watching from the hillsides where he had a good view of the farms and houses. He would break into a house after dark to rape and kill his victims by hacking them to death with an axe and/or bludgeoning them with a hammer. He disposed of his victims by throwing them into the dams. Like a lot of criminals, he was caught because of a stupid mistake: he left his cell phone at a crime scene. He was convicted of 16 counts of murder and 19 counts of rape. On May 3, 2007, he was sentenced to life in prison.

Jha, Chandrakant (b. 1967) was born in Ghosai, Madghepura, Bihar, India. He is responsible for the deaths of seven victims in Delhi between 1998 and 2007. His victims were migrant laborers whom he befriended and helped to get employment. He murdered all of his victims by strangulation, then dismembered the bodies and left body parts around the city, taunting the police to catch him.

He was arrested for the first killing and held in jail until 2002. He was released due to lack of evidence. He then murdered six more before he was arrested.

In February 2013, he was found guilty of three murders. He was sentenced to death on each of two murders and life without parole on the third murder. His sentences of death were commuted to life in prison without parole in January 2016.

Johannesburg Mine-Dump Serial Killer aka **Dube, Sipho** (b. 1976) was a thief and a serial killer in Johannesburg and the northern area of the province of KwaZulu-Natal during the early 2000s. He lured his child victims by promising to give them toys, or posing as a police officer or handyman. All of his victims were children except the first. All of his child victims were kidnapped, raped, beaten, and strangled.

On March 3, 2001, the body of Rashunthee Hariduth Singh, Dube's first victim and the only adult, was found near an Indian residential area in the town of Ladysmith.

The woman had been beaten and her face so badly mutilated it was difficult to identify her race. It was determined by her hair that she was Indian. She had told her mother that she was going to the bank before returning home. She had been robbed but not raped.

On April 13, 2003, Martha Mthimunye sent her son Thabo, age 14, to a shop. He never returned. His body was found 12 days later just a few kilometers from his home in Regents Park. His arms had been cut off.

On August 6, 2003, Nomnikelo Jumba, age 14, was murdered in Bertrams. Even though Dube was in the area, had detailed knowledge of the murder and his shoes were covered in blood, authorities did not question him. Dube led police to the area where they found Nomnikelo's school blazer with blood on it and told them how she had run down a hill after she was raped and then collapsed and died. She had been stabbed in the neck and under her arm.

On September 18, 2003, Lukhanyo Kuwane, age 10, and a friend, age 15, were walking home from school when they were approached by a man pushing a cart loaded down with cardboard boxes. He asked them to help him carry the boxes and he would give them each R20. The friend refused, saying, "I never walk with strangers." Lukhanyo agreed to accompany Dube. His beaten body was found naked the following day on the side of the road in southern Johannesburg.

On September 24, 2003, Anele Mbuku, age 9, and his cousin, Siyabonga Mbuku, age 12, were lured away by the promise of toys. Anele took Dube to his home, so his mother, Sophie Mbuku, could pay for the toy Dube has promised. Sophie told Dube she could not afford the toy and asked him to leave. She then sent Anele and Siyabonga to go to her sister's house nearby to pick up something for her. Dube was still lurking in the area. About two months later, their badly decomposed bodies were found near a dam a few kilometers from their home.

On November 8, 2003, 11-year-old Tina Bernardes disappeared. The following day, her beaten body was found on a mine dump near the Denver off-ramp of the M2 highway.

A homeless man, Alfred Nyanga, who lived under the M2 interchange bridge, identified Dube as the man he had seen walking with a young white girl toward the highway. He told Tina's uncle, Mario Bernardes who was searching for Tina, that he recognized Dube because he had seen him several times at a scrap yard on Eloff Street. Bernardes gave Nyanga 50 rand (about $3.00 US) and asked Nyanga to phone him if he saw Dube again. The following day, Nyanga phoned him and said that Dube was at the scrap yard. Bernardes and his brother hurried to the scrap yard where Nyanga had pointed out Dube. Police were contacted and they arrested Dube.

Under questioning, Dube could remember most of the incidents and sometimes went into great detail about what he had done to his victims. Sipho Dube was convicted of seven murders and three rapes. He was given 10 life sentences plus an additional 114 years for 20 other crimes ranging from kidnapping to theft.

Johns, Ronnie (b. February 23, 1973) was a burglar and drug dealer who shot four people to death during robbery attempts in 1991 in Flint, Michigan. He was arrested in 1992 and given a life sentence with the possibility of parole on one count and 15 years to life on another count on July 9, 1992.

Johnson, James Rodney (April 18, 1949 – January 9, 2002) On December 9, 1991, due to a domestic disturbance at the home of James Johnson in central Missouri, police were called. Johnson was arguing with his wife and adult daughter, and Johnson had forcibly removed his daughter from the house at gunpoint. Deputy Sheriff Leslie Roark arrived at the home and Johnson exited the home and shot the deputy. Hearing the deputy moaning, he shot the deputy in the forehead, killing him.

Johnson then left in his car and drove to the home of County Sheriff Kenny Jones who was having an early Christmas party. Johnson fired shots through a window with his .22 caliber rifle. Sheriff Jones' wife, Pam was struck five times, in the shoulder, face, neck and back of her head, killing her. He then went to the home of Deputy Sheriff Russell Borts and shot him four times in the face, hand, and chest, but he survived.

Next Johnson went to the Moniteau County Sheriff's office where he shot and killed Cooper County Sheriff Charles Smith with four shots. Deputy Sheriff Sandra Wilson arrived about that time and she was shot in the chest with an 8 mm Mauser rifle and died.

Johnson left the area, took a hostage at her home and held her there most of the day. Law officers talked with him and finally he surrendered.

At his trial, his lawyers entered an insanity defense asserting that he suffered Post Traumatic Stress Disorder as a helicopter pilot during the Vietnam War. This was rejected and he was sentenced to death by lethal injection. James R. Johnson was executed on January 9, 2002.

Johnson, Johnny Ray (August 2, 1957 – February 12, 2009) is a suspected serial killer, although he was tried and convicted of only one murder. Johnson was in trouble with the law as far back as 1975 in Harris County, Texas, when he was placed on probation for the felony offense of burglary of a vehicle. His probation was revoked in 1978 when he was convicted of aggravated assault. A few years later he raped a little girl, only eight or nine years old. In 1983, he was convicted of sexual assault (in an unrelated case) and sentenced to five years in prison.

After his release, he worked as a cab driver in Houston, but again was convicted of sexual assault. He picked up a woman and tried to buy sex from her but she refused, and Johnson began choking and hitting her in the face, and raped her in the cab. He was again sentenced to five years.

Upon his release, he met and married a crack addict prostitute and they moved to Austin. He beat his wife so severely that he would have killed her if someone had not called the police. He was held in custody for six months for another beating.

In 1994, he beat a 40-year-old woman for refusing to have sex with him. The woman tried to defend herself with a razor and Johnson bashed her head in and stomped on her before raping her and dumping her body behind a drug store. It is also known that he raped a girl on a big hill across from the Austin police station, and raped another girl and smashed her head into a rock after she tried to steal his crack. In December 1994, Johnson lured a girl into a graveyard with crack and then raped her several times.

He moved back to Houston in 1995 and raped a woman at a party. There were two more brutal rapes and murders, after the rape at the party, to which he confessed. One victim was found lying face down in a water-filled gully, the other was found partially nude beneath a highway overpass and had suffered massive blunt trauma to the head similar to having been struck with a large rock. Both women had died of asphyxia due to strangulation.

On March 27, 1995, Johnson offered to give Leah Joette Smith some of his crack cocaine in exchange for sex. She refused and Johnson became angry. He grabbed her, ripped off her clothes, and threw her to the ground. She fought back with a wooden board. Johnson repeatedly struck her head against the concrete curb until she stopped moving and then he raped her. Smith told Johnson that she was going to file rape charges; this made him very angry and he stomped on her face five or six times. He left, but then returned when he found he had left his wallet. He raped her again, then picked up his wallet and her boots, and left her there to die.

In May 1995, a woman reported that Johnson grabbed her neck from behind, threw her to the ground, held her by the neck while he ripped off her clothes, and told her he would kill her if she kept struggling. He held a knife to her throat and raped her more than once. Because the woman was able to identify Johnson as the person who raped her and due to the similarities between her attack and the murder of Leah Joette Smith, a warrant was issued for Johnson's arrest.

Johnson directed police to the scenes of the murders he had committed and gave written statements confessing to Leah Joette Smith's assault and murder, and the other brutal crimes and murders committed.

On May 21, 1996, Johnny Ray Johnson was found guilty of capital murder. On May 30, he was sentenced to death. On February 12, 2009, he was executed by lethal injection at Huntsville Correctional Institute, Huntsville, Texas.

Johnson, Martha Ann (b. 1955) was a serial killer in Georgia who murdered three of her children by smothering them between 1977 –1982.

By the age of 22, Johnson was into her third marriage. She gave birth to a girl in 1971 during her first marriage; a son was born in 1975 during her second marriage; and a son in 1979 and daughter in 1980 were born during her third marriage to Earl Bowen.

On September 23, 1977, James William Taylor, Johnson's 23-month-old son, would not wake up from his nap and was rushed to the hospital, but he could not be revived and was pronounced dead. His death was attributed to SIDS (sudden infant death syndrome).

On November 30, 1980, Tabitha Jenelle Bowen would not wake up from her nap. Paramedics tried to revive the 3-month-old daughter of Johnson but were not successful. Her death was also attributed to SIDS.

In January 1981, Earl Wayne Bowen, age two years and seven months, was said to have ingested rat poison he had found. He was taken to the hospital where he was treated and released. His parents claimed he had seizures afterward. On February 12, 1981, the 31-month-old went into cardiac arrest and was taken to the hospital where he was revived and placed on life support. Doctors pronounced him brain dead and three days later he was removed from life support.

In early 1982, Johnson claimed her daughter, Jenny Ann Wright, age 11, was complaining of chest pains. The doctor prescribed Tylenol and a rib belt. Paramedics were called on February 21 and they found Jenny face down on Johnson's bed with foam around her mouth. They were unable to revive her. The autopsy indicated Jenny had been asphyxiated.

Several years later, there was an article in the December 1989 issue of *The Atlanta-Journal Constitution* questioning the deaths of these children, which resulted in the case being reopened. It was determined that each child's death was preceded by marital problems between Johnson and Bowen, who separated and divorced after Jenny's death.

Martha Ann Johnson was arrested on July 3, 1989. She confessed to killing two of her children. She said that after confrontations with Earl Bowen, she would suffocate the children by rolling her body over them while they slept. She weighed 250 pounds. Her motive was to punish her husband. She retracted this confession as her trial began in April 1990.

Johnson was convicted of the three first-degree murders of her children and sentenced to death, which was later commuted to life upon appeal. She is currently housed at Pulaski State Prison at Hawkinsville, Georgia but in January 2020 she received a tentative grant of release. No parole date had been set at the time of this writing.

Johnson, Matthew Steven (b. May 24, 1963) of Hartford, Connecticut had a long criminal record before he was identified as a serial killer. He had been found guilty and sentenced to 10 years in prison for the beating and attempt to rob a security guard inside a cathedral in 1982. He served four years and in 1988 was convicted of forcefully restraining a woman on the street; and he was convicted of raping and beating another woman.

On April 16, 2000, the body of Aida Quinones was found murdered at 85 Laurel Street. Four months later, on August 29, 2000, the body of Rosali Jimenez was found at 50-52 Cedar Street. The body of Alexia Ford was found on July 22, 2001 at 1 Myrtle Street. All three of these addresses are in Hartford, Connecticut, in the Asylum Hill neighborhood.

There were no suspects, but in early 2002, the Cold Case Squad tied Matthew Steven Johnson to these murders through DNA testing. Johnson went on trial for these three murders in 2004 and was convicted. He was sentenced to life in prison for each murder. He is currently serving his sentences at the Cheshire Correctional Institution in Cheshire, Connecticut.

Johnson, Milton (b. May 15, 1950) raped a woman in Joliet, Illinois and tortured her with cigarette lighter. In 1969, he was sentenced to 25 – 35 years, with a consecutive term of five to ten years added on for conviction on a burglary conviction. Authorities released Johnson on March 10, 1983, after serving less than half his sentence. This early release resulted in the deaths of 10 more people. Between June 25 and August 25, 1983, Joliet and the surrounding areas were terrorized by the savage violence of the "weekend murders." Local residents stocked up on guns and ammunition since the killer managed to elude law enforcement.

On June 25, two sisters were murdered in Will County on this Saturday. On July 2, another Saturday, Kenneth and

Terri Johnson were shot to death. The woman's body was discarded in southwestern Cook County.

On July 16, five people, including two Will County deputy sheriffs, were murdered in what authorities called a "random wholesale slaughter." The deputies were killed during a routine stop to help a motorist. The rear of the stopped pickup truck was blocking part of the road, and the front bumper was up against a red car stopped in a turn-around area. The assailant yelled, "We need a jump." As the officers exited their patrol car, the gunman shot both of them. Auxiliary Deputy Stephen Mayer died shortly after being shot. Auxiliary Sergeant Denis Foley was seriously wounded in the throat; one bullet had shattered his mouth and teeth. He tried to give their location over the radio, but his words were garbled. He was told to turn on his siren and shine his spotlight in the air. A short time later another car came around the curve and slowed down. The gunman opened fire on it. The driver was killed; his passenger was shot six times. The car stopped in a bean field down the road. The female, who was wounded, went looking for help. A nearby farmer called the county police and told them he could hear a lot of racket behind his buildings, including a siren. Officers met the farmer and quickly located the auxiliary deputies. Another unit located the bodies of a 25-year-old female and a 32-year-old male who were in the car parked in front of the pickup.

Patricia Payne and her boyfriend, Anthony Hackett, had spent the day of July 16 at Six Flags Great American Amusement Park in Gurnee, Illinois, and left the park about 10 p.m. They had over 200 miles to drive to their hometown of Emden and pulled over along I-55 to sleep. Hackett slept in the front and Patricia Payne in the back. Patricia was awakened about 1:30 a.m., on the morning of July 17 by a tapping on the passenger's side window, followed by gunshots which killed Hackett. The killer ordered Patricia to get out of the car and into his pickup truck. He drove down the interstate while sexually assaulting her. He then pulled off the interstate, stopped the truck, and raped her. He pulled back onto the road then back onto the shoulder, where he stabbed Patricia in the chest and dumped her from the truck. She was found about an hour later by a passing motorist. She had no pulse or blood pressure, but she was rushed to a hospital where doctors performed emergency surgery and she survived.

Authorities interviewed Patricia Payne, but other than to say her assailant was an African American with no observable facial hair, she was unable to identify him at that time. Fortunately in August 1983, Ann Shoemaker telephoned the sheriff's office and reported an incident that had occurred on a night in July 1983. She and a friend had been in her car and were being followed by a dark pickup truck that played cat and mouse with them. She and her friend followed the truck and recorded its license plate.

Realizing they did not know the driver, they managed to get away. It was established that the pickup truck was owned by Sam Myers, Milton Johnson's stepfather. Myers gave the police permission to search the truck and found Caucasian hairs, similar to Payne's hair, bloodstains, a steak knife, reddish brown fibers, and a sales receipt for a Tasmanian Devil stuffed doll (Hackett had bought the stuffed doll for Patricia Payne at the amusement park). The police got a search warrant for Myers' home, where Johnson lived. They seized three .357 magnum cartridges from a dresser in Myers' bedroom. On March 6, 1984, Payne identified Johnson from mugshots shown to her by police.

Milton Johnson was convicted of the first-degree murder of Anthony Hackett, plus aggravated kidnapping, deviate sexual assault, rape, and the attempted murder of Patricia Payne. Johnson waived his right to a sentencing jury, and the court found the defendant eligible for the death penalty. He was sentenced to death for Hackett's murder and to 40 years for deviate sexual assault, rape, and attempted murder to run concurrently. Upon appeal, Johnson's death sentence was commuted to life. He is serving his sentence at Menard Correctional Center in Chester, Illinois.

Jones, Daniel O. (b. September 26, 1969) was paroled in 1996 for raping a teacher at a high school in Kansas City, Missouri. In 2002, he was convicted of the March 6, 2001, murder of Candriea White, age 18, who was stabbed 14 times in her home. She was the mother of two small children. Jones was sentenced to life without the possibility of parole.

On March 19, 2004, Jones pleaded guilty to the murders of Jenai Douglas, age 19, murdered on December 2, 1998; Kaliquah Gilliam, age 21, murdered on March 10, 1999; and Roxanne Colley, age 21, murdered on August 16, 1999. This case evolved over several years.

Police matched DNA collected from Jones in 2001 to DNA from the semen found on Colley's body in 1999. Jones was charged with the murder of Roxanne Colley. A plea agreement was reached, and Jones agreed to plead guilty to the murder of Colley and the murders of Gilliam and Douglas. He was sentenced to 20 years to run concurrently with his sentence of life without parole. He is currently housed at the Southeast Correctional Center in Charleston, Missouri.

Jones, Genene Anne (b. July 13, 1950) was a pediatric nurse turned serial killer. It is believed that she murdered as many as 46 infants and children in her care. Her method of murder was an injection of digoxin, heparin, and later, succinylcholine. She injected these babies and children with the intention of reviving them in order to receive praise and attention from her supervisors and co-workers at a pediatric physician's clinic in Kerrville, Texas, where she was charged with poisoning six children. She was also suspected of killing her child patients at the Bexar County Hospital (now the University Hospital of San Antonio) in the Pediatric Intensive Care unit. She was asked to resign.

In 1985, Genene Jones was sentenced to 99 years in prison for killing Chelsea McClellan, only 15 months old, with succinylcholine. Later in 1985, she was sentenced to a concurrent term of 60 years for nearly killing Rolando Jones with heparin. Due to a law that was in effect at the time dealing with prison overcrowding, she will serve only one-third of her sentence. She was scheduled to be released automatically in March 2018. To avoid this, on May 25, 2017, Jones was charged with the murder of Joshua Sawyer, who was only 11 months old when he was killed. When she is released from prison after serving her original sentence, Genene Jones will be transferred to the Bexar County jail to await trial on new murder charges.

Jones, Jeffrey Gerard (b. 1960) attended college in Arizona, but in 1982 was sent home to Sacramento after he began to exhibit abnormal behavior. In 1984, his father awoke to find his son standing beside him with a knife in his hand. Later in 1984, he was charged with robbing a disabled man—he pleaded not guilty by reason of insanity. It was noted that with therapy and medication, he was "stabilized" and no longer a threat to others.

On January 21, 1985, Jones murdered Harry Dong, age 47, using a claw hammer in a public restroom. Later the same day, with a hammer, he battered John Rowland, leaving him for dead in a restroom at the University of California campus medical center in Davis. On January 22, he murdered Dr. Michael Corbett, age 35, with a hammer in another restroom in the same building. On February 18, he murdered Fred Morris, age 34, in an identical fashion at UC Davis physics-geology building. It was revealed that he had threatened to do "something bad" in an effort to get psychiatric care. He was tried and sentenced to death in

1987. He is currently on death row at San Quentin Prison in California, where he is apparently suffering from mental health issues, alternating between catatonia and rabid mania.

Jones, Jeremy Bryan (b. April 22, 1973) was a drifter from Oklahoma who may have murdered as many as 13 or more people between 1992 and 2004 in the states of Oklahoma, Kansas, Louisiana, Alabama, and Georgia.

On February 14, 2004, the body of Katherine Collins, age 47, was found in the Garden District of New Orleans. She had been strangled and stabbed to death.

On March 12, 2004, Amanda Greenwell, age 16, disappeared from her home. Her body was found a month later a few miles from her home. She had been beaten and raped and her neck was broken. She lived in the same trailer park as Jones in Douglas County, Georgia.

On April 15, 2004, Jones stopped at a hair salon to get directions. Realizing that Patrice Tambers-Endres, age 38, was alone, he kidnapped her. He raped and murdered her and then disposed of her body near a Douglas County bridge. A thorough search of the area was made, but Tambers-Endres was not found. Cadaver dogs twice indicated that a body had been there at one time. In early December 2005, remains found behind a Dawson county Church were confirmed, using dental records, as those of the missing Forsyth County hair stylist. Jones has not been charged with this disappearance and possible murder due to lack of physical evidence.

On September 18, 2004, the body of Lisa Nichols, age 45, was found in her partially burned home in Chunchula, Alabama. She had been raped, shot three times in the head, and her body burned in the house fire, which had been deliberately set. A car seen parked in front of her home on the night of the murder was registered to a "John Paul Chapman".

On September 21, 2004, "John Chapman" called the police. They traced the call and apprehended him. After a thorough search of Chapman's background it was determined that he was, in fact, Jeremy Bryan Jones, age 31, a drifter from Miami, Oklahoma, who was wanted in Oklahoma for jumping bail in 2000, where he was charged with two counts of rape and two counts of sodomy.

Charged with the murder of Lisa Nichols, Jones not only confessed to killing Nichols, he also confessed to 13 other murders in six states. Investigators were successful in getting enough evidence to charge Jones with four murders in Alabama.

Jones confessed to the murders of Jennifer Judd, age 20, who was stabbed to death with a kitchen knife in her home in Baxter Springs, Kansas, on May 11, 1992; Doris Harris, age 41, and Daniel Oakley, age 38, were shot in the trailer where they lived and the trailer was set on fire in 1996 in Delaware County, Oklahoma; Justin Hutchings, age 19, was murdered with a "lethal injection" in 1999, in Pitcher, Oklahoma; Danny and Kathy Freeman were shot to death and their home set on fire on December 30, 1999.

Tina Mayberry stepped out of a restaurant in Douglasville, Georgia, and in just a few minutes she came back in bleeding from stab wounds. Paramedics were called, but she died at the hospital shortly after arriving. She had not been robbed or sexually molested; Ashley Freeman, age 16 and daughter of the Freemans above, and her friend Laura Bible, disappeared on the same night that Danny and Kathy Freeman were murdered. Jones said that he threw their bodies down a mine shaft.

Jones later recanted his confessions, saying he was just "playing the system" for better treatment—good food, more phone calls, and more visitation from family.

He was convicted of the murders in Alabama and sentenced to death. He is currently on death row at Holman Correctional Facility in Atmore, Alabama.

Jones, Sydney (? – June 25, 1915) was hanged for murder at the Jefferson County jail in Birmingham, Alabama on June 25, 1915. He left a note in his cell, confessing to 13 homicides. All of the victims were black, except two who were white: a Nebraska Deputy Sheriff and a brakeman on the Mobile & Ohio RR. At the end of the note Jones wrote, "I'm sorry I missed Richard Moore on September 12, 1912. Just one more would have made an even number."

Joshi-Abhyankar Serial Murders were committed by **Jakkal, Rajendra**; **Sutar, Dilip Dhyanoba**; **Jagtap, Shantaram Kanhoji**; and **Shah, Munawar Harun**, all commercial art students of the Abhinav Kala Mahavidyalaya in Pune, India. The murders were committed between January 1976 and March 1977.

On January 15, 1976, the group kidnapped Prakash Hegde, a colleague, and took him to Jakkal's shed on Karve Road. They forced him to write a note to his father stating that he was leaving home. They then gagged him and took him to Peshwe Park, where they strangled him with a nylon rope from the shed, put his body in a barrel along with stones, and dumped the barrel into the lake. A ransom note was mailed to Sundar Hegde, Prakash's father, the following day.

Using knives, the group forced their way into Achyut Joshi's house on October 31, 1976. Joshi and his wife, Usha, the only ones in the home, were tied up. Joshi was strangled with a nylon rope and Usha was suffocated. When the son, Anand, came home, he was stripped naked and strangled with the nylon rope. The killers left with their ill-gotten-gains—a mangala sutra**, a watch, and a few thousand rupees.

On November 22, 1976, Yashomati Bafna's home was attacked. Bafna and her two servants managed to ward off the attack and the group escaped by climbing the barbed wire fence surrounding the home.

December 1, 1976, the home of noted Sanskrit scholar Kashinath Shastri Abhyankar, age 88, his wife Indirabai, age 76, maid Sakubai Wagh, age 60, granddaughter Jai, age 21, and grandson Dhananjay, age 19, was attacked. The intruders stuffed balls of cloth into the mouths of the occupants, tied their hands and feet, and then strangled them with the nylon rope. Jai, the granddaughter, was stripped naked and forced to show the intruders where the valuables were in the house. Then she too was strangled.

On March 23, 1977 Anil Gokhale, a younger brother of one of the group's college friends, was supposed to meet his brother at Alka Talkies. He accepted the offer of a ride on the back of Jakkal's motorcycle. He was taken to Jakkal's shed where he was strangled with the nylon rope. His body was tied to an unused iron ladder, weighed down large rocks, and dumped into the Mula-Mutha River near Bund Garden.

On the evening of March 24, Anil Gokhale's body surfaced near Yerawada. The police investigators realized that the rope used to tie the body to the ladder was tied exactly the way the ropes had been tied in the prior murders. The investigators questioned Jakkal, Sutar, Jagtap and Shah, but their stories contradicted each other's stories about their whereabouts over the past week. A colleague, Satish Gore, broke down and confessed. Another classmate, Suhas Chandak, who was a witness to the Hegde killing, also confessed.

The killers were arrested on March 30, 1977. In September 1978, all four were sentenced to death. The Bombay High Court confirmed their death sentences on April 6, 1979, and their special leave petition against the convictions and sentences was dismissed by the Supreme Court on November 17, 1980. The convicted four then approached the President of India for a pardon, which was denied. All four were hanged on November 27, 1983, at the Yerawada Central Jail.

Mangala sutra is a necklace that a Hindu groom ties around *the bride's neck which identifies her as a married woman. The woman continues to wear the mangala sutra as a sign of her marital status.*

Joyner, Anthony (b. May 26, 1959) was a serial killer of elderly women at Kearsley Home, Philadelphia, Pennsylvania. Kearsley Home is the oldest nursing home in the United States.

Between January and July 1983, Joyner raped and murdered at least six elderly women, ages 80 to 92, at the rest home where he was employed. He was charged and convicted of five counts of first-degree murder and one count of second-degree murder. Jurors were deadlocked over the death penalty in the penalty phase of his trial. He was sentenced to a mandatory term of life in prison. He is currently serving his sentence at Graterford Prison in Schwenksville, Pennsylvania.

Juiz de Fora Strangler aka **Cassimiro, Andre Luiz** (b. 1965) was an ex-con. He was also a serial killer in the town of Juiz de Fora, Brazil, who had a taste for older women. All of his victims were between the ages of 58 and 77 and lived alone. They were all tortured, strangled with electrical cords, and some were raped. He stalked his victims for several days observing their daily routines and entered their houses "to rob them but ended killing them. In those moments I felt hate towards the little old women."

On June 19, 1995, he entered the home of Zilda Araujo Barbuth, 76. She was sleeping and awoke when Cassimiro dropped a clock radio he was stealing. When she tried to scream, he gagged her and tied her to the bed post with electrical cord. He then raped and strangled her. In late 1995, he murdered Odete Barbosa da Silva, age 62, a woman he had dated for a year and a half. In early 1996, he murdered Aldenira Mello, age 58. At a party for senior citizens, he met Maria Malvina de Oliveria, age 77. They danced all evening long. Her body was found three days later with her head brutally crushed. On May 13, 1996, he murdered Celia Nicolini de Farias, age 74. It is believed that Cassimiro raped her post-mortem.

After his arrest, Cassimiro confessed to the murders. He was sentenced to life in prison.

Junni, Ismo Kullervo (June 27, 1943 – November 3, 1995) was a serial killer and arsonist in Finland. Nothing is known of his early life. The one thing that all of the killings had in common was the removal of the victims' teeth.

In August 1980, Junni killed his wife in Knotula, and pulled out her teeth. In June 1986, Junni murdered two of his friends, Seppo Mantyniemi and Jhua Vare, at the Kivinokka summer camp in Herttoniemi. He then set fire to the crime scene. Matti Haapanen, another friend, was murdered in July 1986 and his home set on fire. Matti and Ismo had been drinking and got into a brawl and Matti was killed. Ismo then stole Matti's dental prosthesis. His last known murder was that of Pauli Sironen, whom he burned alive in his summer home.

Ismo Kullervo Junni was convicted of the murders of his wife, Seppo Mantyniemi, Jhua Vare, Matti Haapanen, and Pauli Sironen. He was sentenced to life imprisonment in February 1992. He committed suicide in 1995.

Kakehi, Chisako (b. 1947) was a serial killer in Kyoto, Japan. Her weapon of choice was cyanide. She was convicted of the murder of three, including her husband, and the attempted murder of another, and sentenced to death.

She dated mostly elderly or ill men whom she met through dating agencies. After they made her beneficiary of their life insurance, she poisoned them with her cyanide cocktail. It was reported that she amassed a fortune to the tune of one billion yen (approximately $8.8m US). She lost most of it through unsuccessful financial trading.

During the trial, Kakehi's lawyer argued that Kakehi was not criminally liable because she was suffering from dementia. Judge Ayako Nakagawa rejected the defense lawyer's argument. At the beginning of her trial, Kakehi refused to speak. She stunned the entire court when she admitted that she had murdered her fourth husband because he gave other women "tens of millions of yen" and would not give her a penny. She told the court that she was ready to be hanged.

Kansas City Butcher aka **Berdella, Robert Andrew** (January 31, 1949 – October 8, 1992) was a Kansas City, Missouri serial killer. As a teenager and young adult, Bob, as he preferred to be called, got in trouble with the law for selling amphetamines and received a suspended sentence, and for possession of LSD and marijuana, but the charges were dropped due to lack of evidence. He opened a novelty shop that catered to occult-type tastes.

On April 4, 1988, a young man whom Berdella had been raping and torturing for a week, jumped naked out of the second floor of his house and escaped. In a search of Berdella's house, after his arrest, the police found detailed torture logs and volumes of Polaroid pictures he had taken of his victims, which remain in police possession. By this time, Berdella had abducted and tortured at least six young men and was suspected of two other disappearances. One victim's skull was found buried in the back yard. All of the other dismembered bodies were put out at the curb for weekly trash pickup. The bodies were never recovered.

His known victims were: Jerry Howell, age 20, who disappeared on July 5, 1984; Robert Sheldon, age 18, who disappeared on April 19, 1985; Mark Wallace, age 20, who disappeared on June 22, 1985; James Ferris, age 20, who disappeared on September 26, 1985; Todd Stoops, age 21, who disappeared on June 17, 1986; and, Larry Pearson, age 20, who disappeared on July 9, 1987.

On December 19, 1988, Berdella pleaded guilty to one count of first-degree murder and to an additional four counts of second-degree murder for the deaths of other victims. He was sentenced to life in prison. On October 8, 1992, Robert Andrew Berdella suffered a heart attack at the Missouri State Penitentiary and was pronounced dead at a Columbia hospital.

Kartal, Ayhan/Kornis, Ayhan (1966 – March 13, 2000) was born in Izmir, Turkey. He raped and murdered young boys. He was convicted of two of the murders, but there may have been others.

On April 30, 1985, Kornis murdered Armagan Kayadipli, age 13, by strangulation after raping him in the Ikicesmelik quarter of Kemeralti district in Izmir. Kornis was sent to a mental hospital in Bakirkoy, Istanbul and was released after one year. He changed his surname to Kartal.

On September 23, 1989, Kartal raped and murdered Baris Kurt, age 9, in Sirinyer, Izmir. He was found hiding in a chest at his home in Pinarbasi, Bornova in Izmir.

In 1992, Kartal was in Manisa Psychiatric Hospital for diagnosis and treatment for his mental disorder. He escaped from the hospital on October 14, 1993. He was caught and returned to the hospital after a short time. He told authorities that he felt very close to children and could have intercourse with children only.

Kartal was in the same mental hospital and same ward as serial killer Suleyman Aktas, the "Nailing Killer". He was very afraid of Aktas and was relocated to another ward. On the night of March 13, 2000, his two roommates, serial killer Ali Kaya and Tayfun Sahin, stabbed him once in the throat and three times in the stomach. A physician on duty found him in a pool of blood and arranged for his transfer to an emergency station. Kartal died on the way to the emergency station.

Kasler, Steven Lawrence (March 14, 1967 – November 8, 2014) is a serial killer who is known to have killed in Louisiana, Ohio, and Tennessee. He confessed to 34 murders across the south and midwest states, while in prison in Louisiana serving a 99-year sentence. He later recanted these confessions.

Steven Kasler entered a plea in Madison County Common Pleas Court in Ohio to a charge of aggravated murder in the death of Charlotte Lane, 32, of Columbus, Ohio. Her decomposed body was found Oct. 25, 1992, in a rural area west of Columbus. He confessed to three other murders in Ohio, was convicted and sentenced to four terms of life in prison. He also confessed to a murder in Louisiana.

Authorities in Shelby County, Tennessee have a warrant issued for Kasler in the unlikely event he is ever released from prison in Ohio. He is wanted for the murder of Teresa Butler, age 26, a nurse at St. Francis Hospital where in 1986, he and a buddy named "Ricky Tick" ran her off the road, kidnapped her at gunpoint, and took her to Knoxville where she was held captive by them in a motel for two days before Kasler said he stabbed her to death. He claims that he killed "Ricky Tick" the same way and buried them in Southeast Knox County. Their bodies were never found even though Kasler showed authorities where he had buried them. Authorities have never been able to verify that "Ricky Tick" ever existed.

Steven Kasler was in prison at Lebanon Correctional Institution in Lebanon, Ohio when on November 8, 2014, he died of natural causes.

Katóka Street Killer aka **Nemeskéri, Gusztáv** (b. 1960) is a Hungarian serial killer who was heavily in debt due to buying property with money from loans. He had no means to repay the loans, so he murdered and robbed using an improvised gun.

A dog breeder came to Hungary to buy dogs from some of the Hungarian breeders in 1996. While there, he and Nemeskéri became friends and in February 1996 the dog breeder moved in with Nemeskéri. An argument ensued one day and Nemeskéri shot him, then stole about 1.5 million Hungarian Forints (about $6,000 US) and a gold ring. He put the body in a bag, then into the car parked in his yard. About four to five weeks later, he buried the body in his garden. He was questioned by the police but claimed he knew nothing of his friend's disappearance. He was given a polygraph test, but the test was inconclusive due to an investigative error.

Nemeskéri had the electric meter in his home checked by an electrician in June 1996. He had made falsified measurements which the electrician had found. When he said that he would have to report it to the company, Nemeskéri killed him. He put the body into a bag, left it in his courtyard, and went to Vienna for a dog show. When he returned home, he buried the electrician in his garden.

His next victim was a postwoman. He had spent money on stamps from the postwoman and wanted it back. He shot the woman and stole 750,000 Forints (approx. $2,700 US) on December 12, 1997. He took her body to a lake on the outskirts of the town of Csömör and left it on the shore. The body was found about 60 days later. A witness had seen the postwoman get into the car with a man. From her description, a very good composite was made which aided in his capture.

Nemeskéri also owed a large sum of money to his half-brother, Zsolt, who filed a lawsuit against him after repeatedly trying to get his money back, 2,000,000 Forints ($7200 US). The trial was to begin on April 8, 1999. Nemeskéri invited Zsolt to his apartment to try to settle the loan, but instead Zsolt was shot and killed and his body hidden in the basement.

An investigation was begun, Nemeskéri house was searched, and his half-brother's body was found in the basement along with a few other corpses. Nemeskéri denied any knowledge of the bodies. He attempted to blame his brother for the murders. The investigators did not believe him and Nemeskéri went on trial. He was found guilty of the murders and given a sentence of 40 years to life, which he is serving at the Star Prison in Szeged, Hungary.

Kaya, Ali (b. 1980) was born in Gaziantep, Turkey. Nothing is known of his early life. While in his teens he began to commit assaults in the process of stealing from individuals. At age 17 he was imprisoned and released two years later. He began killing when he was released.

In 1997 he stabbed his uncle, Celal Kaya to death while working at his real estate office in Alanya. He was sentenced to five years, was sent to Silifke Prison, and was released in 1999.

After his release, he murdered a man named Zeynel Abidin Gumus, whom he thought had sexually assaulted his mother. He was sent back to prison, this time to Elazig Prison where he was diagnosed with a mental disorder. He was transferred to a psychiatric hospital but was released because one of the reports attested to the fact that he was claustrophobic.

He began killing again. He murdered three people in Alanya: a music hall owner called Dedo; a procurer called Mehmet of Agri, and someone known as Firat S. He also killed two wardens of Alanya Prison, Kemal Aksakal, and Hasan Askeroglu by stabbing them to death when he met them on a street. He was confined to Manisa Psychiatric Hospital and diagnosed with a personality disorder.

At the hospital he murdered his roommate, Ayhan Kartal, who was a rapist and child killer and nicknamed the *Beast of Izmir.* He was stabbed in the throat and stomach. Kaya was arrested and sent to Sanliurfa Prison.

Shortly after his release, he murdered Mehmet Poyraz in Gaziantep. Kaya was captured after a shootout with Turkish Gendarmerie in November 2013.

Kaya escaped from Sanliurfa Prison in 2003. He was caught in 2004 in the village of Mahmutlar, Alanya. He had a fake ID card with the name of Erdal Yilmaz, and a long "death list" with the names of people he said had abused him during his childhood.

He again escaped from Gaziantep Prison in January 2014, this time during visitation hours. He walked out with a crowd of visitors. He was not missed until the evening check of all inmates. He was captured on March 3, 2014, in downtown Gaziantep. He had a handgun and another death list with the names of 10 people. He was returned to Gaziantep Prison, where he remains today.

Kearney, Patrick Wayne (b. September 24, 1939) aka *Freeway Killer/Trash Bag Murderer* was a serial killer in California who picked up his victims in gay bars or as they were hitchhiking. He was a homosexual and a necrophile. He shot his victims without warning, sexually assaulted the bodies, then mutilated and dismembered them. He wrapped the dismembered bodies in garbage bags and dumped them along the freeway or in the desert. His lover, David D. Hill, was present during some of the murders, but his involvement is uncertain, and he was not charged in any of the cases.

On March 13, 1977, Kearney murdered John LaMay and dumped his body in the desert. The remains were found on May 18, 1977 and identified. LaMay had last been seen in the company of Kearney and David Hill, Kearney's lover. The pair had fled to El Paso, Texas. They turned themselves in to authorities at the urging of their families. Hill was eventually cleared of any involvement in the murders and was released.

It was learned that the lovers argued frequently, and Kearney would get in his car and go for long drives. This was when he picked up his victims.

Kearney confessed to murdering 28 young men. To avoid the death penalty, he pleaded guilty to 21 murders. He was given 21 life sentences. Authorities believe that he was responsible for the additional seven murders, but they did not have enough evidence to charge him. He is currently serving his sentences at Mule Creek State Prison at Ione, California.

Since Kearney pleaded guilty, there was no trial. There is very little information available concerning his victims, i.e. names, ages, method of murder, date of murder, etc.

Kebab Killer aka **Gul, Shirin** (c. 1970) was convicted in Afghanistan of killing 28 men in collaboration with her husband and his in-laws, along with her son, **Samiullah**. The family was part of a large regional gang that specialized in stealing and selling cars, particularly taxis. During a 2004 investigation into the murder of businessman Haji Mohammed Anwar, whose naked body was found near Kabul, police discovered the remains of 18 men buried in the yard of Shirin Gul's home in Jalalabad. Anwar had been invited to Gul's home to discuss a property deal. His uncle was aware of his destination and reported it to the police after he learned of Anwar's disappearance. Six more bodies were found buried in a property in Kabul. In addition, the body of Gul's first husband was found under the floor of her Jalalabad home. Two more bodies were found elsewhere.

Most of the victims were taxi drivers. Rahmatullah and Samiullah took taxis to their home and invited the taxi drivers in for a cup of tea and kabobs (a typical display of hospitality in Afghanistan). Gul would then offer the men kababs laced with sedatives. Once the men were helpless, they were strangled and buried. Their cars were then taken to Miram Shah, a town on the Pakistan border, and sold for more than $10,000.

Four more men have been arrested as accomplices. Prosecutors were seeking the death penalty.

Shirin Gul was sentenced to 20 years and is believed to be still running her business from her jail cell in Nangarhar Women's Prison.

Kelliher, Mary poisoned her husband, three of her children, her sister, and a sister-in-law between the years of 1905 and 1908 in Boston, Massachusetts. An autopsy of her daughter found traces of arsenic. Investigators found a mattress soaked in arsenic in her home. Kelliher escaped conviction by blaming their deaths on sleeping on the arsenic contaminated mattress.

Kelly, Kieron (1928 – 2001) was a native of Ireland who moved to London in 1953. He worked odd jobs and spent most of his earnings on liquor. It is believed by investigators in London that he murdered many gay men over the period of the 30 years he had been in London, but only five murders could be tied to him with enough evidence to go to trial.

On December 25, 1975, Hector Fisher was found in a Clapham church yard. The elderly panhandler had been stabbed repeatedly about the head and neck. He was last seen alive on Christmas Eve with several men dressed as Father Christmas.

On June 2, 1977, Maurice Weighly was found murdered in Soho, a suburb of London. His face and genitals were mutilated, and the neck of a broken bottle had been thrust up his rectum. Kelly and another transient were found in the area with bloodstains on their clothing. Kelly was charged with the murder after his companion described the murder in great detail. Six months later, he was acquitted after his lawyer described the witness (his companion on the night of the murder) as an alcoholic and "blind drunk" at the time of the murder. The witness soon vanished.

An elderly panhandler was pushed onto the tracks at Kensington Station in May 1983, but the driver of the subway train managed to stop his train before hitting the man. Kelly was identified as the one who had pushed the old man onto the tracks. He was arrested on charges of attempted murder, but he was acquitted of the crime.

August 4 found Kelly in jail, this time charged with robbery and public drunkenness. Locked in with other transients, he murdered William Boyd by crushing his skull, and then garroted him. During the interrogation, Kelly confessed to five killings. He admitted to killing Hector Fisher and Maurice Weighly, but he could not be charged with Weighly's murder because he had been previously acquitted. His other victims included the witness who vanished after his first murder trial, an elderly transient he shoved beneath a train several days after the Kensington incident, and William Boyd. Police confirmed that there had been a "fatal accident" at Oval Station on the date stated but had no corroborating evidence to charge Kelly.

Kieron Kelly was convicted of Hector Fisher's murder in June 1984 and was sentenced to life in prison. He was also sentenced to life for the murder of William Boyd. He died in prison in Durham, England in 2001.

Kembo, Charles (b. 1968) is a serial killer who murdered for profit, assumed his victims' identities after their murders, and took over their finances. Kembo arrived in Canada as a government-sponsored "convention refugee" from the African country of Malawi in December 1989 without a passport, using the name Charles Matthew Gwazah. Documents later showed that Kembo made refugee claims under three different names over a three-year period. He attended college in Toronto but dropped out and began a life of crime. In 1992, Kembo moved to Vancouver, British

Columbia. His son, Grant, was born in April 2000. Kembo married his son's mother, Margaret, but they did not live together. He lived with his common-law wife, Genevieve Camara, who gave birth to his daughter in August 2002.

Kembo's wife, Margaret, was last seen alive on December 31, 2002. Her body has never been found. Kembo wrote checks on her bank account and Camara would cash them and give Kembo the money.

On November 5, 2003, the body of Ardon Samuel, Kembo's business partner, was found strangled and castrated in Quilchena Park in Vancouver. On November 5, 2004, the body of Sui Yan Ma, Kembo's mistress, was found in a hockey bag in a slough in Richmond. The RCMP (Royal Canadian Mounted Police) became suspicious of Kembo and began a surveillance of him.

On July 27, 2005, the nearly naked body of Rita Yeung, Kembo's stepdaughter, was found on the shore of the Fraser River. She had either been drowned or suffocated.

A few days later, Kembo was arrested by the RCMP. He was charged with killing his wife, his mistress, and his stepdaughter. He was later charged with the murder of his business partner.

During the trial in 2005, it was learned that he had been ordered deported more than ten years earlier, but was allowed to stay in Canada because he did not meet all of the tests for deportation (he was not considered a public danger). Charles Kembo was sentenced to life in prison with no possibility of parole for 25 years. In April 2014 he appealed his conviction; three months later the B.C. Court of Appeal rejected arguments from his lawyer and his appeal was denied.

Kennedy, Edward Dean (May 5, 1945 – July 21, 1992) was serving a life sentence for the murder of a motel clerk in 1978 when he and two other prisoners escaped from the

Union Correctional Institution north of Gainesville, Florida, on April 11, 1981.

Kennedy fled to the town of Baldwin, west of Jacksonville, and broke into the trailer home of Floyd Cone Sr. He was changing clothes when Fred Jr., Mr. Cone's son and his cousin Highway Patrol officer, Robert Patrick, drove onto the property. They were both killed in a shootout with Kennedy.

Kennedy was sentenced to death. On July 21, 1992, he was led to the gray execution chamber and strapped into the oak chair, known as "Old Sparky". Before he was electrocuted, he said, "Peace be with you all," and added in Arabic, "Allah Akbar," which means, "God is great."

Kennedy, Julian (b. 1943) was an escaped convict awaiting trial on robbery charges in March 1973. He confessed to multiple murders, his first when he was only 15 as part of an initiation into "outlaw" motorcycle gangs in the South. He confessed to at least six murders during holdups across the states of Arkansas, New Mexico, and Texas, plus the murder of a woman in Valdosta, Georgia. He was tried and convicted of the murder in Georgia. He was sentenced to life in prison.

Keyes, Israel (January 7, 1978 – December 2, 2012) was an admitted serial killer, rapist, arsonist, burglar, and bank robber. However, we may never know the whole story because Israel Keyes committed suicide on December 2, 2012, in his jail cell in Anchorage, Alaska, after his confession.

Keyes was born in Cove, Utah, the second of ten children. He was raised a Mormon and was home-schooled. His family moved to Washington near the town of Colville where they were neighbors and friends with the Kehoe family, notorious for being white supremacists. Kirby, the father, and sons, Chevie and Cheyne, made big news back in the late 1990s. Keyes eventually rejected religion and identified himself as an atheist.

Keyes admitted to the violent sexual assault of a teenage girl in Oregon in the mid to late 1990s. He also claimed to have murdered four people in the state of Washington in the late 1990s. Keyes lived in several places in Washington during that time. While in the navy, sometime between 1998 and 2001, he was stationed at Fort Lewis a few miles southwest of Tacoma. He also lived in the Makah Reservation community of Neah Bay on the Olympic Peninsula.

Keyes admitted to the murders of Bill and Lorraine Currier in Essex, Vermont, and a murder in New York State, but did not give the name, age, or gender of the victim. Authorities have enough evidence to link Keyes to some of the murders. He told authorities that he robbed banks in New York and Texas. It was later confirmed by the FBI that he had robbed the Community Bank branch in Tupper Lake, New York, in April 2009. His last known murder was the kidnapping and murder of Samantha Koenig, age 18, in Anchorage, Alaska. He demanded $30,000 ransom and was paid. He dismembered her body and disposed of the parts in Matanuska Lake, north of Anchorage. Police tracked withdrawals from the account and watched as Keyes eventually moved through the southwest, heading east. He was arrested in Texas after using Koenig's debit card. He was extradited to Alaska and was being held in custody at the Anchorage jail when he committed suicide by cutting his wrists and self-strangulation.

Keys, Russell (1957 – 1998) was killed by his wife, Dominique, in Phoenix, Arizona, after he allegedly claimed (in the presence of Dominique and his friend, Paul Gilligan) to have murdered five women in Portugal, France, and Morocco when they rejected his attempts to marry them. After the confession, Gilligan said he heard three shots and found the body of his friend, Russell Keys. Dominique was arrested and claimed to have shot her husband in self-defense as he tried to strangle her. She was found guilty and sentenced to life in prison but will be eligible for parole after serving 25 years.

Kha, Roshu/Khan, Rasu is a confessed serial killer of 11 female garment workers in Bangladesh. In 2015, he was sentenced to death for the rape and murder of a 19-year-old woman in 2008.

Khamarov, Ruslan (b. 1973) was a serial killer in Ukraine who murdered at least 11 women between 2000 and 2003. Khamarov was born in the city of Berdiansk to a father of Uyghur ancestry. His father abandoned the family in 1981. He converted to Islam and moved to Makhachkala in the Republic of Dagestan, Russia. His mother jumped under a train in 1985, committing suicide.

Khamarov grew up in an orphanage and attended the vocational school, graduating in 1991. He was arrested in 1991 for theft and was sentenced to 2-1/2 years in prison. When he was released in 1993, he lived in Zaporizhya until 1997, when he was again arrested for theft. Between 1997 and 2000, he was confined to a psychiatric hospital. He returned to the city of Berdiansk upon his release.

In November 2000, Khamarov murdered a 47-year-old woman. This was his oldest victim. He usually sought out younger girls. He picked them up in the park, bars, or dance parties, invited them back to his house, drank vodka, engaged in sex either willingly or forced upon the victim. He then killed the victim and engaged in sexual intercourse with the corpse. When he was done, he disposed of the corpse down a well.

Between November 2000 and February 2003, he murdered 11 girls and women. His last victim, Polina Izvekova, age 17, was murdered on February 24, 2003.

When she had not returned to her mother's home after three days, the mother called the police. They found Polina's body in the well.

Khamarov was found to be sane at the time of the murders, and he was therefore tried and convicted. He was sentenced to life in prison.

Killer Clown
Gacy, John Wayne

Killer Clown aka **Gacy, John Wayne** (March 17, 1942 – May 10, 1994) was an American serial killer in Illinois in the 1970s. Gacy was the only son and middle child of John Samuel Gacy, a machinist, and Marion Elaine Robinson Gacy. John Gacy grew up being overweight and a nonathletic person. His father was an alcoholic and physically abusive to his wife and children. When Gacy was nine, he was sexually abused by a family friend. When he was 11, he was struck in the head by a swing which caused a blood clot in his brain that was not discovered until he was 16, when he began to have blackouts. He took medication to dissolve the clot. He did not graduate from high school. At age 20, following another argument with his father, he left home and moved to Las Vegas, Nevada, but returned to Chicago after just three months. He enrolled and graduated from Northwestern Business College. He worked as a management-trainee for the Nunn-Bush Shoe Company, then was transferred to Springfield, Illinois as a salesman. He was promoted to manager of his department and became active in local organizations, joined the Jaycees, and by 1965 was the vice president of the Springfield chapter.

Gacy met and married Marlynn Myers. His father-in-law appointed him manager of three KFC (Kentucky Fried Chicken) restaurants in Waterloo, Iowa, and the Gacys moved to Iowa. He and his wife had two children, a son and a daughter.

His move to Iowa not only was his first experience at managing restaurants, but was the place of his first sexual experience with a man, a fellow Jaycee. There was more to the Waterloo Jaycees than business. They were also involved in wife swapping, prostitution, pornography, and drugs. Gacy became involved in these activities. By 1967, he was abusing his teenage male employees. He sometimes paid the boys, claiming that he was carrying out homosexual experiments for scientific research.

In March 1968, two boys, aged 15 and 16, accused Gacy of sexually assaulting them. Gacy was arrested and convicted of sodomy. He was sentenced to ten years. On that day, his wife filed for divorce and requested possession of the couples' home and property, full custody of their two children, and alimony payments. The court awarded her everything she asked for. Gacy never saw his family again. He was paroled on June 18, 1970 after serving only 18 months of his sentence. He went back to Chicago to live with his mother.

In 1971, Gacy was again charged with the sexual assault of a teenage boy, but the charge was dismissed when the boy failed to show up in court. Gacy bought a house in Norwood Park in August 1971 with help from his mother and they moved in together. Gacy met and became engaged to Carole Hoff, a woman he had dated briefly in high school. Carole had two daughters from her previous marriage. The three of them moved into the house and Gacy's mother moved out.

On January 2, 1972, Gacy picked up Timothy Jack McCoy, age 15, at the Greyhound bus terminal and took him on a sightseeing tour of Chicago. Gacy told the boy that he could spend the night at his house, and he would drive him back to the bus station in time to catch his bus in the morning. Gacy awoke to find the boy standing over him with a knife. A fight ensued and Jack McCoy was killed. When Gacy went into the kitchen, he saw that McCoy had been in the process of preparing a breakfast of bacon and eggs, and had probably entered the bedroom absentmindedly carrying a kitchen knife. McCoy was buried in the crawl space beneath the house.

On June 22, 1972, John Gacy was arrested and charged with battery after a young man claimed that Gacy had flashed what looked like a police badge, lured him into his car, and forced him to perform oral sex on him. The charges were dropped when the young man attempted to blackmail Gacy.

John and Carole were married on July 1, 1972. Gacy started his own construction business calling it PDM Contractors (PDM = Painting, Decorating & Maintenance). In the beginning, the work consisted of minor repairs, but later would include interior design, remodeling, installation, assembly, and landscaping. In 1978, Gacy grossed over $200,000.

By 1975, the marriage had gone sour. The couple no longer had sexual relations after Gacy admitted to Carole that he was bisexual, and she saw him bringing teenage boys into his garage. She had also found gay pornography in the house. They divorced in March 1976.

Gacy had become active in the local community, entertaining at picnics and parties as a clown and volunteering to clean the local Democratic Party office. He was rewarded for his volunteer work by being appointed to serve on the Norwood Park Township street lighting committee. He was later the precinct captain. He was appointed director of Chicago's annual Polish Constitution Day Parade (Gacy was of Polish and Danish heritage), a position he held from 1975 to 1978, and was even photographed with First Lady Rosalynn Carter, wife of President Jimmy Carter.

Gacy learned of the Moose Club members known as the "Jolly Jokers" who dressed as clowns and entertained at fundraising events and parades. Gacy created his own clown—Pogo the Clown—designed his own costumes and learned the technique of applying clown makeup. He often spoke of entertaining children at the local hospitals; there is no evidence to support this statement.

In January 1974, Gacy committed his second (known) murder, an unidentified male aged 18-20 who was found buried under the barbecue pit. On July 29, 1975, Gacy murdered for the third time (known), John Butkovitch, age 17. Gacy continued his rapes, tortures, and murders. In 1976, he raped, tortured, and murdered 14 boys and young men. In 1977, he raped, tortured, and murdered 11 boys and young men. In 1978, he raped, tortured, and murdered five young men and boys.

On December 11, 1978, Gacy was at a Des Plaines pharmacy to discuss a remodeling job with the owner. He mentioned that he hired teenage boys to help with the construction jobs. A teenage employee of the pharmacy, Robert Jerome Piest, overheard the conversation and told his mother when she came to pick him up from his job that he was going to talk to a local contractor about a job. He told his mother he would return shortly. When Robert had not returned, his family filed a missing person's report. The owner of the pharmacy told the authorities that Gacy was probably the contractor that Robert had left with. The authorities contacted Gacy, who denied having had any conversation or association with Robert Piest. Police checked Gacy's record and discovered that he had an outstanding battery charge against him in Chicago and had served time in Iowa for sodomy. A search of Gacy's house was authorized and undertaken on December 13. Searchers found a 1975 high school class ring, several different driver's licenses belonging to young men and boys, handcuffs, a 2 x 4 with holes drilled in the ends, books on homosexuality and pederasty (anal intercourse with a boy), a syringe, clothing too small for Gacy, and a photo receipt from the pharmacy where Robert Piest worked. Gacy was put under surveillance while the police continued to investigate Piest's disappearance. Gacy filed a $750,000 civil suit against the Des Plaines police demanding the surveillance cease.

Further investigation linked Gacy to the disappearance of three other males. A former employee of Gacy's and Gacy's second wife, Carole, told of the disappearance of John Butkovitch, age 18. The high school ring found in Gacy's house belonged to John Suzy. The pharmacy receipt found in Gacy's house was traced to a friend of Piest's, who told authorities she had placed it in Piest's parka pocket just before he left the store. Another employee of Gacy's told that Gacy had made him dig trenches in the crawl space of his house.

On December 20, 1978, Gacy invited two of the surveillance team detectives into his house. They were immediately aware of the smell of corpses coming from a heating duct. The search team had previously failed to notice the odor because the house was cold at that time. On December 21, the police obtained a second search warrant for Gacy's house. To hold Gacy in custody while they again searched the house, the police arrested him on a charge of marijuana possession. After digging in the crawl space of Gacy's home, police found human bones. The informed detectives of their find and Gacy was charged with murder.

During the wee hours of December 22, Gacy confessed that since 1972, he had committed somewhere between 25 and 30 murders, all of whom he said were teenage male runaways or male prostitutes, which proved to be untrue.

Gacy's Victims
Name   Age   Date of Murder
Timothy McCoy   15   January 2, 1972
Unidentified Male   18-20   January 1974
Unidentified Male   15-17   July 1975-May 1976
John Butkovitch   17   July 29, 1975

Darrell Sampson   18   April 6, 1976
Randall Reffett   15   May 14, 1976
Samuel Stapleton   14   May 14, 1976
Michael Bonnin   17   June 3, 1976
William Carroll   16   June 13, 1976
Unidentified Male   20-24   June 13-Aug. 6, 1976
Unidentified Male   17?   June-December 1976
Rick Johnson   17   August 6, 1976
Kenneth Parker   16   October 25, 1976
Unidentified Male   19-21   August-Dec. 1976
Unidentified Male   22-28   August-Dec. 1976
Michael Marino   14   October 25, 1976
Gregory Godzik   17   December 12, 1976
John Szyc   19   January 20, 1977
Unidentified Male   25?   Jan. 20-March 15, 1977
Jon Prestidge   20   March 15, 1977
Matthew Bowman   19   July 5, 1977
Unidentified Male   18-20   July-September 1977
Robert Gilroy   18   September 15, 1977
John Mowery   19   September 25, 1977
Russell Nelson   21   October 17, 1977
Robert Winch   16   November 10, 1977
Thomas Boling   20   November 18, 1977
David Talsma   19   December 9, 1977
William Kindred   19   February 16, 1978
Timothy O'Rourke   20   June 16-23, 1978
Frank Landingin   19   November 4, 1978
James Mazzara   21   November 24, 1978
Robert Piest   15   December 11, 1978

Twenty-six of the victims were found buried in Gacy's crawl space and he stated that he would periodically pour quicklime to accelerate the decomposition process. One victim was found beneath the concrete floor of the garage, one was found in a pit beneath a barbecue grill in the back yard, and another was found buried beneath the joists of the dining room floor. Several of the victims were found with a ligature still tied around their necks and some were found with cloth gags stuffed deep into their throats. Three bodies recovered from the Des Plaines River between June and December 1978 were confirmed as being the victims of John Wayne Gacy. Some of the victims were easily identified due to their known connection to Gacy; others were identified from items found in or on the Gacy property. Eight victims are still unidentified.

On February 6, 1980, John Wayne Gacy was finally brought to trial in Rockford, Illinois before Judge Louis Garippo. He was charged with 33 murders. Gacy spent over 300 hours with doctors at the Menard Correctional Center undergoing a variety of psychological tests before a panel of psychiatrists to determine whether he was mentally competent to stand trial. Gacy tried to convince the doctors that he had a multiple personality disorder. He pleaded not guilty by reason of insanity. Three psychiatric experts who appeared for the defense said that they found Gacy was a paranoid schizophrenic and did, in fact, suffer from a multiple personality disorder.

The prosecution, however, was convinced that Gacy was sane, fully in control of his actions, and based their case on these facts. They had their own psychiatric experts who testified that Gacy was sane and did not suffer from any kind of multiple personality disorder. Two of Gacy's employees testified that Gacy made them dig trenches in very specific locations in his crawl space and that he checked frequently to be sure they were dug exactly where he ordered. At one point, Gacy's defense team tried to raise the possibility that all 33 murders were accidental erotic asphyxia deaths which was countered by the Cook County coroner with the evidence that made this assertion impossible. In addition, two of his victims of sexual assault testified against him. The case boiled down to the fact that Gacy had no defense for what he had done. The bodies were found buried under his house and property and he had confessed to the murders.

On March 12, 1980, the jury deliberated for less than two hours and found Gacy guilty of each and every murder. Both sides made their pleas for sentencing. The prosecution requested that they should sentence Gacy to death. The defense asked for life imprisonment. After a little more than two hours, the jury returned with its sentence of death.

Gacy was incarcerated at Menard Correctional Center in Chester, Illinois, for 14 years before his sentence was carried out. During those 14 years, he began to paint; many works were portraits of clowns, which were sold at auction. He also spent a lot of time studying law books and filing numerous exhaustive appeals and motions. His final appeal was denied on March 4, 1985, by the United States Supreme Court.

On May 10, 1994, John Wayne Gacy was finally executed at Stateville Correctional Center in Joliet, Illinois by lethal injection, after some difficulty. Before the execution, the lethal chemicals unexpectedly solidified, which clogged the IV tube in Gacy's arm. The blinds were closed between the execution chamber and the witnesses. The IV tube was changed. After 10 minutes, the blinds were opened, and the execution took place. It was said that Gacy did not express any remorse for his crimes.

After his execution, Gacy's brain was removed and examined by forensic psychiatrists. They stated it revealed no abnormalities.

In July 2017, another victim of John Wayne Gacy was identified as James Byron Haakenson, age 16, who ran away from home in St. Paul in the summer of 1976.

Killing Team aka **Sims, Mitchell Carlton** (b. 1960) and **Padgett, Ruby Carolyn** (b. 1965) tortured and murdered three employees of pizza restaurants during robberies in 1985 in South Carolina and California. Their victims were

Gary Melkie and Chriss Zerr, who worked at a Domino's restaurant, and John Steven Harrigan, age 21, who was a Domino's delivery man. Apparently, Sims was angry that he didn't get the bonus he thought he deserved while working for the pizza chain. Padgett and Sims were arrested on December 25, 1985. Sims was sentenced to death in California in 1987. Padgett was sentenced to life without the possibility of parole. As of this writing, Sims remains on death row at San Quentin State Prison in San Quentin, California.

Kimball, Scott Lee (b. September 21, 1966) was released early from prison, where he was serving time for check fraud, to become an FBI informant. He is also a serial killer who may have murdered as many as 17 people in Colorado and New Mexico.

Kimball was arrested on March 14, 2006, and charged with the murders of Kaysi McLeod, age 19, who disappeared in 1993 and whose body was found by hunters in northwestern Colorado; Jennifer Marcum, age 25, disappeared on February 17, 2003 and whose body has not been found; and LeAnn Emry, age 24, disappeared on January 30, 2003. Human remains found in the Book Cliffs Mountains in Utah were identified as Emry by DNA tests. Kimball's uncle, Terry Kimball, age 60, disappeared in 2004. His body has not been found.

Authorities said that Scott Kimball has provided some credible information, but they believe he has withheld details. Kimball pleaded guilty to two counts of second-degree murder on October 8, 2009. He was sentenced to 70 years behind bars.

In December 2010, Kimball revealed that he was being investigated as a potential suspect in the West Mesa murders in New Mexico.

Kimes, Sante (July 24, 1934 – May 19, 2014) and her son, **Kimes Jr., Kenneth** (b. March 31, 1975) were a mother and son team who murdered, robbed, violated anti-slavery laws, and committed forgery and numerous other crimes.

Sante spent most of her life fleecing people out of their money or possessions. She was the epitome of the term "con artist". When her son, Kenneth, was old enough, he joined his mother in her illegal ways.

Sante committed insurance fraud on numerous occasions, sometimes by arson. She enslaved young, homeless, illegal immigrants and kept them prisoners by threatening to report them to immigration if they did not do exactly as she said. In 1985, Sante was sentenced to five years in prison for violating anti-slavery laws. Her husband, Kenneth Sr., took a plea deal and agreed to complete an alcohol treatment program. He died in 1994.

In one incident, David Kazdin allowed Sante Kimes to use his name on the deed of a home in Las Vegas where Sante and her husband lived. She convinced a notary to forge Kazdin's signature on an application for a loan of $280,000. When Kazdin discovered the forgery, he threatened to expose Sante. She ordered him killed and her son, Kenneth Jr. shot him in the back of the head. Sante and Kenneth Jr. got rid of the body and the evidence. Kazdin's body was found in a dumpster near Los Angeles airport in March 1998.

In June 1998, in Manhattan, New York, Sante and Kenneth Jr. schemed together for Sante to assume the identify of their landlady, socialite Irene Silverman, age 82, and then take over ownership of her mansion valued at approximately $7.7 million at that time. Even though her body has never been found, both Sante and Kenneth were convicted of her murder in 2000. Authorities had discovered notes written by Silverman, who was extremely suspicious of the Kimes, and Kimes' own notes detailing the crime. Kenneth confessed to strangling the woman after his mother had used a stun gun on her. He stuffed her body into a bag and put it in a dumpster in Hoboken, New Jersey.

Kenneth Jr. confessed to the murder of Sayed Bilal Ahmed in the Bahamas in 1996 after Sante had ordered him killed. Kenneth and Sante drugged the man, drowned him in the bathtub, and then dumped his body in the Atlantic Ocean. Even though Bahamian authorities suspected the Kimes of murdering Sayed, charges were never brought against them.

Sante denied any participation in any of the murders and stated that Kenneth's confession was an effort to avoid the death penalty.

Sante and Kenneth were convicted of the murder of Irene Silverman plus other charges including robbery, burglary, conspiracy, grand larceny, forgery—a total of 117 other charges. Sante Kimes was sentenced to life plus 120 years. Kenneth Kimes Jr. was sentenced to life plus 125 years.

In the California trial of Sante and Kenneth Kimes for the murder of David Kazdin, both mother and son were sentenced to death.

Sante was serving her New York sentence of life plus 125 years in New York at Bedford Hills Correctional Facility for Women, when she died there of natural causes on May 19, 2014.

Kenneth is currently housed at the Richard J. Donovan Correctional Facility, San Diego, California.

Kinne, Sharon (b. 1940) was born Sharon Elizabeth Hall. She was only 16 when she became pregnant and married James, the boy responsible, because it seemed like the right thing to do, especially in a place like Independence, Missouri. Neither loved the other. A miscarriage negated the need for the marriage, but they stayed together. By 1960, they had a mortgage and two children. Sharon was not happy and wanted a different life. On March 19, 1960, police were called to the home and found James dead in his bed. He had been shot once in the head. Sharon told police that their 2-year-old daughter must have been playing with the pistol when it discharged. The death was ruled a suicide.

Sharon bought herself a new car with some of the insurance money and got herself a new boyfriend, Walter Jones, the salesman who sold her the car. On May 27, 1960, Sharon again called police to report the discovery of a woman's lifeless body on a rural road in Jackson County. The victim had been shot four times. It turned out that the victim was none other than Walter Jones' wife. Sharon's story was that they were out looking for Walter's wife whom he thought was meeting another man in the secluded "lovers' lane". Police learned that Sharon had recently obtained a pistol with the help of a male coworker. She was indicted for murder in September. However, ballistics tests indicated that her gun was not the murder weapon.

Upon her release she was immediately arrested for the murder of her husband. Homicide detectives did not like the "accident" theory. Experts testified at Sharon's trial in January 1962 that the two-year-old could not have pulled the trigger on the gun that killed her husband James. She was convicted and sentenced to life. Upon appeal the trial was set aside and a new trial was ordered. Sharon was released. The jury deadlocked on the retrial and a new trial was scheduled for October 1964.

On September 14, 1964, Sharon and her new boyfriend, Frank Puglise, checked into a hotel in Mexico City. A few days later, after quarrelling with the newest man in her life, she took up with Francisco Ordonez, a local radio announcer, and the two went to Ordonez's hotel room. The proprietor heard shots a short time later, rushed to the room, and found Ordonez sprawled on the floor with two bullets in his heart. Sharon was standing over him with gun in hand. She shot at the manager as he turned to leave, and they were fighting over the weapon when police arrived.

Sharon claimed self-defense but was not believed. She was sentenced to 10 years in prison. Upon appeal, three more years were added to the original sentence.

Sharon Kinne escaped from the Mexican prison where she was being held on December 7, 1969. Despite an extensive manhunt (or womanhunt, as the case may be), she has never been found.

Kirkland, Anthony (b. September 13, 1968) murdered five people, one as early as 1987. After being released from prison, he murdered three more people in 2006 and one in 2009.

In 1987, Kirkland killed his girlfriend, Leola Douglas, age 27, and set her body on fire. He opted for a "plea" deal and pleaded guilty to manslaughter in exchange for a sentence of 16 years. He was released in 2004.

In April or May 2006, he murdered Mary Jo Newton, age 45, and in May 2006, he murdered Casonya Crawford, age 15. On December 22, 2006, he murdered Kimya Rolison, age 14. On March 7, 2009, he murdered 13-year-old Esme Kenney. Three had been strangled. He burned each of the victims in an attempt to conceal evidence of rape.

Anthony Kirkland was arrested on March 8 near the scene of Esme Kenney's murder and was in possession of her watch and iPod. He was convicted of aggravated murder, gross abuse of a corpse, attempted rape, and aggravated robbery. On March 31, 2010, Anthony Kirkland was sentenced to death. He awaits his sentence at Chillicothe Correctional Institution in Chillicothe, Ohio.

Kirmes Killer aka **Bartsch, Jurgen** (November 6, 1946 – April 28, 1976) was born Karl-Heinz Sadrozinski in Essen, Germany, the son of a young mother who died of tuberculosis soon after giving birth. He lived at the hospital where his mother had left him and was adopted when he was 11 months old by a butcher and his wife from Langenberg (now Velbert-Langenberg). His name was changed to Jurgen Bartsch. His adoptive mother was fixated on cleanliness. He was not permitted to play with other children because he might get dirty. His mother bathed him until he was 19. He was put in a Catholic school after his parents decided that the public school was not strict enough.

In 1960, Bartsch molested his first victim, 10-year-old Axel. He took Axel to a cave in the forest, forced him to undress, lie on his lap on his stomach so that his buttocks were available for just 13 blows, Bartsch promised the boy. In reality, it was more than 13 blows, each harder than the last. Bartsch finally stopped only because his hand hurt and he could do no more. He threatened the boy with death should he tell anyone. Axel told no one. Bartsch's second victim was also enticed into the cave where razor blades were waiting. Fortunately for the boy, he escaped before Bartsch could injure him.

In 1962, Bartsch murdered Klaus Jung. On August 7, 1965, he murdered Peter Fuchs. After meeting him near a fair, Jurgen offered Fuchs a ride home. Bartsch stopped in the forest, forced the boy to take off his clothes, then chained him and took him to the cave where he murdered him. One week later, Jurgen spotted another innocent young boy, Ulrich Kahlweiss, whom he enticed into the car. He drove away to a solitary road where he stopped, then undressed and shackled Kahlweiss. Jurgen hit the child on the head with a heavy hammer and killed him. Bartsch was so shocked at his own behavior that he began to drink and lost his driver's license.

Without a driver's license, Jurgen turned to taxi service— one for the ride to the forest and one for the return. In 1966, using this method of transportation, Bartsch slaughtered Manfred Grassmann while the boy was still alive. A short time later, on June 18, 1966, he took 5-year-old Peter Frese to the cave where he hit Peter, chained him, and then masturbated. Not wanting to get home too late, he left the child in the cave. Peter undid his chains and fled.

Bartsch was arrested, and on November 30, 1967, even though he was a juvenile when he committed the first two murders, he was tried as an adult and sentenced to life in prison. He was sent to a psychiatric nursing home where he would spend the rest of his life.

The psychiatrists at the nursing home offered several therapy concepts: psychotherapy, castration or psychosurgery, but Bartsch declined. After he had served ten years, Bartsch decided to be castrated so he would not have to stay in the mental hospital for the rest of his life.

During the operation on April 28, 1976, Bartsch was given an overdose of halothane (a general anesthetic), accidently causing his death.

Kitakyushu Serial Murders were committed by **Matsunaga, Futoshi** (b. April 28, 1961) and his accomplice, **Junko Ogata**, in the city of Kitakyushu on the island of Kyushu, Japan.

Matsunaga's first victim was a married woman who had three children. He convinced her to leave her husband. He told her that Junko was his sister. While in his custody one of the children died mysteriously in September 1993 and the other two were sent to live with their father. During their relationship, Matsunaga had defrauded the woman of 11.8 million yen. The woman died mysteriously in March 1994. Police could not prove that Matsunaga had murdered the woman or her child.

In 1994 Matsunaga began victimizing Kumio Toraya and his daughter whom he held captive in his room. They were tortured and on February 26, 1996, Toraya died. Junko and Kumio Toraya's daughter threw his remains into the sea after they were pulverized.

Matsunaga's next victim was a woman who was an acquaintance of Kumio Toraya's. He defrauded the woman of 5.6 million yen (approx. $55,250 US). She and her daughter were held captive in Matsunaga's room. The woman escaped by jumping from the second floor in March 1997 and was put into a mental hospital.

His accomplice, Junko Ogata, was often mistreated and more or less held captive by him, but still participated in the tortures and murders. He continued to defraud, victimize, and murder women and members of Junko's family. Matsunaga boiled some of their remains in pots. The pair was finally arrested on March 7, 2002.

Futoshi Matsunaga and Junko Ogata were charged with the murders of Kumio Toraya on February 26, 1996; Takashige Ogata (Junko's father) on December 21, 1997; Shizumi Ogata (Junko's mother) on January 29, 1998; Reiko Ogata (Junko's sister) on February 10, 1998; Kazuya Ogata (Rieko's husband) on April 13, 1998; Yuko Ogata (Junko's nephew) on May 17, 1998; and Aya Ogata (Junko's niece) on June 7, 1998. Police had no physical evidence, nor had they recovered any human remains. The prosecutors relied primarily on the testimony of Kumio Toraya's daughter and Junko Ogata.

On September 28, 2005, both Matsunaga and Ogata were sentenced to die by hanging. On appeal, Junko Ogata's sentence was reduced to life in prison because Matsunaga had control over her and forced her to kill.

Futoshi Matsunaga sits on death row awaiting his death by hanging.

Kiyotaka Fujiwara aka **Katsuta, Kiyotaka** (August 29, 1948 – November 30, 2000) was a firefighter in Nagoya, Japan. He was also a serial killer who is known to have murdered at least eight and maybe as many as 22 people during the ten-year period from 1972 – 1982.

Katsuta committed several murders by strangling or shooting during robberies or attempted robberies. After his arrest, he admitted to seven other murders. It is believed that he may have raped some of his victims before murdering them.

His last known murder was on October 31, 1982, when he shot a man to death during an attempted robbery. Katsuta was arrested on January 31, 1983, during the attempted robbery of a man. He was charged with only eight murders.

On January 17, 1994, the Japanese Supreme Court sentenced him to death for the seven murders between 1972 and 1980, and another death sentence for the murder of the man on October 31, 1982. Katsuta was executed by hanging in Nagoya Detention Center on November 30, 2000.

Klenner Jr., Frederick Robert "Fritz' (July 11, 1952 – June 3, 1985) was born in Rockingham, North Carolina the youngest of three children. His father was a racist who was interested in Hitler, German history, military propaganda, military clothing, and the Ku Klux Klan. In high school, Klenner Jr. joined Demolay (a teen version of the Masons), French Club, Latin Club, the Library Club, and was an audio-visual assistant in the library. His father switched him from public school to Woodward Academy, a private school in Georgia, to escape racial integration. He was accepted to the University of Mississippi in 1960 and attended classes. In 1974, he entered summer school to get the required credits for graduation but did not finish the courses and did not graduate.

In 1977 Klenner moved to Durham, North Carolina, and was supposedly studying to become a doctor at Duke University. He soon met Ruth Dupree. They were married in 1978, but by late 1979, he was having multiple affairs. Klenner and Ruth were divorced in 1981 after she learned about his affairs. His first cousin, Susie Newsom Lynch, and her husband got a divorce and were in the midst of a custody dispute. Susie moved back to North Carolina to be closer to her family and was again in touch with Fritz Klenner. They soon became lovers. Susie was diagnosed with multiple sclerosis by Klenner while he was working at his father's clinic. His father agreed with the diagnosis.

Dr. Klenner died on May 20, 1984 and left $25,000 to Fritz, who spent most of it on weapons and military paraphernalia.

On July 22, 1984, Klenner broke into the home of Susie's ex-in-laws and shot to death Delores Lynch, age 68, Tom Lynch's mother, and Dr. Jane Lynch, Tom Lynch's sister. Their bodies were discovered by a friend of Delores' on July 24. Both had been shot in the back and in the head.

On May 18, 1985, Fritz Klenner went to the home of Susie's parents, Robert Westley Newsom, Jr. and Florence Sharp Newsom, in Winston-Salem, and shot them both. He also murdered Robert's 85-year-old mother, Hannah Carter Newsom. Klenner had made up a story about working for the CIA (Central Intelligence Agency). He told his friend, Ian Perkins, that he had been given an assignment to wipe out a communist cell that had been smuggling weapons to South America, trading them for drugs, and selling them to benefit the communists. This was all controlled by the KGB. Fritz had been told to make a "touch." Klenner and Perkins planned a three-day weekend to the Blue Ridge Mountains which would be their "cover" for that period of time. Perkins had driven Klenner to within ½ mile of the Newsom home.

Investigators came across Perkins in the search for the killer. During their interview, Perkins realized the truth and told them all of his involvement in the murders. He found out during the interview that Klenner was not and never had been a doctor and was not an operative for the CIA. He agreed to wear a hidden microphone in his next meeting with Klenner, but Klenner insisted that he was working with the CIA. He said, before driving off in his Chevy Blazer, "I've got things to do. I won't see you again."

When he got to Susie's apartment, which detectives had already staked out, they saw Klenner and Susie running back and forth from the apartment. Klenner and Susie climbed into the vehicle and then Susie's two sons, John and Jim, came out of the apartment and got into the back seat.

When he was stopped in his van in Greensboro, North Carolina, Klenner began shooting then detonated an explosive charge, killing himself and Susie. Susie's two sons were not killed by the bomb; they had been killed previously by their mother with a shot to the head.

Klimek/Gburek, Ottilie "Tillie"

Klimek/Gburek, Ottilie "Tillie" (1876 – November 20, 1936) was born in Poland and came to America as an infant with her parents who settled on Chicago's Near North Side. As an adult, people believed she was a psychic. She predicted the deaths of her five husbands and a few of her neighbors. She said these predictions came to her in dreams. She was never wrong; she had first-hand knowledge as she was the one who planned the deaths and made sure the "dreams" came true.

Tillie married John Mitkiewicz in 1895. In 1914, she told a friend that she dreamed of finding his corpse on a certain day a few weeks hence. On the very day she had predicted, John became ill and died that evening.

Tillie didn't grieve for long. Two months later, she married John Ruskowski. Again, Tillie had a dream of her husband's demise. Sure enough, Ruskowski died on the specified date.

Frank Kupszcyk, a man of means, became the next husband. Tillie learned that his life insurance entitled her to sole beneficiary benefits. Tillie had another dream. Within six months, Kupszcyk was dead as predicted.

Tillie's next husband was Joseph Guszkowski. Tillie told neighbors about her dream. She even told Guszkowski and he laughed. But she had the last laugh, Guszkowski died on the date Tillie had dreamed.

Tillie predicted that a terrible plague would strike a family who lived on her block. Those who knew Tillie and her dreams began to avoid her. Sure enough, a family's three children became ill and died agonizing deaths.

How Tillie was able to continue to attract men, given her reputation, remains a mystery. Anton Klimek came under her spell and married her in 1921. Although his family was worried, he told them, "She is a goot woman and I am a healsy man who intents to stay healsy." Anton and Tillie signed their last will and testament, leaving all their possessions to each other. The "healsy" man became ill almost immediately. His family, not Tillie, rushed him to the hospital and he survived. A doctor's examination showed that he had ingested a large amount of arsenic. The hospital notified the police and Tillie, afraid that the police would unearth her former husbands' remains, confessed to poisoning Klimek. Tillie stood in the courtroom chanting that she would not be sentenced to death. Again she was right; in March 1923 the court sentenced her to prison for life. Her last known prophecy came true.

Knighton, Robert Wesley (1942 – May 27, 2003), **Brittain, Lawrence Lingle** (b. 1973), and **Williams, Ruth Renee** (c. 1991) robbed and murdered four people in their homes in the 1990s in Missouri and Oklahoma. Knighton was given the death penalty in 1990 in Oklahoma. He was executed by lethal injection at the Oklahoma State Penitentiary on May 27, 2003. Brittain was sentenced to life in Missouri in 1990 and Williams was sentenced to 15 years in Missouri in 1990.

Knoppa, Anthony Michael (b. 1948) and **Lanham, Harry** were suspected of murdering at least four girls and young women in 1971 in Texas. Their modus operandi was to pick up women hitchhikers, women in bars, or those stranded along the highway, transport them to a vacant house where they would be raped multiple times, and drive them into the rural areas to be shot many times with a shotgun.

The body of Adele Crabtree, age 16, was found on November 3, 1972, just outside the city of Conroe, Texas. She had been murdered by several close-range shotgun blasts. Linda Faye Sutherlin, age 22, was reported missing the same day. Her body was not found until five days later near Pearland with her pantyhose tied around her neck, but she had also been murdered by close-range shotgun blasts. Witnessed saw her at a neighborhood bar after work talking with tow-truck driver Harry Lanham. During the autopsy, 72 pellets from a shotgun were found in her back, shoulders, and legs.

The remains of Collette Wilson, age 13, of Alvin Texas, and Gloria Gonzales, age 19, of Houston were found about 35 meters apart where they had been dumped by their killer/s. They had been missing since October 1971.

Lanham and Knoppa were convicted in 1974 of the murder of Linda Faye Sutherlin. Lanham was sentenced to 25 years. Knoppa was sentenced to 50 years.

The case against Knoppa for the other murders fell apart when Lanham lunged for an officer's gun at the Harris County jail and the officer shot Lanham to death. The State now had no case since Lanham was the key witness against Knoppa in the murders.

Knoppa was given an early release from prison on April 7, 1989, after serving 15 years.

Knorr, Frances (December 10, 1868 – January 15, 1894) was a "baby farmer" when contraception was almost nonexistent, and illegitimacy was taboo. "Baby farmers" took in these babies, for a fee, and were supposed to care for them until a home could be found for them. A lot of these babies never left; the "farmers" would murder them and pocket the money.

Frances Knorr began farming babies while she lived in Melbourne, Australia. She buried a couple of the babies' bodies in the back yard. She then moved to Sydney. The next tenant in the house in Melbourne discovered a baby's corpse and called police. Another baby's body was also found. Police focused on the previous tenant—Frances Knorr.

Knorr appeared on trial in Melbourne on November 27, 1893. She was found guilty of the murders and sentenced to death. She was described as being a model prisoner who spent her time praying and singing hymns. She was hanged in Old Melbourne Gaol in 1894.

Kodaira, Yoshio (January 28, 1905 – October 5, 1949) was a rapist and mass/serial killer in both China and Japan. He joined the Imperial Japanese Navy in 1923 and participated in the Jinan Incident in 1928 when over 6,000 Chinese soldiers and civilians (men, women, and children) were massacred and thousands were injured. He admitted to raping and murdering many women in China during the Japanese occupation.

He married after his return to Japan. His wife left him after he had a child by another woman. Kodaira became angry and killed his father-in-law and injured six others on July 2, 1932. He was arrested and sent to prison. He was released in 1940.

It is believed that he raped and murdered ten women in 1945 and 1946 in Tochigi and Tokyo. Kodaira was arrested on August 20, 1946. He denied involvement in three of the murders, but he was still tried for seven of them. He was sentenced to death on November 16, 1948. He was executed by hanging on October 5, 1949. It is reported that on his final day, he said, "I am fortunate to be able to die on such a calm and peaceful day."

Koedatich, James J. (b. June 12, 1948) is a serial killer, having murdered a man in Florida in 1971 and two women in New Jersey in 1982 just two months after being released from prison in Florida for the first murder.

On July 13, 1971, Koedatich murdered his roommate, Robert Anderson, age 40. He was convicted of murder and robbery and served 11 years in Raiford Prison in Florida. Upon release, he received permission from the state to move north to Morristown, New Jersey.

On November 23, 1982, an 18-year-old high school cheer leader, Amy Hoffman, was kidnapped from a shopping mall, raped, and fatally stabbed in the chest and back. Her body was found in a rural water tank three days later. Witnesses gave police a description of the attacker, but they had no suspects.

Twelve days later, Deirdre O'Brian, age 29, was kidnapped from her car on a country road and left for dead. She had been raped and stabbed. She survived long enough to describe her attacker.

On January 16, James Koedatich phoned the police in Morristown and told them that he had been stopped by an unknown assailant and stabbed in the back in Morris Township. Authorities checked out his car as part of the investigation and noted that his tires seemed to match the tracks found at the site of O'Brian's murder. After a further search, Koedatich was arrested and held on $250,000 bond. He was charged with the murder of Deirdre O'Brian on May 12 and on December 15, he was charged with the murder of Amy Hoffman. He was convicted and given a death sentence which was reduced to life in prison on appeal. He is currently serving his sentence at New Jersey State Prison at Avenel, New Jersey.

Kohlhepp, Todd Christopher (b. March 7, 1971) was born in Florida and raised in South Carolina and Georgia. His parents divorced when he was two years old and his mother was given custody of him. In nursery school, he was described as "troublesome." He was known to be aggressive and destroyed toys belonging to other children. He was also cruel to animals. His father said that Todd had only one emotion—anger. He was sent to Arizona to live with his father in 1986, after his mother divorced again. He took his father's surname and began working at various jobs. He started a hobby of collecting weapons, as did his father. His father taught him how to build bombs and how to blow things up.

On November 25, 1986, at the age of 15, in Tempe, Arizona, Kohlhepp threatened a 14-year-old girl with a .22 caliber revolver, kidnapped her, took her back to his home, tied her up, and taped her mouth shut. He then raped her. He told her that he would kill her younger brothers and sisters if she told anyone. Kohlhepp was soon arrested and charged with kidnapping, sexual assault, and committing a dangerous crime against children. He pleaded guilty to the kidnapping charge only, was sentenced to 15 years in prison, and registered as a sex offender. He was diagnosed with a borderline personality disorder. Early on at the prison, Kohlhepp was cited for violations that included violent behavior, but in later years he had no record of disobedience. While in prison he attended and graduated from Central Arizona College with a bachelor's degree in Computer Science. He was released from prison in August 2001 and moved to South Carolina, where he worked as a graphic designer for a company in Spartanburg. He attended Greenville Technical College in 2003, transferred to the University of South Carolina, and graduated in 2008 with a Bachelor of Science degree in Business Administration-Marketing.

He was able to get a real estate license on June 30, 2006, despite being registered as a sex offender. He built a firm that had 12 agents working for him. He was quite successful and was recognized as a top-selling agent. He bought several properties that were out of state, got a pilot's license, and bought nearly 100 acres of land for $305,632. He put a fence around the entire property at a cost of $80,000.

On November 6, 2003, a customer went into the Superbike Motorsports shop and discovered the bodies of four people. They were identified as the owner, Scott Ponder, age 30; service manager, Brian Lucas, age 30; mechanic, Chris Sherbert, age 26; and bookkeeper, Beverly Guy, age 52, mother of Scott Ponder. They had been shot to death. The case went cold.

On August 31, 2016, Kala Brown, age 30, and her boyfriend, Charles David Carver, age 32, were sent to clean the home of Kohlhepp. They disappeared. There were messages posted on Carver's Facebook account after his disappearance, which caught the attention of investigators. Tracking their cell phone signals led investigators to Kohlhepp's house. On November 3 they went to his property. Upon arrival, they saw a large storage container and heard loud banging noises coming from inside. They found Kala Brown chained to the wall in the container. They also found Carver's vehicle down in a ravine, covered with debris. Kala told investigators that she had witnessed Kohlhepp shooting Carver. His body was found on the property. Kohlhepp was arrested on November 3, 2016.

On November 6-7, investigators found two more bodies. They were identified as Johnny Joe Coxie, age 29, and Meagan Leigh McCraw-Coxie, age 26, who had been hired by Kohlhepp to do some work on his property. They had been reported missing on December 22, 2015.

Todd Christopher Kohlhepp was charged with seven murders, four in 2003 and three in 2015-16. He pleaded guilty to these murders, plus two counts of kidnapping and one count of criminal sexual assault. He was given seven consecutive life sentences without the possibility of parole, which he is serving at the Broad River Correctional Institution in Columbia, South Carolina.

Kondro, Joseph (1960 – May 3, 2012) was a full-blooded Chippewa, a millworker, and the father of six. He was thought to be a serial killer in the state of Washington even though he was convicted of murdering only two people. He saved himself from a death penalty in 1999 by pleading guilty to the murders of two young girls; both were daughters of Kondro's closest friends.

On May 15, 1985, Rima Traxler, age 8, was last seen walking home from Mount St. Helens Elementary in Longview. About a block from the school, Rima proudly showed her art project to a neighbor. She never made it home. Police questioned Kondro, who had been drinking with Rima's stepfather near where she disappeared but found no evidence to charge him.

In 1997, Kara Rudd, age 12, left school early because Kondro had invited her to take a ride in his gold Pontiac Firebird along the banks of the Columbia River, west of town. He instead took her to an abandoned house where he raped and strangled her. He then put her body in his car, drove to Mount Solo Road, dragged her body down a ravine, and wedged it under the shell of an old red, rusted-out Volkswagen. Kondro immediately fell under suspicion as he was the last one to have seen her. After six weeks of searching for Kara's body, the lead detective, McDaniel, ordered a search of the Mount Solo area where he knew that Kondro liked to hang out. They soon spotted Kara's black Reebok T-shirt inside the Volkswagen. They had little hope of finding much else since so much time had elapsed, but the VW had acted like a refrigerator and preserved the lower half of her body so they were able to recover enough DNA from semen to name Kondro as the killer.

Kondro was kept in isolation for 18 months before he was offered any kind of deal. He could avoid the death sentence if he admitted to murdering both Kara and Rima. Kondro agreed and gave a detailed statement of Rima's murder. He said that he took her to a swimming hole on Germany Creek where he raped and then strangled her. He said that he left her body in a shallow grave, but searchers failed to find any trace of her. They also questioned him on 70 other murders and disappearances. He was a suspect in some of the cases.

Kondro died at the state prison in Walla Walla, Washington on May 3, 2012.

Kopilov, Dmitriy (b. 1988) was a serial killer in the city of Chelyabinsk in the South Ural region of Russia who robbed and murdered at least six women and one man. The man accidentally witnessed the murder of the sixth woman. Police say that the juvenile killer followed the lone women, then attacked and robbed them. He dragged them to a nearby forest and murdered them with whatever was available— knife, rocks, a metal rod, pieces of pipe, and even animal bones. The court sentenced him to 10 years' imprisonment, the maximum penalty allowed for an underage person.

Koreatown Slasher aka **Danks, Joseph** (b. 1961) is a serial killer who preyed on the transients in Los Angeles' Koreatown. He was vicious and fast with his knife, cutting down his victims from behind and making death almost instantaneous. He was responsible for the deaths of five men and attempted to kill two others. He was caught as the result of witnesses to his last murder in a downtown alley. The witnesses pursued him for five blocks and were finally able to flag down a police car. He was arrested without incident. After his knife blade was matched to the wounds of his victims, Danks confessed.

During his trial in 1993, Danks stabbed one of his lawyers with a knife he had managed to smuggle into court. On April 2, 1993, Joseph Danks was sentenced to death. He is currently sitting on death row at San Quentin State Prison in Marin County, California.

Korn, Donald (c 1944 – October 4, 2004) was a suspected serial killer in the states of Ohio, Florida, and Indiana. He died on October 4, 2004, at the Pendleton Correctional Facility, Pendleton, Indiana, where he was serving a life sentence for the 1974 rape and murder of 72-tear-old Ruth Doench a retired Hamilton, Ohio, high school principal. He was serving the sentence in Indiana along with a 25-years-to-life sentence for the 1975 rape and attempted murder of a 54-year-old woman in Jeffersonville, Indiana.

Korn was also tied by DNA to the 1964 rape and murder of Ethel Strayer in Hamilton, Ohio. This case has now been closed with his death. Authorities believe Korn may be responsible for some of the cold cases still open at the time of his death, in particular, the 1974 rape and murder of a 76-year-old retired school teacher in Madison, Indiana, and at least four rape/murder cases in Florida, where authorities have placed Korn in that state at the time the murders occurred.

Kraft, Randy Steven (b. March 19, 1945) aka *Freeway Killer* (one of) */Scorecard Killer* was a native of Long Beach, California suspected of murdering 67 victims during the years 1971 through 1983. Forty-five bodies have been found. Twenty-two victims are still missing and presumed dead. It is believed that Kraft sometimes had an accomplice due to a second set of shoe prints being present at two murder scenes; DNA from semen was found that did not match Kraft's; Kraft would have difficulty moving the corpses that weighed over 200 lbs.; dumping the bodies from the car alone would be difficult; and Kraft had morbid photos of the dead men. Who or where were they processed? Kraft did not have darkroom expertise or any darkroom equipment.

Police also found a coded list kept by Kraft of cryptic references to his victims. The list included four double murders. Terry Gambrel was not on the list and is known to have been murdered by Kraft. Eric Church could not be found on the list, but the investigators believe that he may be listed in such a way that they have not connected it to Eric Church. Investigators believe that their total of 67 victims may not be all. There could be more – a lot more.

Randy Kraft's known and suspected victims (*Kraft's code name for victim and brief description*):

Wayne Joseph Dukette, age 30, was murdered in 1971 and is thought to be Kraft's first victim. Dukette's decomposing body was found on October 5, 1971, beside the Ortega Highway. The coroner found no signs of foul play and placed his death around September 20, 1971. His clothing and belongings have not been found. *(Stable: Last seen at Stables Bar in Sunset Beach)*

Edward Daniel Moore, age 20, was found strangled on December 26, 1972, along an on-ramp to the 605 Freeway in Seal Beach. Moore was a Marine from Camp Pendleton. *(EDM: Initials of victim)*

An unidentified male was found murdered on February 6, 1973, on the side of Terminal Island Freeway in the Wilmington area. *(Wilmington: Body was found in the Wilmington area)*

Kevin Bailey, age 18, was found on April 9, 1973, at Huntington Beach. He was not identified until March 1995 by a Deputy Coroner using a new fingerprint database of the Western US and his own computerized system. *(Airplane Hill Body was found in area known by locals as Airplane Hill)*

Unidentified head was found on April 22, 1973, at Long Beach. The torso and right leg were found in San Pedro and his left leg at Sunset Beach. *(Hawth Off Head: Head was found, then torso and legs)*

Ronnie G. Wiebe, age 20, was found on July 30, 1973, on the on ramp to the San Diego Freeway. Wiebe was an electrical company worker from Fullerton and was last seen at the Sportsman Bar in Los Alamitos. His car was found in the parking lot with a flat tire. He had been sexually mutilated.

Vincent Cruz Mestas was murdered on December 29, 1973. His remains were found in a San Bernardino Mountains ravine. *(Vince M: Part of name)*

Malcolm Eugene Little, age 20, from Selma, Alabama was traveling with his brother who was a truck driver. The brother dropped him off at the interchange of the Garden Grove Freeway and the San Diego Freeway on May 27 to hitchhike back to Alabama. His body was found on June 2, 1974 on the side of Highway 86. *(Teen Trucker: Had been riding with his truck driver brother before he disappeared)*

Roger Dickerson, age 18, was murdered in June 1974 and his remains were found at Laguna Beach.

Thomas Paxton Lee, age 25, was murdered on August 3, 1974. His body was found on a pier in an oil field area of Long Beach. *(Pier 2: Pier where Lee's body was found)*

Gary Wayne Cordova told his friends he was moving from Pasadena and was going to hitchhike to Oceanside. His remains were found on August 12, 1974, on the side of a highway in southern Orange County.

James Dale Reeves' body was found on November 27, 1974, near San Diego Freeway in Irvine. His car was found later in front of the Ripples Bar in Long Beach, which Randy Kraft frequented. *(Twiggie: A four-foot-long twig was stuffed into a body cavity)*

John William Leras, age 17, was last seen boarding a bus on January 3, 1975, in Long Beach on his way to a roller-skating rink with his new skates. His body was found the next day floating in the surf at Sunset Beach. *(Skates: Carrying skates when abducted)*

Craig Victor Jonaites, age 21, was found on January 17, 1975, in the parking lot of the Golden Sails Hotel along the Pacific Coast Highway.

Keith Daven Crotwell, age 19, from Long Beach was last seen leaving Belmont Shore with Randy Kraft on March 29, 1975. On May 8, 1975, his severed head was found in a bay in Long Beach. His skeletal remains were found in October 1975 in Laguna Hills but were not identified until 1983. *(Parking Lot: Last seen leaving parking lot with Randy Kraft from Belmont Plaza Pool)*

Mark Howard Hall, age 22, was found on January 3, 1976, in Silverado Canyon. He was from Pocatello, Idaho, but was working in Santa Ana at the time. *(New Year's Eve: Last seen leaving a New Year's Eve Party)*

Paul Joseph Fuchs, age 19, of Long Beach, disappeared on December 12, 1976. He was last seen at Ripples Bar in Long Beach. He is still missing and presumed dead. *(Expletive Deleted: Due to mispronunciation of his surname)*

Scott Michael Hughes, age 18, was last seen on April 14 and was found on April 16, 1978, on the on ramp to Riverside Freeway in Anaheim. He was from Seattle, Washington and was a Marine stationed at Camp Pendleton.

Roland Gerald Young, age 23, from Maywood was found in Irvine near the San Diego Freeway on June 11, 1978. *(Jail Out: Had been released from Orange County jail on a misdemeanor violation. Jail release form in his pocket.)*

Richard Allen Keith, age 20, was found strangled on June 19, 1978, along the Moulton Parkway in Laguna Hills. He was another Marine stationed at Camp Pendleton. *(Marine Carson: Was last seen hitchhiking from his girlfriend's house in Carson)*

Keith Arthur Klingbeil, age 23, of Everett, Washington, was found July 6, 1978, just off the northbound outside lane of the San Diego Freeway south of the La Paz exit in Mission Viejo. He was last seen the day before hitchhiking from Everett, Washington to San Diego. *(Hike Out LB Boots: The lace was missing from his left boot and Long Beach matchbook in his pocket.)*

Richard Crosby, age 20, disappeared on September 28, 1978. His body was found the next day about 200 yards north of Highway 71 in San Bernardino County. *(Torrance: Had gone to a movie in Torrance before being abducted)*

Michael Joseph Inderbeiten, age 21, was found on November 18, 1978, on the on ramp from San Diego Freeway to the 605 Freeway in Seal Beach. *(Dart 405: San Diego Freeway is the 405. No explanation for Dart)*

Donald H. Crisel, age 20, was found on an on ramp to the San Diego Freeway on June 16, 1979, after he was thrown there from a moving vehicle. He was from Des Ark, Arkansas, and was a Marine stationed at Marine Corps Air Station, El Toro, California. *(Marine Drunk Overnight Shorts: Found wearing only shorts)*

Unidentified dismembered male body was found on August 29, 1979, behind a Union 76 gas station in Long Beach.

Gregory Wallace Jolley, age 20, from Jacksonville, Florida, was found in Lake Arrowhead-Big Bear area. His body was found less the head and legs on September 14, 1979.

Jeffrey Sayre, age 15, was last seen on November 24, 1979, at a bus stop in Westminster. His body has not been found, but he is believed to be one of Kraft's victims. (*Westminster Date: Last seen with a girlfriend in Westminster*)

Mark Alan Marsh, age 20, last seen on February 18, 1980, was a Marine from El Toro who was last seen hitchhiking toward Buena Park. His body was found near Templin

Highway missing its head and hands. *(Marine Head BP: Was hitchhiking to Buena Park)*

Randy Kraft was sent to Oregon in the summer of 1980 as part of a contractual assignment by his employer. While in Oregon, Kraft is believed to have murdered two more young men.

Michael O'Fallon left his home in Denver, Colorado, to hitchhike to the Northwest. He was murdered on July 17, 1980, and his body was found 10 miles south of Salem, Oregon. He had been hogtied, plied with alcohol and valium, and strangled. *(Portland Denver: His home was in Denver and he was hitchhiking in the Northwest)*

Unidentified male was found the following day, July 18, 1980, estimated to be 35-45 years old, beside a freeway in the city of Woodham, Oregon. The victim had ingested a toxic level of valium and Tylenol. He had been strangled. *(Portland ECK: Prosecutors could not connect the ECK, but this was listed with five other "Portland" code names.)*

Just one month after Randy Kraft returned to California from Oregon, the killings began again.

Robert Wyatt Loggins' body was found in a trash bag on September 3, 1980. He had last been seen alive close to the Pacific Coast Highway on August 23. The 19-year-old was found nude in a trash bag on a dead-end street in El Toro.

On April 10, 1981, the body of Michael Cluck, age 17, was found beside Interstate 5 close to Goshen, Oregon. He had been abducted while he was hitchhiking from Kent, Washington, to Bakersfield, California, the day prior to his body being found. Note: Randy Kraft had been sent to Oregon by his employer at the time of Cluck's murder. *(Portland Blood: Of all the victims, this was the bloodiest murder scene)*

Christopher Allen Williams' partially clothed body was found on August 20, 1981, in the San Bernardino Mountains. This 17-year-old known male prostitute worked the bus stops in Hollywood.

Residents complained of a foul odor coming from the direction of the Hollywood Freeway in the Echo Park neighborhood and this was investigated by a crew from Cal Trans. The body of Raymond Davis, age 14, was found on July 29, 1982, under some leaves and soil. His wrists were tied behind his back and he had been strangled with his own shoelaces. He was last seen about two weeks earlier searching for his missing dog. *(Dog: Was searching for his dog when he disappeared)*

The same crew found the body of Robert Avila, age 16, also on July 29 about 40 feet from where Davis' body was found. He had not been missing as long as Davis, but the body was as badly decomposed. He had been strangled with stereo speaker wire. *(Deodorant: Avila was known as a heavy deodorant user)*

On November 1, 1982, Arne Mikeal Laine, age 24, was abducted while hitchhiking toward Orange County in search of work. His body was not found until January 19, 1984 on a hillside close to the town of Ramona. *(SD Dope: Was a dope user and found in San Diego County)*

On November 28, 1982, the body of Brian Witcher, age 26, was found alongside Interstate 5, close to the city of Wilsonville, Oregon. The coroner found high levels of both alcohol and Valium. *(Portland Head: Last seen in Portland. Prosecutors cannot explain the "Head" connection)*

On December 3, 1982, Anthony Jose Silveira, age 29, disappeared while hitchhiking to a National Guard drill in Medford. His body was found on December 18, 1982, near Medford. He had been strangled and sodomized, and there was evidence of his having been violated with foreign objects prior to his murder. *(Portland Reserve: Was in National Guard)*

At the time of these last two murders, Kraft was known to have been on another business trip to Oregon. The day after his business trip ended and Silveira was reported missing, Kraft drove from Portland to Seattle, Washington, to visit friends. Friends remembered that Kraft was wearing a military jacket inscribed with the name "Silveira" on it. The following day, December 5, Kraft flew from Seattle to Grand Rapids, Michigan, on another business trip.

On December 9, 1982, the bodies of Dennis Alt, age 24, from Comstock Park, Michigan and Christopher Schoenborn, age 20, from Conklin, Michigan, were found in an open field close to the Amway Hotel. Both were cousins of Randy Kraft who had attended a seminar with him and had been seen with him in the reception area of that hotel the previous night. Alt had died of asphyxiation from an overdose of alcohol and Valium. Schoenborn had been plied with the alcohol and Valium, but he lived to be strangled to death with his own belt. Both had been sodomized and their bodies were arranged in sexually suggestive positions. *(GR 2: Murdered in Grand Rapids with Alt)*

On December 8, Kraft traveled back to Portland, Oregon from Michigan. Within one day, he murdered Lance Taggs, age 19, who was last seen hitchhiking from the city of Tigard, Oregon, to Los Angeles on December 9. His body was found the following day discarded alongside a rural road in Clackamas County. He had died of suffocation after a sock was stuffed into his throat. He had suffered the same kind of atrocities as the other victims. *(Portland Hawaii: Had small tote bag marked "Hawaii". Was found in Kraft's house)*

Eric Herbert Church, age 20, was found on an on ramp to the 605 Freeway on January 27, 1983. He was from Hartford, Connecticut, and had been hitchhiking around the country. *(This writer believes that the code name "Angel" could be the code name for Church)*

Geoffrey Alan Nelson, age 18, from Buena Park was found at the entrance to the Garden Grove Freeway from Euclid Street on February 12, 1983. He (and his friend Rodger DeVaul below) were last seen near their homes in the early-morning hours of February 12, 1983. *(2 in 1*

Beach: Nelson and DeVaul [below] were abducted from the beach)

Rodger James DeVaul Jr, age 20, was found on February 13, 1983, next to Glendora Ridge Road near Mount Baldy in the Angeles National Forest. His throat had been cut. He was also from Buena Park. *(2 in 1 Beach: DeVaul and Nelson [above] were abducted from the beach)*

Terry Lee Gambrel, age 25, was found murdered in Mission Viejo in a vehicle driven by Randy Kraft on May 14, 1983.

Other code names on Randy Kraft's list that have not been tied to any known victim:

2 in 1 Hitch
2 in 1 MV to PL
Angel
Carpenter
Diabetic
England
Front of Ripples
Golden Sails
Hari Kari
Iowa
LB Marina
Marine Down
MC Dump HB Short
MC Plants
Navy White
Oil
Oxnard
Portland
User
Van Driveway
What You Got

Kraft had "partners" during the murders, some of whom helped him kill. It is believed that Kraft's roommate, **Jeff Graves**, helped in at least two murders, but he died of AIDS before authorities could question him.

Most of the victims were young men and teenage boys. All had been drugged, savagely tortured, sexually mutilated, and shot in the head or strangled to death. Socks and other foreign objects were placed in the rectums of some victims. Before the investigation was over, prosecutors concluded that Randy Steven Kraft was one of the most prolific serial killers ever in the United States.

On May 14, 1983, at 1:10 a.m., two California Highway Patrol officers pulled over a brown Toyota Celica that had been weaving in and out of traffic on the San Diego Freeway in Mission Viejo. Kraft exited the car immediately after stopping and poured out the contents of a beer bottle. Officer Michael Sterling met Kraft at the front of his patrol car and observed that Kraft's jeans were unbuttoned. Officer Sterling had Kraft walk back to the front of his vehicle and had him perform a series of field sobriety tests, which he failed. While this was going on, Sergeant Michael Howard approached the car and saw a young Marine in the passenger's seat, appearing to be asleep. Sgt. Howard gave him a rough shake in an effort to wake him, but the Marine did not awaken. Sgt. Howard felt for a pulse and finding none suspected they had a homicide. Removing a jacket covering the victim's lap, he discovered the victim's pants had been pulled down to his knees. Investigation of the vehicle yielded color photographs of several young men who were nude and appeared to be dead. Within a day, Randy Steven Kraft had been linked to four other homicides in Southern California, six in Oregon, and two in Michigan. The passenger seat in the vehicle was badly bloodstained, but the victim found there had not bled, he had been strangled. Some of the items found in the car were alcohol, tranquilizers, various other prescriptions, in addition to the envelope with the photos of the dead young men.

The investigation was turned over to the Orange County Sheriff's Department who searched Kraft's house and garage at least three times. They took many items including a flower-patterned couch which, when moved, revealed bloodstains on the wall. Investigators found that one of the photographs showed a young man nude and lifeless on that couch. The young man in the photo was Robert Wyatt Loggins, a 19-year-old Marine from El Toro who was murdered in August 1980. They also found clothing and other items belonging to his victims.

Randy Steven Kraft was eventually charged with 16 homicides committed between December 1972 and May 1983. He pleaded not guilty but was convicted on all counts. On November 29, 1989, he was sentenced to death. This death sentence was upheld by the California Supreme Court on August 11, 2000. Kraft is currently on death row at San Quentin State Prison. He continues to deny guilt in any of the murders. *See separate articles – Bonin, William and Kearney, Patrick.*

Krajcir, Timothy (b. November 28, 1944) has confessed to murdering more than nine women between 1977 and 1982. He murdered women in Missouri, Illinois, Kentucky, and Pennsylvania. Krajcir spent most of his adult life in prison, except for his two years in the navy and the years 1977 – 1982. He has been incarcerated since 1988 on rape and other charges.

Krajcir traveled to towns where he had no connections to anyone or anything. He stalked his victims, broke into their houses while they were gone, waited for them to come home, and then raped them. Rape eventually escalated to murder. Some victims were tied up and left in their beds, others were kidnapped and transported across state lines before being murdered. Some were shot in the head, some were stabbed, and some were asphyxiated. The lack of forensic and DNA technology at that time, plus the varied methods of murder, made it difficult for investigators to tie the crimes to one person.

Krajcir's known and suspected victims:

On August 14, 1977, Mary Parsh, age 58, and her daughter Brenda, age 27, were shot to death in the Parsh home in Cape Girardeau, Missouri. They were found the following day naked, face down laying side by side in bed, their hands tied behind their backs. They had been raped and each was shot once in the head.

In November 1977, Sheila Cole, age 21, was kidnapped from a parking lot of Wal-Mart in Cape Girardeau. Her body was found in a rest room at a rest area close to McClure, Illinois. She was fully clothed and had been raped and shot twice in the head.

On May 12, 1978, Virginia Lee Witte, age 51, was found by her husband in their Marion, Illinois, home. She had been raped, stabbed, and strangled to death.

In March 1979, Joyce Tharp, age 29, of Paducah, Kentucky, was kidnapped from her home. She was found naked amid garbage cans behind a Paducah church.

On April 17, 1979, Myrtle Rupp, age 51, was murdered in her home after answering the door to someone who showed a badge, claiming to be a policeman investigating a burglary. He drew a knife, took her to the bedroom, and ordered her to strip. He tied her hands and ankles with drapery cord, then raped her and strangled her with more of the drapery cord. When Krajcir confessed, he told authorities that he had stalked her and was in her home waiting for her one week earlier, but when he heard two voices, he fled.

On January 27, 1988, Margie Call, age 57, was found in her home face down, arms folded across her back, with a washcloth in her mouth. There was evidence that her wrists had been tied together. She had been raped and asphyxiated.

On April 8, 1982, Deborah Sheppard, age 23, a student at Illinois Southern University in Carbondale, Illinois, was found in the bedroom of her apartment by a friend. She was naked, had been raped and strangled.

On June 21, 1982, Mildred Wallace, age 65, was found in her bedroom, blindfolded, hands tied behind her back. She had been raped and shot in the head.

In the mid-2000s, Deborah Sheppard's murder was finally tied to Timothy Krajcir by DNA evidence left at the crime scene. He was arrested on August 29, 2007. On December 10, Krajcir was sentenced to 40 years in prison. On January 18, 2008, he pleaded guilty to the 1978 murder of Virginia Lee Witte and was sentenced to another term of 40 years in prison. On April 4, 2008, Krajcir pleaded guilty to the murders of the five women in Cape Girardeau, plus seven sexual assaults and one robbery. He was sentenced to 13 consecutive life terms.

Timothy Krajcir is currently incarcerated at the Pontiac Correctional Facility, a maximum-security prison in Pontiac, Illinois.

Kranskop Killer aka **Mfeka, Samuel Bongani** (c. 1970) was a serial killer of six women in KwaZulu Natal province in South Africa during the years 1993 – 1996. He was arrested for rape on September 6, 1996, and during questioning by investigators, he gave the locations of the bodies of the six women he had murdered. His victims were all raped and strangled. Four of the bodies were in Kranskop close to his home. Another body was found in Carletonville and one was found in Vrede. He was sentenced to four life sentences.

Krasnoyarsk Beast aka **Ershov, Vadim Nikolayevich** (b. 1973) was born in Krasnoyarsk, Russia. Nothing is known of his early life.

He was drafted into the Soviet Army in May 1991 and served in the Far East. He was bullied by other solders. He attacked one of the bullies with a brick and stabbed him several times. He deserted the army and returned to Krasnoyarsk.

Soon after, he raped a girl, age 16, who went to a vocational school, on the banks of the Yenisei River. He let her live. On November 28, 1992, he raped a 42-year-old woman and beat her with a stick.

Between 1992 and 1995, Ershov committed 18 rapes and murdered 15 of the women. He raped and murdered girls and women of all ages. He stole from his victims anything he could carry with him. He also committed over 40 robberies and murdered some of those victims.

He was finally caught when he tried to attack a 16-year-old girl and steal her gold chain. Her relatives heard her cries for help and several of them went to her aid. He fought off the first one with a knife, but one of the women knocked him out with a fire extinguisher. He was arrested, but he gave police a false name and claimed to be a tramp. Finally, they forced the information out of him. When they searched his residence, they found two of the knives he had used in the murders, the belongings he had stolen from his victims, and passports from some of them. They also found a diary where he kept detailed records of each attack, the number of the victim, the date, weapon used, if he had injured or killed the victim, scene of attack, etc.

Vadim Ershov was convicted of all charges against him and sentenced to death by firing squad. Due to the moratorium on the death penalty in Russia, his sentenced was changed to life in prison. He is incarcerated at the Black Dolphin Prison in Sol-Ilesk, Orenburg Oblast.

Krist, Gary Steven (b. April 29, 1945) and **Schier, Ruth Eisemann** (b. 1942) are best known for the December 17, 1968, kidnapping of heiress Barbara Jane Mackle and burying her in a ventilated box about 20 miles northeast of Atlanta in the piney woods. The box was fitted with an air pump, food and water, and a battery-powered lamp. Barbara was the daughter of millionaire Robert Mackle, 57, co-owner of the Deltona Corp., a pioneer of planned communities in Florida, with his brothers Elliott and Frank Jr. After the $500,000 ransom was paid, authorities received a phone call giving directions to where Barbara Mackle had been buried 83 hours earlier. She was found alive and well. The kidnappers were put on the FBI's "Ten Most Wanted" list. Krist was captured trying to escape the country in a boat he had bought with part of the ransom money. Schier was captured in Norman, Oklahoma, 79 days after the kidnapping. Both were convicted of the kidnapping. Krist was given a life sentence but was given parole after only 10 years. Schier was sentenced to seven years and was paroled after four years on the condition of deportation back to her native Honduras.

While awaiting trial, Krist confessed to a string of unsolved murders. He said that his first victim, in 1959, was a 65-year-old hermit with whom he had a sexual relationship at age 14 while living in Pelican, Alaska. He confessed that as they were walking on a bridge across a deep ravine, he tripped the hermit and he fell into the ravine. Authorities verified the case, which had been thought to have been an accident.

By 1964, Krist was in California where he killed a girl near San Diego. He said that he strangled and beat her to death, and tried to conceal her body under a pile of rocks. This death was also confirmed, and the victim was identified as Helen Crow, whose body was found on October 3, 1964. The coroner put her time of death at six to eight weeks before discovery.

Krist also confessed to killing a homosexual whom he picked up in Utah. He said that he killed the man in a fit of rage and dumped the body near Wendover, Utah. Local officers confirmed the discovery of a skeleton on July 27, 1967. The coroner's estimate of death roughly matches the time Krist had a period of freedom from custody. He also confessed to a fourth murder, but did not offer any details. These murders have never been prosecuted.

In January 2006, Krist chartered a boat to South America and upon his return on March 6, authorities were waiting for him. They discovered four illegal aliens, who had paid $6,000 each to come to the US and 14 kilograms of cocaine paste valued at approximately $1 million. He was arrested. It was also found that he was running a cocaine operation in Barrow County, Georgia. Krist was sentenced to five years and five months. He spent his sentence at the Federal Correctional Institution in Marianna, Florida, and was released in November 2010.

On August 27, 2012, a federal judge in Mobile, Alabama, revoked Krist's supervised release for violation of his probation; however, he had fled the US and sailed to Cuba and then to South America on his sailboat.

Kudzinowski, Peter (August 13, 1903 – December 21, 1929) was a serial killer of children in New Jersey at the same time Albert Fish was killing children in the New York City area.

On March 8, 1924, Harry Quinn was murdered near Scranton, New Jersey. Kudzinowski confessed to this murder.

On November 17, 1928, Joseph Storella, age 7, met Kudzinowski on First Avenue in New York City. Kudzinowski took the boy to a movie. After the movie, he took the boy to Jersey City, New Jersey, and walked him into the swamps in Secaucus. He began beating the boy. Afraid the boy's cries would attract someone, Kudzinowski slashed his throat and fled.

On August 19, 1928, Julia Mlodzianowski, age 5, was lured away from a school picnic at Lake Hopatcong, New Jersey, and murdered.

Kudzinowski was captured in Detroit, Michigan, and brought back to New Jersey. He was found guilty of first-degree murder on November 17, 1928. On February 24, 1929, he was sentenced to death. Peter Kudzinowski was executed in the electric chair on December 21, 1929, at the New Jersey State Prison in Trenton, New Jersey.

Kudzinowski was a suspect in the 1927 murder of Irving Pickelny and was also a suspect in the disappearance of Billy Gaffney, whose body was never found, but Albert Fish later confessed to this murder.

Kukri aka **Mughal, Javed Iqbal** (October 8, 1956 – October 8, 2001) was a serial killer in Lahore, Punjab, Pakistan, in the years 1998-99.

In December 1999, Mughal sent a letter to both the police and a local newspaper confessing to the rape and strangulation of 100 boys, aged 6 to 16. He claimed he dismembered the bodies and disposed of them using vats of hydrochloric acid and dumped whatever remained into the local river. In the search of his house, investigators found bloodstains on the walls and floor, photographs of some of his victims, and two vats containing partially dissolved human remains. They also found the chain that Iqbal claimed to have used to strangle the boys. In his note he said that he planned to drown himself in the Ravi River. The river was dragged, but Iqbal was not found. The largest manhunt ever in Pakistan was launched.

On December 30, 1999, Iqbal turned himself in at the local newspaper *Daily Jang* because he said he was afraid the police would kill him. He was arrested there. At his trial, he was found guilty and sentenced to death by hanging. The judge said to Iqbal, "You will be strangled to death in front of the parents whose children you killed, your body will then be cut into 100 pieces and put in acid, the same way you killed the children."

On the morning of October 8, 2001, Iqbal and his accomplice, **Sajid Ahmad**, were found dead in their cells. They had apparently hung themselves with their bedsheets.

Kulaxides, Peter (c. 1880) was charged with the murders of his first seven wives on September 22, 1930, moments before his marriage to his eighth wife in Athens, Greece. He was convicted of murdering all seven women, although he confessed only to the seventh murder, saying that he killed her because she had lied to him. His sentence is unknown.

Kulik, Vasiliy (January 17, 1956 – June 26, 1989) was a serial killer in the city of Irkutsk, Irkutsk Oblast, eastern Siberia, between the years 1984 through 1986. He is responsible for the rapes and murders of 13 people, mostly children and elderly women.

In 1984, Kulik abducted an elderly woman on the street, drugged her, and then raped and strangled her. His next victim was an 8-year-old-girl, then a woman, age 53, whom he killed with a gun and a kitchen knife. His six child victims ranged in age from two months to eight years and the seven women from their early 50s to 75.

Kulik was arrested on January 17, 1986 and convicted of 13 murders. On August 11, 1988, he was sentenced to death. He was executed by firing squad on June 26, 1989.

Kumar, Ravinder (b. 1991) was born in Badaun, Uttar Pradesh, India. Nothing is known of his formative years. He began raping and murdering children in 2008. His first victim was a laborer's child in Samaypur. The information is very sketchy. When arrested on July 19, 2015, he confessed to killing more than 30 children, most of them between four and seven years old, and targeted poor families in Delhi, Mundka, Samaypur, Badli, Begampur and Vijay Vihar. He blamed alcohol for his actions, but when asked why he had killed the children, he said, "They made too much noise." No information about his sentencing found.

Kuzikov, Ilshat (b. 1962) was known to be a cheerful and helpful individual who made his living as a street sweeper. He preferred the company of his cat, Dasha, to people. It was known by neighbors that he was an outpatient of the local psychiatric clinic, but they did not know the reason for the visits to the clinic.

A piece of human torso was found in the basement of a deserted house near where Kuzikov lived. A severed head was found in a trash can on Ordzhonikidze Street, the street where Kuzikov lived. Later, the severed head of Edik Vassilevski, a psychiatric patient and a friend of Kuzikov's, was found and Kuzikov became a suspect. When police broke into Kuzikov's home, what they found was horrifying—a bottle filled with semi-dried blood, on the coffee table a jar filled with dried ears and skin, and a cooking pot filled with the remains of Vassilevski cut into portions for a Russian style kebab.

Kuzikov was declared criminally insane in 1997 and sent to a maximum-security psychiatric hospital.

Kuzmin, Vladimir Ivanovich (b. September 14, 1965) was born in Moscow, Russia, to a sick mother who was also blind. In 1975, he began to steal and by age 12 he had several convictions for vagrancy. He did not take care of his mother; he stole her money, starved her, and beat her. At the age of 14, he was sent to a special school in Kashirskaya, a part of Moscow, where juvenile criminals and children from dysfunctional families are sent.

When he was released, by law, he could not live with his mother. He began to rob apartments on the first and second floor where he could get in and out easily, and sold the stolen goods. He was arrested and sentenced to seven years in a youth detention center. He was raped repeatedly and became a passive homosexual. He began to treat the weaker inmates the same way he had been treated. He splashed hydrochloric acid into the face of another prisoner, blinding him, for no apparent reason and was sentenced to an additional five years.

In 1993, he escaped from prison and went to Moscow. His mother had died while he was in prison. He met Denis Kalistratov, age 13, near the Tsaritsyn orphanage. He was lonely as Kuzmin was. Kuzmin treated him to a beer, took him to a construction site, and offered to do oral sex. Denis refused, but when Vladimir put a knife to Denis' throat, he agreed. After a short time, they began to live together. Kuzmin brought another boy to live with them and committed lewd acts on him using threats to accomplish what he wanted. The boy escaped and went to the police. Kuzmin was arrested and sent to prison. When he was released, he returned to Moscow.

He managed to find Denis Kalistratov and found that he lived with a girl he was planning to marry. Kuzmin demanded that Denis break up with the girl, threatening to tell the girl of Denis' past. Denis broke up with the girl and moved in with Kuzmin, but told him that he would not have sexual relations with him. On July 2, 1997, Kuzmin brought another boy, Yuri G., age 15, to the house. They drank vodka and Kuzmin tried to persuade him to have sex with him, but the boy refused. Kuzmin stuck him twice with a knife and raped him. When Kalistratov returned, he finished the boy off by strangling him with a cable. He took his corpse to a barn and burned the body.

On August 30, they met another 15-year-old, Vladimir V., and Kuzmin told him they were setting up an unloading team and offered Vladimir a job if he wanted. An appointment was set for the next day at Kalistratov's apartment to discuss the details. When Vladimir arrived, he was raped by Kuzmin and suffocated with a pillow by Kalistratov. They threw his body into the Moskva River.

Kalistratov fled the area and Kuzmin had to act alone. In September 1997, the body of a young man was found in Borisov Pond. He was identified as Vladimir K. who had disappeared two days before. He was supposed to have gone to Denis Kalistratov's apartment on September 25 to buy some marijuana. Surveillance was set up behind the apartment. Two teenagers, Artyom Malinin and Valery Vassiliev, were detained and questioned when they came to the apartment. They told police they had been looking for Kalistratov for two weeks, but he had not been to his apartment. They checked the apartment and found fresh blood in the bathroom. When they found Kalistratov, he told them that Kuzmin had a set of keys for the apartment. They found Kuzmin at a cousin's house in Moscow. Kuzmin was arrested. He confessed to 11 murders (three teenagers, five men, and three women). The bodies of four of the men could not be found.

Vladimir Kuzmin was convicted of seven murders, rape, and several other crimes. He was sentenced to life imprisonment. The first five years of his sentence were spent in a prison and the remaining years in a special regime penal colony.

Kuznetsov, Oleg Vladimirovich (April 30, 1969 – August 4, 2000) was a serial killer in the vicinity of Balashikha, in the Moscow Oblast, Russia. He confessed to killing 18 women, but eight murders have never been verified.

Kuznetsov began raping at the age of 16 and committed his first murder in May 1991, while working as a truck driver. After raping his victims, Kuznetsov murdered them by stabbing. He also stabbed their eyes because he believed that the eyes carried an image of the killer.

He was arrested on March 26, 1992. He was tried and convicted of 10 murders and sentenced to death. His sentence was commuted to life when Russia suspended capital punishment in 1999. He died of heart failure on August 4, 2000, in prison in the Russian Republic of Mordovia.

Lacenaire, Pierre Francois (December 20, 1803 – January 9, 1836) was born in Francheville, Rhone, near the city of Lyon, France, to Jean-Baptiste Lacenaire and Marguerite Gaillard. His father was a bourgeois merchant. After finishing his education, he joined the French Army. He deserted in 1829 to become a criminal. He was in and out prison frequently.

He recruited two men to assist in his crimes, **Pierre Victor Avril**, whom he met in prison, and **Hippolyte Francois**. It is not known how many people were murdered by Lacenaire, but he was tried for a double murder and sentenced to death. He was guillotined on January 9, 1836. The blue frock coat he wore for his execution was subsequently sold to a collector.

Lady Killer aka **Caputo, Ricardo** (1949 – October 1997) was a serial killer during the 1970s. Caputo was born in Mendoza, Argentina. He came to the United States in 1970 and settled in New York City.

Beginning in 1971 in Flower Hill, New York, he murdered Nathalie Brown, age 19. In 1974, he murdered Judith Becker, age 26, in Yonkers, New York. The following year in San Francisco, California, he murdered Barbara Ann Taylor, age 28. Two years later, 1977, Laura Gomez was murdered in Mexico City. He is also suspected in the deaths of Devan Green in Los Angeles in 1981 and Jacqueline Bernard, age 64, in New York City.

Caputo was No. 1 on the FBI's "Ten Most Wanted" list several times. He remained a fugitive throughout the 1980s.

He surrendered to police on January 18, 1994, and was sentenced to 25 years at Attica State Prison in New York where, in 1997, he suffered a fatal heart attack.

Lainz Angels of Death/La Dama del Silencio (The Silent Lady) were four nurses' aides at Lainz General Hospital in Vienna, Austria. **Maria Gruber** (c. 1964), **Irene Leidolf** (c. 1962), **Stephanija Mayer** (c. 1960), and **Waltraud Wagner** (c. 1960) who jointly confessed to murdering 49 patients during the years of 1983 through 1989 with overdoses of morphine or by forcing water into their lungs.

In 1983, Wagner murdered a patient with an overdose of morphine. She liked the way it made her feel—to actually have the power of life and death. Gruber and Leidolf soon became her partners, as did Mayer. They devised their own murder method: one of them held the victim's nose while one of the others poured water into the victim's mouth and they drowned. The women knew that most of the elderly had fluid in their lungs and felt their deaths would not be seen as murder. Some of the patients murdered were terminally ill, but some were not.

A doctor overheard the women bragging about their latest murder at a local tavern. He notified authorities. After their arrests, they confessed to 49 murders, but they may have murdered many more.

Waltraud Wagner was convicted of 15 murders, 17 attempted murders and two assaults. She was sentenced to life in prison. Irene Leidolf was convicted of five murders and was sentenced to life in prison. Maria Gruber and Stephanija Mayer were convicted of manslaughter and attempted murder. Mayer was sentenced to 20 years in prison and Gruber was sentenced to 15 years.

Mayer and Gruber were released several years before Wagner and Leidolf, who were released in August 2008. They all assumed new identities.

Lake, Leonard (October 29, 1945 – June 6, 1985) and his partner **Ng, Charles** (b. December 24, 1960) were serial killers in California between 1983 and 1985. They murdered at least 11 people and maybe as many as 25, including two infants.

At age six, Leonard Lake and his siblings were sent to live with their grandparents after their parents separated. It is alleged that Leonard developed an obsession with pornography from being encouraged by his grandmother to take photos of his sisters in the nude. It was also alleged that he extorted sexual favors from his sisters. At age 19, he joined the Marine Corps and became a radar operator. He served two tours of duty in Vietnam. He was diagnosed with a schizoid personality disorder and was given a medical discharge. He was married in 1975, but it did not last very long after his wife found out that he was making and starring in pornographic movies with bondage and/or sadomasochism. He served some time in prison for car theft and was released in 1980. He married again in 1981, but this second wife, Claralyn Balazs, left him due to his increasingly erratic behavior and his insistence that she star in pornographic movies. Arrested for a firearms violation in 1982, he skipped bail and moved to a remote ranch is Wilseyville, Calavaras County, California, owned by his wife, Claralyn.

Charles Chi-Tat Ng was born in Hong Kong to a wealthy company executive and his wife. He was reportedly abused by his father. Ng was described as a troubled teenager and had been expelled from several schools. He was arrested for shoplifting at age 15 and his father sent him to Bentham Grammar, a boarding school in Yorkshire, England. He was soon expelled for stealing from other students and returned to Hong Kong. He finally moved to the US and spent one semester at Notre Dame de Namur University at Belmont, California. He enlisted in the Marine Corps but was dishonorably discharged after less than a year for theft of heavy weaponry and machine guns. He was also charged with escape from confinement. He was convicted and sentenced to 14 years in a military prison. He was released after less than two years when his sentence was commuted.

Leonard Lake and Charles Ng met in 1982 and became friends. Ng joined Lake at his remote ranch and they soon began abducting, torturing, raping, and murdering people, some of whom they knew.

Charles Ng was seen shoplifting at a shop in San Francisco and fled the scene before police arrived. Lake was arrested on weapon's charge on June 6, 1985, after police found a .22 revolver with an illegal silencer in his car. He identified himself as Scott Stapley and had a driver's license in that name. The police became suspicious after seeing on the driver's license that Stapley was 26 years old and this man was obviously in his late 30s. Scott Stapley had been missing for several weeks. It was determined that the car belonged to a Paul Cosner, age 39, who had been missing for eight months. Lake was taken to the police station and during questioning he asked for a glass of water. He used the water to swallow the cyanide pill that had been hidden in the lapel of his shirt. He was rushed to the hospital, went into a coma, and was put on life support. He died four days later.

In the search of Lake's ranch in Wilseyville, the investigators determined that Lake was a survivalist who believed there would be a global nuclear war. He had built a bunker where he and his slaves (the women he kidnapped) would live and begin to replenish the earth with their children. They also found videos showing Lake and Ng torturing and raping women. The cinder block bunker is thought to have been where they kept their captives and it had a one-way mirror which investigators believe the captors could keep their captives under watch. All of this led them to start digging up the grounds of the ranch. They found the remains of 11 people in shallow graves. The victims were identified as Harvey Dubs, his wife Deborah and infant son Sean; Lonnie Bond, Brenda O'Connor and their infant son, Lonnie Jr.; Clifford Peranteau; Jeffrey Gerald; Michael Carroll; Kathleen Allen and Scott Stapley. They also found some 45 pounds of charred fragments of human bones, estimated as belonging to as many as 25 people. Paul Cosner's body has never been found.

Charles Ng had fled to Calgary, Alberta, Canada, where he was arrested on July 6, 1985, for shoplifting at The Bay department store. He pointed a pistol at the two security guards. After a brief struggle, one of the guards was shot in the hand, but they overpowered him and placed him in custody. He was charged and convicted of shoplifting, felonious assault, and possession of a concealed firearm. He was sentenced to 4-1/2 years in a Canadian prison. After serving his sentence in Canada and a long extradition battle with Canadian officials—Canada does not have a death penalty law and is reluctant to extradite defendants to countries that do have a death penalty—Ng was finally returned to California to stand trial for the murders of 12 people.

On February 11, 1999, Charles Ng was convicted of the murders of six men, three women, and two male infants. He was not convicted of Paul Cosner's murder. He was sentenced to death and is currently on death row at San Quentin State Prison in San Quentin, California.

LaLaurie,
Delphine Marie

LaLaurie, Delphine Marie (March 19, 1789 – December 7, 1849) lived with her third husband, Louis Nicolas Léonard LaLaurie, a physician, in the French Quarter at the corner of Royal and Governor Nicholls Streets, New Orleans, Louisiana, in the early

1800s. For years there had been rumors of the horrendous things that went on in the LaLaurie house. It was known that the LaLauries treated their servants badly. Delphine had been fined by the courts several times for her horrible treatment of her slaves. She had once been charged with the death of a child whom she had whipped so severely that the child jumped out of a third-floor window to her death.

On April 10, the LaLauries were entertaining guests when a fire broke out in the kitchen of the home. When the fire brigade arrived, they entered through the courtyard and heard screams and moans from the third floor. They entered the room on the third floor by breaking into it because it was locked. What they found was the unmistakable odor of death, vomit, and excrement. Not only were there dead slaves chained to the wall, but there were some who remained barely alive. One woman was so afraid that she jumped out the window. Most of the victims had been severely deformed by medical experiments and surgeries. A man had been transformed into a woman by surgery. A woman had been made to resemble a crab and she was kept in a cage. One woman's arms had been cut off and the skin made into a spiral. There were numerous pails in the room full of body parts, organs, severed heads, and things not identifiable. Some of the dead had faces so disfigured they looked like something out of a nightmare. The survivors were quickly removed to medical facilities. As word spread of the horror, a lynch mob came to the house. But they were too late; the LaLauries had escaped and were never held accountable for their crimes. An old, cracked copper plate found in New Orleans' St. Louis Cemetery No. 1 in the 1930s reads, "Mme. LaLauries, born Marie Delphine McCarthy, died in Paris December 7, 1842." However, according to the French archives of Paris, she died December 7, 1849.

Lambeth Poisoner aka **Cream, Thomas Neill** (May 27, 1850 – November 15, 1892) was a doctor and a serial killer. Cream was born in Glasgow, Scotland, but raised in Quebec City, Canada, his family having moved there in 1854. Cream attended McGill University in Montreal and in 1876 went to London to study medicine at St. Thomas Hospital Medical School. He had good reason to study abroad; he had almost killed his wife, Flora Brooks Cream, while aborting a baby. The bride's family had forced the marriage after finding out their daughter was pregnant. Flora died in 1877, supposedly from consumption. Cream qualified as a physician and surgeon in 1878 in Edinburg. He then returned to Canada to practice medicine in London, Ontario. When he was accused of murdering Kate Gardener, a woman with whom he allegedly had an affair, in August 1879, Cream fled to the United States.

Cream set up his medical practice in Chicago, not far from the Red Light district and offered illegal abortions to prostitutes. In August 1880, he was investigated after the death of Mary Ann Falkner, but nothing came of it due to lack of evidence. In December 1880, a Miss Stack died after receiving treatment by Dr. Cream. He attempted to blackmail a pharmacist who made up a prescription for her. On July 14, 1881, Daniel Stott, age 61, died of strychnine poisoning at his home after Dr. Cream had supplied him with a remedy for epilepsy. Cream again attempted to blackmail the pharmacist who supplied a prescription. Dr. Cream and Mrs. Julia Abbey Stott were arrested and charged with the murder of Daniel Stott. Mrs. Stott turned state's evidence and laid the entire blame on Cream. Mrs. Stott was not prosecuted, but Cream was found guilty and sentenced to life imprisonment in Joliet Prison. In July 1891, Cream was released after his brother had pleaded for leniency (and allegedly bribed the authorities) and Governor Joseph W. Fifer commuted his sentence.

Upon his release, Cream sailed to England using money he had inherited from his father, who died in 1887. Cream quickly resumed his poisonings. On October 13, Ellen

"Nellie" Donworth, age 19, accepted a drink from Cream. She became ill the next day and died on October 16 from strychnine poisoning. Cream wrote to the coroner offering to give the name of the murderer in return for a reward of £300,000. Cream also wrote of W. F. D. Smith, owner of the W. H. Smith bookstalls, accusing him of the murder and demanding money for his silence.

On October 20, Cream met Matilda Clover, a 27-year-old prostitute. She became ill that night and died the next morning. On April 2, 1892, after returning from a vacation in Canada, Cream attempted to poison Louise Harris. She was suspicious of him and only pretended to take the pills he had given her. On April 11, Cream talked his way into the flat of Alice March, age 21, and Emma Shrivell, age 18, both prostitutes. He offered them each a bottle of Guinness. He left the flat before the drinks, laced with strychnine, took effect. The women died in agony.

Cream wrote to the police anonymously accusing two fellow doctors of killing several women, including Matilda Clover. Matilda's death had been attributed to natural causes. The police quickly determined that the two doctors were innocent. They realized that the letter writer was the serial killer, but they did not know who had written the letter.

A policeman from New York City visiting London met Cream and asked what he knew about the poison killings. Cream took him on a brief tour of where the victims had lived. Later the policeman from New York City mentioned this to a British policeman who found Cream's detailed knowledge of the case very suspicious. Scotland Yard police put Cream under surveillance and learned of his habit of visiting prostitutes. They contacted police in the US and learned of Cream's conviction for murder by poison in 1881. On July 13, 1892, Cream was arrested and charged with the murder of Matilda Clover.

Dr. Thomas Neill Cream went on trial on October 17. On October 21, he was convicted and sentenced to death. On November 15, 1892, Dr. Thomas Neill Cream was hanged on the gallows at Newgate Prison. His body was buried the same day in an unmarked grave within the prison walls, as was customary for executed criminals.

The executioner, James Billington, claimed that he heard Cream say, as the trap door was tripped, "I am Jack the . . ." Billington claimed that he had executed the notorious serial killer *Jack the Ripper*. However, records show that Cream was still in Joliet Prison outside Chicago during the *Jack the Ripper* murders in London in 1888.

Lamborgine, Ted (b. February 1, 1941) pleaded guilty to 15 sex-related counts involving young boys, rather than accept a plea bargain that would have required him to take a polygraph test on the Oakland County child killings.

Ted Lamborgine was part of a pedophile ring in Detroit, Michigan, in the 1970s. The group operated out of a bike shop and used the boys from the poor neighborhood for their darkest fantasies. They put money in the boys' pockets and food in their stomachs, and even helped the families by paying their gas bills to get them through the Michigan winters. The men tried to be relatively gentle with the boys so they would come back. The group met at each other's homes and brought a boy to share. The boys were sodomized, photographed, put in the bathtub to clean up, given money, and released.

Lamborgine was arrested in Parma, Ohio, in 2006 and extradited to Michigan. In 2007, Ted Lamborgine was convicted of Criminal Sexual Conduct, three counts with a child under the age of 13, and 11 with a child aged 13 to 15. He was convicted on all charges and given three life sentences and 11 sentences of 10 – 15 years. He is currently incarcerated in the Saginaw Correctional Facility in Freeland, Michigan.

He is a suspect in the *Oakland County Child Murders.*
See separate article.

LaRette, Anthony Joseph (October 1, 1951 – November 29, 1995) traveled all over the US by bus. He is a suspected serial killer. He confessed to murders in Arkansas, Colorado, Florida, Illinois, Kansas, Louisiana, Mississippi, Nebraska, Texas, and Virginia. He was tried and convicted of only one murder.

On July 25, 1980, in St. Charles, Missouri, Mary Fleming was seen running from her apartment by a couple who lived nearby. She was naked except for a bikini top and was covered in blood. She made it to the door of the couple's apartment before she collapsed. Police and medical aid arrived, but Mary died at the local hospital shortly after arriving. She had bled to death from stab wounds to the chest and her throat had been cut from ear to ear. One of her lungs had been punctured. The couple had seen a white male running from the girl's apartment, get into a cream-colored convertible and drive away.

A person who knew LaRette became suspicious after hearing of the murder and the man in a cream-colored convertible. He called LaRette and LaRette admitted that he had gone to the apartment, but only to commit a robbery. This person contacted police and LaRette was arrested. He admitted that he had murdered Mary Fleming because she had lied to him. He told her not to scream and when she did, he attacked her.

Anthony Joseph LaRette was convicted of the murder of Mary Fleming, age 18, and sentenced to death. During his 14 years on death row, he confessed to many murders in at least 10 states dating back to the 1970s, saying that he would strangle his victims and then cut their throats.

Finally, on November 29, 1995, Anthony Joseph LaRette was executed by the State of Missouri.

Las Poquianchis aka **Gonzalez Valenzuela, Delfina** (c. 1930 – October 17, 1968), **Gonzalez Valenzuela, Maria Luisa** (c. 1932 – November 19, 1984), **Gonzalez Valenzuela, Carmen** (c. 1934 – late 1950s), and **Gonzalez Valenzuela, Maria de Jesus** (c. 1936 – mid 1990s) were serial killers in Mexico.

The sisters were born in El Salto de Juanacatlan, Jalisco. Although Isidro Torres, the father, was part of the rural police, the family lived in poverty. Torres was abusive and a strict disciplinarian. When his daughters wore "risqué" clothing or makeup, he would lock them in the town jail to teach them a lesson.

On the job, Torres was a violent man, often abusing his authority. He once shot and killed a man during an argument, which gained him many enemies. He and his wife, Bernardina Valenzuela, and their daughters moved to the small village of San Francisco del Rincon in the state of Guanajuato. Having grown up in poverty, the sisters feared always living that way. They saved and pooled their money and opened a saloon and bar. It did not make them rich, but it did give them enough to eat.

Later they ventured into prostitution, opening brothels in San Francisco del Rincon, Purisima del Rincon, and Leon in the state of Guanajuato; El Salto and San Juan de Los Logos in the state of Jalisco; and one in San Juan del Rio in the state of Queretaro near Mexico City. The sisters bought a bar in Lagos, Jalisco, from a gay man nicknamed "El Poquianchi" and the nickname was passed on to them as *Las Poquianchis* (which they hated). In the late 1950s, Carmen died of cancer.

The sisters searched the countryside looking for the prettiest girls. With job offers of maids and waitresses in the big cities, the poor peasant girls thought their dreams had been answered. Other times, with the help of an army captain or henchman and Delfina's lover, Hermengildo

Zuniga, girls were simply kidnapped and taken to the brothels to work.

The prettiest virgins were saved for the richer patrons, who would pay good money for an untouched girl. The others would be raped and intimidated to work in the brothels. When a girl became pregnant, she would be beaten and forced to abort and the fetuses dumped at the brothels or buried at the sisters' main ranch, Loma del Angel. If a girl got too sick for whatever reason, she would be locked in a room, starved to death, or the other girls would be forced to beat her to death with sticks and heavy logs. The bodies were burned to ashes or buried in mass graves. "Johns" with a lot of cash would also be murdered, their cash taken, and their bodies burned.

In 1963, Ramon Torres, Delfina's son, got into an argument with the police and was shot to death inside one of the brothels. The police closed down the brothel. Delfina ordered Hermengildo Zuniga to track down the cops who had killed her son and kill them on the spot. He did as he was ordered.

In early 1964, Catalina Ortega, one of the sisters' "whores" managed to escape the ranch and with her mother went to the Leon, Guanajuato police. They were lucky to talk to police officers who were not on the sisters' payroll. With a search warrant and arrest warrant for Delfina and Maria de Jesus, they raided the ranch on January 14, 1964. They found 12 starved and dirty women in a locked room. The girls pointed to places on the ground and said, "That's where you will find the bodies." The chauffeur, who was also under arrest, was forced to dig at the places indicated. They found the decomposed bodies and bones of at least 91 women, men, and fetuses. Under heavy guard, Delfina and Maria de Jesus were taken to the jail in San Francisco del Rincon. Fearing a lynching, a judge sent the sisters to the Irapuato City jail. One week later, Maria Luisa went to a Mexico City police station and turned herself in, fearing she would be lynched if she went to San Francisco del Rincon or Irapuato.

Besides murder and extortion, the sisters were also accused of having the girls raped. The "whores" accused *Las Poquianchis* of dabbling in Satanism and forcing the women to practice sexual acts on animals. The sisters were also charged with corrupting and bribing local and state authorities. Each of the sisters was sentenced to 40 years in prison.

Delfina went mad in prison. On October 17, 1968, with Delfina screaming and ranting, workers doing repairs above her cell at Irapuato jail "accidently" dropped a bucket of cement on her head and killed her.

Maria Luisa died alone in her cell at Irapuato jail on November 19, 1984. Her rat- ravaged body was found a day later.

Maria de Jesus was the only one to walk free. Why and when she was freed is not known, but the story goes that she met a 64-year-old man in prison and once both were free, they married and lived their life in obscurity, both dying in the mid-1990s.

In 2002, a new housing development was being built in Purisima del Rincon, Guanajuato, down the road from where the notorious Loma del Angel ranch was located. Workers clearing land found the remains of about 20 skeletons in a pit. Authorities determined the victims had been buried in the 1950s or 1960s and were probably victims of *Las Poquianchis*. If these are indeed victims of the Gonzalez Valenzuela sisters, they bring the total murder victims to 110.

Laser Man (Lasermannen) aka **Ausonius, John** (b. July 12, 1953) is not technically a serial killer, but it is not for wont of trying, as you will see.

Ausonius was given the name Wolfgang Alexander Zaugg when he was born in Lidingö, Sweden. His parents were immigrants, his father from Switzerland and his mother from Germany. He grew up in a working-class neighborhood of Stockholm. He claimed he was bullied as a child because he was born in Sweden. In contrast to those born in Sweden with blond hair and blue eyes, he had very black hair and brown eyes. As an adult, he had bleached blond hair and blue contacts. He had also changed his name to John Wolfgang Alexander Stannerman and later to John Wolfgang Alexander Ausonius.

The prime minister of Sweden, Olof Palme, was assassinated on the night of February 28, 1986, on the streets of Stockholm as he and his wife were walking home from the theater. Ausonius (then using the name John Stannerman) was one of the initial suspects.

Ausonius served in the Swedish Army in 1981-82 and was taught the use of weapons. When he was again a civilian, he purchased several personal weapons, but they were of poor quality after Ausonius modified them. He sawed off the barrel of his rifle to make it shorter and fitted the Smith & Wesson with a silencer and a laser. Due to these modifications, the revolver was very inaccurate. Due to this inaccuracy, his bid to murder immigrants resulted in one murder and ten injuries.

David Gebremariam, age 21 and an immigrant from Eritrea, was shot in the back on August 3, 1991, and survived. His two friends told investigators that they saw a circle of red on his body before they heard the shot.

Shahram Khosravi, age 25, an immigrant from Iran and a student at Stockholm University, was shot in the face on October 21, 1991, and survived.

Dimitrios Karamalegos was a homeless man from Greece who was shot twice in the stomach on October 27, 1991, and survived. He also reported seeing a bright red light prior to being shot.

Heberson Vieira Da Costa, a musician from Brazil, was shot in the head and several times in the stomach on November 1, 1991, during the middle of the day at a restaurant kitchen. He told police that he saw a red light before being shot. He also gave a very good description of the shooter.

Jimmy Ranjbar, also an immigrant from Iran and a student at Stockholm University, was shot on November 8, 1991. He died the following day.

There was a hiatus in the shootings at this point. Ausonius took a trip to the United States. He went to Las Vegas to gamble and then travelled to the Grand Canyon. When he returned to Sweden, the shootings began again.

Erik Bongcam-Rudloff, a Ph.D. student in Medical Science was shot in the head at a café outside the Linnaeus Garden in Uppsala on January 22, 1992. He survived and is now a scientist who represents Sweden in several international scientific networks.

Charles Dhlakama, a bus driver and an immigrant from Zimbabwe, was shot in the chest during the middle of the day on January 23, 1992, in Stockholm. On the same day, in the evening, two men were shot at a Somali club in Stockholm and survived.

Isa Aybar, an immigrant of Syrian/Assyrian/Aramean origin, was shot four times in the head and arm on January 28, 1992. Even thought he was seriously wounded, he was able to call police. He survived.

Hasan Zatara, a store owner of Palestinian origin, was shot in the head on January 30, 1992, in Hägerstensåsen. He also survived, but was paralyzed.

Ausonius had developed a hatred for Communists, Social Democrats, and immigrants. He worked as a taxi driver with low pay but dreamed of becoming wealthy. He began trading in stocks and bonds and was successful. He quickly earned a fairly large fortune and adopted a "Yuppie" lifestyle. By the late 1980s he owned a luxurious apartment and drove a Toyota Supra (instead of a Porsche, which most Yuppies drove, because he hated the company) and had a mobile phone which at that time was a luxury item. Soon he began making bad investments and depleted his fortune. He was also addicted to gambling. Finding himself in dire financial circumstances while in Germany, he successfully robbed a bank. As his only source of income, he committed 18 bank robberies before he was arrested on June 12, 1992, during a bank robbery.

He was convicted of the murder of Jimmy Ranjbar and bank robbery and was sentenced to life imprisonment. In 2016, John Ausonius was extradited to Germany and charged with the February 23, 1992, murder in Frankfurt of Blanka Zmigrod, age 68, and a Holocaust survivor. He was found guilty and sentenced to life in prison, which he is serving in Sweden's largest prison, Kuma Prison. He was also charged with stealing Blanca's handbag after killing her because he believed she had taken an electronic device where he kept his bank account numbers.

Last Call Killer/Gay Serial Killer aka **Rogers, Richard** (b. November 21, 1964) stalked gay bars, killed middle-aged men, and dumped their dismembered bodies at rural sites in New York and nearby New Jersey.

On May 5, 1991, the body of Peter Anderson, age 54, was found stuffed into several large plastic bags at a rest stop on the Pennsylvania Turnpike in Lancaster County. The last time he had been seen was two days earlier at the Townhouse Bar & Restaurant on the Upper East Side of Manhattan. Anderson was a wealthy socialite and Republican city council candidate in the city of Philadelphia.

On July 10, 1992, the head of Thomas Mulcahy, age 57, was found by a crew of state workers at a rest area on Route 72 in Woodland Township, Burlington County, New Jersey. His legs and torso were found some 20 miles away on the Garden State Parkway in Ocean County near milepost 61. He was in Manhattan on a business trip and had last been seen at lunch two days earlier. His body had been washed and sawed into seven parts. He had been bitten on the neck and stabbed in the chest.

On July 17, the limbs and torso of Guillermo Mendez, age 56, were found in garbage bags in Rotterdam, New York, just a few miles from his home in Schenectady. His head was later found in a garbage bag in a cemetery.

On May 10, 1993, the head of Anthony Marrero, age 43, was found in a bag that was ripped open on Crow Hill Road in Ocean County, New Jersey. The rest of his dismembered body was found in woods near the road.

On July 31, 1993, the last known victim of this killer was Michael Sakara, whose head and arms were found in a garbage can along the Hudson River about 30 miles north of Manhattan. About a week later, the rest of his body was found in a garbage container in Rockland County. Sakara had last been seen at a Greenwich Village piano bar when he left arm-in-arm with a "new" friend whose name was either Mark or John.

The killer picked up his victims in gay bars. After Sakara's body was found, the bartender at the Five Oaks, a gay bar in Greenwich Village, told police that Sakara had been there and was drinking with a man named "Mark" or "John" who was a nurse at St. Vincent's Hospital. Police got photos of all the male nurses from several hospitals, but she was unable to make a positive identification.

The case went cold until 1999 when Mulcahy's widow called Lt. Matthew Kuehn of the New Jersey State Police for an update on her husband's murder. The state police then sent the bags holding the bodies of Mulcahy and Marrero to the Toronto, Ontario Police Department where they were using a new technique to lift fingerprints from evidence. They found 33 prints mainly from the bag Mulcahy's body had been in. Shortly after the New Year 2001, Lt. Matthew Kuehn mailed out 51 packets of the prints and an explanation of the case to all the states and Puerto Rico, asking them to check their databases for a fingerprint match. Finally, a call came in from the state of Maine and said, "We got him." Rogers said he had killed Frederick A. Spencer, who lived in the same apartment building, in 1973, after Rogers caught Spencer in his apartment and came at him with a hammer. He said that he managed to take the hammer away and he beat Spencer with it until he was dead. Rogers was charged with manslaughter. He was found not guilty.

On the charges of murder of Thomas R. Mulcahy and Anthony E. Marrero, Rogers was found guilty and sentenced to life in prison. He is currently serving his life sentences at the New Jersey State Penitentiary.

Lastennet, Claude (b. January 19, 1971) was born in Brest, France. He spent time in a psychiatric hospital when he was 18. At the age of 22, he became a murderer who eventually killed at least five elderly women in various regions of France between August 1993 and January 1994.

Marcelle Cavilier, age 87, was murdered on August 24, 1993; Antoinette Bonin, age 76, murdered on November 15, 1993; Raymonde Dolisy nee Fournier, age 72, murdered on November 16, 1993; Augustine Royer, age 91, murdered on December 18, 1993; and Violette de Ferluc, age 92, murdered on January 8, 1994.

Lastennet was arrested on January 12, 1994. During interrogation, he admitted the murders to the police. He was sentenced to life in prison without the possibility of parole for 18 years.

Laurence, Michael George (1964 – November 16, 1995) was a murderer of young boys in Griffith, New South Wales, Australia. Laurence liked little boys, saying, "Young boys turn me on." Laurence claimed that since the age of 11, he often exchanged sexual favors with older men for money. During this time, he discovered that he preferred young boys, ages 8 to 12, not old men. New South Wales is known for its fruit, which brings fruit pickers, with their families, to the area.

Laurence was known by most of the boys as he spent every Saturday at the local football (soccer) field watching the junior football games. The boys relished his enthusiasm, which helped Laurence to gain their trust.

On September 29, 1984, after the football games, Laurence lured two boys to his home. He suggested that they play a game called "tie-ups". Soon after being bound, the boys realized that this was not a game at all. Laurence molested both boys one at a time, then took them into the bathroom where he drowned them in a tub. He buried the bodies in his yard. Sometime later, he dug up the bodies and dumped them into the local lake. The bodies were found the following year by a hunter.

In June 1986, Laurence lured a boy, age 8, from the football field and promised to buy him a hamburger. Instead, he abducted the boy, brutally assaulted him sexually, and suffocated him with a piece of wide tape covering his nose and mouth. He placed the boy's body under a tree trunk in the bush land. Witnesses reported seeing the boy with Laurence. When the police confronted Laurence, he confessed to the boy's murder, plus the murder of the other two boys. On November 16, 1995, Laurence hung himself in his cell at the Long Bay Jail Special Protection Unit in Matraville, New South Wales.

Le Prof aka **Janssen, Ronald** (b. February 6, 1971) was a teacher of technical drawings in a small town in Belgium. He is also a serial killer who may have murdered as many as 15 people between 1996 and 2010. Most of these murders included the rape of his young women victims.

Arrested in January 2010, he first confessed to the New Year's Day murder of his neighbor, Shana Appeltans, age 18, and her fiancé, Kevin Paulus, age 22, who were shot to death. They were found in their burned-out car. Janssen then confessed to the abduction and murder of a third victim, a young girl who had disappeared about two years earlier.

Janssen is also suspected in the unsolved abduction murder of Ingrid Caeckaert, age 27, who was stabbed to death in 1996; the unsolved abduction murder of Carola Titze, age 16, who was murdered in 1996; the abduction murder of Annick Van Uytsel, age 18, who disappeared in April 2006 after a party, was beaten to death and her body was found dumped in a local canal wrapped in a plastic sheet and weighted down with stones; and the unsolved disappearance and suspected murder of Tamara Morris, age 27, in 2006.

Janssen was sentenced to life in prison. Belgian officials are looking into many unsolved murders during the years 1996 – 2010.

Le Thanh Van (c. 1964) is a female serial killer who murdered 13 people in Ho Chi Min City, Binh Province, Vietnam. She had a year of training at an army medical facility which taught her, among good health treatments, how to kill a person with a poison and leave no evidence. Her motive was financial. After she murdered her victims, she took possession of their money and anything that had monetary value.

Her victims would complain of dizziness, nausea, and breathing difficulties. She would take them to a hospital, where they died, and she took possession of their property. Among the items she stole were a passenger bus, a motorbike, a house, and jewelry. Between 1992 and 2001, she murdered 13 people.

She was arrested in 1993 and jailed for fraud after poisoning her first victim, but investigators were unable to find sufficient evidence to try her. She was arrested again in July 2000 after police suspected her of stealing the minivan of a couple she had killed. Police found 1.4 kg (3 pounds) of an unnamed poison, but no traces of it was found in the bodies of the couple.

Arrested again in late August 2001, she confessed to investigators that she had murdered 13 people between 1992 and 2001 to steal their possessions. Her trial began on August 24, 2004. She was found guilty of murdering 13 people and on September 1, 2004, she was sentenced to death.

LeBaron, Ervil Morrell

LeBaron, Ervil Morrell (February 22, 1925 – August 16, 1981) was born in Galena, Chihuahua, Mexico, the son of Alma Dayer LeBaron, Sr. He lived in the United States until the Church of Jesus Christ of Latter-day Saints (LDS or Mormon Church) officially abandoned the practice of polygamy in 1890. Those polygamists were later excommunicated from the LDS Church and moved south to the state of Chihuahua in Mexico. Alma LeBaron was one of these. He moved to Mexico in 1924 with his family of two wives and eight children and started a farm and community called "Colonia LeBaron" in Galeana, Chihuahua. His son, Joel LeBaron, assumed the leadership when his father died in 1951. Joel incorporated the community and named it as the Church of the Firstborn of the Fulness of Times.

In 1972, Ervil LeBaron split with his brother Joel and the Church of the Firstborn of the Fulness of Times. He moved to San Diego and started his own church, the Church of the First Born of the Lamb of God in San Diego, California. Ervil ordered Joel's murder. The youngest LeBaron brother, Verlan, had the leadership of the Baja California church. Ervil tried to have Verlan killed. Ervil was tried and convicted of Joel's murder in 1974 in Mexico. His conviction was overturned on a technicality (more likely a bribe). His followers tried to kill Verlan in Los Molinos, but Verlan was in Nicaragua at the time. The town was destroyed, and two men were killed.

During the following years, Ervil focused his attention on killing his rival polygamous leaders. Ervil ordered the deaths of Bob Simons, who sought to minister to Native Americans; Rulon C. Allred, leader of the Apostolic United Brethren (another Mormon fundamentalist group); Ramon Marston, Ervil's own stepdaughter, murdered by Rena Chynoweth, Ervil's 13th wife; Dean Grover Vest, one of LeBaron's henchmen, who attempted to leave Ervil's church was murdered by Vonda White, LeBaron's 10th wife; Noemi Zarate Chynoweth, father-in-law of Ervil through his wife, Lorna Chynoweth, had been critical of Ervil's practices, was reportedly murdered by Vonda White and Thelma Chynoweth (Lorna's mother and Noemi's sister-wife); and Rebecca, Ervil's daughter who was pregnant with her second child, who wanted to leave the group, is believed to have been strangled to death by Ervil's stepson Eddie Marston and Duane Chynoweth, Ervil's brother-in-law.

Ervil LeBaron was arrested by Mexican police on June 1, 1979 and extradited to the US. He was convicted of having ordered Allred's death and sentenced to life in prison. He was incarcerated at the Utah State Prison in Draper, Utah, where he died of an apparent heart attack on August 16, 1981.

Ervil's brother, Verlan, was killed in an auto accident in Mexico City just two days after Ervil's body was discovered in his cell. Some of the family believes that Verlan's death may not have been an accident.

As many as 25 people are believed to have been murdered on Ervil LeBaron's orders while he was in prison. Many of his family members and others associated with Ervil's church and family remain in hiding for fear of retribution.

Lee, Bruce George Peter (b. July 31, 1960) was born with the name Peter George Dinsdale in Manchester, England, to a mother who was a prostitute. Lee lived in children's homes and suffered from epilepsy and congenital spastic hemiplegia (muscles on one side of the body are in a constant state of contraction). He limped with his right leg and held his right arm across his chest.

After his mother married a man whose surname was Lee, Peter changed his name to Lee and added Bruce to it as homage to Bruce Lee. As an adult, Peter Lee worked as a laborer.

On December 4, 1979, a house on Selby Street, Hull, East Riding of Yorkshire, was set on fire. The sleeping family, Edith Hastie and her sons, Charles and Thomas, both age 15; Paul, age 12; and Peter, age 8, were sleeping inside. Charles rescued his mother by pushing her out a second-floor window. He rushed to try to help his brothers, but because they opened a window, causing a draught, they were trapped. Thomas, who had muscular dystrophy, slept in a different room; he managed to escape through a window in the back bedroom. There were also three daughters, but they were staying with relatives and were not home the night of the fire.

The three boys, Charles, Peter, and Paul were severely burned and were rushed to the special burn unit at Pinderfields Hospital in Wakefield, West Yorkshire. Charles died during the night. Peter lived for two days and Paul survived for 12 days.

During the investigation, police noticed a lack of caring for the family who had suffered such great loss. It was learned that the Hasties were known as a "problem family" whom neighbors believed were responsible for petty crimes and vendettas. The police began looking for someone who may have been seeking revenge against the family. Lee was one of many who volunteered to be questioned.

During the questioning, he confessed to pouring paraffin through the letterbox and setting it on fire in revenge against Charles Hastie, with whom he had sexual contact, and Charles threatened to go to the police and report it because he was a minor. Lee also was infatuated with Angeleena, Charles' sister, but she had rejected him several times. He then confessed to starting nine more fatal fires in Hull over the past seven years. Twenty-six people had died in the fires including a 6-month-old baby, a young mother and three small sons, plus 11 elderly men in a residential home.

To test his confession for the fires, police drove him around the city and Lee pointed out the buildings where he set the fires. As a further test, they took him to the home of a high-profile fire and the person responsible had been convicted. Lee immediately stated that he had nothing to do with that fire.

On January 20, 1981, Lee pleaded not guilty to 26 counts of murder, but guilty to 26 counts of manslaughter on the grounds of diminished responsibility and guilty to 11 counts of arson. He was sent to Park Lane Special Hospital in Liverpool and later transferred to Rampton Secure Hospital, a high-security psychiatric hospital near the village of Woodbeck between Retford and Rampton in Nottinghamshire, England. He was later cleared of 11 counts of manslaughter of elderly men in January 1977.

Bruce George Peter Lee's trial received little publicity, possibly because he had pleaded guilty to manslaughter and not to murder, but more likely due to the fact that there was a high-profile trial being conducted at the same time—the trial of Peter Sutcliffe, the *Yorkshire Ripper*.

Legebokoff, Cody Alan (b. January 21, 1990) is one of Canada's youngest convicted serial killers. Born and raised in Fort St. James, British Columbia, his friends describe him as a popular young man who played ice hockey in school and from whom they had never seen any violent behavior.

After graduating, he lived in Lethbridge, Alberta for a short time and then moved to Prince George, British Columbia.

The violence first showed its ugly head on October 9 or 10, 2009, when Jill Stacey Stuchenko, age 35 and mother of six, disappeared. Her body was found four days later at a gravel pit in a rural area on the outskirts of Prince George.

Natasha Lynn Mongomery, age 23 and the mother of two, was last seen on either August 31 or September 1, 2010. Her remains have never been found, but her DNA was found in Legebokoff's apartment by investigators after his arrest on November 27, 2010.

Cynthia Frances, age 35, was last seen on September 10, 2010. Her body was found in Prince George Park about a month later. She had died of blunt-force trauma to the head and penetrating wounds. Her autopsy showed that she had a hole in her shoulder blade, a broken jaw and cheekbone, and severe injuries to her neck. Her killer not only beat her, but he stomped on her neck.

These three women were reportedly working in the sex trade to support themselves and their children. Legebokoff used them to get him cocaine for his addiction.

On the evening of November 27, 2010, Constable Aaron Kehler, a rookie with the Royal Canadian Mounted Police, saw a 2004 GMC pickup truck being driven erratically as it turned onto BC Hwy. 27 from a remote logging road. Kehler pulled the vehicle over for a routine traffic stop. It appeared odd that someone was using this logging road, especially at night on a frigid November evening. He suspected that the driver was poaching deer. Kehler was joined by another RCMP officer.

They found blood smears on the driver's face and chin, plus blood on his legs and a pool of blood on the driver's floor mat. In searching the vehicle, they discovered a multi-tool and wrench covered in blood, plus a backpack and wallet containing a children's hospital card bearing the name of Loren Leslie. Legebokoff claimed that he had been poaching and had clubbed a deer to death, stating, "I'm a redneck and that's what we do for fun." No deer was found in the truck.

The body of Loren Donn Leslie, age 15, was found some distance back on the logging road. She had met Legebokoff on the website *Nexopia*. Loren was legally blind. She had about 50% vision in one eye and was completely blind in the other. She was originally listed as a victim of the Canada's Highway of Tears killer.

On September 11, 2014, Cody Legebokoff was convicted of these four murders. Five days later he was sentenced to life in prison with no parole for 25 years. He was added to the National Sex Offender Registry. Supreme Court Justice Glen Parrett stated that, "He lacks any shred of empathy or remorse. He should never be allowed to walk among us again." He was first incarcerated at the Kent Institution in Agassiz, B.C., but was transferred in March 2019 to Warkworth Institution, a medium-security prison in Trent Hills, Ontario.

Léger, Antoine (1795/96 – November 30, 1824) left his parents' house in Saint-Martin-Bettencourt, France, to become a hermit. He lived in a cave near Moutmiraux until the time of his arrest on August 12, 1924. He was a sexual sadist who murdered and cannibalized several young women in the 1820s in his native France. He also drank the blood of his victims, and sometimes removed and devoured their hearts. His trial took place on November 23, 1824. He was found guilty of murder and sentenced to death. Antoine Léger was guillotined one week later, on November 30. An autopsy was performed after his death and doctors found abnormalities in his brain, which may or may not explain his behavior.

LeGrand, Devernon (1924 – 2006) and his son, **LeGrand, Steven** (b. 1950), were cultists who murdered two of Devernon's wives, two teen sisters, and two men in New York in the years 1963 – 1975. They each received a sentence of 25 years to life. Devernon LeGrand died in prison in 2006. In February 2009 Steven LeGrand was deported to the U.K., the country of his birth.

Lehman, Christa Ambros (b. 1922) lost her mother at an early age and was neglected by her father, so she grew up undisciplined in Worms, Germany. She was arrested for petty theft and served probation in her early teens. In 1944, she married Karl Lehman, an alcoholic. She had several affairs to compensate for the lack of attention from her husband.

On September 17, 1952, Karl Lehman died during convulsions and the doctor listed the cause of death as a ruptured stomach ulcer. On October 14, 1953, Christa's father-in-law died in the streets just 20 minutes after leaving Christa's house. The death was attributed to natural causes.

In early 1954, Christa began giving chocolate truffles to some of her neighbors. One woman, Annie Hamann, bit into a piece of truffle and said that it was very bitter. She began having convulsions and died within minutes. A dog that ate the remains of the truffle also died. Tests revealed traces of E-605, a phosphorous-based pesticide.

Christa Lehman was arrested on February 23, 1954, and confessed to spiking the truffles in an effort to kill Eva Ruh, an elderly neighbor who lived with Annie Hamann. Eva had criticized Christa's relationship with Annie. Christa Lehman was convicted of multiple homicides and sentenced to life. She was released after 23 years in prison.

Lelièvre, André (c. 1930) and wife, **Lelièvre, Yvette** (c. 1932) were married and in lieu of using some form of birth control, simply drowned at least seven newborn infants and buried them in the 1950s and 1960s in France. They both received life sentences in 1959.

Lemke, Thomas (b. 1969) was a member of the Wiking-Jugend and the Free German Worker's Party, both far-right organizations, was a mercenary in the Hrvatske oružane snage – HOS (Croatian Armed Forces). Police found anti-Antifa lists of enemies with names and addresses of political opponents. He is also a German serial killer, having murdered at least three people.

On July 18, 1995, Lemke drove to Altena, with his girlfriend, Bianka W., and their mutual friend, Dagmar K., where Lemke kidnapped one of Bianka's acquaintances, gagged her, took her to a forested area, and strangled her with a rope. He hit her several times with a spade and then buried her in a hole in the ground.

Lemke went to Oberhausen on February 2, 1996, to visit Marcel M., a friend. They then drove to the apartment of Patricia W. in Bergisch Gladbach. Lemke handcuffed her, undressed her, raped her, hit her, and then murdered her with 91 stab wounds. He had met her previously and developed a deep hatred for her because she wore a sticker on her clothes that read "Nazis out."

Lemke murdered his last known victim on March 15, 1996, when he shot Martin K., age 26, to death on a staircase in the town of Rhade. Lemke considered him a traitor because he was quitting the far-right movement and was going to testify against Lemke.

In March 1997, Lemke was found guilty of three murders and one rape and was sentenced to life imprisonment. The court had sentenced Lemke the maximum penalty allowable for the charges. Bianca was sentenced to six years for murder, and Marcel was sentenced to five years for aiding and abetting.

Lent Jr., Lewis (b. 1950) was a lust killer who murdered five females and three males, all between the ages of 10-21, in the eastern US in 1983 – 1990. He was sentenced to life without parole in Massachusetts in 1995 and to 25 years to life in New York in 1997. In 2019, he confessed to the murder of James Lusher, a Westfield 16-year-old who had been missing since November 6, 1992.

Leonard, Eric Royce (b. 1969) aka *Thrill Killer* was a serial killer who murdered six during petty robberies in 1991 in Sacramento, California. On June 13, 1996, he was sentenced to death. The death sentence was upheld by the California Supreme Court on May 17, 2007. He is still on death row at San Quentin Prison in California.

Lesage, Celine (b. 1971) murdered six of her newborn babies between the years 2000 and 2007, suffocating four and strangling the other two.

She found herself a new boyfriend, Luc Margueritte, and he moved into her flat in Valognes, a commune in the Manche department in Normandy in northwestern France. On October 19, 2007, Luc went to the basement on some kind of errand and found the six baby corpses wrapped in plastic bags. He reported it to police and Lesage was arrested, convicted, and sentenced to 15 years in prison.

Lethal Lovers aka **Graham, Gwendolyn Gail** (b. August 6, 1963) and **Wood, Catherine May** (b. March 7, 1962) met at the Alpine Manor Nursing Home when Graham got a job as nurse's aide after moving to Grand Rapids, Michigan from Texas. Wood was already employed there as a nurse's aide. By 1986, they were lovers. Most of the following information came from Wood.

In January 1987, Wood stood guard while Graham went into the room of an Alzheimer's patient and smothered her with a washcloth. The patient's death appeared to be natural and there was no autopsy. They turned the deaths into a game by killing patients whose surnames would spell out the word "murder." This became extremely difficult, so they changed to counting each murder as a "day."

Wood told the investigators that Graham took souvenirs from the victims, but these souvenirs were never found. Over the next few months, they murdered four more patients. They broke up as couple when Graham began dating another woman at the nursing home. Graham and her new partner moved to Tyler, Texas.

Wood told her ex-husband about the murders and he went to the police. On December 4 and 5, 1988, Graham was arrested in Tyler, Texas and Wood was arrested in Walker, a suburb of Grand Rapids, Michigan. Detectives questioned Wood intensely during several interviews. She painted Graham as the brain and brawn of the murders and maintained that she acted only as lookout. Wood plea-bargained for a reduced sentence in exchange for testifying against Graham. Graham maintained her innocence, testifying that the murders were all an elaborate "mind game" by Wood. Graham's new girlfriend testified that Graham had confessed to her that she had killed five patients.

Gwendolyn Gail Graham was convicted of five murders and one count of conspiracy to commit murder. She was sentenced to five life sentences. She is currently serving her sentence in the Women's Huron Valley Correctional Facility in Pittsfield Charter Township, Michigan.

Catherine May Wood was charged with one count of second-degree murder and one count of conspiracy to commit second-degree murder. She was sentenced to 20 years on each count. She has been eligible for parole since March 2, 2005. She is currently serving her sentence at the minimum security Federal Correctional Institution in Tallahassee, Florida. She is expected to be released on June 6, 2021.

A book written by Lowell Cauffiel, *Forever and Five Days,* tells a different story. After interviewing friends, relatives, coworkers, and others who knew Graham personally stated that the real brain behind the killings was Wood. Psychological testing of Graham revealed that she could be easily manipulated, suffered from borderline personality disorder, and lacked the sophistication to plan or carry out these murders. The book also states that Wood has told inmates two different stories of the murders. One was that she made up the whole story to punish Graham for leaving her for another woman. The second story claims that she had done all of the killing and had framed Graham for leaving her.

Letter, Stephan (b. September 17, 1978) was a serial killer in Herdecke, North Rhine-Westphalia, Germany, between January 2003 and July 2004, while working as a nurse at a Southofen hospital in the state of Bavaria. He was arrested on July 29, 2004, and admitted to killing 16 elderly patients. Authorities exhumed 42 more bodies and stated that they believed he was responsible for those deaths as well. They were unable to check the cause of death of another 38 patients because they had been cremated after their deaths.

Stephan Letter was convicted of 29 murders and sentenced to life imprisonment. He is incarcerated at Straubing, in southern Germany.

Lewis, Gerald Patrick (August 10, 1965 – July 25, 2009) was convicted and sentenced to death for the murders of women in Alabama and Georgia. He admitted to several murders he had committed over the past decade.

On April 11, 1998, Kathleen Bracken, age 32, was murdered in Mobile, Alabama. Her body was found slaughtered at the Twilite Motel. She had been raped and stabbed to death. Lewis was found at his mother's home.

While questioning Lewis about the Bracken murder, he admitted to the murders of two women in Georgia and to the murder of a woman in Chickasaw.

Misty McGugin, age 22, was reported missing by her family on February 4, 1998. They had last seen her on January 30. Her car was found in the parking lot of the Drifter's Lounge in Baldwin County, Alabama, on February 1. She had taken her son for a weekend visit with his grandmother and was to pick him up on Monday, February 2, but did not arrive. After Lewis' arrest, he led police to Baldwin County Rd. 66, east of Daphne and showed police where he left her body. The state medical examiners determined that it was the body of Misty McGugin.

Patricia "Peggy" Lynn Grimes was eight months pregnant when she disappeared in 1992 in Douglas County, Georgia. Her mother reported her missing after she had not heard from her for several days. Grimes' body was found five years later in a wooded area in Lithia Springs.

Gerald Patrick Lewis was convicted in Douglas County, Georgia, of the murder of Peggy Grimes in 2004 and was given a sentence of death. He was also convicted of the murder of Misty McGugin in Baldwin County, Alabama and sentenced to death. Lewis died of lung cancer at Holman Correctional Facility, Atmore, Alabama on July 25, 2009.

Li Pingping (1960 – June 15, 2004) was a Beijing taxi driver and a serial killer. He was rumored to have engaged in transactions with prostitutes from the local nightclubs. He murdered four of them after having sex with each of them in his home. He then dismembered them and dumped the remains in a garbage pit near his home. His claim was that he murdered them because they made money more easily than a taxi driver.

After being fired from the Song Food Company, he stabbed to death his ex-employer, Song Shutian, Song's wife, and their daughter, who was only 12, and set their house on fire.

Li Pingping was captured by police in June 2003. He was convicted of seven murders and sentenced to death. He was executed on June 15, 2004. Dong Meirong, Li Pingping's wife, was sentenced to 15 years for helping her husband commit the murders and keeping stolen money.

Li Yijiang/Li Wenjiang (b. 1980) was born in Changji, Xinjiang, and raised by his grandmother in Shandong. One day, for an unknown reason, he was sent back to his parents in Xinjiang. Unfortunately, his mother had been diagnosed with a mental illness. She lost her temper frequently, licked things, and beat Li. He was afraid of his mother. His father drank alcohol to excess. After he went to high school, his mother's condition improved, but not his father's. He committed his first murder at the age of 14. There were no more murders until 2002.

In 1999, he began his studies in computer science at the Beijing Institute of Technology. He took a part-time job in the second semester. He dropped out of school in his sophomore year. In 2002 he was raped by four men and he decided to kill those men. He murdered them and two others by cutting off their sexual organs. He was arrested in 2003 and executed on August 20, 2004.

Li Yuhui (c. 1952 – April 20, 1999) was a Chinese geomancer (a method of divination that interprets markings on the ground or the patterns formed by tossed handfuls of soil, rocks, or sand) who poisoned three Hong Kong women and two teenage girls. He also stole $1.2 million from them. He killed the women and girls by selling them deadly cups of cyanide by claiming it would add years to their lives. Li was a self-styled master of feng shui (also known as Chinese geomancy, a pseudoscientific traditional practice originating from ancient China, which claims to use energy forces to harmonize individuals with their surrounding environment. The term *feng shui* literally translates as "wind-water" in English.) He pleaded not guilty to the charges, but was found guilty and sentenced to death. He was executed on April 20, 1999.

Lightbourne, Wendell (c. 1940) was a serial killer on the island of Bermuda, a British island territory in the western North Atlantic Ocean.

On Marcy 7, 1959, Gertrude Robinson, age 72, was raped and murdered. Her body was found at Southlands Beach. On May 9, Dorothy Pearse, age 59, was found raped and murdered. Her body was covered with bite marks and scratches. Both women lived alone in beach cottages and no evidence of robbery was found. On September 28, the body of Dorothy Rawlinson, age 29, was found floating in the surf off the southern shore. Her body had been attacked by sharks, but the coroner determined that she had been beaten to death.

Bermuda, being a British crown colony, brought detectives from Scotland Yard to take charge of the investigation. A call was received from a local merchant saying that on the day of Rawlinson's murder a black man had entered his shop in wet clothes and paid his bill with wet currency. Wendell Lightbourne, age 19, was soon arrested and confessed to the crimes. He was sentenced to death, but his execution date was twice postponed before the sentence was commuted to life. He is in prison in England.

Limpopo Serial Killer aka **Mulaudzi, Mukosi Freddy** (b. 1962) was a serial robber, rapist, and serial killer in the Limpopo Province of South Africa. His criminal career began in 1985 for petty theft. In 1991, he was convicted of two murders and 18 other serious crimes and sentenced to two terms of life in prison. He was sent to Baviaanspoort

Prison in Gauteng Province, but he escaped in 1996 and quickly resumed his criminal life.

In 2006, Mulaudzi was arrested and charged with 28 crimes, including 11 murders. His other crimes included attempted murder, rape, assault with intent to cause grievous harm, housebreaking with intent to rob and steal, and theft of a firearm. He was sentenced to 11 life sentences plus over 200 years in prison.

Limpopo Serial Rapist aka **Makamu, Fanuel** (c. 1977) was a serial rapist and killer in the province of Limpopo, South Africa. Makamu had an accomplice, **Henry Maile**, who was shot dead when police raided his house. Makamu and Maile committed their crimes between February and September 2000 in the area of Acornhoek in eastern Limpopo. Makamu was charged with 34 crimes, including six murders and nine rapes, plus charges of robbery, attempted murder, attempted rape, and attempted robbery. His trial lasted five weeks and more than 50 witnesses testified against him. He was found guilty of 32 of the 34 charges against him and sentenced to eight life sentences plus another 165 years in prison.

Lindholm, Jukka Torsten aka **Michael Maria Pentholm** aka **Michael Penttilä** (b. July 1965) is a serial killer in the country of Finland. When he was 16 years old, he kidnapped a 16-year-old girl. He forced her into the basement and then beat and choked her and threatened to rape her. The girl managed to escape. Lindholm was sent to a youth facility in 1984 for his earlier crimes of theft and attacks. He was released in 1985.

On August 26, 1985, he murdered his own mother, Laina Lahja Orvokki Lindholm, age 48. He was a suspect in the murder, as was his mother's male friend.

On July 26, 1986, he persuaded two 12-year-old girls to go to his apartment to get money for alcohol. Once there, he locked one of the girls in the bathroom. Titta Marjaana Kotaniemen, the other girl, was knocked to the floor and choked to death. He then sexually assaulted the other girl, but she managed to escape. He fled to the forest nearby, where the police captured him.

Lindholm confessed to the police that he had been mistreated by his mother and he had worn his mother's blue leather gloves and red scarf while he committed the murders. He was initially sentenced to nine years and seven months, but the Appellate Court held that the killing of the Lindholm girl was not murder and was instead assault or negligent homicide. His sentence was reduced to seven years. He was paroled in May 1992.

On May 31, 1993, he choked a woman with a cloth belt in her apartment. He was arrested. He claimed that he had been set up by someone and had nothing to do with the choking of the woman. He and another man escaped from the Oulu County Police Station on June 23, 1993. He was recaptured. He then admitted that he had killed the woman, but it was an accident, not murder. He claimed to have proposed explicit sex and was "playing around" with her neck and then realized she was dead. He was sentenced to ten years. He was released in November 2008.

While in prison, Lindholm married Hannele Pentholm, who had been sentenced to life for murdering her husband. They stayed married for about two years.

In May 2009, Lindholm invited a woman to his house and tried to choke her. In August, he bought an apartment in Toppila and choked a woman in the living room. In September, he choked the woman he had hired to clean his apartment; she escaped and alerted the police.

Lindholm was arrested and on June 11, 2010, he was sentenced to six years for three murders and numerous assaults. The Appellate Court reduced the sentence to four years and five months. On March 2, 2012 he was sentenced to four years and four months for rape, gross ill-treatment, and false imprisonment.

On October 13, 2015, Lindholm (now calling himself Michael Penttilä) escaped from an open prison during a shopping trip and was caught the following day. His sentence was to be served in a closed prison. He was released on December 25, 2016.

On April 13, 2018, Penttilä murdered a prostitute in an apartment in Helsinki. Her body was found on May 4 and Penttilä was arrested on May 6. He admitted that he had murdered the woman. In July 2018, he was sentenced to life in prison.

Lindsey, William Darrell (March 18, 1935 – April 17, 2001) is the main suspect in the murders of seven women in the St. Augustine area of Florida beginning in 1983. Lindsey was a former construction worker who was in Florida during the time of the murders.

He became a suspect after he was charged in April 1997 with murdering a prostitute in Asheville, North Carolina. Authorities in St. Augustine put together a trail of murder that followed Lindsey after receiving news clippings of his arrest in North Carolina sent to them by several former residents of St. Augustine who now live in North Carolina. Five bodies found in Florida had all been bludgeoned to death. Two other women are missing and presumed dead. Their bodies have not been found. Most of the women were prostitutes and or drug users.

William Darrell Lindsey was convicted of murder and sentenced to 30 years. He died in prison on April 17, 2001.

Lineveldt, Gamal Salie (1919 – 1942) raped and bludgeoned to death at least four women in 1940-41 in Cape Town, South Africa. He was arrested on March 16, 1941. He confessed to the murders, was convicted, and was hanged in 1942.

Lipstick Killer aka **Heirens, William** (November 15, 1928 – March 5, 2012) was a serial killer in Illinois. He was born into a poor family and wandered the streets of Chicago as a young boy. By age 13, he had turned to burglary to relieve the tension he felt at home. In 1941, Heirens was arrested for carrying a loaded gun. A later search of his home revealed a number of stolen weapons hidden in an unused storage shed on the roof of a nearby building along with furs, suits, cameras, radios, and jewelry he had stolen. He never tried to sell any of the stolen items. Heirens admitted to 11 burglaries and was sent to the Gibault School for wayward boys for several months.

Shortly after his release, Heirens was again arrested for burglary. He was sentenced to three years at the St. Bede Academy, operated by Benedictine Monks. Heirens stood out as an exceptional student and he was urged to apply for the University of Chicago's special learning program. Shortly before his release he was accepted into the program and asked to begin classes in the 1945 fall term. At age 16, he was a college student planning to major in engineering. He was also burglarizing homes again. He was arrested and sent to prison for burglary.

Heirens was a 17-year-old University of Chicago student when he confessed to three murders that, at the time, were considered among Chicago's most heinous crimes:

On June 5, 1945, Josephine Ross, age 43, was found dead in the apartment she shared with her daughters. She had been stabbed repeatedly in the neck and shot. No items were taken from her home.

On December 20, 1945, Frances Brown, a woman who lived alone, was discovered by a cleaning woman who found the door to the apartment open and a radio playing very loud. Frances had been repeatedly stabbed the neck. No items were missing from the home. There was a note written in lipstick on a wall in the apartment:

"For heavens
sake catch me
before I kill more
I cannot control myself"

On January 7, 1946, Suzanne Degnan, age 6, disappeared from her first-floor bedroom. After searching the apartment, the family called police. The police found a ladder outside the girl's window and a ransom note which had been overlooked:

Get $20000 reddy & wAITe foR WoRd. do NoT Notify FBI or Police. Bills IN 5's & 10s.

On the reverse side of the note it read:
BuRN This FoR heR SAfty

A man called the Degnan home several times demanding the ransom but hung up before a conversation could be started.

Mayor Edward Kelly also received a note:

"This is to tell you how sorry I am not to not get ole Degnan instead if his girl. Roosevelt and the OPA made their own laws. Why shouldn't I and a lot more."

This note referred to the nationwide meat packers' strike and the OPA currently considering extending the rationing of dairy products. Degnan, an executive with the OPA, had recently been transferred to Chicago. Another OPA executive received threats against his children. A man involved with selling meat on the black market had been murdered. Police thought maybe the killer could be a meat packer.

Hundreds of people were questioned and 170 were given polygraph tests. Two men were arrested but released. Finally, on June 26, 1946, William Heirens was arrested on burglary charges. He was charged with the murder of Suzanne Degnan when police realized a fingerprint found on the $20,000 ransom note found in Degnan's home matched Heirens'. He was soon charged with the murders of Josephine Ross and Frances Brown. On August 7, 1946, Heirens pleaded guilty to all three murders. After spending more than 65 years at Dixon Correctional Institute in Dixon, Illinois for the three murders, Heirens died from complications of diabetes on March 5, 2012, at the University of Illinois Medical Center.

Little, Samuel (1972)

Little, Samuel (b. June 7, 1940) was born in Reynolds, Georgia to a "lady of the night," as claimed by Little. Shortly after, the family moved to Loraine, Ohio, on Lake Erie and about 30 miles west of Cleveland. His grandmother was his main caregiver and authority. He had problems with discipline and achievement as early as junior high school. While in high school, in 1956, he was arrested and convicted for breaking and entering into property in Omaha, Nebraska. He was sent to a juvenile offenders' institution.

In 1961, now an adult, he was arrested for breaking into a furniture store in Loraine and sent to prison. He was released in 1964 and left Ohio, but not to settle down in any one place but to roam and made his living by robberies and theft. By 1975, he had been arrested 26 times in 11 states for various crimes including theft, assault, attempted rape, and fraud.

In 1982, he was arrested and charged with the murder of Melinda LaPree, age 22, in Pascagoula, Mississippi. She had disappeared in September 1982. The grand jury failed to indict Little for this murder.

Little was transferred to Florida to go on trial for the murder of Patricia Mount, age 26. Her body was found in late 1982. Witnesses placed Little with Mount the night before she disappeared, but Little was acquitted in January 1984 because the jury did not believe the witnesses. Little then headed to California and lived in the San Diego area.

Little, Samuel (2019)

In October 1984, he was arrested for attacking and beating two prostitutes. He was found guilty and sentenced to 2-1/2 years in prison and was released in February 1987. He moved to the Los Angeles area where he murdered Carol Elford on July 13, 1987; Audrey Nelson on August 14, 1989; and Guadalupe Apodaca on September 3, 1987. Their bodies were found on the streets of Los Angeles. Little was found at a homeless shelter in Louisville, Kentucky, where he was arrested and extradited to Los Angeles where he was charged with these murders on January 7, 2013. According to authorities, Little was being investigated for his involvement in dozens of murders in many states in the 1980s. In Mississippi, where he was acquitted of the LaPree murder in 1984, authorities were looking at unsolved murders there.

The trial for the murders of Carol Elford, Audrey Nelson, and Guadalupe Apodaca began in September 2014. DNA testing results, along with testimony of witnesses who were attacked at different times by Little, resulted in Little being found guilty of the three murders on September 25, 2014. He was sentenced to life in prison with no possibility of being paroled. He is presently serving his time at the California State Prison in Los Angeles County, California.

As of November 2018, the FBI had confirmed that Little was responsible for at least 34 of the murders and are working to match more of these murders to him. He is suspected of committing as many as 90 murders across the United States.

As of December 2018, Little had been charged with at least 12 more murders.

Liu Pengli was Prince of Jidong, the third son of Liu Wu of Liang (Prince Xiao posthumously), the grandson of Emperor Wen and the nephew of the Emperor Jing in the country of China. Liu Pengli's sons were Liu Mai, Liu Ming, Liu Ding, and Liu Bushi.

In the year 144 BCE, Liu Pengli, the nephew of Han Emperor Jing, was crowned King of Jidong. Liu Pengli went out on marauding expeditions with 20 to 30 slaves, murdered people and seized their belongings just for sport. It was not until the 29th year of his reign that the emperor learned of these atrocities. It was believed that Lin Pengli probably murdered more than 100 people. The court requested that Liu Pengli be executed; however, the emperor could not bear to have his own nephew killed, so he made Liu Pengli a commoner and banished him to the country of Shangyong (now Zhushan in Hubei Province). Two years later in 116 BCE, Liu Pengli's sovereignty was abolished, and his land was reclaimed by Emperor Jing.

Lockett, Will (1896 – March 11, 1920) aka **Petrie Kimbrough** was an African American born and raised in Pembroke, a small town in the western part of Kentucky on the border with Tennessee. Nothing is known of his early years, but when he was but 10 years old, he was arrested for insulting a white woman. He fled from the state of Kentucky and began using the name Will Lockett.

The next known location of him is Carmi, Illinois in 1912-13 when he murdered a white woman near the Louisville-Nashville train tracks. By 1917, he was in Evansville, Indiana, where he raped and beat a black woman.

He enlisted in the army and was stationed at Camp Zachary Taylor in Louisville, Kentucky. In February 1919 he raped and strangled a woman. The decomposed body of Sally Kraft had been found near the camp and authorities tied her murder to February 1919 murder.

Geneva Hardman, age 10, lived in Fayette County. She disappeared on February 4, 1920. A farmer by the name of Speed Collins found her satchel and cap and took them to the school. Anna Young, a teacher at the school, recognized the satchel and cap as belonging to Geneva. She checked with Geneva's mother, who told her she had not seen Geneva since she left for school that morning. Several men including Speed Collins, Claude B. Elkin, a local store owner, and Thomas Foley went to the place where the items were found. They saw large footprints near the location and followed them to a fodder stock where Geneva's body was found. Geneva and the fodder were covered in blood, as was a large rock nearby. The sheriff was called, and his deputies arrived along with Captain Volney G. Mullikin and his bloodhounds. They followed the man's tracks to the town of Keene in Jessamine County then to Nicholasville also in Jessamine County, where they talked to a farmer, Will Hughes, who told them he saw a black man walking along the pike and gave him a ride. The man's name was Will Lockett, who was known in the area as he supported himself as a laborer at the local farms.

A search party was formed, and Lockett was captured by Dr. W. T. Collette and Deputy Sheriff W. C. White near the town of Dixon, Webster County. He claimed that his name was Will Hamilton. He was questioned by Assistant Chief Ernest Thompson Detective Dudley Veal and he confessed to attacking Geneva. He said his intent was only to rape her, but he had to kill her and used a nearby rock. He also confessed that his true name was Petrie Kimbrough.

Kimbrough was tried and convicted of the murder of Geneva Hardman and sentenced to death. On March 11, 1920, Kimbrough was placed in Kentucky's electric chair and died within 15 seconds.

Lockhart, Michael Lee (September 30, 1960 – December 9, 1997) was a rapist and murderer of at least six girls in 1987 in Indiana, Texas, Florida, and Tennessee. He killed police officer Paul Hulsey Jr. while resisting arrest in Beaumont, Texas. He was sentenced to death on two counts in Indiana and on one count in Texas. He was executed in Texas on December 9, 1997.

Locusta (? – 69 CE) was notorious in Ancient Rome for her skill in concocting poisons. She poisoned thousands in mid-1st century CE. She poisoned for pleasure and for monetary gain. In 54 CE, she was hired by the empress, Agrippina the Younger, to supply a poison to murder Emperor Claudius so that her son Nero could take the throne. Emperor Nero saved her from execution, pardoned her for all of her past murders, and asked her for poison to murder Britannicus. He also rewarded her with a vast estate. After Nero's suicide, "Locusta the Sorceress" was sentenced to death by Emperor Galba in 69 CE. According to ancient texts she was led in chains through the whole city before being executed.

London Hammer Killer aka **Bellfield, Levi** (b. May 17, 1968) is 6 ft. 1 in., an ex-bouncer, and a killer. He is accused of five attacks on women, leaving two dead, all near bus stops in West London over a period of three years.

In February 2003, Marsha McDonnell, age 19, was attacked and killed by three blows from a heavy blunt instrument just yards from her home in Hampton, Surrey, after getting off a bus shortly after midnight. Previously, Bellfield had attacked Kate Sheedy, 18, and Anna-Maria Rennie, 17, shortly after they had gotten off buses.

On December 16, 2003, Bellfield told his two companions, who were riding in his car, "Watch this." He then jumped out of the car, jogged up to Irma Dragoshi, an Albanian hairdresser, grabbed her shoulder, spun her around, and smashed her with a hammer. She had just disembarked the bus in Longford Village, near Heathrow, at 7:30 p.m., and was on her mobile phone with her husband when she was attacked. Her husband took a taxi to find his wife drifting in and out of consciousness. She was taken to Hillingdon Hospital and she recovered.

In August 2004, French student Amelie Delagrange, age 22, left her friends in Twickenham, southwest London about 9:20 p.m., and got on the bus to go home. She missed her stop and was walking across Twickenham Green when she was attacked and killed.

Bellfield was charged with two murders, the attempted murders of Kate Sheedy and Irma Dragoshi, and the attempted abduction of Anna-Maria Rennie. He was sentenced to life in prison with a recommendation that he never be released.

Lonely Hearts Killer aka **Cameron, Rodney Francis** (b. 1948) is an Australian serial killer. Cameron claims that his earliest recollection is that of his mother dropping dead while taking a cake out of the oven in their home in Melbourne. Cameron was a vandal by the age of eight and at ten he tried to strangle a young girl. As a teenager, he tried to strangle a woman. As drugs, alcohol, and Devil worship took control of him, his murderous spree began at age 19.

On January 31, 1974, while working at a nursing home in the Blue Mountains west of Sydney, he murdered for the first time, raping and strangling Florence Edith Jackson, age

49, in her Katoomba home. She had a towel stuffed down her throat.

The following week heading south to Melbourne, he hitched a ride with a 19-year-old bank clerk, Francesco Ciliberto, who was found at the bottom of a seaside cliff near Mallacoota. He had been dead for several days. His head was battered, and a pair of socks and a t-shirt had been stuffed in his throat. Sarah McKenzie's body was found in her home in Milsons Point, after falling prey to Cameron while he was on the run for the Jackson and Ciliberto murders. Mrs. McKenzie, age 79, had been stabbed 30 times and bludgeoned to death with a mattock (digging or grubbing tool).

Cameron was tried for Florence Jackson's murder, convicted, and served nine years. Released on parole in 1983, he was extradited to Victoria where he was tried for Francesco Ciliberto's murder. He was convicted and only served seven years. Released on parole in March 1990, he killed again just three months later. This time his victim was Maria Goellner, a lonely 44-year-old woman he met through a radio matchmaking contest. They booked a motel room at Katoomba, paying in advance for several days. Maria Goellner was found by the cleaning woman, lying in a pool of blood on the bathroom floor, a bouquet of carnations on her chest. She had died of asphyxiation, choking on her own blood after being repeatedly bashed over the head with a blunt object. She had also been strangled.

Cameron was again convicted of murder and sentenced to life. He has since confessed to the murder of a man in South Australia in 1974 by bashing in his skull; strangling a woman to death in New South Wales, also in 1974; and murdering two women in separate knife attacks in Victoria in 1990. This brings his murder total to eight, definitely a serial killer. His file has been marked "never to be released." He is incarcerated at the Lithgow Correctional Centre near Lithgow, Australia.

Lonely Hearts Killers aka **Fernandez, Raymond** (December 17, 1914 – March 8, 1951) and **Beck, Martha** (May 6, 1920 – March 8, 1951) were a pair of serial killers who met through a "lonely hearts" ad in 1947.

Fernandez was born in Hawaii to Spanish parents. The family moved to Connecticut when he was still young. He moved to Spain in adulthood where he married and sired four children. He served in British Intelligence during World War II. After the war, Fernandez moved to America, abandoning his wife and children. He served some time in jail for stealing, where his cellmate taught him voodoo and black magic. After his release from jail, he moved to New York City and started answering the personal ads of lonely women. He would woo the ladies, then steal their money and possessions. In 1947, he answered Martha Beck's personal ad.

Martha Beck was born in Milton, Florida. Supposedly she was overweight due to a glandular problem. After she graduated from high school, she studied nursing, but could not find work due to her size. For a time, she worked as an undertaker's assistant. She quit this job and moved to California, where she found a nursing job in an army hospital. She became pregnant. She returned to Florida where she had the baby and told everyone that she had been married to a serviceman who was killed in the Pacific during the war. She again became pregnant and the father, a bus driver, married her. They were divorced six months later. She was now an unemployed mother of two children. Eventually, she found a job at Pensacola Hospital for Children. In 1947 she placed a personal ad.

Fernandez met Beck in Florida and stayed with her for a short time. When he returned to New York, she told everyone they were going to be married. Shortly, she was fired from her nursing job at the hospital, so she and the children packed up and joined Fernandez in New York.

Fernandez liked the way she took care of him and he told her of his wooing women and stealing their money and possessions. She became a willing partner and gave up her children to the Salvation Army.

It is known that the pair murdered three people in 1949, two women and a 2-year-old child; Janet Fay, age 66, who was killed by Beck during a jealous rage on Long Island, New York; Delphine Downing, who was given sleeping pills and then shot by Fernandez; and Delphine's 2-year-old daughter, who was drowned by Beck because she would not stop crying, in Wyoming Township (a Grand Rapids suburb), Michigan,. They buried the bodies of Delphine and her daughter in the basement. Neighbors became suspicious at the disappearance of Delphine and her daughter and called police. Fernandez and Beck were quickly arrested upon arrival of the police.

Fernandez and Beck confessed with the understanding that they would not be extradited to New York, which has a death penalty. Michigan does not have a death penalty. However, they were extradited to New York. They were thought to be responsible for at least 17 murders, but they denied their involvement. They were convicted of three murders and sentenced to death.

On March 8, 1951, both Raymond Fernandez and Martha Beck were executed by electrocution at Sing Sing Prison in New York State.

Long, Neal Bradley (September 11, 1927 – June 12, 1998) was a racist from Dayton, Ohio, who in 1966 confessed to stabbing a black man in 1944, but police records did not show a crime of that nature in 1944. In the early 1970s, six Blacks were shot dead and 14 were wounded. Dr. Charles Glatt, Dayton's desegregation planner, was shot and killed. Long was arrested and charged with seven counts of murder. He was convicted on two counts and was sentenced to two life terms.

Long Zhimin (d. September 1985) and his wife, Yan Shuxia (d. September 1985) were farmers in Sheng County, Shanxi Province, China. They were also serial killers.

Between February 1949 and May 1985, the couple murdered at least 48 people, with most of the murders being committed between January to May 1985. Long Zhimin murdered all of the victims at his home with a pickaxe and buried them in three pits he dug in his courtyard. He robbed all of his victims for a grand total of 573 yuan (estimated $100 US).

Long Zhimin and Yan Shuxia were found guilty and executed in September 1985.

Long-Haul Territory Killer aka **Boyer, John Wayne** (b. April 18, 1957) murdered at least three women in the southern states and is suspected by investigators in North Carolina, Tennessee, and South Carolina of murdering more than just three. Boyer, who was 5 ft. 7 in. and 293 lbs., targeted women who were especially small.

Michelle Yvonne Haggadone of Boliva, North Carolina, was picked up by Boyer at a truck stop on I-20. They argued about money and Boyer strangled her with a wire or cord. Her body was found in April 2000 at a parking area on I-20 near Florence, Darlington County, South Carolina. The body was finally identified more than ten years later using the DNA from one of Michelle's relatives.

Scarlett Wood was murdered by Boyer in January 2003 in Wilmington, North Carolina.

Jennifer Smith, a 25-year-old prostitute, was picked up by Boyer in Hickman County, Tennessee, in April 2005. The two argued over money, Boyer strangled her with his seat belt, and then dumped her body in an abandoned parking lot just off I-40. Her body was found in 2005 by a highway worker and identified about two years later by DNA.

Investigators of all three states were astonished at the hatred toward women shown by Boyer, who had never been married and lived with his mother. At one interview, the first thing Boyer said was, "What bitch are you here about?" At another, he said he had slept with a lot of prostitutes and a lot of them were detectives' and prosecutors' daughters.

In January 2006, Boyer pleaded guilty to second-degree murder in the killing of Scarlett Wood and was sentenced to up to 12 years in North Carolina. He is also the prime suspect in the 2002 murder of Rosie Marie Mallette in North Carolina; the murder of Madelyn Cox Thomas, also in North Carolina; the murder of Pamela Webb in Maine; and the murder of Amy Baker in Virginia.

Having completed his 12-year sentence in North Carolina, Boyer is presently incarcerated at the Trousdale Turner Correctional Center at Hartsville, Tennessee.

Los Angeles ATM Killer aka **Chavez, Juan** (b. 1966 – September 9, 1999) was a serial killer of gay men in Los Angeles in the years 1986 to 1989. He claimed he killed the men in an effort to help stop the spread of AIDS. He allowed himself to be picked up by gay men and taken to their homes, where he tied them up and forced them to give him their ATM code. He used the card and code to steal money from their accounts. His victims were strangled with exercise ropes, neckties, and electrical cords. He then stole their cars and left them in out-of-the-way places.

Alfred Rowswell, age 46, was the first known victim killed by Chavez in June 1986. Other known victims were Ruben Paris, age 57; Donald Kleeman, age 48; Michael Allen Cates, age 46; and Leo Hildebrand, age 52.

Rowswell's car was found in Utah and investigators found fingerprints on the windows. The fingerprints did not match any prints on file. A photo of a man using one of the victims' ATM cards was found and circulated in the gay bars, but this too was of no help. Finally in 1994, one of the fingerprints was matched to a Washington State prisoner. The inmate told detectives that he got the card from Juan Chavez. They tracked down Chavez who was also in prison for a kidnapping, not related to the ATM killings. He confessed to the murders.

Under a plea bargain, Chavez saved himself from the death penalty. It was all for naught. On September 9, 1999, Chavez was found hanging in his cell.

Loskop Killer aka **Msundwana, Mtimane** (c. 1900 – 1937) killed at least eight people in Kwa-Zulu Natal Province in South Africa, in the years 1929 to 1936. His victims included Suliman Ismail Kharva, Hassan Mia Armoordeen, Mohamed Ebrahim Motala, Ismail Hajat, Hassan Mayet and Nkunzana Mazibuko. Most of these men were Indian and were shot to death during robberies. Msundwana was arrested on August 10, 1936. He was convicted and sentenced to death. He was executed by hanging in 1937.

Louding, Michael, age 17, aka *Marlo Mike*; **Johnson, Kendrick**, age 19; **Rogers, Johnathan**, age 17; **Carroll, Ryan "Sneaks"**, age 16; **Stewart, Eddie,** age 16; **Williams, Jared**, age 20; and **Pittman, Adrian**, age 33, were in custody in June 2010 after a rash of murders in the Baton Rouge area of Louisiana. These murders brought together a multi-agency homicide task force that determined that these seven violent criminal offenders were tied together by criminal enterprise. The arrests were made as the result of "good old-fashioned police work" and "some magic worked" by the state police crime lab.

Michael Louding, who was arrested on May 14, 2010, was charged with the first-degree murders of rapper Chris "Nussie" Jackson on February 9, 2009; Charles Matthews and Darryl "Bleek" Milton on April 1; Marcus Thomas on April 25; Terry Boyd on October 21; second-degree murder of Michael Smith on December 18; and attempted second-degree murder in a shooting on February 22, 2010, on Tioga Street. Louding was found guilty of the murder of Terry Boyd and sentenced to life without parole. He is not eligible for the death sentence due to his age at the time of the murders.

Kendrick Johnson turned himself in to authorities. He was indicted on two counts of first-degree murder of Matthews and Milton on April 1. He pleaded guilty to conspiracy to commit the murders of Milton and Matthews and was sentenced to 20 years.

Johnathan Rogers was arrested and was charged with two counts of first-degree murder of Matthews and Milton on April 1. Charges were dropped.

Ryan "Sneaks" Carroll was arrested and charged with two counts of first-degree murder of Matthews and Milton on April 1; and attempted first-degree murder in the shooting on March 6, 2010. Carroll pleaded guilty to two counts of attempted murder and was sentenced to 18 years.

Eddie Stewart was charged with two counts of attempted first-degree murder in a shooting on February 22, 2010 and the shooting on March 6, 2010. Stewart pleaded guilty to one count of attempted murder and was sentenced to 15 years.

Jared Williams was charged with the first-degree murder of Marcus Thomas on April 25, 2009. Charges were dropped.

Adrian Pittman was charged with first-degree murder of Terry Boyd on October 21, 2009. Pittman pleaded guilty to manslaughter and was sentenced to 20 years.

Louis, Emile (January 21, 1934 – October 20, 2013), was a bus driver in France and the prime suspect in the disappearance and murders of seven women in Yonne, Burgundy, France in the late 1970s. The young women reportedly suffered from mild mental disorders and lived in homes for the handicapped. The disappearances did not attract much attention at the time. It was assumed that they had run away. In 1981, Detective Christian Jambert took an interest in the cases and began to suspect that the girls were not runaways.

In 2000, Emile Louis, who had become known as the *Butcher of Yonne*, confessed to two of the murders and furnished information as to where the bodies could be found. They were found in shallow graves in the area Louis described. Emile Louis later retracted his confession, but he was convicted of all seven murders in November 2004. He was sentenced to life in prison and was incarcerated in the Maison Centrale d'Ensisheim in the Haut-Rhin region of France.

Emile Louis died of neurological problems in the secure unit of the hospital in Nancy on October 20, 2013.

Lovers' Lane Killer aka **Mmbengwa, Mbulaheni David** (b. October 10, 1966) was a serial killer in Silverton, an area in the capital city of Pretoria, Gauteng Province, South Africa, during the years 1996 to 1998. Most of his victims were couples he found making love in their cars in "lover's lane" areas. He murdered at least seven people including lover's lane couples, an agriculture department official, a police inspector, and a police sergeant.

On July 24, 2001, Mmbengwa was sentenced to seven life sentences plus an additional 45 years.

Lucas, David Allen (b. 1956) is a convicted rapist and murderer. Between 1979 and 1984, he was convicted of the murders of Suzanne Jacobs, age 31, and her toddler son, Colin, in Normal Heights, a neighborhood northeast of downtown San Diego; Ann Catherine Swanke, age 22, a University of San Diego student who was last seen in La Mesa; and the attempted murder of Jodie Santiago Robertson, age 35, of Seattle, Washington, who was visiting a relative in East County, California. The jury could not reach a verdict in the slayings of Rhonda Strang, age 23, and Amber Fisher, age 3, whom Strang was babysitting in Lakeside. He was acquitted of the murder of Gayle Garcia, age 29, a real estate agent in a home in Spring Valley she had shown to a client. All of the victims had had their throats slashed. Several were almost decapitated.

David Allen Lucas was sentenced to death on September 19, 1989. He is currently on death row at San Quentin Prison in California.

Lucas, Henry Lee

Lucas, Henry Lee (August 23, 1936 – March 13, 2001) killed at least three people in Michigan and Texas. He has confessed to his involvement in approximately 600 other murders, although his confessions have been challenged by many in law enforcement, prosecutors, and court officials. Lucas later retracted most of these confessions.

There are about 350 murders which were deemed as "believable" by a Texas-based Lucas Task Force. This group has been criticized by many who believe the opinions are the result of sloppy police work and sloppy investigation procedures.

Lucas was the youngest of nine children of an alcoholic father, Anderson Lucas, and an alcoholic/prostitute mother, Viola Dixon Waugh. The Lucas family lived in Blackburg, Virginia. Viola was the ruler of the family and the children were regularly beaten by her. Lucas once spent three days in a coma after his mother struck him with a wooden plank. He claimed that he was forced to watch his mother have sex with men, and she often forced him to wear girls' clothes. His sister, Amanda, supports this claim. Lucas says that he was given a mule by his uncle. He saw his mother shoot and kill it. He also says that he was given a teddy bear by one of his teachers and his mother beat him for accepting charity. When he was ten, he says that his brother stabbed him in the left eye with a knife and his mother ignored the injury for four days until it became infected before he was taken for medical care. The eye had to be removed and replaced with a glass eye.

Lucas' father, Anderson, died in December 1949 of hypothermia. He was drunk when he arrived home and collapsed outside the house during a blizzard. Henry quit school and ran away to drift around Virginia. He was soon having sex with animals and committing petty thefts and burglaries. Lucas claimed that he murdered Laura Burnsley, age 17, in 1951 by strangling her after she refused his sexual advances.

Lucas' mother visited with Lucas and his half-sister Opal, with whom he was living in Tecumseh, Michigan. He thought he had killed his mother on January 11, 1960, after an argument about him returning home to care for her as she grew older. He said that all he remembered was slapping her on the neck and seeing her fall. He tried to pick her up and realized she was dead. Then he noticed a knife in his hand and saw that she had been cut. Viola was not dead, however; she was unconscious. Opal found her mother lying in a pool of blood and called an ambulance. Viola died of a heart attack precipitated by the assault by Lucas. Lucas fled to Virginia but decided to return to Michigan. He was arrested in Ohio on the warrant from Michigan for his involvement in his mother's murder. Lucas was convicted and sentenced to 20 – 40 years for second-degree murder. After serving 10 years, he was released from prison in June 1970, due to prison overcrowding.

Henry Lee Lucas drifted around the southern US, working here and there along the way. In 1976, he met Ottis Toole and became involved with Frieda "Becky" Powell, who was then only 12 years old, and had recently escaped from a juvenile detention facility. In 1978, Lucas and Toole began a homosexual murder spree. Lucas told authorities that Toole assisted him in about 108 murders. Most of this has been recanted. Lucas has often been referred to as the *Confession Killer.* Lucas claimed that Becky had become homesick and he agreed to move to Florida with her. Along the way, they argued at a Bowie, Texas truck stop, and Becky left with a trucker. A waitress at the truck stop supported this claim.

Lucas was arrested on June 1, 1983, for unlawful firearm possession. He was then charged with the murder of Kate Rich, age 82, in Ringgold, Texas, and the murder of Frieda "Becky" Powell. Lucas claims that he was stripped naked by police, denied his cigarettes and bedding, put him in a cold cell and denied him access to an attorney. He said that he confessed to the crimes to get better treatment by the authorities. The evidence against Lucas was questionable. A single bone fragment found in a wood-burning stove was said to be from Kate Rich, and a skeleton (missing some bones) from someone about the same age and size was said to be that of Frieda "Becky" Powell. Lucas made the statement that since he was made "to confess to murders I didn't commit, I might as well confess to them all." Which he did. The Lucas Task Force cleared 213 previously unsolved murders by Lucas confessing to them. Phil Ryan, the Texas Ranger who arrested Lucas, said that he was very concerned about the truthfulness of Lucas' confessions and that he would find it difficult to believe more than the original confession of the murders of Rich and Powell.

Dallas detective Linda Erwin had the same problem believing the Lucas "confessions." She made up a totally fictional crime, complete with photographs from an old murder, solved long ago, and gave details from her own imagination. Lucas confessed with details that Linda had fed to him. She admitted she was uncomfortable with fabricating a crime, but felt it was the only way to determine the veracity of Lucas' confessions. Lucas had made claims that he was part of a Satanic cult called "The Hand of Death" which was cannibalistic, he had taken part in "snuff" films, he had killed Jimmy Hoffa, and he had delivered poison to Jim Jones in Jonestown prior to the mass murder/suicide.

Lucas was convicted on 11 counts of murder. He was sentenced to death for the murder of a woman known only as "Orange Socks". Those were the only items of clothing found with her body discovered on October 31, 1969, in Williamson County, Texas. It was later found that Henry Lee Lucas was not in Texas at the time of her murder. He was actually in Florida, working as a roofer, with work records and check cashing evidence that he was definitely not in Texas at that time. In 1998, Governor George W. Bush recommended commuting Lucas' death sentence to life in prison. Henry Lee Lucas died of heart failure at age 64 on March 13, 2001.

Ludena, Pedro Pablo Nakada (b. February 28, 1973) aka *The Apostle of Death* was born Pedro Pablo Mesias Ludena in Lima, Peru to an alcoholic father and a mentally unstable mother. As a child, he was very submissive and often abused by his siblings. His father died at a young age and Ludena was devastated because his father was the only one to come to his rescue when his siblings were abusing him or making him dress like a girl. He later claimed that he was raped by his brothers after they thought he had killed their pregnant dog. He blamed this incident for his hatred of homosexuals. He claimed to have tortured animals when he was a child.

In 2003 Ludena paid 800 soles (Peruvian money) to a Japanese citizen to adopt him as an adult so he could migrate to Japan as a Japanese descendant. He changed his surname to Nakada. This tactic is used by Peruvian criminals as a way to flee Peruvian justice. Ludena never moved to Japan. His brother, Vayron Jonathan Ludena, moved there and was arrested in 2015 for a three-day killing spree during which he stabbed six people to death.

Ludena fitted his 9mm pistols with handmade rubber silencers made from slippers. He claimed that he had been commanded by God to cleanse the Earth by eliminating drug addicts.

He was arrested on December 28, 2006, after a shootout with the police. He confessed to killing 25 people. He was convicted of 17 murders and sentenced to 35 years in prison.

Ludke, Bruno (April 3, 1908 – April 8, 1944) was an alleged serial killer of 51 people in Germany in the years 1928 to 1943. However, there were no similarities in the modus operandi, signature, or motive. There was never any evidence submitted or fingerprints found that tied Ludke to any of the murders.

He was arrested on March 18, 1943, and questioned about the murder of a woman on January 31, 1943. She had been found in the woods near Kopenick and had been strangled with her own shawl. She showed signs of sexual assault after her death and her purse was missing. Ludke confessed to the murder, plus several other murders. Witnesses reported that Ludke showed signs of physical abuse and that he had said, "They would kill me, if I didn't confess."

A retired police chief took an interest in the case and investigated the original police reports. He found that the reports were inconclusive, incoherent, and vague. His conclusion was that Ludke was not responsible for any of the murders. He stated that Ludke, who was semi-illiterate, did not possess the ability to evade the police for some 15 years, let alone being able to get away with murder. He could not tell his interrogators how many minutes were in an hour. It is believed by many that Ludke was the victim of a frame-up by the chief homicide investigator by the name of Franz, the heavily censored *Reichskriminalpolizieamt*, and the budding Nazi government which had no patience with a person with intellectual disabilities.

Bruno Ludke was never put on trial for any of the murders. He was declared insane and sent to the SS-run Institute of Criminological Medicine in Vienna, where he was the victim of medical experiments until his death by lethal injection on April 26, 1944.

Lumbrera, Diana (b. November 21, 1958) was a serial killer of her children. Between 1976 and 1990, she bore six children who all died. The 6-week-old daughter of a cousin also died of mysterious convulsions.

Daughter Joanna was born in 1976 and was barely three months old when Diana brought her to the community hospital in Bovina, Texas. She was dead upon arrival. According to the mother, the baby had experienced convulsions before she suddenly stopped breathing.

Son Jose was born in 1977 and was just two months old when Diana showed up again at the Bovina Emergency Room on February 10, 1978, with the same story. This time, the baby's resuscitation was successful, but doctors failed to find a cause for the convulsions. Jose was moved to the Lubbock, Texas, pediatric intensive care unit. The baby's condition was listed as stable. Shortly after 6:30 p.m. a nurse saw Diana run from the baby's room in tears. The nurse found little Jose cyanotic and after 30 minutes of CPR he was pronounced dead.

Daughter Melissa was born in 1975 and on October 2, 1978, Diana walked into the Bovina emergency for the third time with a child in her arms. This time it was Melissa, her 3-year-old, who was dead upon arrival. Diana again related the story of convulsions and stopped breathing.

Diana and her husband divorced in 1979. After that she was seldom seen without a male companion. She bore three more children, each with a different father. On October 8, 1980, Diana went for a drive with her cousin who had a

6-week-old baby. About 30 minutes later they were in the emergency room of the local hospital. The baby was dead upon arrival. She again told the convulsions and stopped breathing story.

Daughter Melina, age 3, was pronounced dead at home on August 17, 1982. The cause was officially listed as acute heart failure caused by increased taxation on a case of congenital heart disease.

In November 1983, Diana gave birth to a son whom she named Daniel. On March 25, 1984, Daniel was treated by a physician for an ear infection. Three days later he was dead upon arrival at the hospital. Septicemia was listed as the cause of death.

In 1985, Diana moved to Garden City, Kansas. On February 21, 1986, she gave birth to another boy. He managed to survive for four years and three months. In the spring of 1990, Diana carried him into a hospital emergency room, but he was dead upon arrival. The day before her son's death she had taken him to a local doctor complaining about the mysterious convulsions. The doctor could find no cause and simply prescribed an antibiotic. This time, hospital officials were suspicious and called police. They compiled a list of her previous children, and the places and dates of their deaths. It was found that all of the children had been insured for amounts between $3,000 and $5,000, with her last son insured for $5000.

Diana Lumbrera was charged with her son's death. After less than one hour of deliberation, the jury found her guilty and she was sentenced to life imprisonment. She faced three counts of murder in Texas. Facing a death penalty in Palmer County, Texas, Diana pleaded no contest and was sentenced to life. Also facing death in Lubbock County, she again pleaded no contest; she received a third life sentence. Charges against her in Castro County were waived, saving the county some $50,000.

Lundin, Peter Kenneth Bostrøm (b. February 15, 1972) was born in Roskilde Sygehus, Denmark, to Ole Bostrøm Lundin and Anna Schaftner Lundin. They moved to the United States with Peter when the boy was 10 years old. They settled in Ormond Beach, Florida, where they operated a local motel.

In 1984, they moved to Maggie Valley, North Carolina. Ole decided to leave Anna and take Peter with him. They moved to Los Angeles. After a few weeks, they moved to New York City, then Boston, and finally to Miami, Florida, where Peter learned about cocaine and marijuana. He began to sell cannabis to his classmates. Ole and Anna got together again. Peter had worked at several part-time jobs while going to school in Miami. At some point, the family moved to North Carolina. Ole and Anna spent a lot of time drinking and the household was in chaos most of the time. Both Peter and Ole were violent with Anna. Neighbors called the police several times. Sometime around April 1, 1991, Anna was murdered by father and son. They drove the body to Buxton, near Cape Hatteras, buried it in the sand, and fled to Canada. A couple walking on the beach found Anna's body on November 1, 1991. On June 6, 1992, Peter and Ole were arrested at a Toronto, Ontario motel.

Peter was sentenced to 20 years in prison. Ole was sentenced to only two years, as an accomplice. Both were subject to expulsion and extradition back to Denmark at the time they were released from prison. Peter married a woman named Tina in 1996 while still in prison. Peter, Tina, and her teenage daughter moved into an apartment in Maløv.

A violent tantrum against his wife and her daughter resulted in Peter being forced out of their apartment and he moved into a men's home in Nørrebro. He visited a brothel in Copenhagen, where he met Marianne Pederson, an employee. She and her late husband had built a massage clinic in Fasanvej. Lundin and Marianne became lovers. On July 3, 2000, Marianne and her two sons were declared missing. Lundin told investigators that they were on holiday and he had been hired to repaint their house. Police technicians were able to find traces of blood in Marianne's car and the basement of the house. Lundin was arrested and charged with murder. It was determined that Marianne and her two sons had been killed and dismembered. He claimed that Marianne had murdered her two sons with a knife and he had struck her "not seriously," and that she had died. He was afraid to call the police because they would not believe him because of his past and decided to dismember the bodies instead.

On October 10, 2000, he confessed to murdering Marianne and her sons because she "had spoken sweetly" to another man on the phone. They got into a fight; he broke the necks of all three of them and had to dispose of the bodies. He placed the bodies in the house freezers and then placed them outside the house to be picked up as bulky waste and sent to the incinerator.

Peter Lundin was found guilty of intentional murder and sentenced to life in prison. He is incarcerated at the Institute of Herstedvester in Herstedvester, Denmark.

Lusaka Serial Killer aka **Chilala, Bernard Gilbert** (c. 1958) claims to have murdered more than 200 people in the African country of Zambia. In one case, he used a hoe to hack to death a 28-year-old farmer and his pregnant wife. He also murdered the Deputy Speaker of the National Assembly, Leonard Kombe, and his wife, plus two other people, using an axe. Chilala claims that his killings were for business purposes—not being paid for work done. He also claims to have killed using black magic. He turned himself in to police in 1997. Gilbert Chilala was sentenced to death by the High Court, although the sentence was later commuted to life in prison based on his good behavior while behind bars.

Lust Killer / ***Shoe Fetish Slayer*** aka **Brudos, Jerome Henry** (January 31, 1939 – March 28, 2006) was an American serial killer and a necrophiliac.

Jerome Henry "Jerry" Brudos was born in Webster, South Dakota, the younger of two sons. His mother dressed him in girls' clothes because she had wanted a girl. The Brudos family moved frequently before settling in Salem, Oregon. Jerome Brudos developed a fetish for women's shoes by the age of five. It was reported that he tried to steal his first grade teacher's shoes. He also developed a fetish for women's underwear and claimed that he stole underwear from female neighbors. He spent several of his teen years in and out of psychotherapy and mental hospitals. He began to stalk women and would knock them down or choke them unconscious and steal their shoes. At age 17, Brudos was arrested for abducting and beating a young woman and threatening to stab her if she did not follow his sexual demands. He was taken to a psychiatric ward of Oregon State Hospital, where he stayed for nine months. While there, it was found that his sexual fantasies came from his hatred and revenge against his mother and women in general. He was also diagnosed as a schizophrenic. Despite his legal and mental problems, he graduated from high school with his class in 1957. Within a short time, he became an electronics technician.

Brudos married a 17-year-old girl in 1961. They made their home in Salem, Oregon and had two children. He asked that she do housework naked except for a pair of high heels so he could take photos. He began having migraines and blackouts. He relieved his tension by again going out on night raids for lacy underwear and high heeled shoes. He kept these items in the garage where his wife was not allowed to enter unless she informed him first via an intercom he set up for this purpose. After a while, the nighttime prowling and masturbation was not enough. It graduated to rape and murder.

Linda Slawson, 19 years old, worked for a book company and sold sets of encyclopedia door to door. On January 26, 1968, she made the horrible mistake of encountering Jerome Henry Brudos on her rounds of door to door peddling. She was never seen or heard from again. Her company did not have any records of her exact location for selling her books that day.

On November 26, 1968, Jan Susan Whitney, age 23, was on her way home to McMinnville from a visit with friends in Eugene. She did not make it. Her vehicle, a red and white Rambler, was found in a rest area just off the highway near Albany, Oregon. It was locked and there was no sign of Jan. The vehicle was taken to the state Identification Bureau for processing. There was no sign of foul play. There was a minor mechanical problem which prevented her from driving farther. It was surmised that she had either walked away or had been picked up by someone to try to get help for her disabled vehicle. After she exited her car, she had simply disappeared.

On March 27, 1969, Karen Elena Sprinkler, 19 years old, was a freshman at Oregon State University. She had gone home to Salem to visit with her parents on a short vacation from college. She had a date for lunch with her mother that day at the restaurant in the Meier and Frank store, then shopping for clothes to take back to college. Karen was always very prompt, so her mother was a little upset when Karen didn't show up for their 12:00 dinner. By 12:30 p.m. Karen still had not appeared, so Mrs. Sprinkler left the restaurant and found a nearby pay phone. There was no one to answer the phone at home. Mrs. Sprinkler left a message for Karen at the restaurant telling her to call home. She received no call from Karen. They checked with friends, hospitals, and police. No one had seen or heard from Karen. Karen was reported missing by her parents. Salem police were checking through all the levels of the parking garage at the Meier and Frank store for any sign of Karen. On the roof, they found Karen's car, parked and locked. Some of Karen's books were on the seat, but there was nothing else. There had been a report of a "weird person" seen hanging around the garage a few weeks before Karen disappeared. This "weird person" was dressed as a woman, but the girls who saw this were pretty sure that it was a man. One witness said that the person got close to her and she could see that it was definitely a man. At the time, there was no reason to link him to Karen's disappearance.

Just four weeks later on April 23, 1969, Linda Salee, age 22, apparently disappeared from a shopping mall where she had gone to buy a gift for her boyfriend, but she failed to meet him that evening. The clerk at the jewelry store remembered waiting on Linda who bought her boyfriend a leather band for his watch. Also, the clerk at the men's clothing store remembered Linda, who had bought a blue suede-cloth jacket and a pair of walking shorts for her boyfriend. Before leaving the mall, she sat on one of the benches, looked again at the watch band, decided it was not the right one, and took it back to the jewelry store for a refund. The clerk also remembered this transaction. Linda did not show up at the YMCA that night or at work the next day. Her car was found in the parking garage at the mall. It was locked. Linda was gone.

On May 10, 1969, a lone fisherman encountered something just beneath the surface of Long Tom River, a tributary of the Willamette River. He made his way closer and then reeled back, almost losing his footing, as he realized that the object was a human body. These were the days before cell phones, so he had to find the nearest pay phone. Linda Salee had been found, weighted down in the river by an automobile transmission. Investigators saved the nylon rope which was used to tie the body to the transmission. The rope had a specific type of knot, so they cut the rope carefully to save the knot. Copper wire was also used and was twisted in such a manner as an electrician would use. The medical examiner was able to determine that she had been strangled.

Investigators continued to search the river. They had three more missing women who they believed were connected to the same murderer. A few days later, they found more remains. This one was tied to an automobile engine head with the same materials as the first remains and the same knots. This would be used to prove that the same person was responsible for both deaths. This victim had been strangled with a strap used as the garrote. Her breasts had been removed. She was identified as Karen Sprinkler.

They were still looking for two more bodies and continued to search but found nothing more in the river. Knowing that Karen Sprinkler was a student at Oregon State University in Corvallis, the detectives began to question students there. They learned that some of the female students had received strange calls from a man trying to lure them out. They also learned that there had been a suspicious pudgy, red-haired man hanging around the campus. One girl actually went out with him on a brief date. She found him very disconcerting as he wanted to talk about the bodies that had been found in the river. She never wanted to go out with him again. He had actually asked her why she was not afraid that he might strangle her. She described him as a tall man with light-colored hair and a lot of freckles. The description matched those offered by other women who had been fortunate enough to have escaped his attempted abductions. The detectives asked her to call them if she should ever hear from him. To her surprise, and the detectives', he did contact her again on May 25. She made a date for one hour later and immediately contacted the police. They went to the designated meeting place and saw the tall, pudgy man. They learned that his name was Jerry Brudos. He seemed very at ease. Having nothing to justify an arrest, they kept him under surveillance. They learned his address and that he worked as electrician. They researched his background and found a number of coincidences—in January 1968, he lived in the same neighborhood worked by Linda Slawson selling her encyclopedia; in November 1968, he was working in Lebanon, Oregon, right by the I-5 interstate where Jan Whitney disappeared; and he was currently working in Halsey, about six miles from where the bodies were found in the Long Tom River. That was too many coincidences.

Jerome Henry Brudos was arrested on May 30, 1969. He and his family were heading north on I-5 with his wife driving and his two young children in the front seat. Brudos was hiding under a blanket in the back seat. He later confessed to murdering Linda Slawson, Jan Whitney, Karen Sprinkler, and Linda Salee. He was sentenced to three life sentences. Jerome Henry Brudos died in prison on March 28, 2006, from liver cancer.

Luther, Thomas Edward (b. June 23, 1957) was born in Hardwick, Vermont, the first of five children. He began drinking and using drugs at a young age and was a rapist and murderer of at least nine women during the years 1970s – 1994 in Vermont, Pennsylvania, West Virginia, and Colorado. He was sentenced to 15 – 35 years for rape in West Virginia in 1995, 48 years for one count of second-degree murder in Colorado, and two 50-year terms for assault and attempted murder in Colorado in 1996. He is currently serving his sentence at Sterling Correctional Facility, Sterling, Colorado.

For More News About Susan Hall,
Signup For Our Newsletter:

http://wbp.bz/newsletter

Word-of-mouth is critical to an author's long-term success. If you appreciated this book please leave a review on the Amazon sales page:

http://wbp.bz/tweosk2a

BIBLIOGRAPHY

Bellamy II, John Stark. *The Corpse in the Cellar.* Cleveland: Gray & Company, 1999

Bugliosi, Vincent. *Helter Skelter.* New York: Bantam Books, 1973.

Burnside, Scott, and Alan Cairns. *Deadly Innocence.* New York: Warner Books, 1995.

Capote, Truman. *In Cold Blood.* New York: Random House, 1965.

Carlo, Philip. *The Night Stalker.* New York: Kensington Publishing, 1992.

Coston, John. *To Kill and Kill Again.* New York: Penguin Books, 1992.

Douglas, John, and Mark Olshaker. *Mindhunter.* New York: Simon & Schuster, 1995.

Eftimiades, Maria. *Garden of Graves.* New York: St. Martin's Press, 1993.

Englade, Ken. *Cellar of Horror.* New York: St. Martin's Press, 1989.

Fido, Martin. *A History of British Serial Killing.* London: Carlton, 2001.

Finkel, Michael. *True Story.* New York: Harper-Collins, 2005

Ganey, Terry. *Innocent Blood.* New York: St. Martin's Press, 1989.

Ginsburg, Philip E. *The Shadow of Death.* New York: Berkley Books, 1995.

Glatt, John. *Cries in the Desert.* New York: St. Martin's Press. 2002.

_____. *Depraved.* New York: St. Martin's Press, 2001.

Goulding, Warren. *Just Another Indian: A Serial Killer and Canada's Indifference.* Markham, Ontario: Fifth House Books, 2001.

Graysmith, Robert. *Zodiac.* New York: St. Martin's Press, 1986.

Gregson, Jessica. *The Angel Makers*. London: PaperBooks Ltd., 2007.

Hazelwood, Roy and Stephen Michaud. *Dark Dreams*. New York: St. Martin's Press, 2002.

Henderson, Bruce. *Trace Evidence*. New York: Penguin Books, 1998.

Humes, Edward. *Buried Secrets, A True Story*. New York: Signet Books, 1992.

Jackson, Steve. *Monster*. New York: Pinnacle Books, 1998.

Keers, Christine, and Dennis St. Pierre. *The Riverside Killer*. New York: Kensington Books, 1996.

Kelly, Susan. *The Boston Stranglers*. New York: Kensington Books, 2002.

Keppel, Robert D. and William Birnes. *Riverman*. New York: Pocketbooks, 1995.

_____. *Signature Killers*. New York: Pocketbooks, 1997.

Keyes, Edward. *The Michigan Murders*. Toronto: Fitzhenry & Whiteside, 1976.

King, Gary C. *Blind Rage*. New York: Penguin Books, 1995.

_____. *Butcher*. New York: Kensington Books, 2009.

Lasseter, Don. *Dead of Night*. New York: Penguin Books, 1997.

Lourie, Richard. *Hunting the Devil*. New York: Harper Collins, 1993.

O'Brien, Darcy. *Two of a Kind: The Hillside Stranglers*. New York: New American Library, 1985.

Olsen, Jack. *I, the Creation of a Serial Killer*. New York: St. Martin's Press, 2002.

Moore, Kelly and Dan Reed. *Deadly Medicine*. New York: St. Martin's Press, 1988.

Moose, Charles A. and Charles Fleming. *Three Weeks in October*. New York: Penguin Books, 1993.

Mustafa, Susan D. and Sue Israel. *Dismembered*. New York: Kensington Publishers, 2011.

Preston, Douglas and Mario Spezi. *The Monster of Florence*. New York: Grand Central, 2008.

Remsberg, Bonnie. *Mom, Dad, Mike & Patti*. New York: Bantam Books, 1993.

Ressler, Robert and Thom Shachtman. *I Have Lived in the Monster*. New York: St. Martin's Press, 1998.

_____. *Whoever Fights Monsters*. New York: St. Martin's Press, 1992.

Rule, Ann. *Green River, Running Red.* New York: Simon & Schuster, 2005.

_____. *The I-5 Killer.* New York: New American Library, 1984.

_____. *Lust Killer.* New York: New AmericanLibrary, 1983.

_____. *The Stranger Beside Me.* New York: New American Library, 2001.

_____. *The Want-Ad Killer.* New York: New AmericanLibrary, 1983.

Ryzuk, Mary S. *Thou Shalt Not Kill.* New York: Warner Books, 1990.

Schultze, Jim. *Preacher's Girl.* New York: Avon Books, 1993.

Smith, Carlton. *Killing Season.* New York: Penguin Books, 1994.

_____ and Tomas Guillen. *The Search For The Green River Killer.* New York: Penguin Books, 1991.

Spencer, Suzy. *Breaking Point.* New York: St. Martin's Press, 2002.

Spizer, Joyce. *The Cross Country Killer.* Dallas, Texas: Top Publications, 2001.

Stanley, Stephanie A. *An Invisible Man.* New York, Berkley Publishing, 2006.

Vronsky, Peter. *Serial Killers.* New York: Berkley Publishing, 2004.

Walker, Steven. *Predator.* New York: Kensington Books, 2010.

Newspapers:
Charlotte Observer, Charlotte, North Carolina
Chicago Tribune, Chicago, Illinois
Chillicothe Gazette, Chillicothe, Ohio
Cincinnati Enquirer, Cincinnati, Ohio
Daily Star, London, England, UK
Dayton Daily News, Dayton, Ohio
Delano Herald Journal, Delano, Minnesota
Detroit Free Press, Detroit, Michigan
Hamilton Journal News, Hamilton, Ohio
Houston Chronicle, Houston, Texas
Los Angeles Daily News, Los Angeles, California
Los Angeles Times, Los Angeles, California
Madera Tribune, Madera California
New York Daily News, New York City

Post-Gazette, Steubenville, Ohio
Rheinische Post, Dusseldorf, Germany
San Antonio Light, San Antonio, Texas
San Diego Union Tribune, San Diego, California
Seattle Times, Seattle, Washington
Star Tribune, Minneapolis, Minnesota
Times-Picayune, New Orleans, Louisiana
Toronto Star, Toronto, Canada

Websites:
www.abcnews.com
   Aleem Agha
www.aol.com/news
   Ryan Gorman
www.apnews.com
www.bbc.com
www.cbsnews.com
www.tampabay.com
www.cnn.com
www.foxnews.com
   Bradford Betz
   Dom Calicchio
www.msnbc.com
www.adn.com
www.allserialkillers.com/ancestry.com
www.angelfire.com/buzzle.com
www.apnews.com
www.bakersfield.com
www.bbc.co.uk
www.birthfactdeathcalendar.net/people/
   hooijmaijers-franz
www.chinadaily.com.ch
www.cncpunishment.com
www.cor.state.pa.us
www.crimecapsule.com
www.crimeindetroit.com
www.crimelibrary.com/serialkillers.htm
www.crimezzz.net
www.dailymail.co.uk
www.dearmrgacy.com
www.deathpenalty.org
www.digitaljournal.com
www.enca.com/south-africa

www.executedtoday.com
www.fbi.gov/stats-services/publications/serial-murder
www.findagrave.com
www.floridacapitalcases.state.fl.us
www.foxnews.com
www.gov.cn
www.inmatesplus.com
www.instantcheckmate.com
www.irishpost.com
www.jamaica-gleaner.com
www.justicefornativewoman.com
www.kaisanet.altervista.com
www.knoxnews.com
www.koreatimesco.kr
www.lusakavoice.com
www.massimopolidoro.com
www.mayhem.net
www.mur.com
www.mycentraljersey.com
www.mycrimelibrary.com
www.myplainview.com
www.ndtv.com/india
www.newyorkalmanack.com
www.pe.com
www.petticoatsandpistols.com
www.realnameof.com
www.reuters.com
www.serialkillers.briancombs.net
www.serialkillercalendar.com
www.serialkillersink.net
www.skcentral.com
www.telegraph.co.uk
www.theoaklandpress.com
www.trutv.com
www.twistedminds.creativescapism.com
www.unknownmisandry.com
www.upi.com/archives
www.vnnforum.com
www.washingtonpost.com
www.wickedwe.com
www.wikipedia.com
www.withoutremorsebook.com
www.worldofbuzz.com

www.zodiackiller.com

Other:
Associated Press writer
    Monica Rhor
Center for Bibliographical Studies & Research
    California Digital Newspaper Collection
Department of Psychology
    Radford University, Radford, VA

INDEX

F

The World Encyclopedia of Serial Killers | 415

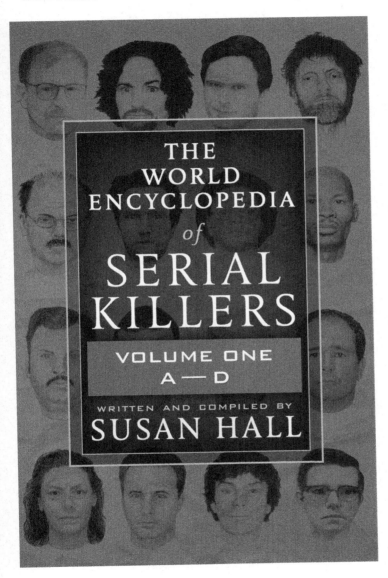

Made in the USA
Monee, IL
12 March 2021